LEGAL WRITING

PARALEGAL TITLES FROM DELMAR PUBLISHERS

Legal Writing, 2d ed., Steve Barber, 1997
Administration of Wills, Trusts, and Estates, 2d ed., Gordon W. Brown, 1997
Basics of Legal Document Preparation, Robert R. Cummins, 1997
Constitutional Law: Cases and Commentary, Daniel E. Hall, 1997
Criminal Procedure and the Constitution, Daniel E. Hall, 1997
Survey of Criminal Law, 2d ed., Daniel E. Hall, 1997
California Estate Administration, Zella Mack, 1997
Torts and Personal Injury Law, 2d ed., Cathy J. Okrent, William R. Buckley, 1997
The Law of Corporations, Partnerships, and Sole Proprietorships, 2d ed.,
    Angela Schneeman, 1997
Texas Legal Research, 2d ed., Pamela R. Tepper, Peggy N. Kerley, 1997

Legal Research, Steve Barber, Mark A. McCormick, 1996
Wills, Estates, and Trusts, Jay H. Gingrich, 1996
Criminal Law and Procedure, 2d ed., Daniel E. Hall, 1996
Introduction to Environmental Law, Harold Hickok, 1996
Civil Litigation, 2d ed., Peggy N. Kerley, Joanne Banker Hames, Paul A. Sukys, 1996
Client Accounting for the Law Firm, Elaine M. Langston, 1996
Law Office Management, 2d ed., Jonathan S. Lynton, Terri Mick Lyndall,
    Donna Masinter, 1996
Foundations of Law: Cases, Commentary, and Ethics, 2d ed., Ransford C. Pyle, 1996
Administrative Law and Procedure, Elizabeth C. Richardson, 1996
Legal Research and Writing, David J. Smith, 1996

Legal Research and Writing, Carol M. Bast, 1995
Federal Taxation, Susan G. Covins, 1995
Everything You Need to Know About Being a Legal Assistant, Chere B. Estrin, 1995
Paralegals in New York Law, Eric M. Gansberg, 1995
Ballentine's Legal Dictionary and Thesaurus, Jonathan S. Lynton, 1995
Legal Terminology with Flashcards, Cathy J. Okrent, 1995
Wills, Trusts, and Estate Administration for Paralegals, Mark A. Stewart, 1995
The Law of Contracts and the Uniform Commercial Code, Pamela R. Tepper, 1995
Life Outside the Law Firm: Non-Traditional Careers for Paralegals, Karen Treffinger, 1995

An Introduction to Paralegal Studies, David G. Cooper, Michael J. Gibson, 1994
Administrative Law, Daniel E. Hall, 1994
Ballentine's Law Dictionary: Legal Assistant Edition, Jack G. Handler, 1994
The Law of Real Property, Michael P. Kearns, 1994
Ballentine's Thesaurus for Legal Research and Writing, Jonathan S. Lynton, 1994
Legal Ethics and Professional Responsibility, Jonathan S. Lynton, Terri Mick Lyndall, 1994
Criminal Law for Paralegals, Daniel J. Markey, Jr., Mary Queen Donnelly, 1994
Family Law, Ransford C. Pyle, 1994
Paralegals in American Law: Introduction to Paralegalism, Angela Schneeman, 1994
Intellectual Property, Richard Stim, 1994

LEGAL WRITING

SECOND EDITION

Steve Barber

Delmar Publishers

an International Thomson Publishing company I(T)P®

Albany • Bonn • Boston • Cincinnati • Detroit • London • Madrid
Melbourne • Mexico City • New York • Pacific Grove • Paris • San Francisco
Singapore • Tokyo • Toronto • Washington

NOTICE TO THE READER

[...]oducts described herein or perform any independent analysis in connection with any [...]er does not assume, and expressly disclaims, any obligation to obtain and include information other than that provided to it by the manufacturer.

The reader is expressly warned to consider and adopt all safety precautions that might be indicated by the activities herein and to avoid all potential hazards. By following the instructions contained herein, the reader willingly assumes all risks in connection with such instructions.

The publisher makes no representation or warranties of any kind, including but not limited to, the warranties of fitness for particular purpose or merchantability, nor are any such representations implied with respect to the material set forth herein, and the publisher takes no responsibility with respect to such material. The publisher shall not be liable for any special, consequential, or exemplary damages resulting, in whole or in part, from the readers' use of, or reliance upon, this material.

Cover Design: Linda DeMasi
Background by Jennifer McGlaughlin

Delmar Staff
Acquisitions Editor: Christopher Anzalone
Editorial Assistant: Judy A. Roberts
Developmental Editor: Jeffrey D. Litton
Project Editor: Eugenia L. Orlandi
Production Manager: Linda J. Helfrich
Art & Design Coordinator: Douglas J. Hyldelund

Copyright © 1997
by West Publishing
an imprint of Delmar Publishers
A division of International Thomson Publishing

The ITP logo is a trademark under license.

Printed in the United States of America

For more information, contact:

Delmar Publishers
3 Columbia Circle, Box 15015
Albany, New York 12212-5015

International Thomson Editores
Campos Eliseos 385, Piso 7
Col Polanco
11560 Mexico D F Mexico

International Thomson Publishing–Europe
Berkshire House
168-173 High Holborn
London, WC1V 7AA
England

International Thomson Publishing GmbH
Königswinterer Strasse 418
53227 Bonn
Germany

Thomas Nelson Australia
102 Dodds Street
South Melbourne, 3205
Victoria, Australia

International Thomson Publishing Asia
221 Henderson Road
#05-10 Henderson Building
Singapore 0315

Nelson Canada
1120 Birchmount Road
Scarborough, Ontario
Canada, M1K 5G4

International Thomson Publishing–Japan
Hirakawacho Kyowa Building, 3F
2-2-1 Hirakawacho
Chiyoda-ku, Tokyo 102
Japan

1 2 3 4 5 6 7 8 9 10 XXX 02 01 00 99 98 97 96

Library of Congress Cataloging-in-Publication Data

Barber, Steve, 1948–
    Legal Writing / Steve Barber.—2nd ed.
        p.   cm.
    Rev. ed. of: Legal writing for paralegals, c1993.
    Includes bibliographical references and index.
    ISBN 0-8273-7539-5
    1. Legal composition.   2. Legal assistants—United States.
    I. Barber, Steve, 1948–   Legal writing for paralegals. II. Title.
    KF250.B37   1997
    808'.06634—dc20
                                    96-21164
                                    CIP
                                    AC

DEDICATION

This text is dedicated to
my wife, Mary Ann Hughes,
and my children, Kathryn and Michael.

Their presence and encouragement made this project enjoyable.
Without their support, it would not have been completed.

CONTENTS

≡ CHAPTER 4:   Diseases of Legal Writing   67

≡ CHAPTER 5:   Style: Polishing Your Writing   88

≡ CHAPTER 6:   Editing   108

≡ CHAPTER 7:   Litigation Documents   133

≡ CHAPTER 8:   Legal Correspondence   162

≡ CHAPTER 9:   Transaction Documents   177

≡ CHAPTER 10:   Legal Memoranda   203

≡ CHAPTER 11:   Legal Briefs   224

≡ Appendices   248

PREFACE

Most legal writing texts are aimed at graduate students of law and presuppose more background information about the legal process than most students actually have. This text starts with the basics of legal writing and builds on these basics before introducing more advanced concepts.

This text demonstrates the relationship of legal writing to the entire legal process, introduces the basics of technical writing, and guides the student through both theoretical and practical applications of the craft. With a focus on straightforward language devoid of "legalese," *Legal Writing* repeatedly prompts legal writers to be aware of the audience for which they are writing.

Legal Writing is adaptable to a wide range of legal professionals and offers a solid foundation to students bound for all types of legal experiences.

About the Textbook

Legal Writing presents its material in three basic segments—introductory, methodological, and document-specific. Chapters 1 and 2 introduce the components of legal writing as a communication form and examine the prewriting process.

Chapters 3 through 6 explore methodology. Structure—design, parallelism, division, classification, and sequencing—is treated in Chapter 3, while writing "diseases" and how to avoid them are presented in Chapter 4. Chapter 5 takes a thoughtful look at style and offers numerous suggestions for polishing the final document. The exploration of methodology concludes with a study of editing procedures and techniques in Chapter 6.

Chapters 7 through 11 examine the five most common forms of legal writing: memoranda, briefs, correspondence, pleadings, and transaction documents. Their similarities, differences, requisite formats, and individual characteristics are addressed in detail.

Supplementing and illustrating the text is an extensive appendix, to which the student is frequently referred. Sample documents drawn from actual cases are designed to enliven the material and help students relate to situations they are likely to encounter in their legal professional careers.

Each chapter contains both **Writing Exercises**, so the student can practice the concepts taught in that chapter, and more challenging projects in a section called **Enrichment Activities**. All new terms used in text are in **boldface** type. There are two glossaries for these new terms—a **running glossary** located in close proximity to the new term, and a more traditional **end-of-the-text glossary** that is alphabetized for quick reference. The glossary terms that do not correspond to *Ballentine's Legal Dictionary and Thesaurus* (Delmar/LCP, 1995) are indicated by a dagger (†) following the terms.

About the Instructor's Guide

To help the instructor derive maximum benefit from *Legal Writing,* each chapter of the Instructor's Guide opens with a list of specific **Learning Objectives.** The objectives are followed by several pages of **Lecture Material** designed to serve as a guide for initiating classroom discussion on the chapter topics. A number of **Teaching Suggestions** are offered, and answers are given for the **Writing Exercises** that appear in the text.

Each chapter of the Instructor's Guide contains a **Chapter Test** and provides answers for these questions.

About the Author

Steve Barber earned his Juris Doctor degree from Indiana University School of Law, where he was inducted into the Order of the Coif. It was also at Indiana University that Mr. Barber earned his Bachelor of Arts degree and membership in Phi Beta Kappa. He was an adjunct instructor in the Paralegal Program at the University of Evansville, Indiana, where he taught legal research and legal writing. The author has published a companion text entitled *Legal Research* (1996).

Acknowledgments

Steve Barber thanks his staff, especially his secretaries, Janet Williams and Jo Jackson. He also would like to acknowledge the assistance of Elizabeth Richardson, who was a consulting editor, and to thank Barry Corrado for his early direction of this project, as well as Chris Anzalone for his direction in this latest edition.

Many colleagues read early versions of the manuscript and freely offered their criticism. In this regard, the author thanks Ross Rudolph, Clark Robinson, Frank Hahn, Debbie Howard, Joseph Vreeland, Stan Levco, and the Honorable Scott Bowers. Ted Lockyear, Daniel McGinn, David Shaw, Clark Robinson, and Jack Schroeder all provided materials that were used in this text.

Some students read early versions of the manuscript and offered their insight, and many of them offered materials that were adapted into the text. Particularly helpful was Helen Reed, a law librarian and former student, as well as Evelyn Hansen-Davis and Shannon Barnes. Finally, the author would like to thank Linda Ireland Falk who copyedited this text and made it readable.

CHAPTER 1

INTRODUCTION TO LEGAL WRITING

Legal writing is one of those rare creatures, like the rat and the cockroach, that would not attract sympathy even as an endangered species.

Richard Hyland
"A Defense of Legal Writing," 134 University of Pennsylvania Law Review *599, 600 (1986)*

The public would be surprised to learn how much of a legal professional's day is spent writing. In fact, when they are not talking, legal professionals spend most of their time writing. In any given day, a lawyer might prepare a court pleading, a demand letter, a will, and a brief. Every legal professional must have a working familiarity with a wide variety of legal documents.

§ 1.1 Variety of Legal Documents

On the first day at work, a legal professional must be able to write an intraoffice memorandum (an expository form of writing), a brief (an argumentative form of writing), a contract or lease (a descriptive form of writing), or a motion to file with a court. So it is helpful to know what these documents are. Because the function is different for each form of writing, this text groups documents into the following categories: litigation documents, briefs, memoranda, transaction documents, and correspondence.

Litigation Documents

The first documents to examine are court pleadings and motions. A civil action is usually commenced when one party (the **plaintiff**) files a **complaint** against another party (the **defendant**) in a lawsuit or files a petition such as

---

TERMS

plaintiff A person who brings a lawsuit.

complaint The initial pleading in a civil action, in which the plaintiff alleges a cause of action and asks that the wrong done him or her be remedied by the court; a formal charge of a crime.

defendant The person against whom an action is brought.

that required in an adoption or an estate proceeding. A complaint states the basis of the lawsuit and identifies the relief sought. The complaint is usually accompanied by a **summons**, the document advising the defendant that some action must be taken within a specified period. When a complaint is filed, the statute of limitations is tolled or stopped.

The defendant must file a response to the complaint. One response is an **answer**, which admits or denies the allegations made in the complaint. Instead of answering the complaint, a defendant may ask the court to dismiss the complaint or petition. More typically, the defending party may ask the court for more time to prepare an answer or a motion to dismiss. Legal writers must know how to draft and file these documents and others. If a defendant decides to assert a claim against the plaintiff, a pleading known as a **counterclaim** is used. In some lawsuits, defendants make claims against codefendants, which is accomplished by filing a **cross-claim**. The complaint, the answer, the counterclaim, and the cross-claim are all pleadings filed in a lawsuit. Pleadings are forms of litigation documents and are used to assert or defend against a claim.

As a lawsuit progresses, each party will want to learn more about the facts of the adversary's case. Such information is obtained through what lawyers refer to as the **discovery process**. Most courts permit liberal discovery of information from the adverse party. One party may file **interrogatories** (written questions) to the other party for this purpose. The legal professional will need to consult with the client and prepare answers to these questions. If the client wants the opposing party to be examined by an impartial physician, a **request for examination** must be filed. If the client wishes to inspect documents held by

---

TERMS

summons In a civil case, the process by which an action is commenced and the defendant is brought within the jurisdiction of the court.

answer A pleading in response to a complaint. An answer may deny the allegations of the complaint, demur to them, agree with them, or introduce affirmative defenses intended to defeat the plaintiff's lawsuit or delay it.

counterclaim A cause of action on which a defendant in a lawsuit might have sued the plaintiff in a separate action.

cross-claim A counterclaim against a coplaintiff or a codefendant.

discovery process A means for providing a party, in advance of trial, with access to facts that are within the knowledge of the other side, to enable the party to better try his or her case.

interrogatories Written questions put by one party to another, or, in limited situations, to a witness in advance of trial.

request for examination† A written request that the opposing party in a legal action be examined by an impartial physician; part of the discovery process.

the opposition, a **request for production of documents** is necessary. To admit that certain facts are true requires filing a **request for admissions**. Each of these discovery documents is a litigation document.

Throughout a lawsuit, parties file various motions with the court. A **motion** is simply a request to the court to take some sort of action. Some motions are accompanied by **affidavits**, written statements of facts made under oath. The **affiant** (person making an affidavit) signs the document before a notary public.

When a court rules on a motion or on the merits of a case, it may ask the attorney who has prevailed to provide an entry or a decree for the court to sign. This document is sometimes called a **court order**. The **decree** or order is another document often drafted by a legal professional.

If a case proceeds to a trial, the legal professional prepares subpoenas for witnesses. A **subpoena** is an order by the court for a witness to appear at a particular place at a designated time. A subpoena may direct the witness to bring certain documents or items to court. This is a **subpoena duces tecum**. As trial approaches, the legal professional usually prepares witness lists and exhibit lists to advise the opposition as to witnesses and exhibits that will be used at the trial. Jury instructions are required for a jury trial.

After the case is decided, certain motions may be needed to initiate an appeal. These pleadings vary from jurisdiction to jurisdiction. One

---

TERMS

request for production of documents† A written request to examine documents held by the opposing party in a legal action; part of the discovery process.

request for admissions† A method of discovery in which one party submits a written request that another party admit to the truth of facts, the genuineness of documents, or the application of law to fact.

motion An application made to a court for the purpose of obtaining an order or rule directing something to be done in favor of the applicant.

affidavits Voluntary statements reduced to writing and sworn to or affirmed before a person legally authorized to administer an oath or affirmation.

affiant A person who makes a sworn written statement or affidavit.

court order A determination made by a court.

decree The final order of a court of equity, as opposed to a judgment, which is the final order of a court of law.

subpoena A command in the form of written process requiring a witness to come to court to testify.

subpoena duces tecum The *Latin* term *duces tecum* means "bring with you under penalty." A subpoena duces tecum is a written command requiring a witness to come to court to testify and at that time to produce for use as evidence the papers, documents, books, or records listed in the subpoena.

jurisdiction may require the filing of a simple notice of appeal while another jurisdiction may require an elaborate assignment of errors.

The legal professional must have a working knowledge of how to prepare court pleadings for filing. Although some pleadings may be found in form books, many of the necessary documents must be written from scratch. Even if drafting begins with using forms, each document must be carefully tailored to the particular facts of the client's case.

How to prepare litigation documents is discussed in depth in Chapter 7.

Briefs

At times during litigation, the court may expect the parties to prepare a **brief** in support of or in opposition to a motion. If a judge is unsure whether a motion should be granted, he or she will ask the parties to provide a written argument.

A brief is an argument of factual and legal reasons as to why the client's position should prevail. Before a brief is written, the applicable law must be researched. The brief may be on a topic as simple as the speed limit in a school zone, or it may focus on more complicated issues. The opposition will also file a brief to argue its side of the question. Because it is an argumentative form of writing, a brief is functionally different from the other court documents discussed previously.

When a party files a motion to dismiss or a motion for **summary judgment** (a motion asking the court to dispose of the case without trial), the court almost certainly will require a brief to support the motion. If the parties argue over whether they should be required to answer certain discovery requests, again the court may require supporting briefs. The parties must research the applicable rules and court cases to see if precedent supports their arguments. The resulting documents are called trial briefs.

A trial brief is filed with a trial court or court of original jurisdiction. A trial court is where the parties usually present evidence through witnesses and exhibits. A judge or jury hears the testimony and decides which party should prevail.

TERMS

brief A written statement submitted to a court for the purpose of persuading it of the correctness of one's position. A brief argues the facts of the case and the applicable law, supported by citations of authority.

summary judgment A method of disposing of an action without further proceedings.

Sometimes after a case is lost, a party may decide to appeal the case to a higher court—a court with appellate jurisdiction over the trial court. In such a proceeding, the parties file appellate briefs. Usually the **appellant** (the appealing party) files the first brief, and the **appellee** (the party who defends an appeal) files a response brief. The appellant then files a reply brief. Many appellate courts set forth rigid rules for the form of trial briefs. They may require certain information in the brief and demand adherence to specific page limitations, margin requirements, and color standards for the covers. If a party fails to comply with these rules, that party may lose the appeal.

Brief writers attempt to persuade courts that points of law should be applied to benefit their clients. Parties may ask the court to either establish a precedent or apply an existing precedent to decide the case. The parties may have a dispute over a court rule or a constitutional provision. Chapter 11 deals with writing briefs.

Memoranda

Similar to a brief is a **memorandum**. A memorandum of law is prepared to explain or summarize the law or the facts on a certain subject and is usually used within the law office or by the client for informational purposes. The memorandum may contain recommendations to the client or may be used by other legal professionals within the law firm. Writing a memorandum may involve looking up a few cases on a topic, or it may involve researching and reporting on a rather complicated issue. In a brief, the writer argues a position. In a memorandum, the writer describes what he or she believes to be the existing law. Although some may refer to a brief as a memorandum, in this text, a memorandum is strictly an intraoffice document.

The purpose of a legal memorandum is to tell the reader what the law is on a given subject. It is descriptive and objective. Chapter 10 examines the techniques of writing legal memoranda.

TERMS

appellant   A party who appeals from a lower court to a higher court.

appellee   A party against whom a case is appealed from a lower court to a higher court.

memorandum   A writing made for the purpose of preserving events or ideas in one's memory or communicating them to someone else; a writing made for the purpose of recording and evidencing the terms of an agreement prior to drafting it.

Transaction Documents

A law professor once quipped that lawyers are usually only involved when there is tragedy or something of value exchanges hands. Transaction documents are prepared by legal professionals when something of value exchanges hands. Lawyers are routinely asked to document large transactions. In fact, as transactions become more complicated, the work of the legal professional becomes more complicated as well.

Centuries ago, a real estate transaction was memorialized by a ceremony. The ceremony was a way to remember the transaction. Even today a few deals are sealed with a handshake. Today, however, almost all transactions are documented in writing. Lawyers typically prepare **transaction documents** to memorialize events. Wills, trusts, corporate minutes, and bills of sale are all transaction documents.

Other documents, such as **bilateral agreements** (agreements containing mutual promises of performance), must be prepared to record ongoing relationships. Common examples include the lease and the contract. In a bilateral agreement, the drafter is not only recording an event or transaction but also planning a future relationship for the parties. Unlike the parties to pleadings, the parties to transaction documents do not want their documents read by a court. In fact, they prepare these documents in an effort to stay out of court. A legal professional should be able to prepare simple contracts and leases with minimal supervision from a lawyer. The drafting of these documents is discussed in Chapter 9.

Correspondence

Most texts on legal writing omit instruction on the most common task of legal professionals: writing correspondence. Preparing quality correspondence may be the most neglected activity of a law office, yet often the clients' only impression of the law firm derives from the correspondence they receive. Demand letters (letters demanding payment of debt), settlement proposals, client reports, and letters between counsel are just a few of the letters a legal professional prepares in the course of a week. Some correspondence may be as uncomplicated as confirming a telephone call or telling the client of a date for a hearing, but other correspondence

---

TERMS

transaction documents† Documents that memorialize events: *e.g.*, deeds, wills, trusts, contracts, bills of sale, and corporate minutes.

bilateral agreements Agreements in which each party promises performance to the other, the promise by the one furnishing the consideration for the promise from the other.

may be expository or even argumentative, such as in a settlement demand letter. Because this activity is so common, it deserves special treatment. Chapter 8 discusses legal correspondence, including examples of several commonly written letters.

§ 1.2 The Importance of Legal Writing Skills

Clients pay substantial fees to have lawyers prepare legal documents. As noted previously, legal professionals probably spend more of their time writing than doing any other single activity. As a result, good writing skills are a prerequisite to success as a legal professional. Cases may be won or lost and deals may close or go sour based on the documents that have been prepared. Thus, a measure of the firm's success depends on the legal professional's performance.

Those who may be intimidated by the legal writing process may be surprised to learn that many lawyers have little formal writing training. Perhaps this lack of training is part of the reason that federal and state laws have been passed requiring some legal documents to be written in simple English so they can be read and understood by the people who use them. Remember the last time you read a signature card to open a bank account? How about an insurance contract or an apartment lease or mortgage? Even lawyers have trouble understanding the meaning of some of these documents, but gradual improvement in readability has occurred over the past two decades. Under the federal pension reform legislation (ERISA), for example, the plan description that is distributed to employees must be written in language the average participant can understand. Leases in New York must now be written in simple language. When Jimmy Carter was president, he ordered the simplification of federal regulations. The 1975 Magnuson-Moss Warranty Act required that warranties for consumer products be written in "simple and readily understandable language."

Numerous other laws have been passed or proposed calling for consumer documents to be written in understandable language. These laws are part of what is known as the **plain-English movement**—a movement away from so-called legalese. This text illustrates how court rules mandate "simple" pleadings, consumer documents must be readable, and briefs should be written so the court can easily follow the gist of the argument.

TERMS

plain-English movement† A movement away from so-called legalese; *e.g.,* plain English activists promoted the passage of laws calling for consumer documents to be written in understandable language.

If a document is written clearly, if it is logical and understandable to the writer, the document should pass muster with any audience. No law says that legal documents must be written in archaic legalese! But before being paid to prepare that first legal document, the legal professional should understand how legal writing compares to other forms of writing.

§ 1.3 Characteristics of Legal Writing

A legal document is a form of communication. All written communication has four components: an author, an audience, a writing, and a speech community. It is helpful to consider the role of the legal professional in relation to these components.

The Author

The legal profession claims the exclusive right to prepare legal documents. Laws in most states boost this claim by prohibiting nonlawyers from engaging in the unauthorized practice of law. In fact, it is a crime in most states to perform the work of a lawyer for a client unless you are admitted to the bar. Even filling in forms may violate these statutes. As a result, lawyers enjoy a virtual monopoly in this area. Lawyers as authors of legal documents enjoy a unique privilege. Legal professionals can prepare legal documents and not violate these laws only if their work is properly supervised by an attorney.

The Legal Author's Goals

Most authors write with a goal to entertain, to sell books or articles, to teach, to sell products, or to create. In contrast, legal professionals use language as a tool to help clients. Lawyers use **nonemotive language** (language without emotional content) to make a contract or file a motion with a court. Lawyers also use language to help parties set up relationships such as that of landlord and tenant, bank and borrower, or buyer and seller.

TERMS

---

nonemotive language† Language that lacks emotional content.

At other times the legal writer uses **emotive language** (language meant to induce an emotional response such as in a sales pitch) in a brief to persuade a court to take a particular course of action. Always the legal writer composes these documents without providing a clue as to what he or she personally feels about the transaction, motion, or argument.

The legal writer owes a duty to the client but owes no duty to the other side of a suit or transaction except to act within the bounds of ethics and the law. Lawyers exercise the duty to a client by coloring a motion or contract to favor that client. Another author (the opposing lawyer) may rewrite the document to recolor it for another client's advantage. Still another lawyer may research the same document years later and try to interpret it differently from the intended meaning of the original authors.

The Legal Author's Responsibilities

With these privileges associated with the practice of law come responsibilities. In the filing of court pleadings, court rules protect against abuses. A court may impose fines on a party for filing frivolous or sham pleadings. In the filing of briefs, practical restraints help ensure that arguments are presented fairly. In the drafting of contracts and leases, the *contra proferentem* **rule** may protect against a drafter sneaking questionable provisions into a transaction document. This *contra proferentem* rule says that ambiguity in a document is construed against the document's author. So if the author of a legal document creates doubt as to how the document should be interpreted, the doubt will be resolved against the author.

Legal professionals provide services, and their time is charged to the client. When they prepare legal documents for a client, they need to start the writing process knowing that they are professional writers who represent the interests of the client and that they, too, have constraints on the manner in which that role is satisfied.

The Audience

Most writers want a wide audience. Usually the wider the audience, the better the compensation. This rule does not apply to legal professionals. The legal professional might think that the audience for a legal

---

TERMS

emotive language† Language meant to provide an emotional response; *e.g.,* a sales pitch or an attorney's summation to a jury.

contra proferentem **rule†** A court rule providing that ambiguity in a document be construed against the document's author.

document is the client, but it is not always that simple. Certainly the client is part of the audience. The audience, however, is more varied than the immediate parties to the transaction.

Publishers target an audience. Although lawyers are professional writers, they seldom consider who is their audience. The ultimate reviewer of legal documents is a court. The immediate audience is the parties to the event or transaction. A secondary audience is the possible assignees, beneficiaries, heirs, and successors to the transaction. A peripheral audience includes attorneys and other persons who may review the document years later in connection with future transactions.

Courts

Obviously, the ultimate audience for most legal documents is a court, yet the good drafter of a contract or lease tries to avoid this audience. The legal professional normally does not want a contract or lease to end in a court dispute. A drafter, however, cannot ignore the possibility that the document may end in a dispute no matter how well it is drafted. The drafter must anticipate that the document may end in litigation.

Trial lawyers who dream of writing the script for their next trial often fail to realize that whenever they draft a document, they are preparing the "testimony" relating to a transaction. These lawyers are forgetting their audience. An agreement prepared by the legal professional may be the only material testimony introduced at trial regarding the transaction.

Each time a document is drafted, the legal professional should remember that even if the document fails in meeting the primary goal of avoiding litigation, the drafting of the script may still succeed if it is done so a court can understand it and interpret it to the client's benefit. Every document should be prepared as if it will ultimately be read in court.

Clients

Clients are the immediate audience for most legal documents. If an agreement is written so that it can be understood by the client and disputes arise during its term, attorneys may not have to become involved in the interpretation process. Clearly written transaction documents enable clients to solve problems without legal assistance.

A good drafter writes so that clients (the first audience) understand the documents. After all, the client pays the legal professional for the legal work. It is the client who will consult the document in the future. The document should be drafted in anticipation of any problems that later may arise between the parties to the transaction.

When amicable parties first appear at a lawyer's office, it is sometimes difficult to believe there will ever be a problem between them. But while parties may be eager for an agreement at the time a document is prepared, it does not follow that they will be on the same friendly footing throughout the term of the agreement. Moreover, an attorney who has handled estates realizes that even close-knit families cannot always agree on the disposition of a deceased's property. That is why any loose ends should be taken care of at the time of the consummation of the agreement, if possible, while parties are eager to do business.

Successors to the Transaction

The immediate parties to the legal document do not make up the total universe of its users. If the document is assignable (that is, if its rights or duties can be transferred to a person not a party to the document) or if one of the parties dies, other persons may claim rights under the document. When a document is initially executed, the parties may have little anticipation of ever litigating any disputes. Yet as any practicing attorney should know, their in-laws and spouses may eventually spark a controversy that can be solved only by litigation. A drafter may believe that a contract between two siblings will never be litigated, yet if one of the siblings dies, the in-laws may not be quite as friendly. The party eager to start a new business and the party eager to retire may both change their minds as time goes on. During negotiations, the typical layperson tends to doubt that the other party would ever breach the agreement, yet contracts are broken every day.

Suppose that a legal professional haphazardly drafts an agreement between two friends or relatives and later finds that the agreement ends in litigation after both have assigned their interests to third parties. The drafter can mutter about unforeseeability, but this problem was not unforeseeable. The drafter merely failed to consider the wider audience.

Thus, the audience for a legal document encompasses third parties (friends, relatives, or others with whom the original party has legal relationships) and parties who might step into the shoes of the original parties (such as a receiver or a trustee in bankruptcy). The wider audience may be quite expansive. Shareholders may change, a corporation may merge or expand, partners may die. The Internal Revenue Service may audit the transaction, and the accountant may take a deduction or credit based on its tax ramifications. Third parties, such as a trustee or a creditor in a bankruptcy proceeding, will not read a document with the view of the friend or relative with whom your client originally negotiated the transaction. These events are not unforeseeable or even unexpected. They represent daily possibilities. A legal writer must be aware of the audience beyond the immediate parties, including all possible assignees, beneficiaries, heirs, and successors to the transaction.

Subsequent Reviewers of the Transaction

The audience may include attorneys who may review an instrument of title in an abstract decades later or an attorney consulted to find a loophole in the agreement. It may include a bank that is asked to lend monies on the basis of the agreement. This peripheral audience cannot be ignored. Legal professionals must remember that it is difficult to know every person who might read the documents they prepare. Some will read them with a friendly view and others may read them with disgust. The writer must try to look far beyond the client when envisioning the audience.

The Writing

The writing has an important function in law. In fact, some transactions must be in writing to be enforceable. The written document is used to memorialize the transaction. If a transaction later ends in litigation, the document the legal professional prepared may be used as evidence in the case.

The Necessity of the Writing

The laws that require certain transactions to be documented in writing are called **statutes of frauds**, and they vary from state to state. Most state statutes of frauds require written documents for contracts that will not be performed within one year, real estate contracts, and contracts involving certain minimum values. Although there are exceptions, an oral contract is unenforceable if it does not comply with the statute of fraud requirements.

In addition to statutes of frauds, there are **parol evidence rules**, which provide that a party cannot by means of oral testimony contradict or vary the terms of a written document. If a written contract specifies payment of ten dollars, for example, parties are not usually permitted at trial to testify that they meant five dollars. Although there are various exceptions to parol evidence rules, the law favors the written word over sworn

---

TERMS

---

statutes of frauds   Statutes, existing in one or another form in every state, that require certain classes of contracts to be in writing and signed by the parties.

parol evidence rules   Rules stating that evidence of prior or contemporaneous oral agreements that would change the terms of a written contract are inadmissible.

testimony. (One such exception is the partial integration doctrine, which permits the use of oral evidence to prove provisions not inconsistent with the written terms.)

Written agreements serve as evidence of the parties' agreement. The writing cautions and reminds parties of their obligations. In our society, written documents to record information replace the ritual ceremonies of earlier ages. A legal document defines relationships between parties, provides for sanctions, and grants privileges or rights to a party. A deed, a power of attorney, or a will memorializes an event or an intent. When times were less litigious, oral agreements or handshakes may have been sufficient. But as the complexity of transactions increased, it became unrealistic to rely solely on the memory of individuals who witnessed an agreement between parties.

The complexity of our legal system is a direct response to the complexities of everyday society. Legal professionals must be aware of these complexities as they prepare documents for clients, remembering that the function of any legal document is to anticipate and avoid litigation as much as is foreseeably possible.

Functions of the Writing

The drafter of a transaction document such as a contract creates a relationship. The relationship may have been partially negotiated before the parties appeared at the law office, but usually it is still forming at that time. Typically, when a legal professional first meets a client, the parties announce they have reached an agreement and need only the "paperwork." Seldom is this the case.

In the situation where an individual has just sold his or her house on contract, for example, it is not unusual for the client to inform the attorney that all "terms and conditions" of the agreement have been established, when in fact all that has been established is the price and perhaps the terms of payment. Legal professionals preparing their first contract consult a **form book** and suddenly realize (usually after the client has left the office) that such concerns as taxes and insurance have not even been discussed. Most parties do not anticipate future problems in their relationships. They fail to anticipate what would happen if the house were to burn before the purchaser took possession or if the purchaser could not secure

---

TERMS

form book† Book that provides forms for court-related documents (*e.g.*, complaints, answers, motions) or transaction-related documents (*e.g.*, wills, trusts, leases).

financing. Just as frequently, the parties overlook such obvious concerns as who must pay the taxes or the insurance premiums.

A legal document may be consulted at various times by the parties—and the expectation is that the parties will find ready answers to future problems when they look at that document. The law permits parties to fix the rules that will be used by them to solve difficulties that occur during the life of the transaction. This concept of freedom of contract is fundamental to understanding the role of a drafter in preparing bilateral agreements for parties.

All legal writers must approach the drafting process with Murphy's Law in mind—what *can* go wrong probably *will* go wrong. Drafting is a litigation-avoidance process, but if a document does end in litigation, the drafter wants sufficient evidence to record the transaction favorably for the client. Even though this aim should be evident, many lawyers tend to overlook it.

In summary, important observations of the function of a written record should be made. First, in every type of legal document, the drafter attempts to reflect either past, present, or future intentions of the parties. Second, the document may create rights, duties, privileges, or responsibilities. An important function of legal writing is to encapsulate agreements, but more often, the function is to *finish* the agreement for the parties. Finally, the drafter must ensure that the writing is in compliance with the applicable statute of frauds and any other legal requirements.

The Speech Community

A speech community shares common cultural and language rules. A legal professional is a member of a narrow speech community. To become accepted in the community, the legal professional must learn the rules. For example, legal professionals use many words and expressions unique to their profession:

motion in limine	*per curium*
personal jurisdiction	*sua sponte*
ratio decidendi	*weight of evidence*
obiter dictum	*summary judgment*
res ipsa loquitur	*directed verdict*
prima facie	*ejusdem generis*

From the first day, the legal professional student needs to begin to learn the vocabulary of the law.

In addition, the legal professional student needs to avidly read law and about law whenever possible. The law is contained in constitutions, cases, statutes, court rules, and ordinances. The basic language of the law is found in these source documents. In addition to the law, there are many works written about the law such as encyclopedias, periodicals, articles, and books. These works explain the law. By reading these works, the legal professional student will begin to understand the necessary vocabulary and concepts of the law. Much of the student's success as a writer depends on how much the student reads and understands law.

Learning the language of the law, however, involves more than merely learning new words and expressions. Legal professionals prepare legal documents according to certain rules or conventions. For example, a brief may need a section on the jurisdictional basis of the appeal, another section on the procedural posture of the case, and a section with the argument. By referring to cases or statutes in a brief, the legal professional student will learn how lawyers cite such authority. Lawyers follow very precise rules on citation. The student must learn to format legal documents.

In addition to vocabulary and format, the law has developed certain rules for interpreting legal documents—so-called rules of construction. These rules are used to settle language disputes and to interpret statutes, contracts, or other legal documents. Courts are always deciding how to interpret a word or phrase in a statute, an ambiguity in a contract, or the language of a lease. Over the centuries, the courts developed the rules of construction so there would be an objective basis for deciding language disputes. By understanding these rules of construction, the legal professional student begins to appreciate the kinds of problems caused by sloppy drafting.

§ 1.4 The Rules of Construction

Language experts call the study of the rules of our speech community **semiotics**. Semiotics consists of the study of **semantics** (the meaning of words), **syntactics** (the relationship of words to one another), and **pragmatics** (the effect of words on us). Chapter 4 examines the way in which semantics and syntactics can help the legal professional write more clearly.

TERMS

semiotics† The study of the rules of our speech community.
semantics† The meaning of words.
syntactics† The relationship of words to one another.
pragmatics† The effect of words on those who hear or see them.

In the legal arena, the courts are ultimately responsible for resolving any controversy over the meaning of words. Courts have developed their own speech rules to resolve language disputes. Many of these rules have Latin names, such as *ejusdem generis, noscitur a sociis,* and *expressio unius est exclusio alterius.* These terms are not as difficult to understand when we explain them in English. Other rules such as consistency principles and the precedent-antecedent doctrine are somewhat self-explanatory. Because the legal professional drafts legal documents for clients, it is helpful for the legal professional student to understand the speech rules used by courts. The end of this chapter shows that although these rules have been used for centuries, they are not always effective at providing a means to resolve language disputes. Nevertheless, the student should acquire familiarity with the concepts.

The Consistency Principles

Unless technical terms are used, a court attempts to read a disputed document to ascertain the intent of the parties according to the common meaning of the terms. All words in an agreement must be considered in determining the meaning of the contract without rendering any word, phrase, or paragraph ineffective or meaningless, if possible. Each word, phrase, or term is presumed to have the same meaning throughout the document. Each time a different word, phrase, or term is used, a different meaning is presumed. The consistency requirement provides the underpinning for many of the basic rules used by the courts in construing documents. Throughout this text are examples of errors that resulted from inconsistency. The first drafting principle is that every term must be consistent with every other term. This principle flows, of course, from logic. But it also flows from the court decisions that hold that the intention of the parties must be determined by reading the instrument as a whole.

The Specific Limits the General

Specific words limit the meaning of more general words. Lawyers refer to this rule by its Latin name, *ejusdem generis. Ballentine's Legal Dictionary and Thesaurus* defines this rule as follows:

> The rule of construction that when things are enumerated in a document (such as a contract, will, or statute), followed by a more general

────────────── **TERMS** ──────────────

ejusdem generis†   Of the same kind or class; specific words limit the meaning of more general words.

description, the general description will be understood to relate only to things similar in kind to those enumerated.[1]

But what does the rule actually mean? Suppose a teacher says, "Peter, Paul, and the other students will be permitted to go to recess." Does this include all the rest of the students? Use of the *ejusdem generis* rule might lead to the conclusion the boys can go but not the girls. A list of people or things does not give them their widest meaning but, instead, limits the meaning to those in the same class as those specifically listed. If only boys are enumerated, girls may not be included under "other students."

The following examples illustrate how this rule has been applied in court cases. Where a pornography statute used the words "book, pamphlet, picture, motion picture film, paper, letter, writing, print," the statute was held not to include phonograph records, since it listed only objects that can be seen or viewed.[2] Similarly, where a person promised to pay "all unpaid taxes and mortgages shown of record and all other liens . . .," the phrase "all other liens" was construed to include only *recorded* documents, and not an unrecorded mortgage.[3]

The *ejusdem generis* doctrine is applied frequently when words of enumeration are followed by words such as "other," "any other," or "otherwise." This doctrine applies when the enumerated terms can be classified with similar characteristics.

Context Clues

Often the meaning of a word or phrase is interpreted by surrounding words. According to *Black's Law Dictionary*, **noscitur a sociis** means that "general and specific words are associated with and take color from each other,"[4] restricting a general word to a less general meaning in relationship with other words in the sentence. This rule simply says that when there is a word of doubtful meaning, the meaning for that word can be ascertained by looking at the words associated with it. This is the same rule you learned in grade school about using context clues to discover the meaning of other words in the paragraph. The courts use the Latin word to indicate that the meaning of a doubtful word can be found by looking at other words associated with the doubtful word in the document.

TERMS

noscitur a sociis†   A rule suggesting that the meaning of a word or phrase be interpreted by surrounding words.

Intended Omissions

Expressio unius est exclusio alterius (expression of one thing is the exclusion of another) provides that if a writing specifies an exception or condition, then other exceptions or conditions not mentioned are intended to be excluded. A simple example would be where a man leaves his estate "to my children except for my oldest son." An illegitimate son attempts to claim his share of the estate. The *exclusio alterius* doctrine holds that if one thing or category is specifically identified, the others are meant to be excluded. Since the man specified an exception, there would be no other exception intended, so the illegitimate son would be able to share in the estate.

In another case, a physician withdrew from a partnership. The partnership agreement limited a physician who quit the partnership from practicing for two years in a defined area. The partners sued to enforce this agreement. The applicable statute voided contracts that restrained a person from "exercising a lawful profession, trade or business of any kind." Another section, however, made an exception, permitting those in "business" to contract not to compete. Is a professional partnership a business? Using the *expressio unius* doctrine, the court held that the exception did not apply to a professional partnership.

Simply put, the *expressio unius* doctrine presumes that omissions are intended.

§ 1.5 The Counterrules of Construction

The rules of construction best illustrate the errors made by legal writers. These rules of construction actually are not nearly as important as one might think at first blush, since for each of these rules or canons, there is a counterrule. As Karl Llewellyn noted:

> When it comes to presenting a proposed construction in court, there is an accepted conventional vocabulary. As in argument over points of

TERMS

expressio unius est exclusio alterius† A rule providing that if a writing specifies an exception or condition, then other exceptions or conditions not mentioned were intentionally excluded.

caselaw, the accepted convention still, unhappily requires discussion as if only one single correct meaning could exist. Hence there are two opposing canons on almost every point. . . .

Plainly, to make any canon take hold in a particular instance, the construction contended for must be sold, essentially, by means other than the use of the canon: The good sense of the situation and a simple construction of the available language to achieve that sense, by tenable means, out of the statutory language.[5]

What this means is that a court can reach a result, and then select the canon of construction to validate that result, since there is an opposing canon on each point. Every rule has a counterrule that will permit the court to reach a result opposite the rule if necessary. The following are examples of some construction rules and counterrules:

Rule	Counterrule
• A statue cannot go beyond its test.	• To effect its purpose a statute may be implemented beyond its text.
• If language is plain and unambiguous it must be given effect.	• Not when literal interpretation would lead to absurd or mischievous consequences or thwart manifest purpose.
• Words and phrases which have received judicial construction before enactment are to be understood according to that construction.	• Not if the statute clearly requires them to have a different meaning.
• Every word and clause must be given effect.	• If inadvertently inserted or if repugnant to the rest of the statute, they may be rejected as surplusage.[6]

The point here is that a student of the drafting process gains little insight by studying the court decisions to learn legal writing, except perhaps in identifying problem situations. Judges are not linguistics experts. Decisions are made and then rationalized.

The important thing to understand is that each document is a communication. When the law requires that a deed use precise words such as "convey and warrant" or that an option to purchase real estate use "binding or irrevocable," these legal rules for this speech community must be followed. A brief also may have precise format requirements that must be followed. In most situations, however, the writer simply must write precisely and accurately.

§ 1.6 Applying Writing Skills to the Legal Writing Process

Most good writers will make good legal writers, but legal writing skills are not always commensurate with general writing or grammar skills. Examples better illustrate this point. English teachers often advise students not to repeat the same word over and over in writing, and young students take this rule to heart. Yet this rule is contrary to a fundamental rule of drafting that holds that consistency is of paramount concern. The consistency principle states that every time the same meaning or concept is expressed, the same word or phrase or clause should be used. Every time a different meaning or concept is intended, a different word or phrase or clause should be used. If the foremost principle of drafting is to write as simply as possible for the transaction, the second most important rule is to follow this consistency principle. Most inexperienced drafters find it difficult to use the same word over and over again in the same document, yet consistency demands this approach.

As students become more sophisticated, English teachers teach them to write "impersonally." This maxim leads to the use of passive voice constructions, inversions such as "there are . . ." and windups such as "it is evident. . . ." Scholarly writers tend to prefer passive voice. From a legal drafting standpoint, however, the conscious use of active voice ensures that the party who is delegated a duty or responsibility has been properly identified. After all, legal documents involve people. Use of active voice in legal drafting ensures that who does what to whom is identified.

Many legal professionals are not taught how to transfer general writing rules to the drafting process. Consider the problem of *ejusdem generis*, the doctrine that if a general word follows a series of specific words, the general word becomes limited by the special words. In the example "cars, trucks, and other motor vehicles," the drafter may have intended to expand the words to include more than cars and trucks. The *ejusdem generis* doctrine, however, tells us that "other motor vehicles" must be in the same class as a car or a truck. Certainly one may argue, as many scholars do, that the drafter did not intend to limit the words "other motor vehicles" to vehicles precisely like cars and trucks. Whether the drafter also intended to encompass a motorcycle, jeep, or moped by the term "other vehicles" may have been frustrated by the *ejusdem generis* rule. The legal scholars bicker about whether this rule reflects what was really intended.

Doubtless these same scholars were once chastised by their writing teachers for using the word "etc." Such usage, they were told, left what was being included open to question. The drafter who uses the general words "other vehicles" commits the same offense as the elementary student who uses the abbreviation "etc." Neither usage is acceptable. Just as any competent writer avoids "etc.," so must any competent drafter avoid situations that lead to the application of the *ejusdem generis* doctrine.

Another universal grammar lesson is that of the vague referent. Most first-year college students are required to take an English composition course. Many of them encounter instructors who pretend not to understand what the word "it" or "this" refers to at the beginning of a sentence. Teachers of English composition seem to enjoy circling the word "it" and asking in the margin, "What does 'it' refer to?" Unfortunately, the same students who learn this lesson may later become lawyers and turn to such legal abominations as "such," "said," "hereinabove," and "hereinafter." These terms are the legal counterparts of the vague referents the students were taught to avoid. Just as the student learned when not to use "it" in English composition, as a legal writer, the student must learn to use "such," "said," "hereinabove," and "hereinafter" as sparingly.

Beyond Technical Writing

Legal writers must become familiar with rules of technical writing, but rules alone are not enough. Legal writers must also master the unique features of the legal writing process. For example, the rule of consistency discussed earlier—the premise that each time the same meaning or concept is intended, the same word or phrase is used—is uniquely important to the legal drafting process.

By integrating theories from technical writing, editing, and legal drafting, the legal professional student will acquire the requisite skills for legal writing. The student must develop a propensity to spot problem words as well as problem grammatical constructions. Successive prepositional phrases, the participle, and certain conjunctives are symptoms of equivocation. As the student learns and applies this knowledge, the student should develop a readable style that is compatible with the aims of the plain-English movement.

Although it is helpful to categorize and understand the problems of legal writing, it is more helpful to find solutions for these problems. Consider again the *ejusdem generis* situation of "cars, trucks, and other motor vehicles." Students typically opine that no legal professional can be expected to enumerate all possible situations: it would take pages of words to solve this problem. Unfortunately, that is how most drafters think, but the answer is just the opposite. If the problem is reconceptualized, a simple phrase—"any motor vehicle"—may solve the problem. *Ejusdem generis* situations are avoided through reconceptualization, not further enumeration. When strings of words are used, the words should be reduced to the "lowest common denominator." Faced with the temptation to write "give, devise and convey," for example, the drafter need only use "give." Reduction to the lowest common denominator is accomplished by deleting the extra words.

Sometimes the worst student of legal writing is one who has already been exposed to the language of law and has accepted lawyers' use of centuries-old jargon without asking why this archaic language survives in a modern age. In one lamentably true-to-life cartoon, a client hands a document to a lawyer with an instruction to "add some legalese." Sadly, some legal writers perceive this as their role and are amazed to be told that it is not only acceptable, but preferable, to draft documents in simple English. This may be the foremost principle of legal writing: *The drafter should write so that he or she and the client can understand the transaction.* A crude agreement drafted by a layperson can be just as valid a contract as the most sophisticated document drafted by a Wall Street law firm. There is no one correct method for approaching legal writing. The purpose of writing is to communicate, and communication is the goal of every legal professional.

Transaction documents and pleadings are among the forms of legal writing that require great precision and accuracy. In these areas, this text stresses principles to achieve such precision and accuracy. Rationales for rules and principles set forth in this text have been explored. The student who decides to discard a writing principle will do so with full awareness of the risks of that decision. Every time a principle of drafting is ignored, the risk of ambiguity lurks.

As the student begins to understand the techniques for drafting agreements, even the newspaper will be read differently. The student will notice how a reporter uses ambiguity in writing a news article, how a cartoonist uses equivocation for humor, and how deliberate ambiguity calls attention to a sales pitch. Learning writing skills helps develop reading skills as well.

Learning About Your Subject Matter

In some respects, a good legal writer is like any other good writer. A good writer, like a good actor, learns as much about the subject matter as possible before beginning to write. A skilled legal writer tries to learn as much as possible from the client. If the client is a retailer, the writer must learn about retailing. If the client is in the fishing business, the writer must know the problems of the fishing business. The hardest lesson to learn is that law is fact-intensive: A complaint is a story about a wrong, and the writer must learn about the story. A contract is a map of a relationship, and the writer must learn the details of the relationship. A real estate agreement is likely to concern the sale of a house, and the writer must learn what can go wrong in a house. A skilled legal professional learns all the facts.

This book sets forth the rules for competent writing techniques. After reading it, the student should be able to draft a document that can be understood by a reasonably intelligent client. Throughout the student's professional life these legal writing techniques will be continuously practiced and polished.

Writing Exercises

1. Use the lowest-common-denominator principle to correct the flaw in this sentence opening.

   I hereby give, devise, bequeath, transfer, and convey to you . . .

2. Identify the rule of construction that best describes this writing flaw.

   I like cows, dogs, and other farm animals.

   Rewrite the sentence to correct the flaw.

3. Identify the rule of construction that best describes this writing flaw.

   I like dogs. These wolf-like animals are smart. I own a mutt. Do you like canine-type animals?

   Rewrite the sentences to correct the flaw.

4. Identify the rule of construction that best describes this writing flaw.

   It shall be unlawful to spit or expectorate on any public sidewalk or other public place, or on the floor or walls of any store, theater, hall, public vehicle, or other place frequented by the public or to which the public is invited.

   Rewrite the sentence to correct the flaw.

5. Go to a law library. Find several truck leases in a book of legal forms. Copy two of them. Which one is more complete? Which one is better written? Explain.

6. An attorney hands you the complaint form that appears in Figure 1–1 and tells you his clients are John Doe and Mary Doe. The vehicle in which they were traveling was struck at the intersection of Oak and Maple when an automobile driven by Joe Hotrod ran a stop sign. The attorney tells you to use the form to prepare a complaint.

   a. Find two other complaint forms at a law library. Copy them.

STATE OF INDIANA   )   SS:
COUNTY OF _____)   IN THE _____ _____COURT
)
_____)
         Plaintiff   )
)   CAUSE NO. _____
         vs.   )
_____)
        Defendant   )

COMPLAINT

Comes now the plaintiff, _____, by _____ of _____, h_____ attorneys, and for h_____ cause of action herein states and alleges as follows:

1. The plaintiff, _____, is a resident of _____ County, residing at _____, _____, Indiana 4_____.

2. The defendant, _____, resides at _____, _____, _____ County, Indiana, 4_____.

3. On _____ _____, 19___, plaintiff, _____, was operating a vehicle owned by _____, and traveling _____ on _____ at the intersection of _____.

4. At said time and place the vehicle being operated by plaintiff, _____, was struck broadside by a vehicle being operated by defendant, _____, when defendant failed to stop at a stop sign located at the intersection of _____ and _____.

5. The defendant, _____, was negligent in the following particulars, to-wit:

    a. The defendant, _____, did not obey a traffic sign;
    b. The defendant, _____, failed to yield right-of-way to a moving vehicle;
    c. The defendant, _____, failed to keep a proper lookout;
    d. The defendant, _____, was operating a motor vehicle without a driver's license.

6. As a result of the negligent and careless actions of the defendant, _____ the plaintiff, _____, sustained the following injuries directly and proximately by reason of the negligent acts or omissions to act on the part of the defendant in this, to-wit:

    a. Multiple abrasions, contusions and lacerations;
    b. Injury to right arm;
    c. Injury to face and scalp;
    d. Disfigurement and scarring of arm; and,
    e. Severe physical pain and mental anguish.

7. As a result of the injuries sustained, the plaintiff has incurred medical and hospital expenses and will continue to do so in the future. Plaintiff is unable to state the exact amount of h_____ losses at this time.

FIGURE 1–1
Complaint Form

FIGURE 1–1
(continued)

WHEREFORE, the plaintiff, _____, prays judgment of and from the defendant, _____, in an amount that will fairly and equitably compensate h_____ for h_____ losses, damages, for h_____ costs herein laid out and expended and for all other just and proper relief in the premises.

_____ & _____

Attorneys at Law
123 N.W. 4th St., Suite 402
Evansville, Indiana 47708
Phone: (812) 555-5555

By: _____

_____
ATTORNEYS FOR PLAINTIFF

DEMAND FOR JURY TRIAL

Plaintiff respectfully requests a trial by jury in this matter.

_____ & _____

Attorneys at Law
123 N.W. 4th St., Suite 402
Evansville, Indiana 47708
Phone: (812) 555-5555

By: _____

_____
ATTORNEYS FOR PLAINTIFF

    b. Compare the complaint forms from the law library with the one from the attorney. Which one would you use? Are any of them better than others in some ways? Explain.

    c. Prepare a complaint. Are there other questions you need to ask? List the questions.

7. An attorney hands you the real estate purchase agreement form in Figure 1–2 and tells you that her clients are John Doe and Mary Doe. They are buying a house located at 630 Oak Street from Mary Breach. They need a purchase agreement. The deposit is $5,000. The purchase price is $60,000. The clients need to acquire financing, and the house must be inspected for termites. The attorney instructs you to initiate the transaction by preparing the agreement.

FIGURE 1–2
Real Estate
Purchase
Agreement
Form

REAL ESTATE PURCHASE AGREEMENT

THIS Real Estate Purchase Agreement is made this _____ day of _____, 19___, between _____ and _____ ("Purchasers") and _____ and _____ ("Owners").

Recitals:

The purchasers agree to purchase from owners, the real estate located at _____, Vanderburgh County, Indiana and more particularly described as follows:

The _____ (_____) feet of Lot_____ (_____), adjoining Lot _____ (_____), all of Lot _____ (_____) and the West or adjoining _____ (_____) feet of Lot _____ (_____) in Block _____ (_____) in a Subdivision of Blocks _____ (_____), _____ (_____), _____ (_____), _____ (_____), _____ (_____), _____ (_____), _____ (_____) and _____ (_____) of _____ Addition to the City of _____, as per plat thereof, recorded in Plat Book _____, pages _____ and _____ in the office of the Recorder of _____ County, Indiana.

Subject to all roadways, highways, easements, rights of way, assessments, building and use restrictions of record or affecting the use or occupancy of said real estate.

for the purchase price of _____ Thousand Dollars ($_____,000.00) upon the following terms and conditions:

1. PURCHASE PRICE: The purchase price of _____ Thousand Dollars ($_____,000.00) is payable at closing.
2. ABSTRACT OR TITLE INSURANCE: Evidence of good and merchantable title shall be furnished in the form of an abstract of title certified to date OR title insurance in an amount not less than the purchase price, at Owner's option. Evidence of title shall be billed in accordance with local title company billing procedures, and shall be furnished within _____ (_____) days after request therefore; such request to be made within a reasonable length of time. Owners shall have a reasonable period to correct any title defects and shall make diligent efforts to correct such defects.
3. CLOSING: This transaction shall be closed within _____ (_____) days after delivery of an abstract or title insurance binder to Purchasers, or their designee.
4. DEED: At the closing, upon the Purchase Price being paid as provided in Paragraph 1 hereof, Owners shall deliver to Purchasers a good and sufficient Warranty Deed conveying the real estate to Purchasers with merchantable title. PURCHASERS shall assume and agree to pay the real estate taxes due and payable _____, 19___, and all subsequent taxes. The deed shall be subject to all covenants, restrictions and easements of record, and all applicable building and zoning ordinances.

FIGURE 1–2
(continued)

5. POSSESSION: Possession shall be given to Purchasers within _____ (_____) days after delivery of deed.
6. LOSS OR DAMAGE: The risk of loss or damage to the premises by fire or otherwise until delivery of deed is assumed by Owners and Owners agree to deliver the property in the same condition as when the contract is accepted, normal wear and tear excepted.
7. INSPECTION: Purchasers have inspected the property and agree to take same in its present condition, normal wear and tear excepted. No verbal agreements or representations regarding condition or quality of the property not specifically set forth herein shall be binding upon either of the parties, or their agents.
8. DAMAGES FOR BREACH: If Purchasers default in any of Purchasers' obligations hereunder, all sums paid hereunder may be retained by Owners in accordance with their agreement, as liquidated damages and not as a penalty, without affecting any of Owners' further remedies. Either party may demand specific performance of this agreement.
9. GENERAL: All oral statements or representations are merged into this agreement. Any reference to the plural shall include the singular where applicable.

EXECUTED this _____ day of _____, 19___.

        "OWNERS"   "PURCHASER"

_____   _____
_____   _____

_____   _____
_____   _____

_____
_____

This document prepared by _____, 123 N.W. 4th St., Suite 402, Evansville, Indiana 47708

a. Find two other real estate purchase agreement forms at a law library. Copy them.

b. Compare the real estate purchase agreement forms from the law library with the one from the attorney. Which one would you use? Are any of them better than others in some ways? Explain.

c. Prepare the agreement. Are there other questions you need to ask? List the questions.

Enrichment Activities

Complete the following exercises.

1. Look at a newspaper. Find examples of sentences that illustrate each of the following:

    a. Consistency principle

    b. The precedent-antecedent principle

    c. *Expressio unius est exclusio alterius*

2. The so-called rules of construction are rules used by courts to construe ambiguous documents. Which of the rules make sense to you? Explain.

3. Compare the functions of a complaint and a contract.

4. Invent a game or select a game already on the market and in your own words write rules for the players. Write the rules so everyone can understand them.

Notes

[1] Jonathan S. Lynton, *Ballentine's Legal Dictionary and Thesaurus* 207 (Delmar/LCP, 1995).

[2] *State v. Alpen*, 338 U.S. 680 (1950).

[3] *Whicker v. Hushaw*, 159 Ind. 1, 64 N.E. 460 (1902).

[4] *Black's Law Dictionary* 1209 (5th ed. 1979).

[5] Karl Llewellyn, *Remarks on the Theory of Appellate Decision and the Rules or Canons About How Statutes Are to Be Construed,* 3 Vand. L. Rev. 395, 401 (1950).

[6] Christopher G. Wren and Jill Robinson Wren, *The Legal Research Manual* 88 (A-R Editions, Inc., 1983).

⚖

CHAPTER 2

THE PREWRITING PROCESS

The average lawyer is essentially a mechanic who works with a pen instead of a ball-peen hammer.
    ***Bob Schmitt, 4** American Journal*
    for Legal Reform No. 3 (Spring 1984)

The legal writing process seems intimidating to the uninitiated. The student should keep in mind, however, that writing is simply a process of putting thoughts into words, and legal writing is simply a process of putting legal thoughts into words. Any good writer, with or without any legal training, can put legal thoughts into words. That is why analyzing the law is an important part of the prewriting process.

§ 2.1 The Importance of the Prewriting Process

The most neglected, and perhaps the least analyzed, stage of the legal writing process is the prewriting process—the point before beginning to write but after completing the legal research. Of course, the prewriting process is not a completely separate stage. Sometimes the writer begins to write during the research phase, and sometimes the writer is still researching during the writing phase.

The research phase involves taking notes on the research. Thorough notes made during research make the writing process much easier. Sometimes the writing begins during the research phase if an outline for the project is settled on, but other times, the writer discovers that the thinking process is just beginning as the writing begins and that research steps need to be retraced.

§ 2.2 Stages of the Prewriting Process

Law is complex, contradictory, uncertain, and ambiguous. As a result, legal professionals need to learn techniques for dealing with complexity, contradictions, uncertainty, ambiguity, and much more. It should not be assumed that the prewriting process can be taught as a series of steps, but it is helpful to look at the various means by which legal professionals reason through a legal situation. It is easier to understand this process by viewing it as a series of stages: identifying the law, reading the law, analyzing the law, applying the law, and evaluating the law.

Identifying the Source Law

Litigation attorneys prepare pleadings, motions, memoranda, and briefs. Real estate attorneys prepare opinion letters, deeds, contracts, and leases. Business attorneys engineer mergers and acquisitions and prepare contracts and corporate minutes. Different writing and thinking skills are required to prepare these different types of documents. Yet there is one common rule that must be followed when any document is prepared: the writer must know the law applicable to the document. That is why the legal thought process begins and ends with legal research.

No one should ever write about law without first gathering all the law applicable to a given situation. Rules of law are contained in constitutions, statutes, regulations, ordinances, court rules, and cases. This law is **primary authority,** that is, the source law, in contrast to **secondary authority,** which is something written about the law. Examples of secondary authority are encyclopedias, articles, and books. Because secondary sources are interpretations of the law, the primary source law should always be read before legal writing begins.

In the United States, many different institutions make law. This fact is significant because it means there are many different primary sources that may have an impact on how the writer writes about the law. A successful legal writer must be able to find and read the various primary sources of law. The language of the law is found in these primary sources. They are the building blocks of the legal thought process.

Constitutions

Law in the United States stems from the United States Constitution, the highest law in the nation. In addition to a federal Constitution, each state has its own constitution. Thus, there exists both a federal system and various state systems of government. No law can conflict with the federal

---

TERMS

primary authority† Rules of law contained in constitutions, cases, statutes, court rules, regulations, and ordinances.

second authority† Something written about the law (*e.g.*, encyclopedia, article, or book).

Constitution, but otherwise, a state constitution is the highest authority within a particular state.

United States Constitution. The federal Constitution is the foundation for the United States legal system. It sets up the three branches of government. The legislative branch (Congress) has the power to pass statutes. The executive branch administers and enforces the law. The judicial branch (the courts) resolves disputes regarding the interpretation of the laws.

Constitutional amendments grant certain rights to the people. For example, the First Amendment to the United States Constitution is the basis of the right to freedom of the press. Figure 2–1 contains the text of the First Amendment.

State Constitutions. State constitutions are typically modeled after the federal Constitution. State constitutions provide for state legislatures to pass laws. They also establish state court systems and grant rights to citizens. Within the territory of a state, the state constitution supersedes all other laws except for the United States Constitution.

Statutes

A statute is a law enacted by the legislature. There are both federal and state statutes. These statutes must conform with the provisions of the federal and state constitutions. Most people understand that laws are contained in statutes. In fact, much law in the United States is made by statutes. Courts interpret and apply statutes. Statutes are primary authority.

Federal Statutes. Federal statutes are passed by the United States Congress. State statutes are passed by state legislatures. Examples of federal statutes include the Social Security Administration program, the Internal Revenue Act, the Occupational Safety and Health Act (OSHA), and securities laws. The legal professional can find federal statutes in the *United States Code* (U.S.C.).

AMENDMENT I

Congress shall make no law respecting an establishment of religion, or prohibiting the free exercise thereof; or abridging the freedom of speech, or of the press; or the right of the people peaceably to assemble, and to petition the Government for a redress of grievances.

FIGURE 2–1
First Amendment to U.S. Constitution

State Statutes. A state legislature passes laws that are enforceable within that state's borders. Examples of state statutes are divorce, insurance, and property laws. Figure 2–2 is a copy of a state statute dealing with divorce.

Regulations

Administrative agencies promulgate law in the form of regulations. These regulations have the force of law. When dealing with a problem involving an administrative agency, the writer must consult the regulations as well as any statutes applicable to that situation. Figure 2–3 is an example of a federal regulation dealing with safety in the workplace.

State agencies are similar to federal agencies. They also promulgate regulations. Examples of state administrative agencies are bureaus of motor vehicles and state environmental protection agencies.

Ordinances

Counties and cities also pass laws. These laws are called ordinances. City ordinances may deal with zoning, building permits, sewer tap-in fees, and sidewalks. Local ordinances are usually published at the local level and can be located by contacting a county or city clerk. The ordinances are enforceable within the boundaries of the county or city. Figure 2–4 is an example of an ordinance dealing with animal control.

Court Rules

Courts adopt rules to direct the course of litigation. These rules prescribe how to initiate a case by filing a complaint, gather information about the case from other parties through the discovery process, and bring the case to trial. The Federal Rules of Civil Procedure (FRCP) govern practice before the district courts. The Federal Rules of Appellate Procedure (FRAP) govern practice before the United States circuit courts of appeals. The Supreme Court Rules tell how to take a case before the Supreme Court.

The Federal Rules of Civil Procedure apply to all district courts. Most individual district courts, however, issue specific rules dealing with practice before that court. These are referred to as local rules. Local rules govern ministerial matters, such as how many copies of a brief should be filed.

The federal circuit courts of appeals operate according to the Federal Rules of Appellate Procedure, and the United States Supreme Court has its own rules. Before deciding to seek a writ of certiorari or of appeal, for example, a practitioner must thoroughly review the pertinent rules to see if all requirements for the writ or the appeal have been satisfied.

State court rules are usually modeled after federal rules, but these rules vary from jurisdiction to jurisdiction. Like the Federal Rules of Civil

§/401. Dissolution of marriage

§ 401. Dissolution of marriage. (a) The court shall enter a judgment of dissolution of marriage if at the time the action was commenced one of the spouses was a resident of this State or was stationed in this State while a member of the armed services, and the residence or military presence had been maintained for 90 days next preceding the commencement of the action or the making of the finding; provided, however, that a finding of residence of a party in any judgment entered under this Act from January 1, 1982 through June 30, 1982 shall satisfy the former domicile requirements of this Act; and if one of the following grounds for dissolution has been proved:

(1) Th at, without cause or provocation by the petitioner, the respondent was at the time of such marriage, and continues to be naturally impotent; the respondent had a wife or husband living at the time of the marriage; the respondent had committed adultery subsequent to the marriage; the respondent has willfully deserted or absented himself or herself from the petitioner for the space of one year, including any period during which litigation may have pended between the spouses for dissolution of marriage or legal separation; the respondent has been guilty of habitual drunkenness for the space of 2 years; the respondent has been guilty of gross and confirmed habits caused by the excessive use of addictive drugs for the space of 2 years, or has attempted the life of the other by poison or other means showing malice, or has been guilty of extreme and repeated physical or mental cruelty, or has been convicted of a felony or other infamous crime; or the respondent has infected the other with a communicable venereal disease. "Excessive use of addictive drugs", as used in this Section, refers to use of an addictive drug by a person when using the drug becomes a controlling or a dominant purpose of his life; or

(2) That the spouses have lived separate and apart for a continuous period in excess of 2 years and irreconcilable differences have caused the irretrievable breakdown of the marriage and the court determines that efforts at reconciliation have failed or that future attempts at reconciliation would be impracticable and not in the best interests of the family. If the spouses have lived separate and apart for a continuous period of not less than 6 months next preceding the entry of the judgment dissolving the marriage, as evidenced by testimony or affidavits of the spouses, the requirement of living separate and apart for a continuous period in excess of 2 years may be waived upon written stipulation of both spouses filed with the court. At any time after the parties cease to cohabit, the following periods shall be included in the period of separation:

(A) any period of cohabitation during which the parties attempted in good faith to reconcile and participated in marriage counseling under the guidance of any of the following: a psychiatrist, a clinical psychologist, a clinical social worker, a marriage and family therapist, a person authorized to provide counseling in accordance with the prescriptions of any religious denomination, or a person regularly engaged in providing family or marriage counseling; and

(B) any period of cohabitation under written agreement of the parties to attempt to reconcile.

FIGURE 2–2
An Excerpt From an Illinois Divorce Statute

Part 404, Subpt. P, App. 1

4.01 Category of Impairments, Cardiovascular System

4.02 *Congestive heart failure (manifested by evidence of vascular congestion such as hepatomegaly, peripheral or pulmonary edema).* With:

A. Persistent congestive heart failure on clinical examination despite prescribed therapy; or

B Persistent left ventricular enlargement and hypertrophy documented by both:

1. Extension of the cardiac shadow (left ventricle) to the vertebral column on a left lateral chest roentgenogram; and

2. ECG showing QRS duration less than 0.12 second with S_{v1} plus R_{v5} (or R_{v6}) of 35 mm. or greater *and* ST segment depressed more than 0.5 mm. *and* low, diphasic or inverted T waves in leads with tall R waves, or

C. Persistent "mitral" type heart involvement documented by left atrial enlargement shown by double shadow on PA chest roentgenogram (or characteristic distortion of barium-filled esophagus) and either:

1. ECG showing QRS duration less than 0.12 second with S_{v1} plus R_{v5} (or R_{v6}) of 35 mm. or greater *and* ST segment depressed more than 0.5 mm. *and* low, diphasic or inverted T waves in leads with tall R waves, or

2. ECG evidence of right ventricular hypertrophy with R wave of 5.0 mm or greater in lead V_1 *and* progressive decrease in R/S amplitude from lead V_1 to V_5 or V_6; or

D. Cor pulmonale (non-acute) documented by both:

1. Right ventricular enlargement (or prominence of the right out-flow tract) on chest roentgenogram or fluoroscopy; and

2. ECG evidence of right ventricular hypertrophy with R wave of 5.0 mm. or

20 CFR Ch. III (4-1-90 Edition)

greater in lead V_1 *and* progressive decrease in R/S amplitude from lead V_1 to V_5 or V_6.

4.03 *Hypertensive vascular disease.* Evaluate under 4.02 04 4.04 or under the criteria for the affected body system.

4.04 *Ischemic heart disease with chest pain or cardiac origin as described in 4.00E.* With:

A. Treadmill exercise test (see 4.00 F and G) demonstrating one of the following at an exercise level of 5 METs or less:

1. Horizontal or downsloping depression (from the standing control) of the ST segment to 1.0 mm. or greater, lasting for at least 0.08 second after the J junction, and clearly discernible in at least two consecutive complexes which are on a level baseline in any lead; or

2. Junctional depression occurring during exercise, remaining depressed (from the standing control) to 2.0 mm. or greater for at least 0.08 second after the J junction (the so-called slow upsloping ST segment), and clearly discernible in at least two consecutive complexes which are on a level baseline in any lead; or

3. Premature ventricular systoles which are multiform or bidirectional or are sequentially inscribed (3 or more); or

4. ST segment elevation (from the standing control) to 1 mm. or greater; or

5. Development of second or third degree heart block; or

B. In the absence of a report of an acceptable treadmill exercise test (see 4.00G), one of the following:

1. Transmural myocardial infarction exhibiting a QS pattern or a Q wave with amplitude at least 1/3rd of R wave and with a duration of 0.04 second or more. (If these are present in leads III and

§ 90.04   **EVANSVILLE ANIMALS**   6

§ 90.04 Prohibited Acts.

(A) No person shall do the following prohibited acts.

　　(1) Be a custodian of a prohibited animal as identified in § 90.05.

　　(2) Be a custodian of, or permit, an animal nuisance.

　　(3) Be a custodian of a dangerous animal; however, the exemptions provided under § 90.03(C) shall also be applicable to this provision.

　　(4) Be a custodian of a dog that is not under restraint, or of a nuisance animal.

　　(5) Confine an animal in an area which is unclean, overcrowded, or inadequately ventilated.

　　(6) Deprive an animal from the opportunity for adequate exercise or access to fresh air, or maintain a large animal in a lot of less than 10,000 square feet per animal.

　　(7) Be a custodian of an animal that has not been properly licensed pursuant to this chapter, nor be a custodian of any animal that has not been vaccinated with a rabies vaccine approved by the State Board of Health if the animal is capable of carrying or transmitting rabies.

　　(8) Abandon an animal.

　　(9) Sell chickens or ducklings younger than eight weeks of age in quantities of less than 25 to a single purchaser.

　(10) Give away any live reptile, bird, or mammal as a prize for, or as an inducement to enter, any contest, game, or other competition, or as an inducement to enter a place of amusement, or offer such a vertebrate as an incentive to enter into any business agreement whereby the offer was for the purpose of attracting trade.

　(11) Be the custodian of an animal and fail to provide the animal with sufficient, good, and wholesome food and water, proper shelter, protection from the weather, veterinary care when needed to prevent suffering, and with humane care and treatment.

　(12) Expose any known poisonous substance, whether or not mixed with food, so that such poisonous substance shall be liable to be eaten by any domestic animal.

　(13) Leave an animal unattended in a vehicle when conditions in that vehicle would constitute a health hazard to the animal.

　(14) Fail to confine in a secure building or enclosure a female dog or cat in heat so as to prevent conception except during instances of planned breeding.

　(15) Be a custodian of a vicious animal. A finding that an animal is a vicious animal shall supersede a finding of an animal being an animal nuisance or a dangerous animal.

FIGURE 2–4
Evansville
Ordinance on
Animals

FIGURE 2–4
(continued)

(B) No person shall fail to obey the provisions of this chapter or any restrictions, regulations, or orders issued by the Commission pursuant to the terms of this chapter.

(C) No person shall fail to maintain in a sanitary manner the premises occupied by an animal, whether the animal is kept in a structure, fence, pen, or fastened, hitched, or leashed. Custodians of an animal shall regularly, and as often as necessary, maintain all animal areas or areas of animal contact to prevent unsanitary conditions on the property and to prevent odor from escaping from the property of the custodian.

('62 Code, Art. 2, Ch. 20, 57) (Ord. G-80-49, passed 4-13-81; Am. Ord. G-87-4, passed 4-6-87; Am. Ord. G-87-37, passed 12-14-87) Penalty, see § 90.99.

Procedure, state court rules describe how to initiate a case, obtain information about the case through discovery, and make motions. A legal professional must consult court rules whenever the dispute concerns a procedural issue.

Cases

Most people know that law is made by statutes but have only a vague notion of how law comes from cases. It is critical to understand the manner by which law is made through cases.

The Common Law. In England, much law was initially decreed by judges through their court decisions and was referred to as the common law. Much of the English common law was adopted by state courts in the United States and continues to grow and change as judges make new decisions in court cases. This law is also called common law.

In a sense, this is an odd way to make law. Two parties have a dispute, and the dispute ends in court. One party prevails. The loser appeals the case to an appellate court. Both sides file briefs with the appellate court, which consists of a panel of judges. An appellate judge renders a written decision, which explains the rationale used deciding the case. The case becomes a precedent to be followed in later cases. In other words, it becomes law. A case, which is sometimes referred to as a decision or judicial opinion, is a primary authority just like a statute.

Stare decisis, the doctrine that says legal precedents must be followed, is the basis for the development of the common law. A precedent is an earlier decided case. It can be either binding or persuasive. A binding precedent is a case decided by a higher court in the same jurisdiction. A persuasive precedent is a case decided by a court in another jurisdiction or by a lower court in the same jurisdiction. In deciding cases, courts are, in effect, laying down rules for other courts to follow.

Use of *stare decisis* ensures uniformity of results and predictability, so that clients can act accordingly. It also ensures equality of treatment and fairness in decision making. Courts can change precedents, however, if they were wrongly decided or changes in society require a different look at the dispute.

When parties do not agree about how a statute, regulation, or court rule should be interpreted, the courts resolve the dispute. These cases are also law and are used as precedents in resolving future statutory disputes. In this regard, federal and state courts operate the same way. A legal professional must learn techniques for reading and understanding cases.

Reading the Law

Law is the process of applying legal rules to events and transactions. These rules can be simple, such as a speed limit of fifty-five miles per hour, or extremely complex and technical. The legal professional must be able to deduce legal rules and principles from reading the primary sources (cases, statutes, regulations, and so on) before writing about them. In other words, the legal writer must be able to read a fifty-page case and summarize the basic principles of that case in a few sentences or locate the exact sentence in a lengthy statute that pertains to the situation about which he or she is writing. Because the law is so technical, the legal professional must learn techniques for reading the law before writing about it, especially if he or she is to grasp the nuances and fine points of the law.

Case law, in particular, can be difficult to understand (for example, see *Griswold v. Connecticut* in the appendix of this book). Even experienced legal professionals struggle when reading some cases. That is why legal professionals have developed techniques to help them to read the law. One technique used to grasp the meaning of a case is called "briefing a case."

Briefing a case is different from writing a brief, which was discussed in Chapter 1. Briefing a case is a technique for sifting out the important information. The student makes an outline and then reads a case, putting information found in the case under the appropriate headings in the outline. Legal professionals must be able to competently brief a case because the technique is so valuable for understanding hard-to-read cases.

The steps used to brief a case vary from text to text. Some teachers use five steps while others use as many as eleven or sixteen. This text presents the technique in five steps: the facts, the issue, the procedural posture, the holding, and the legal reasoning.

Majority, Dissenting, and Concurring Opinions

Before briefing a case, however, it is important to understand which part of the case is to be briefed. There are nine justices on the United States Supreme Court. They vote on how a case should be decided, usually after the parties have filed briefs on the case and presented oral arguments. A justice is then assigned the task of writing the majority opinion. If a justice disagrees with the reasoning and logic by another justice but agrees with the result, he or she may write a separate opinion, called a concurring opinion. If a justice disagrees with the majority, he or she may write a dissenting opinion. The *Griswold v. Connecticut* case in the appendix contains examples of each, but the following text on briefing a case uses only the majority opinion written by Justice William O. Douglas. The student should take note, however, while reading the case, whether Justice Douglas's reasoning was adopted by a majority of the court.

Not every published decision has a majority, dissenting, and concurring opinion. In federal district courts, only one justice hears each case and issues a decision, thus there is only one judicial opinion. Only in courts that have more than one judge to agree or disagree do dissenting and concurring opinions exist.

The Five-Step Brief: An Example

The following text uses a five-step technique to read and understand *Griswold v. Connecticut*, a decision that has had important consequences on later cases in the United States Supreme Court. Although constitutional law cases can be difficult to understand, the step-by-step briefing process will help the student understand what happened in this case.

Step 1—The Facts.   First the parties must be identified: the student needs a scorecard as to who was the prevailing party in the lower court, whether that party was the plaintiff or defendant in the lower court, and which of the parties is the appellant (the party taking the appeal) and which is the appellee (the party defending on appeal) in the current case. Keeping the parties straight is important to understanding the case.

When students brief their first case, they usually include too many facts. Only relevant facts (facts that relate to the issue decided) and material facts (facts that have an impact on the outcome of that issue) should be included. Only the facts that gave rise to the dispute, not the events in the lower courts, are important in the brief. The facts in *Griswold* might read:

> The Griswolds counseled couples about available contraceptive devices for the Planned Parenthood League of Connecticut. They were charged with a criminal offense of aiding and abetting a person who

used a "drug, medicinal article, or instrument for the purpose of preventing contraception."

Note that these facts are written so what the parties are fighting about can be understood. Would you include more facts? Why?

SIDEBAR

When writing a memorandum or a brief, the student should focus on how the relevant and material facts are separated from court opinions. Remembering the learning process involved will strengthen this skill, which is an important one that should be practiced again and again.

Step 2—The Issue. The party who has lost a case is usually unhappy about more than one ruling. When losing parties list what the judge did wrong, they commonly do so by framing issues. In the *Griswold* case, an issue might be stated as follows:

Whether sections 53-32 and 54-196 of the General Statutes of Connecticut constitute an unconstitutional invasion of privacy in contravention of the Third, Fourth, Fifth, Ninth, and Fourteenth amendments to the United States Constitution.

An issue is a legal question that the court considers. Usually, many issues are raised on appeal. Notice how the issue helps to frame the legal dispute so the court knows what questions it must decide. The issue in a case serves the same function as a question in a formal debate. A well-written issue focuses the debate.

Step 3—The Procedural Posture. The procedural posture is the present status of the case. Cases end in many ways. Sometimes a complaint is dismissed. Sometimes a motion for summary judgment is granted. Some cases are decided by jury. In each of these situations, the judge must look at the case in a different way. If a party files a motion to dismiss a complaint, for example, the court must assume that all the facts in the complaint, as well as any reasonable inferences from these facts, are true before ruling on the motion. If the court grants a motion for summary judgment, the parties cannot have any genuine issues of material fact in dispute.

The procedural posture might be a pretrial motion, a motion to compel discovery, or a motion for summary judgment. If the issues are before an appellate court, the status might be "an appeal from a judgment" or "an appeal from the granting of a motion for summary judgment."

Preparing the procedural posture of the case helps focus the questions. The court usually identifies the standard that has been used to review the case. In most cases, this information is available in the opinion.

The procedural posture of *Griswold* is as follows:

> The Griswolds were convicted after trial to the court and were sentenced to pay a fine of one hundred dollars each. After appeals to the state appellate and supreme courts, the convictions were affirmed. This case is on appeal to the Supreme Court of the United States.

Step 4—The Holding. The holding is the decision of the court. When a legal professional writes the holding for the first time, it usually reads something like this:

> The Connecticut statutes are unconstitutional as violating the marital right of privacy, a fundamental right guaranteed by the First, Fourth, Fifth, Ninth, and Fourteenth amendments of the United States Constitution.

Justice Douglas said there was a right of privacy. He said that the right of privacy prevented the state of Connecticut from regulating the sale of contraceptives. Two people reading this decision, however, may disagree about how narrowly or broadly this holding should be stated. One person might think the court was announcing a broad right of marital privacy, while another might conclude this right of privacy applies to some other right, such as a right to have an abortion. Still another might conclude *Griswold* should not be so broadly interpreted and might read the right of privacy as applying only to situations where the state is preventing the sale of contraceptives. Holdings are interpreted differently by various lawyers.

Step 5—The Legal Reasoning. The last step in briefing a case is describing how the court reasoned to the holding. In this case, Justice Douglas said there was a right of privacy. Where did this right come from? Notice Justice Arthur J. Goldberg agreed there was a right of privacy. But how did Justice Goldberg disagree with Justice Douglas about where this right came from? Legal reasoning answers these questions. Understanding the legal reasoning often is the key to answering how broadly or narrowly a case should be applied.

A court may reason to a decision in different ways. It might use a settled principle from a case or statute and apply it to the facts of the case, or it might narrow or expand the principles from a precedent or statute. In briefing the case, the student should consider how the principle was derived from other cases. Perhaps it was taken directly from another case, or perhaps it was derived from a pattern in other cases. A legal professional should be able to trace how the legal principles used in a case were derived and applied.

Now that *Griswold* has been briefed, the student should reread the case. The student should have a better grasp of what this case is saying and what everyone is arguing about because the case has been briefed.

Whenever a case that has bearing on a project is read, a brief of that case should be prepared. This provides insight into the meaning and ramifications of the case. As more and more cases are read and briefed, the process becomes shorter and shorter until a case brief can be done mentally, without actually writing out the five steps. It takes practice. Legal professionals should hone their skills by preparing a case brief any time they read a case that has an impact on their research project.

Briefing a case breaks down the case so it can be understood no matter how complex the issues. Although a case may be fifty pages in length, briefing the case reduces the case to rules or principles. Instead of facing a stack of cases, the legal professional deals with a list of rules or principles deduced from the stack. These rules then need to be organized, ranked, and compared with each other. The more cases are briefed, the easier the process becomes.

Reading Statutes and Other Laws

The case brief works well with case law but is not applicable to statutes and other authority. A case has more information than just straightforward legal principles. The reader who briefs a case strips words from the case until any legal principles are discovered. In statutes and other laws, however, the reader is given only the rules. There are no facts to clutter the statute, no statement of the issues, and no legal reasoning. In a sense, reading a statute would seem to be an easier process—and often it is. Nevertheless, reading statutes and other laws requires different types of skills than those required in reading cases.

Step 1. The statute should be read for meaning. Reading statutes is like reading a rule book. The reader finds rule after rule, so he or she must select those that apply to the facts of the problem. The first reading is to determine the context and scope of the statute. The researcher needs a general understanding of the reasoning of the law, including any exceptions to that law. All relevant statutes must be located.

Step 2. The meaning of the statute must be dissected. Statutes are passed by the legislature. In the legislative process, various compromises are made to ensure passage of a bill. Words are selected with care. Words are used to patch over differences of opinion. As a result, in reading a statute, each word must be considered and reconsidered for meaning. Unlike a case, a statute has no dictum: every word must be considered significant. Then the words must be considered together to see why particular words were used. In a sense, this process is like studying a line of poetry.

Step 3. A flowchart should be prepared. In reading more complicated statutes, a chart or outline of the statute can be developed. If, for example, the researcher was reading the Uniform Commercial Code (UCC), which deals with commercial transactions, and the client had purchased some defective widgets, the different provisions that deal with nonconforming or defective goods might be listed to help the researcher decide what the client's remedy might be. The client would have different options depending on whether the client had accepted the widgets, the defect was discovered soon after acceptance, there was an express warranty, or the widgets were fit for the purpose for which they were purchased.

Step 4. When a dispute arises over the meaning of a statute, the courts must resolve the dispute. In studying a statute, the researcher should always search out any cases that explain the meaning of the statute or that resolve ambiguities in the statute. This step is particularly necessary if the first and second steps do not provide clear answers to the question or there is any ambiguity or vagueness in the statute.

In rare situations, the legislative history of a statute may be considered. That history includes the debates over the passage of the statute, the legislative committee reports, and any committee hearings.

Organizing and Ranking Authority

As the researcher begins to understand the cases, statutes, and other laws pertaining to a situation, the authority must be organized and ranked. At this stage, the law is sifted to find the most relevant rules, and then these rules are sorted to find the controlling rules. For instance, at the beginning of research, a volume of cases on a particular subject may be found. Some of these cases may be several centuries old. Some may not exactly fit the facts of the problem. Some of the cases may be from other jurisdictions or lower courts. If the researcher cannot organize and rank authority, his or her thinking and writing will be rambling and inaccurate.

Law is hierarchical. An appellate court's decision determines the law for the trial courts, and a decision of a state's highest court determines the law for all lower courts in that state. Constitutional provisions supersede statutes, which in turn supersede regulations and ordinances. A case can interpret a statute. On the other hand, a statute can be passed to change case law.

At this stage, cases must be ranked. Higher level cases in the same jurisdiction control over lower level cases. A more recently decided case typically carries more weight than a case decided earlier. A case with facts more analogous to a factual situation will likely control a case with distinguishing facts.

In addition, the writer must notice the subtle differences between cases. Starting with the assumption that the cases are consistent until proven otherwise, the researcher should try to distinguish how different facts have produced different results. In other words, the reader must see whether there are different rules for different situations and, if so, categorize these distinctions.

Analyzing the Law

There probably would be no need for lawyers if law fit into neatly sorted piles of rules and principles. In some situations, a legal professional only needs to read a case or a statute to answer a legal question. In these situations, the legal professional is simply applying a rule to the facts. In many cases, however, as the writer begins to read and sort authority, the writer finds that the law is inconsistent or even contradictory. In other cases, the writer notices a trend that is not clearly enunciated in the cases. The cases may be suggesting that a law should be broadened or narrowed. Sometimes this suggestion must be deduced from how the cases are decided. Law is, indeed, ambiguous and contradictory, and the writer must learn to accept this uncertainty. To deal with this uncertainty, the legal professional must learn to integrate the various sources into a pattern and harmonize the sources, which means the legal professional must analyze and synthesize the law.

In a typical situation, the legal professional finds a relevant statute that has been interpreted by a number of cases and several relevant regulations. The cases might be conflicting or not specifically **on point** to the issue the researcher is resolving. In another typical situation, there may be ten cases affecting the analysis of the client's case. The holding in each case may be deducible only by a careful reading of each case. Each of the cases may contain *obiter dicta* that are not really necessary to the determination of that particular case. Once this extraneous information is extracted from the holding or *ratio decidendi* of these cases, the

---

TERMS

---

on point   Refers to a judicial opinion that, with respect to the facts involved and the applicable law, is similar to another case.
obiter dicta   Means "comments in passing."
ratio decidendi†   A holding or principle of law decided by a court.

researcher may discover that the cases are inconsistent or contradictory with each other. At this stage, it is helpful to ask questions such as the following: Were the same legal issues addressed? Were the facts different in any of the cases? Were meaningful distinctions made between legal principles?

The goal is to try to deduce a rule that is consistent with *all* the law on the subject. Just as the holding of a case may be explained in the form of legal principles, all the law relating to the issue may be reduced into basic rules or principles. For example, the researcher looks for a common explanation for the results of ten cases pertaining to the issue and, if a common explanation cannot be found, tries to explain the inconsistencies. The process of harmonizing law into principles and discovering trends and patterns is sometimes referred to as synthesizing the law.

An Example of Synthesizing the Law

A case read by itself is seldom meaningful. Related cases must be read together. This approach can be examined from the right-of-privacy perspective. In *Griswold*, the court said there was a marital right of privacy. In *Roe v. Wade*, 410 U.S. 113 (1973), the court said this right of privacy extended to the right to an abortion (prior to viability). The court held that a state did not have a justifiable interest prior to viability. After *Roe*, Ohio wrote a statute that required all abortions after the first trimester to be performed in a hospital. In *Akron v. Akron Center for Reproductive Health*, 462 U.S. 416 (1983), the court held that this law unduly burdened those seeking abortions. In another case, the court held that a state could not determine viability because this is the function of a physician. *Coluotti v. Franklin*, 439 U.S. 379 (1979). After all, only a physician can consider gestational age, weight, and lung maturity.

A legal professional reading these cases at this point would have concluded that the state cannot place restrictions on abortions and that physicians, not the state, must determine viability. The state of Missouri, however, wanted to challenge these principles, so Missouri wrote a statute that read as follows:

> Before a physician performs an abortion on a woman he has a reason to believe is carrying an unborn child of twenty or more weeks gestational age, the physician shall first determine if the unborn child is viable by using and exercising that degree of care, skill, and proficiency commonly exercised by the ordinary skillful, careful, and prudent physician engaged in similar practice under the same or similar conditions. In making this determination of viability, the physician shall perform or cause to be performed such medical examination and tests as are necessary to make a finding of gestational age, weight, and lung maturity of the unborn child and shall enter such findings and determinations of viability in the medical record of the mother. Mo. Ann. Stat. 188.029 (Vernon 1989).

This statute said that every physician intending to perform an abortion in Missouri *had to* determine viability. Notice how this statute challenged the prior logic of the cases. Missouri was placing a burden before viability on the right of a woman to have an abortion. Yet this statute required a physician to do what was only a physician function according to *Akron*—test for viability. But this testing was obviously a burden on abortion.

The state of Missouri was using the Socratic method on the Supreme Court in testing the principles it had previously set. This case was resolved in *Webster v. Reproductive Health Services*, 109 S. Ct. 3040 (1989). The result is not important to the point. The point is that cases seemingly consistent can conflict when facts are changed. Missouri found an inconsistency and tested it with a statute.

Strategies When There Is No Controlling Rule of Law

In some instances, there may be no rule of law that addresses the given problem. For example, before *Griswold* was decided, no right to marital privacy was recognized in any recorded case. No matter how hard researchers looked, they would have found no rule dealing with a right to marital privacy.

When a researcher discovers that no existing cases or statutes apply, the research process does not stop. Instead, it is simply refocused or expanded, and the legal professional must look at the existing law from a different perspective. One approach is to extrapolate or analogize a principle from the existing case principles. Another approach is to either expand or narrow an existing principle to cover the problem. The research can merge several principles to make a new principle or identify a new principle from the pattern of other cases. The courts use both inductive and deductive reasoning in these situations.

Legal professionals must rid themselves of any notion that rules of law are totally fixed or predictable. Most legal research does not result in exact answers. That is why lawsuits involve more than one party. The parties argue both sides of the question. In many educational experiences, students are taught there are correct and incorrect answers. In legal research, however, there is not always a correct or incorrect answer, nor is there necessarily a correct or incorrect way to analyze a legal problem. This lack of definitive answers frustrates many legal professionals.

Applying the Law

Until now, the process has focused on how to deal with legal rules and principles. Now these rules and principles must be applied to a set of facts. Applying the law to the facts is like using a slide rule: on the one side of the slide rule are the facts of the situation, and on the other side are the different laws that might apply to that situation. When the facts are aligned to a particular rule, there is a certain result, but never is there absolute certainty. This process is not a science, and different legal professionals reach different conclusions about what rules should apply, sometimes because the cases are inconsistent or contradictory. Ten experts reading the same cases may reach ten different conclusions. Some may reach a narrow conclusion, and some may reach a broader interpretation.

Legal professionals often are working with different versions of the facts. There may be different witnesses to the same event, or there may be facts the client did not reveal. Even if each legal professional were given exactly the same set of facts, there could be some disagreement about which facts were more significant to a resolution of the problem.

As the student prepares to write about the law, he or she must never forget that the facts and law must be woven together. A writer should seldom write about law without reference to facts.

Evaluating the Law

The last step of the prewriting process involves a prediction of how current law applies to the fact situation. The law has been gathered, read, and analyzed. Now a conclusion about how the law applies to the client's situation must be reached. In writing a contract, the writer wants to know what language to use or not use to best favor the client. In writing a memorandum, the writer wants to explain the most likely outcome in a case. In writing a brief, the writer wants to know the strongest argument that can be advanced. Based upon the prediction, a client might decide not to file a lawsuit or might decide to settle a claim.

At this stage, the legal professional assesses the logic and reasoning of the law, looking for trends in the law. The legal professional makes subjective judgments about the law by asking questions such as the following: Do earlier cases reach different results from later cases? Do courts in industrial states reach different results from courts in agricultural states? Has a precedent been accepted or rejected in other jurisdictions? Is the rationale of the case still valid? Is the reasoning of the court divided? Are there suggestions in other cases that the precedent should be changed?

As part of this process, the legal expert may be asked to predict the outcome of the case. Then the legal professional must apply the facts of the case to the law, which might include evaluating the continuing viability of the law on the subject. As with the other stages of the legal thought process, different experts have different opinions. The researcher must strive to render an opinion based upon sound legal principles and reasoning, taking into account all the relevant facts of the situation.

§ 2.3 Tips for the Prewriting Process

It is not difficult to spot an inexperienced legal professional in the law library. He or she carries a stack of photocopied cases, unorganized and inches thick, that have been read and underlined. The topic has been researched and researched. These individuals have a look of despair. They have no idea where to begin. Following are some ways to avoid such frustration in the prewriting process.

1. Make notes during research. Note-taking is an art in legal research. If the researcher makes too many notes, the research will never be completed. On the other hand, taking no notes means the researcher will spend hours looking for a quote or citation. When preparing term papers, students often learn to organize subjects on index cards. When a new subject appears, a new card is used. Then students organize the index cards before starting the writing process. Lawyers use legal pads rather than index cards. As the research progresses, subtopics or subissues emerge. A new page or card should be started for each new category of issues or line of cases.

2. Separate the issues. If issues are kept separate, the materials organize almost automatically as part of the process. If a case is particularly pertinent to the issue or there is a quote that answers the query, the researcher should either copy it or note the page number on which the quote appears. Researchers will find it helpful to copy the title page of the case (for the citation later) and any pages dealing with the researched issue if the case is lengthy. Cases dealing with particular issues should be kept separate from one another. As the research process progresses, the facts from the researched cases should be reviewed to see if more factual information is necessary or if the facts differ from the researched materials.

To help separate the issues, cases can be compared to see why results changed. If there is a lead case (a case cited frequently as precedent), the facts of later decided cases can be examined to see how they changed the legal rule used in the later decisions.

Sometimes the splintering process can become arduous. Nonetheless, the more the researcher organizes the cases during the research stage and pays attention to factual differences in them, the easier will be the writing process. This is not to imply that the research and writing stages are mutually exclusive. They are not. A writer may go back to the research stage many times before the writing project is complete. By starting the writing thought process in the research stage, however, the actual writing will flow much easier than if the thought process were to begin at the computer or typewriter.

3. Develop a working outline. Some students work better from an outline than others. In any event, a working outline of ideas should be jotted down. This does not have to be a formal outline or even an outline for the final project—it is just a means by which to see how the ideas can best be presented in some organized way. Chapter 3 discusses the importance of outlines and structure.

4. Learn the vocabulary. The law has a unique vocabulary. While reading a case or statute, the writer should learn the unique words and phrasing used by the courts or the legislature and then incorporate the language into the writing. The legal professional needs to learn to talk and write like a lawyer. A good legal dictionary and thesaurus (such as *Ballentine's Legal Dictionary and Thesaurus*) should be kept with the writer at all times and used to understand what has been read.

5. Write and rewrite. Writing facilitates the thinking process. Writer's block happens frequently when writers begin to write. It is not unusual for any writer to tear up sheet after sheet while writing the first sentence. This is simply a symptom that the writer's thought process is not complete. The writer should write early and try not to get frustrated, although frustration is sometimes a part of the thinking and writing process.

6. Pay attention to the client's situation. The legal professional must learn as much as possible about the client's situation. In legal writing, there are two main concerns: the facts and the law. The more the writer knows about the client's business, the better the writer can see how to approach that client's legal problem. Some legal professionals tend to focus too much on the law and not enough on the facts, yet the facts determine which rule to use or not use. If the writer pays attention to the facts, the law will make more sense.

7. Never give up looking up the law. A legal professional should never write about the law unless he or she has first looked up all the relevant law and thoroughly understands it. Writing should never precede this research. Sometimes writers have trouble starting to write because their research is not complete.

8. Consult other sources. Inexperienced legal professionals sometimes have problems reading law, especially statutes and cases. With cases, it is usually helpful to do some background reading, which usually means reading secondary sources. With law, there are many secondary sources that are written simply and understandably. Reading these sources first may be all that is needed to understand the meaning of a case or statute so that the writer can begin writing about it.

Writing Exercises

1. Prepare a case brief of *Lucas v. Hamm,* 56 Cal. 2d 583, 15 Cal. Rptr. 821, 364 P.2d 685 (1961), which appears in the appendix. The case brief should include the following sections: facts, issue, procedural posture, holding, and legal reasoning.

2. Prepare a case brief of *Smith v. Lewis,* 118 Cal. Rptr. 621, 530 P.2d 589 (1975), which appears in the appendix. The case brief should include the following sections: facts, issue, procedural posture, holding, and legal reasoning.

3. Compare the principle of law in *Lucas v. Hamm* with the principle of law in *Smith v. Lewis.* Are these principles consistent? Consider the following in your answer:

   a. How are the procedural postures different? What is the effect of these different postures on a court deciding the issues?

   b. What was the law with regard to a federal pension when the plaintiff was divorced? How was the law different in regard to the state pension?

Enrichment Activities

Complete the following activities.

1. Prepare case briefs on the opinions of each of the justices in *Griswold v. Connecticut.* Prepare a report explaining how the various opinions disagree with one another.

2. Read *Roe v. Wade,* 410 U.S. 113 (1973). Prepare a case brief on the opinions of each of the justices. Prepare a report explaining how the various justices disagree.

3. Compare the holding of *Griswold v. Connecticut* with the holding of *Roe v. Wade.* Can you develop a rule of law deducible from these cases? Name as many areas as you can where this right of privacy might lead in the future.

4. The appendix to this volume contains the briefs filed by the appellant and appellee in *Griswold v. Connecticut.* Read the different opinions of the justices in *Griswold v. Connecticut.* Trace the arguments made in the briefs to the conclusions drawn by the different justices.

CHAPTER 3

STRUCTURE IN LEGAL DOCUMENTS

If I had eight hours to cut down a tree, I would use six of them sharpening my axe.

———— Abraham Lincoln

At some point in the writing process, usually at the beginning, every writer must pay attention to structure. More than any other writing focus, structure determines how coherently the message is communicated. In fact, checking the structure of a document is often an internal check of logic. Unfortunately, many legal professionals spend too much time on the particulars of a document at the expense of its overall design.

§ 3.1 The Design of a Legal Document

The **design** of a legal document is the format in which ideas are organized within the document. Design is an important concern in all forms of writing. The rule is that the design should omit nothing important and add nothing superfluous.

Omit Nothing Important

The writer must be careful not to leave out anything material to the document. In construing legal documents, courts presume that if something is left out, the writer intended to do so. They do not make allowance for carelessness. A legal writer cannot leave out ideas any more than a mechanic can leave out a few nuts and bolts when assembling a machine.

Add Nothing Superfluous

The writer must not add material that is extraneous to the thought being communicated. Students often find it difficult to cut a paragraph or strike a sentence, but unnecessary verbiage only diminishes the clarity of the document. Cutting is necessary if there is any superfluous material.

Use Parallel Structure

Parallel ideas should be presented using parallel structure: words with words, phrases with phrases, clauses with clauses, adjectives with adjectives, participial phrases with participial phrases, prepositional phrases with prepositional phrases, and noun clauses with noun clauses.

Caesar said: "I came, I saw, I conquered." This statement has parallel structure. Sentences expressing parallel ideas should be given parallel structure. So should paragraphs expressing parallel ideas. When correcting for parallel structure, the writer has two choices: either put words into the same grammatical structure or eliminate the need for the structure by reorganizing the ideas.

Make Words Joined by Conjunctions Parallel

When words are joined together with conjunctions such as *and* or *but*, the words should be the same part of speech. Verbs should be joined with other verbs, nouns with other nouns, and participial phrases with other participial phrases. Disparate parts of speech should not be joined together by conjunctions. This principle that words joined by *and* and *or* should be grammatically compatible applies also to the use of correlative conjunctions such as *either . . . or, neither . . . nor*.

Make Lists Parallel

When a list or enumeration of ideas is made, the writer should check for parallel structure. Consider this list:

1. apples
2. the oranges
3. bring the laundry
4. did I buy a gift for my spouse?

If the list were rewritten with parallel structure to conform to 1, each entry would need to be a noun. To conform to 2, each entry would need to be a noun preceded by an article. To conform to 3, each entry would start with a verb. To conform to 4, each entry would ask a question.

Make Headings Parallel

Parallelism is particularly important when you write headings for contracts or briefs. Each heading should be of the same grammatical structure as other headings. One heading should not begin with a verb and another with a noun phrase.

Use Parallel Structure to Provide Eloquence

Parallel structure also can be used to provide eloquence in writing. Consider this example:

> That plaintiff's argument is contrary to law is seen simply by reading *Smith v. Jones*. That plaintiff's argument is absurd is seen by the countless contradictions in plaintiff's brief. These contradictions include . . .

The writer should be conscious of parallel structure. Parallel structure tells the reader that the writer is discussing parallel ideas. Parallel structure adds emphasis to writing. When similar ideas are presented, parallel structure should be used.

§ 3.2 Outline: The Basics of Design

The design should begin with an outline. An outline consists of three components: division, classification, and sequencing.

Division

Division means the main headings of the outline. Students are taught in math class that the whole must equal the sum of the parts. In an outline, each heading or grouping is exclusive, but when considered together, the headings must constitute a whole. If a writer were writing about sports, for example, he or she could divide the material according to different types of sports and use main headings such as Basketball, Baseball, Football, Tennis, and so on. Or the material might be divided chronologically or by individual or team sports. There is no restriction on dividing the subject matter as long as the divisions constitute a whole.

Division in Transaction Documents

In preparing a transaction document, division is important for outlining its main points. In a will, for example, an outline might be based upon a sequence of events:

- Pay the debts and taxes.

- Give A a piano.

TERMS

division†   The main headings of an outline for a document.

- Give B a sum of money.

- Give C all the residuary.

A contract might be broken down by responsibilities:

- Rent payments.

- Possession.

- Payment of taxes and insurance.

- Security deposit.

- Contingencies (default, eminent domain).

- Pets.

A good way to write headings for transaction documents is to base the headings on the actions the parties will be taking under the agreement. After all, an agreement governs a relationship between parties.

It is generally helpful to use numbers and letters for paragraphs and subparagraphs, especially for purposes of cross-referencing a document. Just as there is no particular outline that must be used, there is no particular numbering or lettering system that must be used.

Division in Briefs and Memoranda

Sometimes the main components of a brief are specified by court rule. A court rule may require a document to have a jurisdictional statement, the statement of facts, the issues, the argument, and a conclusion.

In the discussion section of a memorandum and in the argument section of a brief, headings correspond with the issues presented. Hence, these sections are divided by legal issues. Look at the headings used in the briefs filed in *Griswold v. Connecticut*, which are set out in the appendix.

Classification

Classification is the arrangement of the information under the appropriate grouping or subgrouping. Whether a concept fits under heading A or heading B is a classification concern.

TERMS

---

classification† In a document, the arrangement of information under the appropriate grouping or subgrouping.

Use Correct Classification in Contracts

In a contract, whether information fits under paragraph 1.1 or paragraph 9.5 is a classification concern. If classification is done with headings, fitting the information under the appropriate heading obviously aids access and clarifies the terms of the agreement. For instance, all provisions relating to a default should be put under one heading, not scattered throughout the document. If the same concern is addressed in several sections of the agreement, a court might not give proper consideration to the displaced terms.

Check Classifications When Editing

In editing a document, cross-checking for classification problems helps the writer spot conflicting language. An issue may have been addressed in two separate parts of a document, or conflicting statements may have been made.

Sequencing

Sequencing simply refers to the order of the outline. Whether heading A or heading B comes first is a sequential concern.

Sequencing in Transaction Documents

The writer must decide what provision of a lease or contract should come first. In most cases, the writer has complete freedom in ordering the provisions. Some commonsense guidelines, however, apply. First, the provisions that have the most financial impact should be near the beginning. The rent provisions, for instance, should be near the beginning rather than at the end. Second, the provisions that the parties will be most likely to use most frequently should be placed before provisions that the parties will be least likely to use with any frequency. Third, the exceptions or conditions should be placed nearer the end and after the general provisions. In other words, the general comes before the specific. Fourth, provisions should be placed in the order the events will occur. For instance, a provision dealing with the length of the lease is placed before a provision dealing with renewal of the lease. Fifth, a provision dealing with a default should be placed nearer the end. Finally, the boilerplate language common to all such agreements should appear toward the end of the document.

Although these rules are sometimes contradictory, the writer should try to arrive at a reason for the way transaction documents are sequenced.

Sequencing in Briefs and Memoranda

In writing briefs and memoranda, the writer must decide what issue to present first. The general rule is that stronger issues should be presented before weaker ones. If the issues are equal, those that will benefit the client the most should be presented first. For example, in a criminal case, two issues might be of equal merit, but one issue might result only in a remand and a new trial whereas the other might result in the client going free through a reversal. Obviously, the second issue would be more beneficial to the client.

These are just general rules, however, and there are many reasons for selecting a different sequencing approach. The writer, for example, may decide to lead with a weak issue if, by developing it, a sympathetic picture of the client's situation can be painted and the court prompted to rule for the client on another issue.

The Importance of Headings

A headline in a newspaper is used to capture attention. For years, legal professionals were more concerned with the content than the layout of a document, but now they recognize that the format and layout of the document can enhance readability. Type size, margins, and typefaces are important factors. Headings break up the material and make reading the page more pleasant.

Use Headings as a Road Map

Headings provide a context for the material that follows. Headings in a contract can lead the reader directly to a specific provision. Headings in a brief can help the reader follow the argument.

Develop Customized Headings

The writer should spend some time on headings and not simply write generic ones. Legal documents deserve headings that are as well thought out as newspaper headlines. For example, consider these headings for an apartment lease:

Before	*After*
Term	Length of this lease
Rent	Rent owed for apartment
Security deposit	How the security deposit is handled
Taxes	Taxes that must be paid
Insurance	Insurance that must be paid

Maintenance	Your duty to maintain apartment
Default	What happens if a default occurs?
Pets	No pets!
Subleasing	How to handle subleasing the apartment if you must move

Review Headings to Check Structure and Readability

Headings play a significant role both in checking structure and in aiding readability. The writer needs to pay attention to the headings in a legal document.

A Basic Outline for Memoranda and Briefs

General outlines serve as guides in legal writing. As a legal issue is analyzed in a memorandum or an argument is developed in a brief, an outline similar to this might be followed:

1. Background or introduction

   ■ Set the tone for the discussion

   ■ Focus the discussion

   ■ State the theme or purpose

   ■ Give the theory

2. Statement of the issue
3. Discussion of the applicable rule of law

   ■ Show how rule was derived

   ■ Show reader that the correct rule is used

4. Application of rule to facts of your case
5. Disprove opponent's position or argument

   ■ Distinguish cases of opponent

   ■ Show logical inconsistencies of opponent's position

   ■ Show how facts change the analysis

6. Conclusions

Multiple Issues

If there are multiple issues in a memorandum or brief, each issue can be discussed according to the preceding outline.

Customized Outlines

Although the generic outline is useful, cases differ from one another. Often the writer finds that it is it better to develop his or her own outline. The writer has considerable freedom to develop that outline in whatever way enables the writer to best present his or her ideas. The important thing is that an outline is prepared for any complex document.

Paragraph Design

The basic unit of structure in legal writing is the paragraph. How paragraphs are sequenced adds to or detracts from how effectively an idea is communicated. Transitions between paragraphs also add to or detract from readability. In fact, the strength or weakness of an argument can be detected by looking at the topic sentences in each paragraph. Isolating the individual topic sentences in a brief, for example, can help the reader trace the opponent's logic. Although there are no fixed rules on paragraph structure, there are some general rules that can lead to better development of ideas.

Paragraphs Should Flow in Logical Sequence

In expository or argumentative writing, such as memoranda and briefs, the first paragraph should set the tone or provide a background to the reader. It might set out the theories or outline the development of an argument. The opening paragraph might even lead with the most persuasive statement (an anticlimactic approach) as opposed to building the argument to a climax. The anticlimactic approach presents the reader with the gist of the argument at the outset, and the remainder of the writing attempts to reinforce this conclusion.

The middle paragraphs should develop or prove the concepts outlined in the opening paragraph. These paragraphs may follow a chronological or historical development, use a compare/contrast approach, follow a general-to-specific or specific-to-general development, or focus on cause and effect.

A good way to make transitions in the middle paragraphs is through the use of adverbs. Emphasis can be expressed with adverbs such as *indeed, that is,* or *certainly.* An illustration or example can be introduced with *for example, for instance,* or *namely.* A contrast of ideas can be expressed with *however, nevertheless,* or *on the contrary.* Points can be enumerated with such words as *first, second,* and *finally.*

The final paragraph should finish what the reader was told in the first paragraph that the writer would accomplish. In other words, the final paragraph should prove the point of the discussion. The final paragraph can be used to summarize the point of the discussion or detail an opinion or course of action. Transition adverbs such as *accordingly, consequently, thus, therefore*, or *as a result* might be used in a concluding paragraph. In any event, the first and last paragraphs should always be reread to see if the development has been completed. One of the most common mistakes of inexperienced legal writers is not following through on the idea started at the beginning of a document, especially when preparing briefs and memoranda. The same principles discussed here also apply when writing correspondence.

Paragraphs Should Contain Topic Sentences

As in other forms of writing, a paragraph in a legal document should contain a topic sentence, although the topic sentence does not necessarily have to be the first sentence of the paragraph. In legal writing, a topic sentence may summarize a proposition of law. Then, in the remainder of the paragraph, the writer can show how the legal proposition was derived or the effect of the legal proposition on the facts of a case. The topic of a paragraph can be implied. Opening each paragraph with a rigid topic sentence only results in a boring piece. A topic sentence aids structure, but there is no set formula for writing topic sentences.

Paragraphs Should Vary in Length

No standard rule dictates paragraph length. A one-sentence paragraph may be appropriate, especially to make a transition between two adjacent paragraphs. Correspondence typically contains shorter paragraphs than a brief. Paragraphs break up the material for the reader. Shorter paragraphs often are easier to read. If paragraphs are too short, however, it usually means that the ideas are not being covered adequately. If paragraphs are too long, it usually means that the discussion is too convoluted.

The rule is that a paragraph should complete the thought of the topic sentence. Each paragraph should deal with only one topic. If the topic is finished, the writer should move to the next paragraph.

Paragraphs Should Utilize Transitions

Paragraphs should be unified. Each paragraph should be connected to the adjacent paragraphs. If each paragraph is connected to the others, the reader is better able to grasp the writer's logic. Transitions lead the reader through the writer's thought process. Writing isolated rather than connected paragraphs is a common error—a poor practice that usually stems from failure to think the position through sequentially. The student should remember that adverbs can aid the transition between paragraphs.

§ 3.3 Sentence Structure

There is more to writing sentences than starting with a capital letter and ending with a punctuation mark. There is more to it than avoiding dangling modifiers and ensuring that subject and verb agree. A sentence is used to communicate an idea or a complete thought. Like the paragraph, the sentence can either add to or detract from an argument. Sentence structure can cause a reader's attention to drift from the analysis, or it can cultivate great interest in the theory. Some guidelines for using sentence structure to help the writing process follow.

Vary Sentence Length

The movement to simplify legal documents tends to advocate shorter sentences. Although the skillful use of short sentences does aid readability, the advantage is lost when a document consists entirely of short sentences. The best practice is to vary sentence length, a technique that serves to accent an argument well. The writer can use a series of longer sentences and end the paragraph with a brief one, or the writer can lead with a series of short sentences for cadence and build up to a point that is made with a longer sentence.

The writer should not hesitate to use shorter sentences when they will do the same job as longer sentences, but developing the habit of varying sentence length is important.

Vary Sentence Type

The writer should favor the simple sentence. As with sentence length, however, variety in sentence type aids the presentation of thought. There are simple sentences, compound sentences, and complex sentences.

I like simple sentences. (simple sentence)

I like simple sentences, but I do not like compound sentences. (compound sentence)

I like sentences that read like this. (complex sentence)

A simple sentence contains a subject and predicate. A compound sentence contains two or more independent clauses, both of which are complete sentences. A complex sentence contains one independent clause and one or more dependent clauses. In other words, a complex sentence contains a complete sentence and at least one clause that is not a complete sentence. Compound-complex sentences combine the properties of the two types.

Avoid Overloaded Sentences

Several ideas should not be crammed into one sentence. A good way to check on how many ideas are crammed into a sentence is to look for the verbs (including the different verb forms such as infinitives and participles). The presence of several verbs is a sign of too many ideas in a sentence.

Use Sentences to Create Special Effects

Strategically placed sentences create special effects. An exclamatory sentence can drive home a legal argument. A parenthetical sentence can highlight an aside. (So can a footnote.) A rhetorical question can focus a dispute.

A sentence is used to communicate an idea. The main idea of the sentence should be in the main clause. Subordinate ideas should be placed in subordinate clauses. A sentence that contains the main idea at its beginning is called a **loose sentence**. A loose sentence is usually more readable. A sentence that contains the main idea at its end is called a **periodic sentence**. A periodic sentence is used to build suspense.

A sentence can be made easier to understand by opening with a familiar idea before introducing an unfamiliar idea. Emphasis can be provided by putting a key word at the end of a sentence. An idea can be buried by placing it in a dependent or restrictive clause. The writer should learn to use sentences creatively to drive home points. Understanding sentence structure will broaden the student's writing ability.

TERMS

---

loose sentence†   Sentence that contains its main idea at the beginning.
periodic sentence†   Sentence that contains its main idea at the end.

Writing Exercises

1. Rewrite the following list, paying attention to parallel structure.

   The elements of a battery include (1) a rude or insolent touching (2) the person does not consent to the touching (3) intending to harm the other person.

2. Correct the following list for parallel structure.

   the candy, the cake, pie and the gum

3. Rewrite this sentence using shorter sentences.

   (a) That the wife shall have, keep and retain the sole ownership, control and enjoyment of, and during her life, or by last will and testament, or by other testamentary disposition, shall have the exclusive right to dispose of any and all property, real, personal or mixed, of every nature and description and wheresoever located, which she now owns or is possessed of, or hereafter may acquire or receive as her own absolute property, without interference by or from the husband, and in like manner as if said contemplated marriage had not taken place and the wife had remained unmarried.

4. Put the main idea of this sentence at the beginning.

   The students were listening to the teacher as gunshots were fired on the playground.

5. You start to work at a business that classifies symbols. On the first day you are shown the symbols with which you will be working.

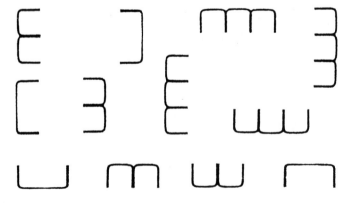

Your job is to divide, classify, and sequence them. Explain your methodology.

6. Write a paragraph using the climactic approach and then write one with the same idea using an anticlimactic approach.

7. You work as a legal professional for a prosector in the state of Ames. Your supervisor will be trying a drunk-driving case in misdemeanor court next week. The facts are most unusual.

> The defendant was seen sitting on a curb next to a moped that was lying on the side of the road. A citizen stopped to help. The citizen concluded that the defendant was intoxicated. The defendant told the citizen that she had been pedaling the moped and had fallen when she hit the curb.
>
> The police arrived and a blood alcohol test was administered. The defendant tested .20, which was clearly in excess of the .10 that is the statutory standard in the state of Ames for intoxication.

The applicable statutes in the state of Ames provide:

> It is unlawful for any person who is under the influence of intoxicating liquor or a drug or a combined influence of intoxicating liquor and a drug, to drive a vehicle. Ames Statutes, Section 101.
>
> A "vehicle" is a device by which any person or property may be propelled, moved, or drawn upon a highway, excepting a device moved exclusively by human power or used exclusively upon stationary rails or tracks. Ames Statutes, Section 102.

Your supervisor has told you that he has serious doubt about whether a moped is a vehicle. He said even if a moped is a vehicle, he does not think the defendant was operating the vehicle. He also said that he doubted whether there was sufficient evidence to show that the defendant was actually riding the moped. The supervisor hands you a synopsis of the relevant cases. The supervisor is always complete and there are no other cases in your jurisdiction. The synopsis is not arranged in any particular order.

Case 1:   Held that a snowmobile was a motor vehicle within the meaning of Ames Statutes, Section 102.

Case 2:   Held that a moped was not a motor vehicle but did not decide whether it was a vehicle within the meaning of Ames Statutes, Section 102.

Case 3:   Held that a motorcycle was a motor vehicle within the meaning of Ames Statutes, Section 102.

Case 4:   Defined the word "drive" as meaning "steering and controlling a vehicle while in motion."

Case 5:   Held that the word "exclusively" must be given effect.

Case 6:   Held that evidence was sufficient to support conviction for drunk driving even though defendant was not seen in car. When police officer arrived at the accident scene, police officer found defendant's car in ditch and several people milling around car. Defendant admitted he had been driving the car.

Case 7:   Held that a defendant who entered a car involved in a collision, started the engine, and with the help of others who pushed, moved the car four to five feet was not "driving" the vehicle. The front wheel had been demolished in the collision.

Case 8: Upheld a conviction wherein an intoxicated person was steering a vehicle towed by others.

Case 9: Held that an intoxicated person found behind the steering wheel of a car with the engine running is not "in motion." Ames Statutes, Section 102.

Case 10: Upheld a conviction wherein a defendant steered an inoperative vehicle as it coasted down a steeply inclined driveway.

a. The supervisor tells you there are three good legal issues. He asks you to prepare an outline of the argument section for a trial brief. Using the outline discussed in the text, prepare a detailed outline of the argument section for the trial brief. Include the cases in your outline.

b. For each of the three legal issues you outlined, write a topic sentence for each outline heading.

Enrichment Activity

1. Discuss the use of parallel structure and organization principles in the Gettysburg Address.

Four score and seven years ago our fathers brought forth on this continent, a new nation, conceived in Liberty, and dedicated to the proposition that all men are created equal.

Now we are engaged in a great civil war, testing whether that nation, or any nation so conceived and so dedicated, can long endure. We are met on a great battle-field of that war. We have come to dedicate a portion of that field, as a final resting place for those who here gave their lives that that nation might live. It is altogether fitting and proper that we should do this.

But, in a larger sense, we can not dedicate—we can not consecrate—we can not hallow—this ground. The brave men, living and dead, who struggled here, have consecrated it, far above our poor power to add or detract. The world will little note, nor long remember what we say here, but it can never forget what they did here. It is for us the living, rather, to be dedicated here to the unfinished work which they who fought here have thus far so nobly advanced. It is rather for us to be here dedicated to the great task remaining before us—that from these honored dead we take increased devotion to that cause for which they gave the last full measure of devotion—that we here highly resolve that these dead shall not have died in vain—that this nation, under God, shall have a new birth of freedom—and that government of the people, by the people, for the people, shall not perish from the earth.

CHAPTER 4

DISEASES OF LEGAL WRITING

Legal writers are professional writers. In many situations, the legal writer must be concerned with problems that are not of concern to other professional writers. For example, the wrong word in a legal document can lead to an expensive dispute. In fact, too many legal disputes are actually caused by poor legal drafting. One survey found that twenty-five percent of all contract disputes arose from poor drafting.

A legal professional prepares many types of technical documents. Although certain rules that apply to technical writers also apply to legal writers, many problems are unique to the legal professional. This chapter explores the unique problems of legal writing.

§ 4.1 Avoid Ambiguity

Avoiding ambiguity is a critical concern of the legal professional. Ambiguity develops when two different interpretations are possible.

Words with Multiple Meanings

Words with multiple meanings can be ambiguous. For instance, the word *ton* can mean a short ton or a metric ton. Similarly, the word *profit* can refer to either gross or net. A *quart jar* can mean a jar that holds a quart of liquid or a jar that displaces a quart of liquid. Ambiguity also arises from the misuse of the simple words *and* and *or* and the words *shall* and *may*.

> Does "P or Q" mean "P or else Q or else both," "P or else Q, but not both" or "P, that is to say Q"? Does "P and Q" mean "only both P and Q" or "P or else Q or else both"?[1]

The classic example of this problem is seen in an old English case that involved a charter party who was required "to load a full and complete cargo of sugar, molasses, and/or other lawful produce."[2] What can be loaded? There are at least seven different combinations. For example, the ship can be loaded with only sugar or only molasses—or the ship can be loaded with no sugar or molasses. Words with multiple meanings, however, are not the only source of ambiguity.

Syntax Problems

Ambiguity can arise from syntax problems. Syntax is the relationship of words to one another. For example, consider an insurance policy that covers any "disease of organs of the body not common to both sexes."[3] Does this policy cover a fibroid tumor (which can occur in any organ) of the womb?

Ambiguity can even arise from the punctuation of a sentence. Consider a contract for sale of "approximately 10,000 (heaters), all in perfect condition."[4] Is this a warranty of the heaters (all heaters must be in perfect condition, as the buyer would argue)? Or is it a limitation of quantity (the buyer can buy all the heaters that are in perfect condition)?

Vagueness

Ambiguity is present in a situation where two different interpretations are possible. Vagueness occurs in a situation where there is a question of degree. Exactly when yellow turns into orange on a color wheel is an illustration of vagueness.

In most cases, ambiguity is an undesirable disease of legal writing. In contrast, vagueness in legal drafting is sometimes appropriate. In fact, conscious use of vagueness is a necessary and sanctioned practice in certain forms of legal drafting. Suppose the parties have reached a snag in negotiations over a situation that might never occur. The parties, however, may be able to agree on language that will cover the contingency satisfactorily for both of them. Inserting a vague term in the agreement can resolve the dispute, so parties sometimes "agree to be vague." Judicious use of vagueness can be an effective bargaining technique, but the writer should remember that if a dispute later arises, the controversy has only been delayed, not resolved.

In child custody agreements, lawyers frequently provide for "reasonable visitation" for the noncustodial parent. Reasonable visitation is a vague concept. By using the word *reasonable,* the lawyer makes an assumption that the parties themselves can discover through the process of trial and error what is reasonable for them under the circumstances. Those parties may apply that concept differently from other parties, yet the phrase *reasonable visitation* is a concept that a court can enforce if the circumstances warrant. Rather than working out detailed specific visitation hours, the attorneys, or in some cases the courts, delegate responsibility to the parties. The concept of reasonableness in any case is vague, but it can be an appropriate problem-solving approach.

An able legal professional frequently completes a transaction by finding solutions to stagnated negotiations. Often the use of vague or elastic terms such as *reasonable, as soon as practical, appropriate, good faith,* or *proper* provides a vehicle for resolving an impasse. Again, the use of vagueness in this context is neither improper nor inappropriate. If the client is cautioned that a vague concept has been inserted, the client can complete the transaction by assuming the risk. If the eventuality occurs and intervention is necessary, a court can resolve the conflict. That is a business risk accepted by the client to reach the agreement in the first place.

§ 4.2 Avoid Inconsistency

Grade school teachers want students to explore a variety of words and urge their students not to use the same words again and again. Students who use a word repeatedly are likely to find it circled boldly in red on their papers.

The consistency principle in legal writing is contrary to this early lesson. The consistency principle dictates using the same word, phrase, or clause in the legal document whenever the same meaning is intended and using a different word, phrase, or clause when a different meaning is intended. Word variation offends the consistency principle. No principle of drafting is more important than being consistent throughout the document. The consistency principle is immaterial to students in disciplines other than law. In legal drafting, inconsistency of expression courts litigation.

The rationale for this rule is that the drafter has carefully and logically selected the words for a legal document. Although this may or may not be the situation, legal writers must pay attention to the consistency rule.

The ultraquistic subterfuge and the elegant variation are two examples of the consistency principle.

The Ultraquistic Subterfuge

Many words have more than one dictionary meaning. When a word with multiple meanings is used to express different ideas in the same document, it is termed an **ultraquistic subterfuge** or legerdemain with two senses. An example of an ultraquistic subterfuge is seen in this sentence: "The real *property* shall be the *property* of the wife." Here the first *property* refers to a specific piece of land. The second *property* refers to ownership.

TERMS

ultraquistic subterfuge†   The use of a word with multiple meanings to express different ideas within a single document.

Another example is seen from an actual case: "A defendant is not *responsible* if at the time of his unlawful conduct his mental or emotional processes or behavior controls were impaired to such an extent that he cannot be held *responsible* for his act."[5] Here the word *responsible* is used in two different contexts. The first *responsible* means "able to discharge one's obligations." The second *responsible* means "accountable for one's actions."

The ultraquistic subterfuge results from using homonyms in the same document. Homonyms are two words that have the same spelling but different meanings. This often results in confusion because the same word is used with two different meanings in the same document. The use of homonyms should be avoided in legal documents.

The Elegant Variation

The converse of the rule that applies to homonyms applies to the use of synonyms. The error of using synonyms to mean the same thing is termed an **elegant variation**. Courts assume that if different words are used, different meanings are intended. When synonyms are used, the courts assume different shades of meaning are intended.

Unfortunately, most legal professionals who use elegant variations do not intend any difference in meaning. They are simply practicing what they were taught to do long ago—using different words for the sake of variety or to show off their vocabulary. Again, the rule is that if the same meaning is intended, the same word should be used. Less-experienced writers believe that repetition of words means lack of imagination. They do not understand that each word has a specific meaning and function. The elegant variation—changing words for the mere sake of change—is a flaw of inferior writers. In legal drafting, the flaw creates ambiguity.

The writer should not substitute synonyms but should choose an appropriate word and use that word throughout the document.

§ 4.3 Avoid Redundant Pairs

Consider the words "last will and testament." What is the difference between "will" and "testament"? Historically, some experts believe that a

---

TERMS

elegant variation† The use of more than one word (synonyms) to indicate a single meaning within a document; courts assume different words intend different meanings.

will dealt with real estate and a testament dealt with personal property, but today a will disposes of all property. Yet legal professionals continue to use the redundant "will and testament."

There is no legal or logical reason to use redundant pairs. The writer should choose the one word that accomplishes the objective. For example, instead of saying "I authorize and direct you," the writer should say "I direct you." Someone cannot be directed to do something without being given authority to do it. Consider this list of redundant pairs and notice how one word can always be used:

alter or change	assumes and agrees
convey and transfer	covenant and agree
deemed and considered	due and owing
each and all	each and every
for and during the period	full and complete
full force and effect	kept and performed
made and entered into	mentioned or referred to
null and void	remise and release
sole and exclusive	give and devise
then and in that event	true and correct

§ 4.4 Avoid Noun and Verb Strings

A problem related to redundant pairs is the problem of **encircling the concept.** This situation frequently occurs when the writer is unsure of the right word so uses a string of words to capture the concept.

This pattern is seen, for example, in a string of verbs such as "The trustee shall serve until he *resigns, dies,* or *leaves* the country." What happens if the trustee becomes incompetent? The simple solution would be to say ". . . until he is unable or unwilling to serve."

Another example is seen in the string of nouns in this provision: "Seller assumes no liability for interruptions to service due to strikes, riots, war,

---

TERMS

encircling the concept†   Using a string of words to capture the concept of a provision.

floods, fire, or acts of God." What happens if vandalism prevents service? A proper solution might be to rephrase the clause to read, "Seller is not liable for service interruptions due to events beyond Seller's control." Trying to anticipate every eventuality without meeting the problem head-on frequently results in missing an eventuality.

The problem of noun and verb strings often arises in statutes, especially where the substantive law requires that the statutes be strictly construed. Does the phrase "business and all furniture, fixtures, and personal property used in connection thereof, and all accounts receivables . . . "[6] include bank accounts? Does the phrase "personal effects, jewelry, and furniture" include silverware? Does "all jewelry, wearing apparel, silver, silverware, china, pictures, paintings, books, house furniture and furnishings, and articles of household or personal use or ornament of all kinds" include statues?

In the preceding examples, the drafter attempted to exhaustively provide for every possible eventuality, but in each situation, the drafter overlooked a pertinent fact. The drafter did not anticipate all eventualities because he or she did not recognize that whenever encircling is used in a document, the danger of missing an important possibility exists. The oversight is not a product of laziness, because the drafter may have spent a lot of time agonizing over how to enumerate all eventualities. But that time would have been spent more constructively in trying to reconceptualize the problem.

Whenever the writer begins to use a string of words to define a concept, the writer should consider whether he or she is creating a conceptualization problem. Overspecificity does not enhance conceptualization. Consider for example, the phrase ". . . to prevent garbage from leaking, spilling, falling, or blowing out of such vehicle." If the word *escaping* is substituted for "leaking, spilling, falling, or blowing," no substance is lost. Likewise, the word *convey* or the word *assign* can be substituted for "grant, bargain, sell, alien, release, confirm, and enfeoff" or for "bargain, sell, assign, transfer, give over, and conform" without loss of substance. The writer should not be afraid to break the habit of redundancy that only fogs the pages of legal documents.

§ 4.5 Avoid the Vague Referent

Most attorneys recognize that words such as *it, there,* and *this* when used as pronouns should be avoided because they are vague referents. These words are meant to refer to "closely adjacent antecedent nouns," but in legal documents they cause problems for readers and, worse, create ambiguity. Yet the same legal professional who avoids using the pronouns *it, there,* and *this* to begin a sentence may use *said, such,* or *hereabove* without hesitation in legal drafting. Vague referents are frequently utilized by attorneys out of intellectual laziness.

When any of these terms are used, the reader does not know whether they refer to the preceding clause, sentence, paragraph, or the entire agreement. A case will best show this point:

> In a California case the phrase, "except as herein expressly provided," was the subject of litigation. It went through three courts: trial court, an intermediate appellate court, and the Supreme Court of California. The trial court held that "herein" in that phrase meant *in the entire statute,* that is, "except as expressly provided in this statute." In the intermediate appeal court consisting of five judges, it was held by a three-to-two vote that "herein" meant "in this particular section," not in the statute. Then it went up to the Supreme Court of California, a court of seven judges. And that court held, by a four-to-three vote, that "herein" meant "in the statute itself." Here we have trial court holding one way, a three-to-two decision in the appellate court holding the opposite, and a four-to-three decision in the Supreme Court of California holding the way the trial court held.

> The District Court of Appeals explained its holding with the following reasoning:

> "In the expression 'Except as *herein* expressly provided' the term 'herein' means 'in this section,' and the words that follow, 'the provisions *of this act* shall not apply, . . .' refer to the entire statute. The placing of the words 'herein' and 'of this act' in the same sentence and their proximity in the sentence make it manifest that the Legislature did not intend and did not achieve vagueness or obscurity. Hence the section means that the provisions of the entire act, except as provided in that section, are not applicable to the sale of the vendor's own securities. . . ."

> "*The conclusion expressed above is affirmed, if confirmation is necessary, by the legislative history of subdivision 3 of section 2(c)*" (italics supplied).

> But the majority in the California Supreme Court reasoned:

> "It is argued that the introductory phrase in that section, 'Except as herein expressly provided' does not refer to the remainder of the act, but is confined to section 2 in which it appears. The meaning of the term 'herein' is determined by the context of the statute in which it is used (see In re Pearsons, 98 Cal. 603, 608, 33 P. 451). *Here it is clear that the word refers to the entire act.* If the reference were to section 2, the language would be meaningless since no exceptions appear in that section. *The all-embracing application is compelled by the manifest purpose of the act* which discloses a comprehensive scheme for controlling the issuance and sale of corporate securities. It is also indicated in the codification of section 2(c). In rephrasing the section for inclusion in the Corporation Code there is substituted for the words 'Except as herein expressly provided,' the phrase: 'Except as expressly provided in this division.' The reference is to division 1, title 4 of the Corporations Code (secs. 25000–26104; Stats.

1949, ch. 384, p. 698) which comprises all of the Corporate Securities Act. It is therefore significant that the intended application of the word 'herein' in Section 2(c) is likewise to the entire act" (italics supplied).[7]

Specific Troublesome Words and Phrases

The legal writer who uses words like *aforesaid, such,* and *hereinabove* evidently believes that they sound professional. But these words create the same problem that *it* and *there* create at the beginning of a sentence. Certain words and phrases invariably cause problems. The writer should avoid them.

Such

From a readability standpoint, it is almost always preferable to substitute the articles *a, an,* and *the* for the word *such. Such* is a demonstrative adjective that should be used with *as.* Using *such* as a synonym for *the* is an illiteracy.

Notwithstanding the Foregoing

Legal professionals love the phrase *notwithstanding the foregoing.* But like other relics of legalese, the phrase raises an immediate question. Does it mean the preceding sentence, paragraph, or the entire document? The mystery deepens when this phrase becomes a double negative. The author once reviewed a statute concerning leases of public property. The first sentence excepted "not-for-profit entities." In the succeeding sections, all other leases of public property required an appraisal before the public authorities could lease the property. Then a section provided that "notwithstanding anything else," no lease could be for a rental value less than two-thirds of the fair market value of the property. Question: Did this section apply to a "not-for-profit entity"?

§ 4.6 Avoid Legal Jargon

Too many legal professionals believe there is a certain way lawyers must write. These writers use archaic legal jargon to make their documents seem "legal." Only infrequently must certain words be used to meet legal requirements. For example, a warranty deed might require use of the words *warrant and convey,* and an option might require the words *irrevocable and binding.* In most cases, however, a legal professional has considerable freedom in preparing a legal document. The writer should exercise this freedom to write so that both the writer and the client can understand the document, if possible.

Ideally, the words in a legal document should express the idea of the parties. The words should be within the vocabulary of the audience. The words should not cause confusion or ambiguity. Choosing the right word, however, requires more than using the common—or dictionary—meaning of words.

In any profession there develops a specialized language. For instance, the language of the physicist has changed dramatically in the past fifty years. There is no reason why legal language should not change also. There is no reason why legal professionals—or any technical writer—should continue to use multisyllable words when simple words will suffice. A writer should find a simple word instead of the more difficult word, if possible. Here are some sample words that legal professionals can avoid entirely:

above (as an adjective)	same (as a substitute for *it, he, him*, etc.)
above-mentioned	thenceforth
aforementioned	thereunto
aforesaid	therewith
henceforward	to wit
herein	unto
hereinabove	wheresoever

The legal connotations of words must be appreciated in choosing them, but just because a word has an established legal meaning does not mean that the writer must use that particular word. The fact that legal professionals of an earlier era used certain language does not suggest that the writer today also needs to use that language. Yet, that logic leads writers to use many archaic expressions in legal instruments. Language usage changes both outside and within the legal community.

§ 4.7 Learn the Difference Between *Shall* and *May*

A sentence in a legal document either commands, authorizes, or declares a result. Legal writers must choose their words carefully in order to ensure the proper result.

The Proper Use of *Shall*

Many legal professionals think that every sentence in a transaction document must use the word *shall*. However, *shall* should be used only to impose a duty. In practice, this word is overused in legal documents.

Many legal writers think that *shall* is a legal word that should be used in almost every sentence of a contract. Whenever a writer uses the word *shall*, however, he or she should test whether that word is really proper by substituting the phrase *has a duty* for the word *shall*. If this substitution does not work, another appropriate word should be selected. *Shall* should not be used in legal drafting to express future tense but should be used only to impose a duty. In some cases, the writer is trying to create a condition rather than a duty. If this is the intent, the word *must* should be used.

In many cases, *shall* and *may* are unfortunately interchanged by the parties, leading to unintended results. In legal drafting,

> "shall" is always used to impose a duty, regardless of whether the duty is affirmative or negative, and "may" is always used to convey authority (but not to deny authority).[8]

The writer needs to learn to recognize the difference between *shall* and *may*.

The Proper Use of *May*

The word *may* causes problems. First, there is the potential ambiguity of *may* as authorization and as possibility. *May* can be read to mean that someone is being given the authority to act or that a possibility is being described. The sentence "I may go to the store" can mean either that someone has given the speaker permission to go to the store or that the speaker is considering whether to go to the store. *May* can mean either permission or a possibility. A writer should read each sentence containing the word *may* with both definitions in mind.

A second dimension of the problem with *may* is the use of the negative, or *may not*. *May not* does not negate authority:

> A second difficulty in the use of "may" is that the negative of authority is not expressed by "may not"; rather, the negative of authority is expressed by the negative duty, "shall not." Thus, if a provision reads, "if a person does not have a license . . ., he may not exhibit a sign . . .," there is doubt about whether the phrase "may not exhibit" means (1) "may possibly not exhibit," (2) "is authorized not to exhibit" or (3) "is not authorized to exhibit."[9]

The legal professional must be aware of the dimensions of the use of the word *may*. The writer should remember that *may not* does not negate authority and that the word *may* can mean either permission or possibility. The writer should always ask: Is *may* meant to confer authority, or is it used to connote a possibility?

This concise synopsis solves many problems:

1. To create a right, say "is entitled to."
2. To create discretionary authority, say "may."
3. To create a duty, say "shall."
4. To create a mere condition precedent, say "must" (*e.g.*, "To be eligible to occupy the office of mayor, a person must . . .").[10]

§ 4.8 Know How to Use *and* and *or*

Choosing between the conjunction *and* and the conjunction *or* appears to be rather simple: *and* is used in the conjunctive sense, and *or* is used in the disjunctive sense. The conjunctive sense connotes "togetherness," whereas the disjunctive sense connotes "take your pick." Although this choice seems simple, consider these problems:

- Someone is told to pick up the red and white flags. If there is a red flag, a white flag, and a red and white flag, which of them does the person pick up?

- Someone is told to pick up the red or white flags. Which flags does that person pick up?

- A statute says that a city may build a skating rink or a swimming pool. Can the city build both?

- A statute says that a city may build a skating rink and a swimming pool. Can the city build just a skating rink?

- Someone is given an invitation that says "husbands and wives may attend." Can one party go without the other?

- A statute says that a tax is imposed on manufacturers of bows and arrows. Is the tax imposed on a manufacturer that makes only bows?

These situations demonstrate that the words *and* and *or* can have different meanings. These words have a joint or inclusive sense as well as a several or exclusive sense. To prevent confusion, the writer should say, "A and B or either of these" or "either . . . or . . . (but not both)." The writer needs to be precise when using either *and* or *or*. Too many drafting problems are created when *and* or *or* are used. The writer should pay attention to the different meanings of these words.

Do not use *and/or*

Although the courts have condemned the use of *and/or*, lawyers continue to claim the right to use it in legal instruments. The use of *and/or* is an invitation to a lawsuit. Consider the comments of one court on this subject, which held that *and/or*

> should not be used in an affidavit and threatened to order costs against anyone so using it. In *Bonitto v. Fuerst Bros.*, Viscount Simon, in discussing the confusion in the pleadings, spoke of "the repeated use of that bastard conjunction 'and/or' which has, I fear, become the commercial court's contribution to basic English."
>
> In *Millen v. Grove*, a notice to quit under the National Security (Landlord and Tenant) Regulations gave as the ground that the premises were reasonably required by the lessor "for her personal occupation and/or for the occupation of some person who ordinarily resides with and is wholly or partly dependent upon her." Gavan Duffy J. said that "the draftsman invited trouble by the common and deplorable affection for the form "and/or"; but he thought that the notice substantially stated the two grounds provided for in the Regulations, namely the premises being required for her personal occupation *and* for the occupation of some person, etc.[11]

Or as another commentator put it:

> A custom has grown among many lawyers to use the words "and/or" in many documents. The expression is an anachronism and should be avoided. Either the word "and" or the word "or" is proper but never both. Don't be an "andorian."[12]

§ 4.9 Avoid Problem Modifiers

A modifier limits the meaning of a word or phrase: "It is the function of a modifier to limit the scope of the idea that is communicated by an unmodified word."[13] Many problems are caused by misuse of modifiers.

The Unnecessary Modifier

Both the Thirteenth and Fourteenth amendments to the United States Constitution provide that Congress has the power to enforce the provisions "by appropriate legislation." Notice that the word *legislation* is modified by the word *appropriate*. Why add the adjective *appropriate*? Logically, this implies that some legislation is inappropriate. The word *appropriate* incorporates an undefined standard. The courts must tell us what is appropriate legislation on a case-by-case basis.

Another example is from a jury instruction that provided that the plaintiff was to prevail if a "fair preponderance of the evidence" was in the plaintiff's favor. Is there an unfair preponderance? Or if a document refers to a "duly licensed physician," is there an unduly licensed physician? In drafting, a modifier that incorporates an undefined standard can cause vagueness.

Further, in some instances, a modifier creates a double standard. This situation occurs when the writer attempts to define the modifier. Consider this example:

> A second modifier fault arises out of an attempt to be clear; the draftsman says too much. If he writes that a hauler of garbage "shall properly cover the vehicle," the provision is defective, as has been suggested, in that the term "properly" calls for a judgment for which no standard is provided. If, on the other hand, the draftsman writes that the hauler "shall keep the vehicle properly covered so as to prevent the contents from leaking, spilling, falling or blowing out of the vehicle," the phrase which begins "so as to prevent" offers a standard for interpreting "properly"; but it also offers the possibility of a double standard. The question is whether "properly" means the same thing as "so as to prevent the contents from leaking . . ." If the draftsman intended by the word "properly" to say something different from "so as to prevent . . .," there is the ambiguity of a double standard. If not, the word "properly" is superfluous and should be omitted to avoid the risk of ambiguity. Thus, one would say, the hauler "shall keep the vehicle covered so as to prevent the contents from leaking . . ."
>
> Usually the risk of a double standard is created by use of a modifier, such as "properly," to precede a word, such as "cover," which it modifies, plus some "purpose" which is added for clarification. In most instances, the "purpose" states the draftsman's idea more clearly and accurately than the modifier does.[14]

The initial concern of the legal drafter is to determine whether the modifier is even necessary. When the writer says "the landlord may by his designated representative . . .," the adjective *designated* connotes something other than just a representative. The representative somehow must have a designation. The problem is that the tenant can cause a delay by asking for a designation.

Another example of an unnecessary modifier is the adjective intensifier (*e.g., very, extremely, greatly*). Seldom do these intensifiers add anything meaningful to the document. In the context of legal drafting, adjective intensifiers can almost always be deleted.

Sometimes it is difficult to tell whether a word is a modifier or part of a noun. Consider the following:

- Cow killer (a wasp or a killer of cows)

- NCAA basketball (a game sponsored by the NCAA or a basketball with an NCAA trademark)

To the extent that modifiers are necessary to provide flexibility for a transaction, there is no reason not to use them. The legal drafter is cautioned, however, that many modifiers are unnecessary.

The Squinting Modifier

Grammar classes teach that a misplaced modifier appears to modify the wrong referent and a dangling modifier is one that has no referent in the sentence. To a legal drafter, a misplaced modifier is a problem only if it causes equivocation. Most drafting experts agree, for example, that splitting an infinitive is acceptable practice if it prevents ambiguity of reference.

Legal drafters, however, must be aware of a special kind of misplaced modifier—a **squinting modifier,** which is a modifier ambiguously placed between two possible referents. When a squinting modifier is used, it is unclear what word or group of words attaches to another word or group of words. Consider the following examples:

- "No child may be employed on any weekday when the school is not open for more than four hours."

- "No person may molest an animal on the highway."[15]

These sentences show squinting-modifier problems. In the first example, the question is whether the child may be employed on days when school *is* open for less than four hours or whether the child may be employed for more than four hours on weekdays. The second example presents the question whether it is the animal or the person that must be on the highway to make the provision operative.

Squinting modifiers are caused by recurrent sentence patterns. The simplest examples are seen in sentences having adjectives or adjective phrases that can modify two nouns. More difficult to spot may be squinting modifiers involving (1) successive prepositional phrases, (2) problems with the conjunctions *and* and *or*, (3) the terminal *because* clause, and (4) the vague participle. Examples of each of these situations are provided in the following text.

TERMS

squinting modifier†   A modifier placed ambiguously between two possible referents.

Successive Prepositions

The use of two successive prepositional phrases routinely causes squinting-modifier problems. The following is the classic example of this problem:

> Every shareholder of a company in Canada.

Does the phrase *in Canada* relate to *shareholder* or to *company*? The phrase relates to a noun, and there are two, namely, the subject *shareholder* and the object of the first preposition. One remedy is to convert one of the phrases to a clause.

> A shareholder of a company who is in Canada.

The pronoun *who* is personal and must refer to *shareholder*. Another remedy is to convert a prepositional phrase to a participial phrase.

> A shareholder of a company incorporated in Canada.

The word *incorporated* can refer only to company; but *domiciled*, for example, could refer to both.[16]

The author's own acquaintance with ambiguity resulting from two successive prepositional phrases is from *Alvey v. G.E.*,[17] when the Seventh Circuit Court of Appeals, in reversing and remanding the case, wrote, "In the context of this case under the present complaint, . . ."[18] Because the case was remanded, there was concern whether the plaintiff could file a new complaint to remedy the pleading problem. After remand, the plaintiff filed leave to amend the complaint, arguing that "under the present complaint" implied that an amended complaint could be filed. The defendants argued that "in the context of this case" meant that the facts of this case foreclosed an amendment. Both interpretations were plausible. The district court granted leave to amend, and the Seventh Circuit upheld the district court's decision.

The Use of *and* or *or* with Adjectives or Adjective Phrases

Consider this sentence: "I give you the black cows and horses." Did you give me the black cows and *all* the horses, or did you give me the black cows and *just* the black horses? The same situation exists in saying "charitable institutions or organizations." Does this mean a charitable institution or any type of organization? Or does it mean charitable institutions or charitable organizations?

The problem also occurs when a modifying phrase rather than a modifying word either precedes or follows a word in a series. For example, in the sentence "No pupil shall, on the ground of religious belief, be excluded from or placed in an inferior position in any school, college or hostel *provided by the council*,"[19] do the italicized words modify only *hostel*, or do the words modify *school* and *college* as well?

A statute from an actual case illustrates how this problem occurs when multiple conjunctions rather than simple conjunctions are used:

> No person shall engage in or institute a local telephone call, conversation, or conference of any anonymous nature and therein use obscene, profane, vulgar, lewd, lascivious or indecent language, suggestions or proposals of an obscene nature and threats of any kind whatsoever.[20]

The reader who tries to identify which words relate to what other words will get dizzy. Consider, for example, just one question: Must the call, conversation, or conference contain *both* a "threat" *and* "obscene, profane, vulgar, lewd, lascivious or indecent language, suggestions or proposals"? Whenever a conjunction appears with a modifying word, this type of problem may arise.

Terminal *Because* Clause

Consider this example: "The developer may not delay construction during the preliminary phase because of financing." There are two plausible interpretations. First, the developer might claim the right to delay construction on the ground that the developer is experiencing financing problems. Second, the developer cannot delay construction because the delay would endanger financing or a financing commitment.

The double meaning in this example results from the terminal *because* clause. The problems are not always easily spotted by the inexperienced drafter. The writer should look for problems whenever the *because* clause is used.

The Vague Participle

A participle is a verb converted to an adjective. It can modify a noun or pronoun. The present participle usually ends in -ing: shipping, running, examining. A past participle ends in -d, -ed, -t, -n, or changes to a vowel: seen, rung.

Problems with a present participle usually arise when the participle can be interpreted as either describing a duty (or a state of condition) or describing when the action is to be performed. In the sentence "A contestant racing a car in the Pinewood Derby shall not be near the track," the question is whether the sentence means that a contestant cannot be near the track *during* the race or that a contestant must never be near the track.

In fact, one writer says that the "use of the participle as a modifier is a major cause of vagueness and inadequacy in documents."[21] Consider the following example and explanation:

"The license requirements of this ordinance do not apply, until three years have expired, to a person transporting garbage upon a public way before (at the time of) the effective date of this ordinance." Presumably "person transporting" could be used as "person who transported" or "person who was transporting" before the effective date . . ." Would a person who transported garbage once prior to the effective date qualify? Is this provision limited to persons who are engaged in the business of transporting garbage?[22]

Equivocation can arise with the past as well as the present participle.

In the description

Every person who was imprisoned on the 1st day of January, 1970

there is doubt whether the verb is the passive of *to imprison* or the active *to be* plus an adjective as subjective complement. Does the description refer to persons upon whom a sentence of imprisonment was pronounced on the named day, or to a person who on that day was in a state of imprisonment?[23]

The solution in many of these cases is to recast the sentence using another structure, such as a subordinate clause.

§ 4.10 The Importance of Spotting Diseased Writing

Legal professionals must be able to recognize that certain sentence structures lead to certain predictable equivocation problems. By recognizing recurrent problem grammatical constructions, the drafter can spot problems before the client sees the document. As a rule, when a writing precept has been violated, problems will surface.

Writing Exercises

1. Read this provision carefully.

   No animal of the dog kind shall be allowed to go at large without a collar or tag, as now prescribed by law, and no person owning, keeping or having custody of a dog in the district shall permit such dog to be on public space in the district, unless such dog is firmly secured by a substantial leash not exceeding four feet in length, held by a person capable of managing such dog, nor shall any dog be permitted to go on private property without the consent of the owner or occupant thereof.

   a. Identify an example of elegant variation. What problems does it cause?

   b. Identify an example of encircling the concept. How would you cure the problem?

   c. Identify a vague referent.

   d. What is the problem with the phrase *owner or occupant*?

2. Rewrite the dog provision given in the preceding exercise.

3. Identify the unnecessary modifier in this sentence.

   The plaintiff must prove his or her case by a fair preponderance of the evidence.

4. Identify the squinting modifier in this sentence.

   The answer only can be filed by mail.

5. Identify the problems in these sentences and correct them.

   a. I represent, warrant, and covenant that the car will run.

   b. You are ordered to cease and terminate the actions by noon.

6. What is wrong with this sentence?

   No person shall violate the law.

7. What is the problem with these sentences?

   I give my money to athletic and artistic pursuits.

   I give my money to athletic or artistic pursuits.

8. Discuss the problems in the following sentence.

   A hauler of garbage shall properly cover said vehicle so as to prevent the contents from leaking, spilling, falling, or blowing out of the garbage truck.

9. Identify a double standard in this sentence.

   It shall be unlawful to exhibit any picture that is obscene because it offends the prurient interest of the viewer.

10. Who has the duty under this statute?

   It shall be the duty of the chief of police and fire marshal to see that every public show is inspected to ensure conformity with the provisions of this chapter.

11. Discuss the following provision from a consistency standpoint.

   It shall be unlawful to spit or expectorate on any public sidewalk or other public place, or on the floor or walls of any store, hall, public vehicle or other place frequented by the public or to which the public is invited.

12. Discuss how encircling the concept affects this provision.

> No garbage or refuse of any kind shall be deposited in any street, alley, or public way, excepting as is provided in this article; and no such refuse shall be placed so that it can be blown about or scattered by the wind.

Is there a difference in treatment of garbage and refuse? Explain.

13. Discuss the problems with modifiers in this provision.

> No vicious, dangerous, ferocious dog or dog sick with or liable to communicate hydrophobia or other contagious or infectious disease shall be permitted to run at large in the city.

14. Discuss the unnecessary modifier in this provision.

> It shall be unlawful for the habitual user of narcotic drugs to operate any motor vehicle on any street.

15. Discuss modifier problems in this provision.

> Every bicycle shall be equipped with good and adequate brakes.

Enrichment Activity

Complete the following activity.

1. Discuss the problems of inconsistency in this statute:

> Be it enacted by the Senate and House of Representatives of the United States of America in Congress assembled, that, until June 30, 1958, notwithstanding the provisions of law of the United States restricting to vessels of the United States the transportation of passengers and merchandise directly or indirectly from any port in the United States to another port of the United States, passengers may be transported on Canadian vessels between ports in southeastern Alaska, and passengers and merchandise may be transported on Canadian vessels between Hyder, Alaska, and other points in southeastern Alaska or the continental United States, either directly or via a foreign port, or for any part of the transportation.

Notes

[1] E. Allen Farnsworth, *Some Considerations in the Drafting of Agreements: Problems in Interpretation and Gap-Filling*, 39 Okla. B.A.J. 917, 918–19 (1968).

[2] *Id.* at 918.

[3] *Id.* at 919.

[4] *Udell v. Cohen*, 282 A.D. 685, 122 N.Y.S.2d 552 (1953).

[5] *United States v. Brawner*, 471 F.2d 969 (D.C. Cir. 1972).

[6] *Hooper v. Hightower*, 119 Ind. App. 144, 81 N.E.2d 707 (1948).

7 Elliott L. Biskind, *Simplify Legal Writing* 100–101 (New York: Arco, 1975).

8 Maurice B. Kirk, *Legal Drafting: Some Elements of Technique*, 4 Texas Tech. L. Rev. 297, 302 (1973).

9 *Id.* at 303.

10 F. Reed Dickerson, *Materials on Legal Drafting* 182 (St. Paul: West Publishing, 1981).

11 E. L. Piesse, *The Elements of Drafting* 108–109 (Sydney: The Law Book Company Limited, 5th ed., 1976).

12 J. B. Thomas, *Problems in Drafting Legal Instruments*, 39 Ill. State Bar J. 55 (Sept., 1950).

13 Maurice B. Kirk, *Legal Drafting: Some Elements of Technique*, 4 Texas Tech. L. Rev. 297, 315 (1973).

14 Maurice B. Kirk, *Legal Drafting: Curing Unexpressive Language,* 3 Texas Tech. L. Rev. 23, 42–43 (1971).

15 F. Reed Dickerson, *Materials on Legal Drafting* 231 (St. Paul: West Publishing, 1981).

16 *Id.* at 234.

17 622 F.2d 1279 (7th Cir. 1980).

18 622 F.2d at 1291.

19 E. L. Piesse, *The Elements of Drafting* 26–27.

20 *State v. Hill*, 245 La. 119, 157 So. 2d 462 (1963).

21 Maurice B. Kirk, *Legal Drafting: Curing Unexpressive Language*, 3 Texas Tech. L. Rev., 23, 45 (1971).

22 *Id.* at 45–46.

23 Elmer A. Driedger, *The Composition of Legislation; Legislative Forms and Precedents* 23 (Canada: The Department of Justice, 2d ed., 1976).

CHAPTER 5

STYLE: POLISHING YOUR WRITING

"No writer long remains incognito," asserts coauthor E. B. White in the third edition of *The Elements of Style*.[1] When a writer writes, he or she reveals something about his or her disposition, personality, and outlook. When preparing a transaction document or pleading, the writer does not intentionally reveal anything to the reader, but nevertheless, if ten legal professionals were to write the same paragraph of a contract, each version would be different. That difference is attributable to **style.**

In the past, writing style has not been a focus for legal professionals, but that lack of concern has earned them a reputation for generating obscure, cluttered documents and is probably why Will Rogers quipped that lawyers make a living out of trying to figure out what other lawyers have written. Awareness of the principles of style is no less important to a legal writer drafting a will than to a novelist writing a best-seller. Style aids precision and readability. Style is the mark of a good writer. A chapter in a legal writing text will not make the student a master of legal writing—only talent, a few good ideas, and a lot of practice can do that—but here are some ways to begin.

§ 5.1 Build Sentences Around Verbs

When writing a sentence, the writer should consider the verb first. The verb expresses the action in the sentence. The writer may say, "The court held that the lawyer's conduct was unethical." Or the writer may state, "The court disbarred the lawyer for her unethical conduct." Although the first sentence is technically accurate, the verb *held* does not capture the action of the court. Consider the following sentences: "There was a collision of a car with a truck." "The truck rammed the car." The second sentence uses a descriptive verb. The writer should always select a verb that describes the action of the sentence.

TERMS

style† The individualized way someone writes.

Avoid Overuse of Inert Verbs

When a writer fails to use words describing the action, inert verbs—that is, verbs that show no action—are likely to be used. The verb *to be* is an example of an inert verb. Overuse of inert verbs leads to awkward sentences.

> A rambling, unwieldy sentence generally hangs from an inert verb—the verb *to be* (*am, are, is, was, were, being, been*), some other vague, actionless verb like have or exist, or a passive form (the verb *to be* plus a past participle; e.g., *is believed, was seen*). Pay attention to the verbs you use, and when you find a weak one, try substituting something more vigorous.[2]

The verb *to be* does not indicate action. The writer should always ask what is the action in the sentence and then recast the sentence with a verb that describes that action.

Avoid Superfluous Verbs

Another problem is the use of superfluous verbs. Consider these examples:

make an attempt	*change to*	try
make a study of	*change to*	study
provide a summary	*change to*	summarize
do an investigation	*change to*	investigate
give consideration to	*change to*	consider
have a tendency to	*change to*	tend to
reach a decision	*change to*	decide

The cure in these cases is to convert the noun to a verb and eliminate the superfluous verb.

§ 5.2 Choose Active Rather than Passive Voice

Almost every writing manual recommends active voice over passive voice. Active voice is when the subject is doing the action described by the verb. Passive voice is when the subject expresses the object of an action:

- Rick hit the ball. (active voice)

- The ball was hit by Rick. (passive voice)

Overuse of passive voice is a symptom of a writing problem. Many legal professionals tend to overuse passive voice, perhaps because students are taught to depersonalize their writing or to hide their opinions. Surprisingly, the more educated the writer, the more the writer tends to use passive voice.

Active Voice Identifies the Person Responsible for an Action

In preparing transaction documents, style is only a secondary reason for choosing active voice. Consider the following provision: "A dog must be kept on a leash." Because this sentence is written in passive voice, the person whose duty it is to keep the dog on the leash is not identified. If the dog is not kept on the leash, who pays the fine—the owner or the person walking the dog? Using active voice, the writer might say, "Owner must keep dog on a leash." In using active voice, the writer confronts the question of *who does what to whom* in selecting a subject for the sentence. Active voice aids the process of identifying the person who is being granted a privilege or given a duty.

A contract might provide the following: "Insurance shall be maintained on the premises." The fallacy of passive voice in this context is that the party who must pay the insurance is not defined. Context sometimes supplies an answer. In many situations, however, the reader does not have any other reference for discerning who is the actor. Consider another example: "A car parked in such a zone may be ticketed." Here it cannot be ascertained who must pay the fine: the owner of the vehicle or the driver. If this sentence were written in the active voice, the writer would recognize the problem.

As the complexity of a document increases, active voice helps the writer check the proper delegation of duties and responsibilities. Conscious concern with voice helps double-check how duties and responsibilities are to be apportioned.

Active Voice Aids Readability

Active voice also aids readability. With active voice, the writer starts with an actor who performs an action, and this development is followed as the sentence is read.

When to Use the Passive Voice

Passive voice is sometimes appropriate. If the object is important, there is no reason not to use passive construction. For example, "The weapon was found by the child." In active voice, the sentence would read "The child found the weapon." Since the object (weapon) is more important than the actor, the use of passive voice emphasizes "weapon" by making it the subject of the sentence. Passive voice is also appropriate when the actor performing the action is unimportant. For example, "This lease was terminated by a default." In this sentence, who defaults is unimportant. A legal writer may use passive voice to focus emphasis away from the actor if, for instance, the client has committed a less than exemplary act. For example, in the sentence "The money was taken by my client," the passive construction deemphasizes the wrongdoing. As a general rule, less than one-third of the writer's sentences should be passive.

§ 5.3 Do Not Overuse Prepositional Phrases

A problem related to the use of passive voice is the overuse of prepositional phrases. In fact, passive voice leads to overuse of prepositions. Chapter 4 discusses how the use of successive prepositional phrases causes modification problems. In addition, strung out prepositional phrases make sentences unnecessarily wordy—a condition known as **prolixity.** If the writer wants to add a person to a passive construction, a prepositional phrase must be added. If the writer says, "The money was taken from the home on Monday," and the writer wants to say who took the money, another prepositional phrase—"by my client"—must be added. Most works on technical writing caution against overuse of prepositions. One writer notes,

> A ratio of one preposition to every four words is a bad prognostic sign. The overuse of prepositions is a severe and extremely common fault. Indeed, if I wanted to offer a single rule for improving the quality of writing, I would unhesitatingly say, reduce the number of prepositions.[3]

TERMS

---

prolixity† The state of being unnecessarily wordy, often the result of strung out prepositional phrases.

Addressing how many is too many, he continues,

> Long sentences that are not easy to understand and that have only one or two verbs, either active or passive, should make you aware that the entire sentence has too many prepositions.[4]

The writer should be aware of the placement and number of prepositional phrases. Changing passive voice to active voice usually imposes an automatic limit on prepositional phrases.

§ 5.4 Avoid Fat Nouns

It is too bad that there is no scale with which to weigh sentences. If there were, the writer could easily avoid the overweight sentence burdened with inactive verbs and fat nouns. A fat noun is usually a **nominalization**—a verb or an adjective changed to a noun—or a superfluous noun.

The Nominalized Noun

A nominalization converts a verb or adjective into a noun by adding a suffix such as *-tion, -ment,* or *-ence* to a verb or *-ity* or *-ance* to an adjective. The following are nominalized words common to legal documents:

appurten*ances*	enforce*ment*
amortiza*tion*	applicabil*ity*
acquitt*ances*	enforceabil*ity*
assign*ments*	specific*ity*
posse*ssion*	determina*tion*

The problem with a nominalized word is that it is inefficient at doing the work of a verb. In most instances, the solution is to rebuild the sentence by converting the nominalized word back to its original form as a verb or an adjective.

Before   The *applicability* of that statute to this case is arguable.

After   The parties can argue whether that statute *applies* to this case.

TERMS

nominalization†   A verb or an adjective changed into a noun.

Usually nominalization results from using passive voice. Writing in active voice usually prevents the problem.

The Superfluous Noun

Legal writers seem to share a fondness for inserting nouns that do nothing to enhance their sentences. Look at the following list:

- **The case of** *Smith v. Jones* is directly on point.

- **The concept of** reasonable doubt is a significant focus of the criminal trial.

- **The extent of** the damages in this case is not controverted.

Case, concept, extent—these nouns add nothing but length to the sentences. Superfluous nouns should be deleted.

§ 5.5 Be Positive, Not Negative

The writer should always write in positive terms unless there is a good reason for using the negative. The positive makes a statement; the negative only denies the positive.

Negatives Convey Imprecision

Negative terms are often imprecise. A negative pregnant is a negative statement that does not actually deny an accusation. Consider the following negative pregnant examples: "The deceased was not dishonest." "I deny I owe you $10.00." In the first sentence, the writer is not saying that the deceased was honest. In the second sentence, the writer is not claiming that nothing is owed: it could be that an amount of $1.00 or $100.00 is owed.

At times the legal professional wants some imprecision. For example, "My client's actions were not unlawful." "My client is not unwilling to accept the offer."

The negative statement is usually more difficult to understand than the positive statement, especially a statement with a double negative. The negative, however, is appropriate to emphasize a command: "Do not play in the street." "No smoking." According to Maurice Kirk, switching to the negative "permits a more specific identification of the supposed duty and of the consequences that can flow from the breach of it."[5] And sometimes the negative is more accurate: "I am not unhappy." "The defendant did not commit perjury."

Negatives Emphasize Important Points

Sometimes the writer deliberately selects the negative for emphasis. For example, in a brief, the writer might write the following: "The bank's argument is not logical." "The defendant's facts are not stated accurately." In most cases, however, use of the positive rather than the negative is recommended. The rule is to use the positive unless there is a good reason to use the negative.

§ 5.6 Use Correct Tense

There are certain conventions to follow in using the present and past tenses in legal writing.

Briefs and Memoranda

1. Past tense is used to describe the facts of a case, unless the actions are ongoing.

   The accident happened at 4:00 A.M.

   The bank refused to honor the check.

   The defendant was questioned at police headquarters about the robbery.

2. Past tense is used to describe the procedural posture of the case.

   The jury deliberated for four hours.

   The complaint was filed on January 2, 1991.

   The trial court denied the motion to dismiss.

3. In writing about a statute, court rule, regulation, or ordinance still in effect, the present tense is used.

   The town ordinance prohibits public drinking of alcoholic beverages.

   The mail fraud statute contains criminal penalties.

4. In writing about a court decision, the past tense is used.

In *Smith v. Lewis,* the court analyzed the issue of legal malpractice and held that . . .

Judge Douglas sentenced Pamela Smart to life imprisonment.

Transaction Documents

A transaction document should be written in the present tense. Although the parties may not consult the document until a future time, the provisions should speak as of the time they are read. In other words, the present tense is used in a contract or lease because the writer assumes that it is being read when it applies, not when it is written. It is simpler to say "if the tenant fails to pay" than "if the tenant shall fail to pay." An exception to the use of present tense in transaction documents occurs, however, if the event is a past event when the problem arises—for example, when a condition or a duty to act is imposed. Thus, a lease might read "if the damage was *caused* by a third party, then the landlord shall make any repairs."

§ 5.7 Think Singular (Even When Using Plural)

Transaction documents in particular should be drafted in the singular rather than the plural. When the plural is used, the writer tends to overlook problems that might arise in particular situations. By rethinking the problem in the singular, the writer often spots problems that might not be apparent if the plural were used:

So far as substantive meaning permits, it is desirable to use the singular rather than the plural. This will avoid the question whether the predicate applies separately to each member of the subject class or jointly to the subject class taken as a whole.[6]

Consider this example: "The plaintiff must give the parties a notice of the filing of a motion." Does each party get a notice, or is one notice sufficient? Consider another example: "My beneficiaries will be paid a monthly allowance of $1,000." Does each beneficiary get $1,000 a month, or do the beneficiaries divide the $1,000? The writer should think in the singular even if the plural is used.

§ 5.8 Use Third Person Except for Correspondence

In a pleading, motion, transaction document, or memorandum, the first person should not be used. The writer should avoid saying "I think," "I submit," "I suggest," "we think," "we submit," or "we suggest." Instead of the first person, the third person should be used: "the Smiths contend that . . ." or "the Bank submits . . ." In most instances, the legal professional is writing for the client and should not refer to himself or herself even in the third person (*e.g.*, "this writer feels . . .") In most cases, the inappropriate reference can simply be deleted:

Before   My opinion is that the bank would have no claim.

After   Thus the bank has no claim.

Transaction Documents

Some readability experts advocate using "I" and "you" in transaction documents, which is a considerable improvement over the awkward designations "party of the first part" and "party of the second part." The objection to using personal pronouns in transaction documents, however, is that one never thinks of oneself as the "you." A better practice is to use the parties' last names ("Smith agrees to deliver 500 completed units to Jones") or some other abbreviated terms ("Southern Bank," "Acme Store").

Correspondence

In correspondence, the first person is often used because there is less formality and less reason to write the writer out of the discussion. Use of the first person is appropriate in most correspondence. The client would consider strange a legal professional who wrote "The writer needs these documents by Friday" rather than "I need these documents by Friday." First person can be used in informal memorandum as well.

§ 5.9 Use Nonsexist Language

Language reflects trends of society. Years ago, few women were involved in business. Many terms, therefore, evolved with a male bias:

chairman, draftsman, draftsmanship, businessman, salesman, foreman, mankind, manpower. The same vestige is seen in letters addressed "Dear Sir" or in references to *he* or *him* when meaning either sex.

Today women assume equal responsibility for supporting themselves and their families. Sex-biased words offend the concept of equality. If the writer is sensitive to the audience, he or she will change sexist words to neutral terms: draftsman to drafter, chairman to chairperson, foreman to supervisor, and so on.

Avoid Standard "Gender Definition" Paragraphs

In the past, contracts and leases commonly used the words *he* and *his*. At the end of those documents, a standard clause said that reference to a male included a female where appropriate. This clause would be offensive today.

Replace Gender Pronouns

In most cases, a sentence can be rewritten without using gender pronouns. One method is to replace the pronoun with a noun.

Before   A default occurs when he does not pay the rent.

After   A default occurs when the party does not pay the rent.

or

A default occurs when the rent is not paid.

or

The nonpayment of rent constitutes a default.

Another method is to replace a possessive pronoun with an article.

Before   The defendant must file his answer on time.

After   The defendant must file an answer on time.

Personal pronouns should be completely removed from the sentence to avoid gender problems. *She or he* and *his or her* should be used only when all other possibilities have been exhausted. The writer should never use *she/he* or *his/her*. Avoiding sexist language is simply an off-shoot of the general rule that the writer must respect the audience.

§ 5.10 Avoid Intrusive Words

The basic sentence consists of subject-verb-object. As the writer builds on this structure, the object can be removed or words can be put between the basic elements. Language experts study the most opportune placement of words in the sentence. Here are a few basic ideas on the most effective placement of words.

Keep the Subject and Verb Together

When words are inserted between the subject and the verb, the actor-action thought tends to be interrupted. The reader is distracted. This problem occurs whether the subject-verb is a simple sentence or the main clause of a complex sentence. Consider this example: "The argument *that the guest act does not apply because the guest had painted the drivers' home prior to the accident* is certainly consistent with the applicable case law." This sentence is classic sprawl. The cure is simply to remove the intruding clause: "The guest act does not apply because the guest painted the driver's house prior to the accident. This conclusion is consistent with the applicable case law."

The subject and verb should be kept together.

Keep Objects with Their Verbs and Prepositions

A writer should not separate a verb or a preposition from its object by placing words between them. The result is the same as when the writer separates the subject from the verb.

§ 5.11 Put Modifiers in Their Place

The general rule is that a modifier should be placed immediately next to the word it modifies. For instance, most adjectives appear immediately before the words they modify. In legal writing, however, some adjectives follow the object of a verb that gives an opinion (*e.g., consider, think, find*). An example: "I consider the evidence irrelevant and immaterial." Here the adjective phrase *irrelevant and immaterial* follows the object, *evidence*. (An adjective phrase usually appears immediately after the word it modifies.)

Split Infinitives Only to Prevent Ambiguity

The most common problem with adverbs involves the infinitive verb (*to belong, to be, to find*). An old rule cautions against splitting an infinitive by placing an adverb after the word *to*. The rule does not apply to a past participle—the *ed* form of a verb ("to have been poorly represented").

Most legal experts advocate splitting an infinitive if the split prevents ambiguity. Consider this example: "To understand the result in that case, you have to carefully weigh decided opinions versus public policy." The adverb *carefully* is best placed between the words *to* and *weigh* rather than after *weigh*. If *carefully* were placed after *weigh*, it could modify *decided*.

The fundamental rule is to place modifiers where there can be no mistake about reference. This rule is usually satisfied by placing the modifier next to the word it modifies.

Use Familiar Words

Legal professionals deal with abstract subjects, principles, and analysis. Because they use abstract ideas, they tend to select abstract words. When concrete or familiar words are used, however, the writing is much clearer. Why use a pretentious word when a simple word will suffice? Table 5–1 is a guide for replacing some commonly used legal terms with simpler words.

§ 5.12 Omit Needless Words

Most writers can immediately improve their writing by heeding Strunk and White's famous admonition: "Omit needless words." Sadly, most legal professionals add words rather than delete them. Rare indeed is the legal writer who errs by using too few words. This text has already covered how to delete noun and verb strings, superfluous nouns and verbs, redundant pairs, and overspecificity. Following are some examples of unnecessary words.

Intensifiers

The writer should avoid using the so-called intensifiers—*very, extremely, intensely, overly*—in legal documents. These words add nothing to a sentence and are characteristic of writers who are trying to bolster a weak point.

TABLE 5–1 A GUIDE FOR REPLACING LEGAL JARGON
WITH SIMPLER WORDS

Do not use this	if this will work as well	Do not use this	if this will work as well
accord	give	on the part of	by
adequate amount	enough	originate	start
afford	give	per annum	a year
allocate	give, divide	prior to	before
applicable	that applies	procure	get
as to	about, relating to	promulgate	issue
attain	reach	provided that	however, if
attributable to	from, by	pursuant to	under
by reason of	because of	retain	keep
cease	stop	render	make, give
commence	begin	shall	must, may, will
conceal	hide	solely	only, alone
effectuate	carry out	sufficient	enough
exclusively	only	submit	send, give, contend
expiration	end	subsequent to	after
for the duration of	during	said, same, such	the, this, that
for the purpose of	to, for	terminate	end, finish
for the reason of	because	unto	to
furnish	give, provide	utilize	use
has the option	may	without the United	outside the United
indicate	show	States	States
in excess of	more than	adequate number of	enough
initiate	begin	afforded	given
in lieu of	instead of	approximately	about
accorded	given	at the time	when
admit of	allow	by means of	by
all of the	all the	category	kind, class, group
attains the age of	becomes . . . years old	cease	stop
		commence	begin, start
attempt (as verb)	try	complete (as verb)	finish
calculate	compute	contiguous to	next to
cause it to be done	have it done	corporation organized	Indiana corporation
institute	begin	and existing under	
in the event that	if	the laws of Indiana	
maintain	keep, continue support	deem	consider
		does not operate to	does not
necessitate	require	during such times as	while
on or before	by	effectuate	carry out

TABLE 5–1 *(continued)*

Do not use this	*if this will work as well*	*Do not use this*	*if this will work as well*
enter into a contract with	contract with	inquire	ask
excessive number of	too many	interrogate	question
expend	spend	in the interest of	for
feasible	possible	is authorized	may
for the purpose of holding (or other gerund)	to hold (or comparable infinitive)	is empowered	may
		is unable to	cannot
		it is directed	shall
forthwith	immediately	it shall be lawful	may
hereafter	after this . . . takes effect	manner	way
		minimum	least, smallest
incases which	when, where	necessitate	require
indicate	show	occasion (as a verb)	cause
in order to	to	no later than June 30, 1992	before July 1, 1992
in sections 2023 to 2039, inclusive	in sections 2023–2039	on his own application	at his request
		on the part of	by
is able to	can	paragraph (3) of subsection (a) of section 2000(e)	section 2000(e)(a)(3)
is binding upon	binds		
is entitled (in the sense of "has the name")	is called		
		party of the first part	(the party's name)
it is the duty	shall	per annum, per day, per foot	a year, a day, a foot
law passed	law enacted	per centum	percent
maximum	most, largest, greatest	period of time	period, time
		portion	part
modify	change	proceed	go, go ahead
obtain	get	prosecute its business	carry on its business
consequence	result	purchase	buy
donate	give	require	need
during the course of	during	retain	keep
endeavor	try	specified	named
evince	show	summon	send for, call
expedite	hasten, speed up	to the effect of	that
expiration	end	until such time as	until
frequently	often	of a technical nature	technical
in case	if	on and after April 13, 1992	after April 13, 1992
inform	tell	on or before April 13, 1992	before April 13, 1992
in lieu of	instead of, in place of	or, in the alternative,	or
		possess	have

TABLE 5–1 *(continued)*

Do not use this	if this will work as well	Do not use this	if this will work as well
preserve	keep	remainder	rest
prior	earlier	state of Indiana	Indiana
prior to	before	the manner in which	how
procure	obtain, get	under the provisions of	under
provision of law	law		

Legal professionals do use elastic words (*e.g., reasonable, duly, necessary*) to solve difficult questions, but elastic terms should not be used unless there is a reason to do so.

The Unnecessary Windup

A common mistake made by those who write briefs and memoranda is beginning sentences with an unnecessary wind up. Consider these two examples: "*We will set out to show that* a host in an automobile is not liable unless the host acted willfully and wantonly." "*It is submitted that* the law is against the plaintiff in this case." The italicized words can almost always be eliminated. This habit probably stems from poor writing instruction or insecurity. In either case, the unnecessary windup should be avoided. If it is avoided, the writing will be more confident.

Other common windups include the following: "It is important to note that . . .," "We intend to discuss . . .," and "We would like to stress that . . ."

Words Between *the* and *of*

Many nouns that appear between *the* and *of* can be eliminated (along with the *of* that goes with them). These words add no meaning to the sentence.

- the amount of

- the area of

- the case of

- the concept of

- the extent of

- the number of

- the purpose of

- the sum of

The writer should try to delete the entire phrase and begin the sentence from that point. Does it disturb the meaning? The student should make it a habit to determine what words are baggage and delete them. Only then will the student begin to become a *good* writer.

§ 5.13 Include All Necessary Words

Converse to the rule to omit needless words is the rule to include all necessary words. Two examples make this point: *that* and the *whiz deletion*.

That

When the author started his legal career, he sometimes wrote briefs for a talented lawyer. The lawyer would edit the briefs that the author had prepared and strike most of the *thats*. The attorney said they were unnecessary, but the author disagreed, arguing that they aided readability. The author continued to use *that* and forgot this debate until starting to write this text. Another talented lawyer read an early version of the manuscript and struck most of the *thats*. The author did not reinsert them, but the consulting editor, a lawyer and writer, put the *thats* back in. Although there is some debate on this issue, the general consensus of the writing experts is that the word *that* can aid comprehension. *That* may not be an unnecessary word.

The word *that*, however, should be omitted at the beginning of a sentence in a complaint or other document. It is often used in that situation just to make the sentence seem more legal sounding, but it is unnecessary.

The Whiz Deletion

The whiz deletion says that when you have a relative pronoun (*e.g., which, who, that*) and the verb is a form of *be,* both the verb form of *be* and the relative pronoun can be deleted.

Before	The lawyer *who is* assigned the case . . .
After	The lawyer assigned the case . . .

Before	The court *that is to* decide . . .
After	The court deciding . . .
Before	The text *that is* in my locker . . .
After	The text in my locker . . .

The whiz deletion results in shorter sentences, but language experts claim the sentences may be harder to read after the deletions.

The point is, the writer must be satisfied that each word in a sentence is performing some function. If it is, the word should be kept. If it is not, the word should be deleted. Legal professionals tend to use too many words rather than too few.

§ 5.14 Write Naturally

The rule that seems to bother legal professionals most is the rule to write naturally. Many legal professionals believe they must try to impress others. That belief clouds more writing than the breach of any other rule discussed in this book. The idea, not the words, should impress the reader.

Words that mirror the ideas should be selected. Familiar words rather than pretentious words should be used. Concrete words are preferred over abstract words. The objective of writing is to communicate. Anyone who criticizes a writer for writing clearly and concisely knows nothing about writing.

Writing naturally does not mean writing informally or colloquially. It means saying what the writer means so that the reader understands it. The rule to write naturally applies to all writers—not just legal writers.

Writing Exercises

1. Rewrite the following sentences using active voice.

    a. The cash was stolen by the defendant.

    b. The defendant was questioned by the court.

    c. An analysis of the law by this court indicates that the defendant should prevail.

2. Rewrite these sentences using active verbs or eliminating superfluous verbs.

    a. I will make an investigation of the case.

    b. We will cause an audit to be performed on the books.

3. Rewrite this sentence, deleting the superfluous noun.

    The idea of fair play is of paramount importance in that sport.

4. Discuss the writing flaw(s) in these sentences.

    a. It is submitted that the defendant is not guilty.

    b. The consideration given to this project by our firm was quite substantial.

    c. I deny that I took all of the tools.

    d. The process of law is taught by the Socratic method.

    e. We will make a decision about that issue in two weeks.

    f. This answer was prepared by me.

    g. An employee must report his hours on his time card.

    h. A legal professional must study legal writing if she wants to be successful.

5. Discuss any problems from these excerpts from a brief.

    a. We submit that the case of *Barber v. Smith* should be overruled.

    b. Our client believes that the case of *Barber v. Smith* should be reversed.

    c. We would argue that *Barber v. Smith* should be reversed.

6. Discuss any problems in these sentences.

    a. If a dog owner has more than one pet, then a fee of $50.00 shall be paid for licenses.

    b. I deny that I went to the mall and the movie.

    c. A truck may not be parked on the grass.

7. Discuss any tense problems in these excerpts from a trial brief.

    Section 50 of the New Angeles Ordinances provided that a dog must be kept on a leash. This ordinance has not been amended.

8. Discuss any tense problems in this provision from a lease.

    The landlord shall have insured the premises against fire and other casualty.

9. Discuss the problems of using the plural in this sentence.

    The plaintiff must file claims against the defendants within the statute of limitations.

Enrichment Activities

Complete the following activities.

1. Discuss these statements from the standpoint of style concerns.

    a. It is acceptable to use legalese in a letter threatening litigation because the legalese would be "intimidating."

    b. We need not change references to gender in designations such as "Dear Sir" where there is no real alternative.

    c. It is acceptable to use first person in a legal memorandum prepared for internal use by your law firm.

2. The brief submitted by the appellee in *Griswold* was written in the 1960s. What styles changes should be made?

3. A common question asked by legal professionals is: What if my attorney commits some of the style errors I have been taught to avoid? What should I do? Discuss this issue.

Notes

[1] William Strunk Jr. and E. B. White, *The Elements of Style* (New York: MacMillan, 3d ed., 1972).

[2] Claire Kehrwald Cook, *The MLA's Line by Line: How to Edit Your Own Writing,* 3 (Boston: Houghton Mifflin).

[3] Lester S. King, *Why Not Say It Clearly* 34 (Boston: Houghton Mifflin, 1985).

[4] *Id.* at 34.

[5] Maurice Kirk, *Legal Drafting: Some Elements of Technique,* 4 Texas Tech. L. Rev. 297, 307–308 (1973).

[6] F. Reed Dickerson, *Materials on Legal Drafting* 183 (St. Paul: West Publishing, 1981).

CHAPTER 6

EDITING

There are two cures for the long sentence: 1. say less; 2. put a period in the middle. Neither expedient has taken hold in the law.

David Mellikoff,
The Language of the Law 366 (1963)

Perhaps the most difficult step in the drafting process is editing—especially editing one's own work. The tendency in writing is to quit too soon or to read over the same mistake. Editing skills are different from writing skills. The best editors are not necessarily the best writers. In fact, in most professional writing, a separate specialist performs the editing function. Although some larger law firms have editing specialists, most legal professionals do not have the luxury of any editing specialists. In any case, every writer has some responsibility for editing his or her own writing.

Editing is an important stage of the writing process. Unfortunately, some legal professionals skip this stage altogether or give it only cursory attention. It is wise to remember that a legal professional is paid substantial fees for legal writing, and a client may long remember a misspelling or a grammatical mistake.

§ 6.1 The Difference Between Macro and Micro Editing

Legal writers commit a wide gamut of mistakes ranging from simple misspellings to critical errors of logic. The editor must catch all the mistakes. A legal editor must check the broad picture, a process that involves looking at the flow of an argument, for example, or considering whether a transaction will work. This is termed **macro editing.** A legal editor also must examine the myriad details of a legal document: spelling,

TERMS

macro editing† Checking the broad content of a drafted document for order, sense, and coherence; *e.g.,* examining the flow of an argument or considering whether a transaction will work.

grammar, punctuation, citations, word usage, capitalization, tabulation, and so on. This process is termed **micro editing**.

§ 6.2 Macro Editing

Legal professionals must review legal documents to determine whether the main ideas have been expressed as clearly as possible.

The most difficult editing is the editing of one's own writing. If at all possible, the first step in the macro editing process should be to put the writing away for several days. What the writer was so proud of on Friday may seem like a sorry excuse on Monday. Time dampens infatuation with the writing. Time also helps the writer see errors that might have been overlooked earlier.

Before a legal professional submits any legal document for an attorney's review, a number of questions must be addressed.

Is the Tone Appropriate?

Tone is the expression of attitude through writing. Almost everyone has heard a parent or other authority figure bark: "Don't use that tone of voice with me!" In writing, the word *tone* has the same connotation.

A letter can be too formal or too informal. A brief can be written with too much sarcasm. A memorandum can be written with too much levity. If the writer is angry while writing, that anger usually filters through the writing. The same is true for most other emotions.

In some forms of legal writing, such as memoranda or transaction documents, the tone will be deliberately neutral. In other forms of writing, such as briefs, some emotion will be deliberately injected. The basic concern, however, should always be the *appropriateness* of the tone. How will the sarcasm be interpreted by the judge who reads the brief? Does the humor detract from the argument? The writer should remember that what he or she finds clever may seem banal to the reader.

When tone is intentionally inserted, the document should be read and reread from the standpoint of the reader. The writer should not assume

---

TERMS

micro editing† Checking the details of a drafted document: spelling, grammar, punctuation, consistency, citations, word usage, capitalization, and tabulation.

the reader shares his or her bias on the issue being presented. Sometimes it is helpful to assume the reader will be reading the document when in a bad mood, then try to envision how the sarcasm, humor, or anger will be received. All final copy should be read for tone.

Is the Writing Coherent?

In a memorandum or legal opinion, the conclusion should follow from the proof. In a brief, the argument should be coherently developed. In a transaction document, the deal must be workable. At some point in the writing process, the writer must read beyond the words to see if the ideas are coherent.

Coherency in Expository and Argumentative Writing

It is always difficult to spot one's own errors of logic. A legal professional, however, should be acutely sensitive to logic faults. Here are some common examples.

Improper Cause and Effect   Suppose a person had never seen a horse but peeks into a barnyard through a slit in a fence. A horse walks by the slit, and this person sees the horse's head first, then its tail. That person might conclude that the horse's tail was caused by its head. This is an improper conclusion about cause and effect. Now consider a more realistic example. Someone sneezes every time they visit a friend's house. That person might erroneously conclude that he or she is allergic to the friend, whereas perhaps the allergy is only to the friend's cat.

Wrong Proof, Right Conclusion   A conclusion depends on proof. If the assumption is wrong, if the wrong rule or wrong data or facts are used, a seemingly valid conclusion may be false.

Consider this syllogism:

> A tells B, "I give you my ring." As A says this, A puts the ring back into his pocket. Now A will not give B the ring. B sues A.

> A student concludes the following:

> A made a gift to B. The rule is that a completed gift entitles the donee to the right to the ring as against the donor. Thus B should prevail.

The flaw here is the conclusion made in the student's first sentence, "A made a gift to B." A gift is made only when there has been a delivery of the gift to the donee. If there is no delivery, there is no gift. The conclusion is wrong because the premise is wrong. In legal writing, often the error of logic is in the basic assumptions made about the facts of the case or in selecting the wrong rule of law to apply to the case.

Right Proof, Wrong Conclusion   Sometimes the conclusion is not warranted by the proof. Consider the following:

A plus B = 2

$A \neq 1$ or 0

Conclusion: A must equal 2 and B must equal 0.

This conclusion is not necessarily true, however, since A could be a negative number.

Absolute Right and Wrong   Some arguments assume that only one of two claims is correct. Abortion is either right or wrong. The argument is framed in terms of an absolute right or wrong. In fact, the argument may permit a middle judgment. The fault is in framing issues as absolutes when other options are possible.

Insufficient Sampling   Suppose a coin is flipped 1,000 times and it happens to come up heads 600 times and tails 400 times. One might conclude that flipping that coin results in a 60% chance that it will come up heads on the next toss. This is a hasty generalization. Here the problem is that the sample is not sufficient. In law, one who sees several courts rule favorably for a particular class of litigants might conclude that the law favors that class when, in fact, the results might be explained by other conditions.

The Personal Attack   In the personal attack, the writer denigrates the other party without focusing on the real issues. The attack distracts the reader from the real issues. Such an attack is termed an *ad hominem* **attack**. The converse of this approach is when one tries to curry sympathy for a client. Law should be based on principles, not personal feelings.

In expository and argumentative writing, logic is critical to the writing. The writer must be able to spot logic flaws in his or her own writing just as he or she tries to spot them in an opponent's writing. All writing should be edited for logic.

Coherency in Transaction Documents

Coherency is a concern in transaction documents. A transaction document puts a deal together. Every transaction document should be

---

TERMS

ad hominem **attack†**   Personal attack in which a writer denigrates the opposing party without focusing on real issues.

read to see if the deal will work. A transaction document engineers a relationship. The relationship must be workable. The writer needs to see the transaction as a series of events and make sure these events appear in a logical order. For instance, a purchaser usually will not complete a real estate closing before inspecting the house, nor will a seller usually transfer title to real property before the buyer pays for the house or makes acceptable arrangements for the payment. A landlord usually will provide for a security deposit to protect the landlord if the tenant leaves the premises in a damaged condition.

Legal writers must edit transaction documents looking for ways a transaction might be misinterpreted and for any loopholes that the opposing side may spot. In checking for coherency in transaction documents, the editor must ensure that all the concepts are consistent. If there are related documents between the parties, they each must be checked against the others to be sure that all are consistent.

Many copy editors use a style sheet to ensure that style remains consistent throughout an article or text. Such an approach is beneficial in self-editing a transaction document, but instead of checking style, the editor should check first for consistency of words and phrases. If the document is complicated or lengthy, a style sheet can be helpful to make sure the same words, phrases, and clauses are used throughout. If several documents are used, the editor should ensure that the same words and expressions are used consistently in each of the documents.

Is the Writing Complete?

Most legal professionals think a document is complete when all the fine details are added. However, there are other dimensions to deciding whether a writing is complete.

The Background

After spending months researching a legal issue, a writer gains insights into the law that the readers lack. A judge may know nothing about the legal issue being argued. All documents must be read to see whether a thorough background has been provided for the reader. The reader should be led through the steps of the writer's logic. The reader may not follow a logic leap. The writer should not assume that the reader knows everything the writer knows on the subject.

The Oversight

Sometimes, in the hurry to put a document together, a writer leaves out a critical point. For example, in many contracts, there are standard clauses to cover various eventualities. In editing, one must ensure that all critical provisions have been included. A court presumes that omissions are intentional, so the writer who omits an important provision should make sure it was done intentionally.

Does the Document Comply with All Laws?

The most artfully drawn deed will do a client little good if it has not been notarized. The most cogently drawn complaint will not be accepted by the clerk for filing if the complaint is typed on the wrong size paper. A detailed will has no effect if not properly witnessed. A brilliantly crafted brief will not be accepted for filing if presented one day late. The editor must be familiar with all requirements affecting the legal document. A document is complete only if it satisfies all applicable legal requirements.

§ 6.3 Micro Editing

Publishing houses employ copy editors—professionals who edit each individual line of copy for style and substance. Most law firms employ no one who performs this function exclusively. Hence, the writer will often have to fill the copy editor's role. Tackling the detail work is not fun if the writer has already spent too much time drafting the document. There is a point in the drafting process when the writer cannot read the draft "one more time." The suggestions that follow help at that point.

These editing techniques are not necessarily exclusive to legal documents or the drafting process. They apply to most types of writing and should serve as tools for evaluating the writer's own work objectively.

Check Style

It is tough to look at one's own copy to see if the style is clear. Here are several ways in which a writer can diagnose his or her own writing faults.

Circle All Prepositions

The editor should turn to a random page and circle all the prepositions, and then count the circles. If there is more than one preposition for every four words, passive voice has probably been overused. The student should reread the section in Chapter 5 on active voice.

Underline Nominalized Words

On the same page where all the prepositions were circled, all words ending in *-ance*, *-ity*, and *-ant* should be underlined. These are nominalized words, which were discussed in Chapter 5. These nouns should be converted back into their original verb and adjective forms, and the sentence should be rewritten without nominalized words.

Circle All Sentences with the Verb *to be*

With a different color pen, all sentences containing the verb *to be* should be circled. Then each sentence should be rewritten without that verb. The writer should remember that *to be* is an inert verb. The fewer inert verbs the writer uses, the better the writer will write.

Strike All Unnecessary Words

All unnecessary words should be stricken. The editor should look for windups, superfluous nouns and verbs, and unnecessary modifiers. In editing one's own work, deleting words usually proves to be the most difficult task. Most writers find it easier to add than to delete, but deleting is the way to fine-tune the writing.

Count Words in Sentences and Paragraphs

Words in a sentence can be counted to see whether sentences are short enough or paragraphs are too long. Experts disagree on the optimal length of paragraphs. (Some advocate four to six sentences and some like seven. Others specify 75 to 125 words per paragraph.) Although longer sentences may be used in a brief than in correspondence, the writer needs to know the length of the sentences used. Actually counting the words in the sentences will help in determining whether the length is within reason.

Check Spelling

Certain legal words are commonly misspelled. The following is a list of frequently misspelled words:

admissible	When writing about *admissible* evidence, the word ends in *-ible*, not *-able*.
allege	There is no *d* in allege.
breach	You *breach* a contract. (Your *breech* is behind you.)

causal	If something is related to the cause, the word is *causal*—not *casual.*
decedent	A person who is dead is a *decedent.* An offspring is a *descendant.*
defendant	The person sued in a case is a *defendant.* The word ends in *-ant.*
exercise	There is no *z* in *exercise.*
foreseeability	This word consists of the words *foresee* and *ability.*
judgment	Judgment drops the *e* from the word *judge.*
merchantability	This word consists of the words *merchant* and *ability.*
personalty	This word refers to personal property.
plaintiff	A party who files a lawsuit.
realty	This word refers to real property.
rescission	When you put an end to a contract, you *rescind* it.
separation	As in *separation* agreement. The writer must resist the temptation to make the second vowel in *separation* an *e* instead of an *a.*
supersede	There is no *c* in *supersede.*
tenant	A person who leases property from a landlord.
therefore	Unless an *e* is put at the end of *therefore,* the word will mean "for this or that."
waiver	An *i* must be put in *waiver* unless the reference is to a person who waves.

SIDEBAR   Almost all law offices now use word-processing systems. Most word processors have spell-check features. The writer should make sure this feature is used. The vocabulary on the computer may not be complete, but the spell checker will catch many mistakes the writer might have overlooked.

Check Word Usage

The following are some words frequently confused by legal professionals:

advice, advise	*Advice* is a noun meaning an opinion. *Advise* is a verb meaning to give advice.

affect, effect	To *affect* is to influence; to *effect* is to bring about or to cause: "The argument visibly *affected* the jury and it ultimately *effected* a settlement of the case."
	Effect as a noun can mean either influence or result. For instance, "The *effect* of the argument was apparent." "The discussions led to the desired *effect*." The noun *affect* is a psychological term: "The patient had a flat *affect*."
appellant, appellee	The person taking an appeal is an *appellant*. The person who defends the appeal is an *appellee*.
assure, insure, ensure	*Assure* means to make sure, as in "I *assure* you that I am honest." It also means to promise, as in "I *assure* you that the news is true." To *insure* means to guarantee against loss. *Ensure* means to make certain of, as in "I will *ensure* the shipment gets to you."
by law, bylaw	When something is required or permitted under a law, it is *by law*. A *bylaw* is an organizational principle for a corporation or local unit of government.
can, may	*Can* refers to the ability to accomplish something. *May* refers to permission.
compare to, compare with	*Compare to* is used in making an analogy between unlike items. *Compare with* is used in comparing like items.
connote, denote	*Connote* is what a word suggests. *Denote* is what a word means.
counsel, council	*Counsel* means to advise. A *council* is a group of people serving in an administrative, legislative, or advisory capacity.
disinterested, uninterested	If someone is impartial or has no bias or gain, that person is a *disinterested* person. If someone is not interested in a subject, the correct word is *uninterested*.
guilty, liable	*Guilty* refers to a conviction of a crime. *Liable* refers to the responsibility to pay civil damages. The distinction depends on whether the matter is criminal or noncriminal.

imply, infer	To *imply* means to hint. To *infer* means to interpret from something known or assumed.
lessor, lessee	The landlord is the *lessor,* and the tenant is the *lessee.*
libel, liable	*Libel* is written or printed defamation. *Liable* refers to the responsibility to pay civil damages.
mortgagor, mortgagee	The person who gives a mortgage is the *mortgagor.* The person to whom the property is mortgaged is the *mortgagee.* The mortgagee is usually a banking institution.
oral, verbal	*Oral* means spoken, not written, and literally means "from the mouth." *Verbal* means "in words" whether the words are spoken or written. Hence, a contract not in writing is an *oral* contract.
principal, principle	*Principal* is a noun meaning the main thing or the head person, as in the *principal* of a school. *Principle* is a noun meaning a rule.

When any word with a legal connotation is first used, the word should be checked in a legal dictionary. A professional needs to learn the words of the trade.

Check Grammar

It is beyond the scope of this text to review the basic principles of grammar, but after grading thousands of pages of student papers, the author is aware of several areas that deserve particular attention.

Sentence Fragments

A sentence fragment is an incomplete sentence. The most frequent cause of a sentence fragment is the substitution of a participle for the finite verb.

Sentence fragment	The court resolving the issue.
Complete sentence	The court resolved the issue.

Sentence fragments sometimes occur in legal writing when sentences begin with *whereas, because, although, if, where, when,* and *since.* For example, "Because the reasoning of the court led to that result."

The writer should check final copy for sentence fragments.

Run-on Sentences

A run-on sentence is two or more sentences improperly joined together. For example, "This text for legal professionals discusses run-on sentences, editors must control these errors." The remedy for a run-on sentence is to either remove the comma and insert a period or link the sentences together where appropriate with a semicolon.

Dangling Modifiers

When a sentence contains a dependent clause and a main clause, the subject in the main clause has to agree with the implied subject of the dependent clause. For example, "Having worked as a legal professional, I had the experience of preparing my own will." The subject of the dependent clause, "Having worked as a legal professional," is an implied "I," as in "I have worked as a legal professional." Hence, the subject of the dependent clause is the same as the subject in the main clause.

The following sentences are examples of dangling modifiers: "Being free on bond, the victim was shot by the felon." "Hitting the brakes, the car went out of control." In these sentences, the subjects do not agree. In the first sentence, the implied subject of the dependent clause is "the felon," while the subject in the main clause is "the victim." In the second sentence, the implied subject in the dependent clause is "the driver," but in the main clause, the subject is "the car."

Dangling modifiers have clumsy meanings and interfere with comprehension.

Subject-Verb Disagreement

In most sentences, the writer automatically makes the subject and verb agree without much thought. In English, except for the verb *to be*, the third person singular (*he, she*, or *it*) is the only verb that changes form. In other words, we say:

	Singular	*Plural*
First person	I talk	We talk
Second person	You talk	You talk
Third person	She talks	They talk

Only she *talks* (*he talks, it talks*) changes form. The third person changes form by adding an *s* or *es* to the verb. The following sections demonstrate some problem situations.

Compound Subjects   When a sentence contains two or more subjects, it needs a plural verb. Consider the sentence "You and I are both legal professionals." In this example, *You and I* requires a plural *are* as opposed to a singular *is*. Problems usually occur when the subject is not at the beginning of the sentence.

Wrong   Enclosed is the letter and the check I referenced.

Right   Enclosed are the letter and the check I referenced.

If, however, the compound subject refers to the same person or thing, a singular verb is used. For example, "The *sum and substance* of the report was that the corporation was experiencing serious financial problems." *Sum and substance* has a singular meaning, and therefore, it requires a singular verb.

Subject Complements   At times a subject does not take the same number as the complement. For example, "The critical concern of the parents was the speed limit on that road." Here the subject, *concern*, is singular although the complement, *parents*, is plural. The subject, not the complement, determines number.

Alternative Subjects   When subjects are linked by *or* or *nor*, the rules are simple. First, if both subjects are singular ("a dog or pony is in the show"), a singular verb is used. Second, if both subjects are plural ("the dogs or the ponies are in the show"), a plural verb is used. Finally, if one subject is plural and another subject is singular ("neither the legal professional nor the attorneys agree on this subject"), the verb should agree with the nearer subject. In this last situation, however, some experts disagree. Some suggest using separate verbs or rewriting the sentence.

Check Punctuation

Punctuation breaks up material for the reader. Without punctuation, reading is difficult. A period concludes a thought. It tells the reader that one thought is complete and a new thought will begin in the next sentence. A comma tells the reader to pause briefly before completing the thought. Punctuation errors can cause equivocation problems:

> Sometimes such ambiguity is the result of inadequate punctuation, as in an unpunctuated telegram, or as in the sentence, "Woman, without her man would be a savage." Do you add a second comma after "her," as the ladies are inclined to do or after "man," as the gentlemen prefer?[1]

The following are some punctuation rules that writers should heed.

Restrictive and Nonrestrictive Elements

A restrictive modifier limits the meaning of the word or words it modifies. Restrictive modifiers are not set off with commas or other punctuation marks. A nonrestrictive modifier provides additional information about the word or words it modifies. Commas are used to set off nonrestrictive elements.

Restrictive   The federal statute that deals with mail theft can be applied when mail is taken from an apartment floor.

Nonrestrictive The mail theft statute, which has been discussed in Chapter 2 of this text, applies to situations where a credit card has been taken from an apartment floor after it has been dropped through a mail slot.

The test here is whether deleting the modifier changes the meaning of the sentence. If it does not change the meaning, commas should be used.

Parentheses, Dashes, Colons, and Semicolons

Inexperienced writers tend to use only periods and commas. A writer should not be afraid to use parentheses, dashes, colons, and semicolons for special effects.

In math, parentheses are used for precision. Consider the following:

$$a \times b + c$$

At this point, the reader does not know whether to add b and c or multiply a by b. Parentheses solve the problem:

$$(a \times b) + c$$

or

$$a \times (b + c)$$

Occasionally parentheses are used in the same way in legal writing:

> . . . in the phrase "active duty (other than for training) performed before July 1, 1964," it is clear that the phrase "before July 1, 1964," refers to "active duty (other than for training)" and not "training."[2]

A dash can be used for emphasis, as in the following sentence: "The defendant's position is contrary to the decision of *Smith v. Jones*—not to mention that it is contrary to logic and common sense."

A colon can be used to signal that a list or explanation follows. For example, "Hence the defendant's position is simple: first, the statute is unconstitutional; second, the statute does not apply to this situation; and third, the defendant did not commit the offense charged."

A semicolon binds together two sentences that contain linking ideas: "My legal professional and I make a good team; working together, we have won all our cases."

The writer should use a variety of punctuation marks.

Check Pronoun Reference

An interesting problem of pronoun reference occurred in a missile treaty:

> "Both sides would agree to confine itself [*sic*] to research, development and testing which is permitted by the ABM treaty for a period of five years . . ." went the language of the first proposal on this subject submitted to the Russians, according to the text provided later by the State Department.
>
> Wrong. *Itself* does not agree with *both sides*. To fix it, the framers could have tried "both sides would agree to confine *themselves*," which is correct, but the plural construction ill fits a singular "side." Another way, "Each side would agree to confine itself," matches up the pronoun with the antecedent, but makes it appear that the side is agreeing with itself.
>
> I would like to think that we created this grammatical bind to confuse the Russians, but it is more likely that it was the result of last-minute drafting by negotiators under great stress.[3]

This problem could have been solved by drafting in the singular. In editing, the writer should pay attention to pronoun reference. Personal and relative pronouns require special consideration.

Personal Pronouns

Subjective case pronouns are *I, he, she,* and *they*. Objective case pronouns are *me, him, her,* and *them*. The subjective case is used when the pronoun is the subject of a sentence or clause. For example, "The legal professional and I will be going to the seminar." The objective case is used when the pronoun is the object of a sentence or clause or the object of a preposition. For instance, "My professor will take my roommate and me to the seminar."

The correct choice between the objective and the subjective personal pronoun can be made by mentally reciting the pronoun and verb together.

Relative Pronouns

Many legal professionals have difficulty with deciding whether to use *who* or *whom*. The rules are simple: If the relative pronoun is the subject of a sentence or clause, *who* is used. If the relative pronoun is the object of a sentence or clause or the object of a prepositional phrase, *whom* is used. A good test is to substitute a personal pronoun for the *who* or *whom*. If the substitution requires a subjective case pronoun, *who* should be used. If the substitution requires an objective case pronoun, *whom* should be used. For example:

The boy (who/whom) is sitting on the porch is very quiet.

The boy (who/whom) the parent reprimanded was subdued.

Using the substitution rule, the first sentence can be changed to read: "The boy (he) is sitting on the porch. . . ." The second sentence can be changed to read: "The boy (the parent reprimanded him) was subdued." Therefore, the first sentence requires the word *who*, while the second sentence requires the word *whom*.

Another decision is whether to use *that, which,* or *who (whom). That* is used in a restrictive clause when the preceding noun is nonhuman. For example, "The stolen truck that struck the plaintiff's vehicle was unregistered." *Which*, preceded by a comma, is used in a nonrestrictive clause when the reference is nonhuman. For example, "The plaintiff's vehicle, which was totaled, was hauled to a junkyard." *Who* is used in both a restrictive and a nonrestrictive clause when the preceding noun is human: "The youth who drove the stolen truck fled the scene." "The plaintiff, who is still hospitalized, was unable to appear in court."

Check Capitalization

In legal documents, there are some unique practices regarding capitalization. The following are some rules.

Capitalize Titles and Headings of Court Documents

Titles of court documents are usually capitalized, as are headings and subheadings within them. Often headings appear in all capitals. The student should examine the way in which headings are capitalized in the briefs filed by the appellants and appellee in *Griswold v. Connecticut*, which is in the appendix.

Capitalize Introductory Words and Phrases in Legal Documents

As a matter of practice, some beginning words of legal documents appear in all capital letters. For example:

IT IS HEREBY ORDERED. . .

RESOLVED, THAT. . .

FOR VALUE RECEIVED. . .

IN WITNESS WHEREOF. . .

These words are capitalized more for show than for substance. Nonetheless, some firms follow this practice.

Capitalize Trade Names

When a trade name (Kleenex, Kodak, Vaseline) is used, a capital letter should be used. If the word is a generic term, lowercase is appropriate.

Capitalize Names of Corporate and Governmental Entities

Official government names are capitalized.

Equal Employment Opportunity Commission (EEOC)

Social Security Administration (SSA)

Environmental Protection Agency (EPA)

Names of companies also are capitalized. However, words such as *federal, government,* and *company* are not capitalized unless they are part of a title or name.

Do Not Capitalize Words to Make Them More Important

Although some firms do capitalize words to highlight them, the general rule is that words should not be capitalized merely to make them more important or to show respect. Legal professionals tend to capitalize the word *court* in pleadings or briefs when referring to the court in which the pleading or brief is filed. Even in that situation, however, *court* should not be capitalized. An exception to this rule is in situations where the writer refers to the United States Supreme Court. Then any reference to the Court should be capitalized.

Check Enumeration

It has become customary in legal drafting to use enumeration as a means to express coordinate ideas. One writer explains:

> A drafter will find it convenient to be systematic in the use of numbers and letters for sub-clauses and paragraphs: (1), (2), (3), etc., for sub-clauses each ranking equally in arrangement, without introductory words; (a), (b), (c), etc., for the paragraphs in a sub-clause, or in a clause with introductory words; (i), (ii), (iii), etc., for sub-paragraphs in a paragraph; small Roman capitals, (I), (II), (III), etc., or capitals (A), (B), (C), etc. for further subdivision. The same pattern of numbering or lettering should be used throughout the document.[4]

Related paragraphs can also be grouped by a numbering system such as 1.1, 1.2, 1.3; 2.1, 2.2, 2.3; and so on. Careful enumeration eliminates equivocation problems and serves as a useful drafting tool. Here are some enumeration rules:

(1) All items in the tabulated enumeration must belong to the same class. (The enumeration must have a common theme or thread.)

(2) Each item in the tabulated enumeration must be responsive, in substance and in form, to the introductory language of the enumeration (the material immediately before the colon).

(3) If the sentence of which a tabulated enumeration is a part continues beyond the end of the enumeration, the part of the sentence that follows it must be appropriate to each item.

(4) All of each item in the enumeration must be indented.

(5) Material immediately preceding or following the enumeration must not be indented, unless it marks the beginning of a paragraph.

(6) If the tabulated material takes the form of a sentence in which the enumeration is an integral part, each item should begin with a small letter and end with a semicolon, except that (1) the penultimate item should end with a semicolon followed by an "and" or an "or" and (2) if the last item ends the sentence, it should end with a period.

(7) If the tabulated material takes the form of a simple list following a sentence that is otherwise complete, each item should begin with a capital letter and end with a period. No "and" or "or" follows the penultimate item.[5]

When enumeration is used, parallelism should always be maintained. The enumeration system must not be varied. Overuse of enumeration can inhibit readability, so the writer should limit enumeration to places where it enhances understanding.

Tabulating simply means setting materials in an indented format such as columns or rows. A list is made in a tabular format. Here are some rules for tabulating items:

- Indent the tabulated items.

- Use parallel structure for each item.

- Use numbers, letters, or bullets for each item.

- Use a comma or semicolon after each item except the last one.

- Put an *and* or *or* after the next-to-last item.

Tabulating provides visual variety for the reader and often makes material more readable.

Check Dates, Ages, and Weights

Some dates leave the reader wondering whether the date being referred to is included:

- This act is effective until April 13. (Is it effective *on* April 13?)
- The act is effective from April 13 to December 30. (Is it effective *on* April 13? *On* December 30?)
- This option to purchase must be exercised by April 13, 1992. (Can it be exercised *on* April 13, 1992?)

This problem can be avoided if the writer is specific:

- This act is effective beginning on April 13 and ending on December 30.
- This option to purchase must be exercised on or before April 13, 1992.

The same problem arises in some sentences when age ranges are given: "A trust shall be imposed for any beneficiary between the ages of 21 and 30." (Does it include a 21-year-old person and a 30-year-old person?) Again, the problem is avoided if the writer is specific: "A trust shall be imposed for any beneficiary 21 years of age or older and under 31 years of age."

When weights are being given, the appropriate units of weight must be designated. The writer also must determine whether there is any ambiguity about the inclusion or exclusion of a certain weight.

Check Definitions

Most drafting books reserve a separate chapter for the use of definitions. Definitions, however, are too often abused as a drafting device. The rules relating to when and how to use definitions are not particularly complicated.

Use Definitions for Shorthand References

The simplest use of definitions in a legal document is the abbreviated word or phrase indicating what the topic or subject will subsequently be called. The word or phrase is placed parenthetically after the referent: "The Northern Sand & Gravel Company, Inc. (Northern Sand)." This method is commonly used to refer to parties or real property after the legal description has been given.

Use Definitions Consistently

A frequent problem with definitions arises when the drafter substitutes another word for the defined term. A drafter may give a legal description and refer to the property as the "leased premises." Later the drafter may refer to "the premises" or "the property." Adherence to the consistency doctrine obviates this problem.

Omit Unnecessary Definitions

Students sometimes define a word that is used only once in a document. This definition can almost always be worked into the sentence where the word appears.

A definition should be used only if the definition assists understanding and only if the word or phrase is used in a common or natural sense. As Abraham Lincoln said, "If you call a tail a leg, how many legs has a dog? Five? No; calling a tail a leg won't make it a leg." In other words, when deciding to use a definition, the writer should make sure the definition fits the idea. For example, it would be inappropriate to say, "The term *fixture* as used in this contract includes the land and all personal property owned by seller," since a fixture is neither real estate nor personal property. Such a definition would be unnatural.

Check Citations

The Bluebook: A Uniform System of Citation covers most of what the writer needs to know about citations. It is published and distributed by the Harvard Law Review Association, Cambridge, Massachusetts. The legal professional needs to learn the proper format in which to cite law. Each citation should be checked with the original to make sure that the reference is accurate. As a citation is copied and typed and retyped, many mistakes may be made.

References to Specific Points

Legal authority is cited in the body of briefs and memoranda rather than in footnotes. In editing legal writing, the editor must make sure that if the writer refers to a specific point, a specific page reference is given for that point. When a quotation is used from a particular source, the exact page for the quotation must be given. This rule aids the reader. In looking at the final copy, the editor should check the accuracy of the information, making sure that pages have been accurately cited and that any quotations are on the pages cited. A misspelling of a case name can raise questions about the accuracy of the writer's ideas. A typographical error in the numbers can send a judge on a wild goose chase through the law library—a chase the writer would prefer did not take place.

Repeating Citations

If a case, such as the case of *Griswold v. Connecticut,* 381 U.S. 479 (1965), has been referenced once in a writing, the next time it is referenced in the same writing, a shortened version can be used:

> *Griswold,* 381 U.S. at 485.

or

> *Griswold v. Connecticut,* 381 U.S. at 485.

If *Griswold* is the immediately preceding citation, the abbreviation *Id.* may be used. For example, if the next citation is page 487 of the *Griswold* decision, the citation is *Id.* at 487.

Once a citation has been given for a particular point, it need not be repeated for the same point.

Check Quotations

Legal professionals frequently use quotations from cases or statutes. On the final copy, quotations should be proofread like the rest of the text. Like citations, quotations fall prey to typographical errors.

The following are rules to follow in editing quotations.

Use Quotations Sparingly

When legal professionals are told to use quotations sparingly, they tend to use none at all. Instead, they should try to strike a reasonable balance. Too many quotations cause the reader to lose interest in the text material, but too few quotations in legal writing raise doubt about the authenticity of the analysis.

The guiding rule is to use quotations to state a precise rule (*e.g.,* language from a case or statute), to state a precise point, or to state something more succinctly or eloquently than the writer could say. This does *not* mean a writer can use a quote when he or she fails to understand the material. In that situation, the writer needs to take extra time to understand the subject matter about which he or she is writing.

Use Short Quotations

Just as too many quotations cause a reader to lose interest, so do quotations that are too long. Quotations need to be edited for the main point or points. They also can be paraphrased or summarized. Key words can be taken from a quotation, and the remainder can be deleted.

Fit Quotations to the Text

The sentence preceding the quotation should lead directly into the quotation. The sentence following the quotation should pick up the idea of the quotation. Quotations must be integrated into the textual materials.

§ 6.4 Some Final Editing Tips

Often there is little time to edit copy because of deadline pressures. The easiest solution is to anticipate deadlines by beginning to write as early as possible. The more time the writer has, the better job he or she can do when editing copy.

Edit and Reedit

The longer the writer works on a project, the harder it is to edit the final copy. To change the routine, the writer might try to read the document aloud. The best approach is to put it away and read it another day if possible.

Shorten the Document

The author once prepared a brief for the Seventh Circuit, which had a fifty-page limit for printed briefs. He called the printer to see how many typewritten pages constituted fifty printed pages to make sure he observed the limit. Unfortunately, the printer was wrong and the brief ran twenty pages too long—a brief that the author thought was letter perfect. Yet, with only hours until deadline, he sliced twenty pages from that brief. Most of the verbiage and surplusage was eliminated. What could not be changed earlier proved reducible by twenty pages without harm to content. That experience forced the author to approach the editing process more earnestly. Most documents can be shortened and in the process made more readable by simply excising the surplusage.

Proofreading Symbols

Figure 6–1 is a list of common proofreading symbols. Support staff should be taught to read these proofreading symbols so the legal professional can use them to edit text materials efficiently with minimal directions.

§ 6.5 Conclusion: The Importance of the Redraft

H. G. Wells wrote: "No passion in the world, no love or hate, is equal to the passion to alter someone else's draft." Whenever a substantial writing project is completed, the writer tends to become materialistic toward it, eschewing anything but a cosmetic change to what has been drafted.

Drafters must learn to deal objectively with their work product. The document should always be viewed as if it were someone else's work. From that perspective, it is easier to make changes. If a document is reused, the writer should try to make some improvement on the previous effort. Each improved redraft leads toward a more litigation-proof document.

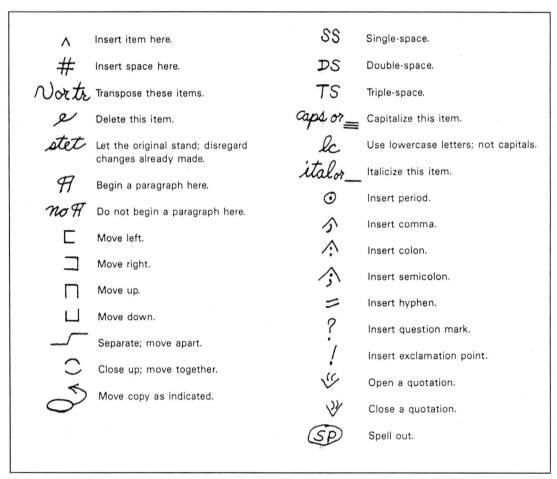

FIGURE 6–1 Common Proofreading Symbols

Writing Exercises

1. Edit these sentences.

   a. The pepsi bottle was held to be admissable into evidence.

   b. Whereas the buyer is desirous of exercizing the option.

   c. The polaroid picture of the document lead to the implication that the defendant was liable for the crime of forgery.

2. Edit and rewrite this sentence using the steps for editing for style discussed in the text.

   The allegations of the complaint filed by plaintiff are that the plaintiff collide with the defendant in an accident on Highway 1.

3. Edit this page from a sample brief, using the principles discussed in the text and the proofreading symbols in Figure 6–1.

   Plaintiff persist's in her mistaken idea that foreseability alone creates duty, in a seperate section in her brief on foreseebility, she says:

   accidents arise out of the ordinary use of an automobile. One would have to be an idiot not to foresee that an automobile could be involved ihn a side impact collision.

   Of course and what was foreseeable to defendant was foreseeble to plaintiffs husband as well.

   It is submitted that a manufacturer's duty is not equated to what he can foresee. A danger must be foreseeble to the manufacturer before he has a duty to take action, but the reverse is not true. Because a manufacturers must forsee against that which would make his product dangerous for the purpose for which it is made.

4. Discuss the grammatical errors in these sentences.

   a. Studying to be a legal professional, legal writing is quite important.

   b. The legal professional who I had as a student.

   c. Legal writing is an art, the legal professional needs to study this subject.

5. Which of the following clauses are restrictive and which are nonrestrictive?

   a. Red, which is my favorite color, is not appropriate in that painting.

   b. My instructor, who is also my supervisor, teaches both English and Law courses.

     c. An instructor who teaches legal writing must know basic grammar.

     d. The dog that tore up my front lawn also attacked my cat.

6. Explain the logic problems in these sentences.

     a. Because nearly all fifty states have guest statutes, only the laws from the more populous states are examined in this memorandum.

     b. Since most of my experience as a legal professional has been in litigation, I am qualified to accept a position with your law firm as a legal professional in your corporate department.

     c. Because I have written so many legal briefs and transaction documents, I have a problem with splitting an infinitive.

Enrichment Activity

Complete the following activity.

1. Take a sample page of a legal document that you have written for this course. Now edit the page, following each of the steps outlined in Chapter 6. Use the proofreading symbols. Then rewrite and submit the page.

Notes

[1] E. Allen Farnsworth, *Some Considerations in the Drafting of Agreements: Problems in Interpretation and Gap-Filling*, 39 Okla. B.A.J. 918 (1968).

[2] F. Reed Dickerson, *The Fundamentals of Legal Drafting* 74–75 (Boston: Little, Brown, 1965).

[3] William Safire, "The Erroneous Eagle and the Cross-Eyed Bear," *New York Times Magazine*, Nov. 2, 1986, p. 10.

[4] E. L. Piesse, *The Elements of Drafting* 35 (Sydney: The Law Book Company, 5th ed., 1976).

[5] F. Reed Dickerson, *The Fundamentals of Legal Drafting* 85–86 (Boston: Little, Brown, 1965).

CHAPTER 7

LITIGATION DOCUMENTS

In law it is good policy never to plead what you need not, lest you oblige yourself to prove what you can not.

— *Abraham Lincoln*

In England, there once were nonlawyer experts called "special pleaders not at the bar." These special pleaders would prepare litigation documents for filing with the courts in both civil and criminal proceedings. They had mastered the highly technical pleading rules required by the common law. Today legal professionals working in a litigation practice also need to develop specialized skills and techniques.

§ 7.1 Background of Pleading Practice

During the first stage of a lawsuit, the parties plead their case. Pleading a case under the current federal rules is rather simple compared to practice under prior rules.

Common Law Pleading

Pleading under the common law was highly formalistic and technical. The purpose of early pleading rules was to frame in detail a single issue for trial. If a party failed to obey the technical requirements of the pleading rules, the action would be dismissed. As a result, many meritorious claims never made it to trial. The plaintiff had to fit his or her claim within a rigid form in order to obtain a writ. If the facts failed to fit the precise pleading category (such as trespass, covenant, debt, replevin), there was no remedy. Likewise, a defendant had to choose between denying the facts, entering a dilatory plea, or denying that the facts alleged a cause of action.

Pleading a case was quite onerous under the common law practice. The plaintiff would file a complaint or declaration, and the defendant would file an answer or plea. The plaintiff then would file a replication, the defendant a rejoinder, the plaintiff a surrejoinder, the defendant a rebuttal, and so on.

Code Pleading

In 1848, New York adopted the Field Code, and other states followed this lead. Code pleading supplanted the highly formalistic common law rules with a method called fact or code pleading. Under code pleading, the plaintiff only had to plead facts that established the cause of action. As with the present rules, a party could plead alternative theories. Although code pleading removed some of the anachronisms of common law pleading, there was still considerable time spent squabbling over the technicalities of the pleading and the legal sufficiency of the facts alleged in the pleading.

Notice Pleading

In the 1950s, the federal courts adopted the Federal Rules of Civil Procedure, and most state courts followed the direction of the federal courts in the 1960s. The philosophy of these new rules was to permit cases to proceed to trial without the strict pleading requirements of code pleading. Thus, the primary purpose of a pleading is no longer to frame issues but to notify another party of a claim, which is why a pleading under the modern rules is called **notice pleading.**

Under the modern rules, most of the technical requirements of the common law have been eliminated. For example, subpart (e) of rule 8 of the Federal Rules of Civil Procedure says simply:

(e) *Pleading to be Concise and Direct, Consistency.*
(1) Each averment of a pleading shall be simple, concise, and direct.
No technical forms of pleading or motions are required.

Hence, the only requirement is that a pleading contain a "short and plain statement of the claim."

Under code pleading, there were complaints, answers, pleas, replications, rejoinders, surrejoinders, and rebuttals. The Federal Rules of Civil Procedure have simplified the types of pleadings allowed. Rule 7 says:

Pleadings. There shall be a complaint and an answer; a reply to a counterclaim denominated as such; an answer to a cross-claim, if the

---

TERMS

notice pleading†   Pleading under the modern rules, which provide that the primary purpose of a pleading is not to frame issues but to notify another party of a claim.

answer contains a cross-claim; a third-party complaint, if a person who was not an original party is summoned under the provisions of Rule 14; and a third-party answer, if a third-party complaint is served. No other pleading shall be allowed, except that the court may order a reply to an answer or a third-party answer.

Under rule 7, a party states the initial claim in a complaint. The defendant's responsive pleading is an answer. A defendant who asserts a claim against a plaintiff files a counterclaim. The plaintiff's response is a reply. A party stating a claim against another party (*e.g.*, coplaintiff against coplaintiff) files a cross-claim. Parties against whom cross-claims are filed state their defenses in an answer.

Practice Under Notice Pleading

An example can be used to illustrate the change in pleading practice under the new rules. In *Conley v. Gibson,* 355 U.S. 41 (1957), a plaintiff filed a simple complaint in the federal district court, claiming race discrimination. This was all the plaintiff said. He was not represented by an attorney. The district court dismissed the complaint, saying the plaintiff had not alleged a sufficient basis for a claim, but the United States Supreme Court heard the case and said this simple complaint had alleged sufficient facts to state a claim.

Most states follow the practice of notice pleading. There is now little formality required for pleadings filed in civil cases, although courts continue to expect professional documents.

The current Federal Rules of Civil Procedure have radically changed the way trials are conducted. Prior to the adoption of these rules, trial lawyers withheld information about their cases until the witnesses were on the witness stand. Under the new rules, parties are given various ways to discover information about the other party's case. This is referred to as the discovery process.[1] Parties may request that the opposing party produce documents. They also may take depositions of witnesses and send interrogatories to the opposing party. All legal professionals should know how to prepare pleadings and motions for filing with a court.

§ 7.2 Distinction Between Pleadings and Motions

The rules of most jurisdictions make a distinction between pleadings and motions. Generally, a pleading asserts a claim against another party or is used to defend against a claim, and a motion asks the court to take some action against one party or in favor of the moving party.

Pleadings

A pleading is a document filed in a lawsuit to assert a claim against another party or to defend against a claim. A party begins a lawsuit by filing a complaint. A complaint is a pleading. The complaint describes the claim of a plaintiff. Rule 3 of the Federal Rules of Civil Procedure says simply:

> *Rule 3. Commencement of Action.*
> A civil action is commenced by filing a complaint with the court.

When a complaint is filed, it stops (or tolls) the statute of limitations. Other pleadings used to make a claim against a party in a civil lawsuit include counterclaims, cross-claims, and third-party claims.

When a complaint is filed, the defendant is required to file an answer. In an answer, the defendant admits or denies every allegation made in the complaint. The defendant also may respond that it is "without information" to answer the allegations.

The defendant may also have a claim against the plaintiff, in which case the defendant files a counterclaim. A counterclaim is a complaint in which the original defendant takes the role of plaintiff and the original plaintiff takes the role of defendant. The plaintiff must answer the counterclaim by filing a reply.

There can be two defendants in a lawsuit. A defendant also may have a claim against another party, in which case that defendant can file a cross-claim. A cross-claim is a complaint. The defendant who is named in a cross-claim has to answer the cross-claim. A third-party complaint is a complaint against a nonparty to an existing lawsuit.

The function of a pleading is to notify the adverse party of the nature of a claim or defense. Pleadings are still used to frame issues in a lawsuit, but this is no longer their main purpose under the modern rules. Issues are formulated more fully through pretrial procedures and the discovery process.

Pleadings are filed in noncivil cases as well. In criminal cases, a charge is made by an indictment or information. If a grand jury is called, an indictment is used. If a charge is filed by a prosecutor, an information is used.

In some states, a petition rather than a complaint is used to initiate proceedings such as divorces or will contests.

SIDEBAR

Motions

A motion is a document filed with a court to ask the court for an order against another party or in favor of the moving party. For instance, motions might be made to request that a court grant a restraining order against another party, dismiss a case, or order a party to answer a question at a deposition.

Parties file motions at every stage of a lawsuit. Courts today generally encourage the use of short, concise documents. The technical requirements of the common law no longer apply to motions. Although some litigation documents still have strict requirements (a criminal indictment is one example), most motions have few rigid form or content imperatives.

§ 7.3 Form of Court Documents

The court rules encourage the drafting of short, plain pleadings and motions. Rule 8(a) of the Federal Rules of Civil Procedure provides:

> **(a) Claims for Relief.** A pleading which sets forth a claim for relief, whether an original claim, counterclaim, cross-claim, or third-party claim, shall contain (1) a short and plain statement of the grounds upon which a court's jurisdiction depends . . . (2) a short and plain statement of the claim showing the pleader is entitled to relief, and (3) a demand for judgment for the relief the pleader seeks . . .

Federal Rules of Civil Procedure 10 states the general form requirements:

> **Rule 10. Form of Pleadings**
> **(a) Caption; Names of Parties.** Every pleading shall contain a caption setting forth the name of the court, the title of the action, the file number, and a designation as in Rule 7(a). In the complaint the title of the action shall include the names of all the parties, but in other pleadings it is sufficient to state the name of the first party on each side with an appropriate indication of other parties.
> **(b) Paragraphs; Separate Statements.** All averments of claim or defense shall be made in numbered paragraphs, the contents of each of which shall be limited as far as practicable to a statement of a single set of circumstances; and a paragraph may be referred to by number in all succeeding pleadings. Each claim founded upon a separate transaction or occurrence and each defense other than denials shall be stated in a separate count or defense whenever a separation facilitates the clear presentation of the matters set forth.

Federal Rules of Civil Procedure 7(b)(2) provides that the form requirements in rule 10 apply to motions as well.

Caption

Most court documents must begin with a caption (Figure 7–1). A caption contains the names of the parties, the court in which the pleading is filed, the docket number assigned to the case by the court, and a heading or title identifying the pleading. The title may simply be "Complaint" or "Answer." Legal secretaries usually know how to format the caption.

Introductory Paragraph

Following the caption, a litigation document might contain an introductory paragraph. The first paragraph of a pleading, for example, might read:

> John Doe, by counsel, Maria Lawyer of Lawyer and Lawyer, for his complaint against the defendant, Mary Roe, alleges and says:

This introductory paragraph usually identifies the parties involved in the pleading or motion and the nature of the document.

Recitation of Basis of Relief Sought

Following the introductory paragraph comes a recitation of the facts supporting the pleading as well as the basis for the pleading. The basis for the pleading is usually a court rule or a statute that gives the party the

---

```
              UNITED STATES DISTRICT COURT
              SOUTHERN DISTRICT OF NEW YORK

JOHN E. HEAD,        )
                     )
          Plaintiff, )
                     )
                     )
     vs.             )     CAUSE No. _____
                     )
DONALD LEGG,         )
                     )
                     )
         Defendant.  )

                          COMPLAINT
```

FIGURE 7–1 Sample Caption for Action Brought in the Southern District of New York

right to ask the court for the relief sought by the pleading. The pleading explains in simple terms the facts and the rule of law that entitle the party to the relief sought. Rule 8 of the Federal Rules of Civil Procedure states that " [E]ach **averment** of a pleading shall be simple, concise, and direct." These paragraphs are usually numbered separately and are sometimes referred to as **rhetorical paragraphs.**

Demand or Prayer

A pleading or motion ends with a **demand** or request for relief. In a pleading, this demand is made against another party. The request may be for more damages, an injunction, or mandamus. Sometimes this demand is referred to as the **prayer** of the complaint. The request for relief in a motion asks the court for a specific order—for example, for an order requiring another party to produce documents, for an order dismissing the case, or for an order to show cause. A pleading or motion is signed by an attorney, whose address and telephone number must appear on the document. A certificate of service follows.

Certificate of Service

Any pleading filed with a court must be mailed to or served on the other parties to the case. The **certificate of service** at the end of the pleading certifies that a copy of the pleading and the certificate have been mailed to or otherwise served on all other parties at the time the pleading is filed. (See Figure 7–2.)

 SIDEBAR   No certificate of service is included in a complaint. Instead, the defendant is issued a summons, which shows that the defendant received the complaint.

$$\text{TERMS}$$

averment   The act of alleging, pleading, asserting, or stating.

rhetorical paragraphs†   Within a pleading, numbered paragraphs reciting the supporting facts and the basis for the pleading.

demand   A claim of legal entitlement or a request to perform an obligation; the assertion of a right to recover a sum of money.

prayer   Portion of a bill in equity or a petition that asks for equitable relief and specifies the relief sought.

certificate of service†   A signed statement at the end of a pleading indicating that the certificate and the pleading have been mailed to or otherwise served on all other parties at the time it is filed.

```
CERTIFICATE OF SERVICE

    The undersigned, attorney for the plaintiff (defendant) herein, certifies that a
copy of the foregoing instrument was served upon the attorneys of record of all
parties to the above cause by enclosing same in an envelope addressed to such
attorneys at their business address as disclosed by the pleadings of record herein,
with postage fully prepaid, and by depositing said envelope in a U.S. Post Office
mailbox this _____ day of _____, 19___.




                                              _____
                                                 Signed by attorney
```

FIGURE 7–2
A Certificate
of Service

§ 7.4 The Importance of Deadlines

Litigation professionals may be responsible for filing and mailing pleadings or motions, so it is essential for them to understand the importance of filing pleadings on time. Most legal work must be completed before a deadline. Inexperienced legal professionals sometimes fail to appreciate the critical nature of deadlines: *A case can be lost if a deadline is missed.* If a complaint is filed beyond a statute of limitations, the lawsuit is barred. If an answer is not filed within the allotted time period, a party can be defaulted. If a party misses a deadline for filing a brief on an appeal, the appeal may be dismissed or decided without the brief.

New legal professionals are likely to be accustomed to an academic environment where deadlines are excused. Courts are less tolerant than a student's least tolerant professor. Litigation documents must be mailed on time. The legal professional should read the court rules to determine how time periods are calculated. The most common mistake made by legal professionals is missing a deadline, and it often happens because time periods are miscalculated. Usually the first day is not counted. Court rules generally specify how to calculate the period when it ends on a weekend or holiday. The legal professional who receives documents that have been served by mail may have additional time under the rules for filing, but not always. Again, if there is any doubt, the writer should consult the rules.

The Federal Rules of Civil Procedure provide for the manner in which the documents are to be filed or served. For example, rule 6(a) makes the following provision:

(a) Computation. In computing any period of time prescribed or allowed by these rules, by the local rules of any district court, by order of court, or by any applicable statute, the day of the act, event, or default from which the designated period of time begins to run shall not be included. The last day of the period so computed shall be included, unless it is a Saturday, a Sunday, or a legal holiday, or, when the act to be done is the filing of a paper in court, a day on which weather or other conditions have made the office of the clerk of the district court inaccessible, in which event the period runs until the end of the next day which is not one of the aforementioned days. When the period of time prescribed or allowed is less than 11 days, intermediate Saturdays, Sundays, and legal holidays shall be excluded in the computation. As used in this rule and in Rule 77(c), "legal holiday" includes New Year's Day, Birthday of Martin Luther King, Jr., Washington's Birthday, Memorial Day, Independence Day, Labor Day, Columbus Day, Veterans Day, Thanksgiving Day, Christmas Day and any other day appointed as a holiday by the President or the Congress of the United States, or by the state in which the district court is held.

§ 7.5 The Tools of the Litigation Professional

Every artisan must learn to use the available tools of the profession. The tools of a litigation professional for preparing court documents are the court rules and legal form books. Both types of tools are critical to the litigation professional.

Court Rules

No legal professional should ever draft any court document without first reading the court rules pertaining to that pleading. If the pleading is to be filed in a federal district court, the Federal Rules of Civil Procedure must be consulted. These rules apply to all actions filed with a federal district court and can be found in the *United States Code* and the annotated codes, as well as in commercial publications.

Each state has trial rules for practice in its courts. These state court rules are usually found in an annotated code. In addition, West Publishing Company and other publishers produce booklets containing these rules. A litigation professional should keep one of these booklets at his or her desk. Court rules are like the rules to a board game. Unless they are consulted, the function of the pleading will not be understood.

The Federal Rules of Civil Procedure set out the rules for filing complaints, answers, motions for discovery, and pretrial, trial, and posttrial motions. District courts, however, also have rules that supplement the federal rules. These rules are referred to as **local rules.** Figure 7–3 is an example of a local rule of the Southern District of Indiana.

Suppose one party asks for the production of documents and the opposing party refuses to produce the documents requested. The requesting party would then need to ask for a court order to force compliance with the request. In some district courts, the judge would not order the production of the documents if the motion did not allege that the attorneys have personally met and tried to resolve the issue. The Federal Rules of Civil Procedure do not require such a meeting, but local rules of some federal courts do. The court might send the parties back for the meeting. Pleading practice runs more smoothly if the rules are followed.

The legal professional should read the applicable rules before beginning to draft and review the rules before filing the document. No legal professional should draft any court pleading before consulting the rules of the court in which the pleading is to be filed. Figure 7–4 is a chart of the federal rules matched with the appropriate courts.

Form Books

In addition to the court rules, the legal professional should consult a good form book before preparing any court document. Court documents do not have to be drafted by the legal professional without help, but neither does an attorney have to be asked for assistance. Help can be found in good forms. Private publishers prepare pleading form books, some of which pertain to particular states or jurisdictions, and some of which cover certain types of cases. For example, Lawyer's Cooperative Publishing Company has published a multivolume set entitled *American Jurisprudence Pleading and Practice Forms, Revised Edition.* The forms contained in this set include litigation documents pertaining to almost any type of case. For an automobile accident claim, for example, there are forms for a complaint, a cross-claim, and the affirmative defenses needed for pleading such cases. Form books contain representative motions for filing. Matthew Bender's *Federal Practice Forms* is a similar set designed for use in the federal district courts. Many publishers have compiled form books for practicing in the various state courts.

There is no reason to draft original pleadings for every case. If a form has already been prepared, that form can be used, but it should be changed to conform to the particular situation. The legal professional is free to improve the form, if possible, and should always tailor the form to the facts of the case.

─────────── **TERMS** ───────────

local rules Rules of court that are applicable in a single judicial district.

FIGURE 7–3
A Local Rule of
the Southern
District of
Indiana

Rule 13

**Attorney's Conference
Concerning Motions and Objections Relating to
Discovery**

To curtail undue delay in the administration of justice, the court shall refuse to rule on any and all motions having to do with discovery under Rules 26 through 37 of the Rules of Civil Procedure unless moving counsel shall first advise the court in such motion that after personal consultation and a good faith effort to resolve differences, they are unable to reach an accord. This statement shall recite, in addition, the date, time, and place of such conference and the names of all parties participating therein. If counsel for any party advises the court in writing that opposing counsel has refused or delayed meeting and discussing the problems covered in this Rule, then the court may take such action as is appropriate to avoid delay.

FIGURE 7–4
Matching the
Federal Rules
with the
Appropriate
Courts

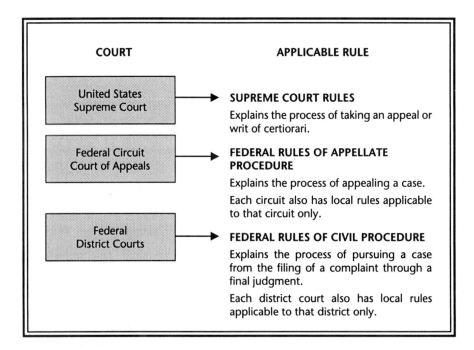

COURT	APPLICABLE RULE
United States Supreme Court	**SUPREME COURT RULES**
	Explains the process of taking an appeal or writ of certiorari.
Federal Circuit Court of Appeals	**FEDERAL RULES OF APPELLATE PROCEDURE**
	Explains the process of appealing a case.
	Each circuit also has local rules applicable to that circuit only.
Federal District Courts	**FEDERAL RULES OF CIVIL PROCEDURE**
	Explains the process of pursuing a case from the filing of a complaint through a final judgment.
	Each district court also has local rules applicable to that district only.

SIDEBAR

Often more appropriate forms than those in form books can be found by consulting other files in the office to find forms used in similar cases.

§ 7.6 Guidelines for Preparing Legal Documents

At the beginning of this chapter, it was noted that nonlawyer experts in England prepared litigation documents for filing with the courts. Today, under supervision of an attorney, legal secretaries, paralegals, and law clerks can prepare litigation documents for filing with a court. With a good sample form and some knowledge of the court rules, most writers can draft basic pleadings and motions for filing with a court. In many situations, however, the drafting of pleadings and motions requires an expertise that is acquired only through years of practice.

The following text provides some insights into the writing process involved in the preparation of pleadings and motions.

Be Precise and Accurate

Perhaps the most important rule to follow when drafting legal documents is to write accurately and precisely. As each sentence is written, it should be tested to determine whether each fact in that sentence can be supported by the evidence. There are several reasons for this emphasis on accuracy and precision.

First, the person who signs a pleading, motion, or other paper is certifying to the court that

> the signer has read the pleading, motion, or other paper, that to the best of the signer's knowledge, information, and belief formed after reasonable inquiry that it is well grounded in fact and is warranted by existing law or a good faith argument for the extension, modification or reversal of existing law . . .

The signature on a pleading, motion, or other paper filed with a court also certifies that the document "is not interposed for any improper purpose, such as to harass or to cause unnecessary delay or needless increase in the cost of litigation."

The signer of a pleading or motion is subject to sanctions if the pleading or motion is found by the court to have been filed for an improper purpose. These sanctions

> may include an order to pay to the other party or parties the amount of the reasonable expenses incurred because of the filing of the pleading, motion, or other paper, including a reasonable attorney's fee.

All legal professionals must be aware of this rule when preparing any pleading or motion to be filed with a court.

A second reason why accuracy and precision is so important is that statements made in a pleading or motion may be used against the client later in the case as "pleading admissions." If the client signs an affidavit prepared by the legal professional without reading it, that affidavit may be used to impeach the client at a later hearing in the case. This situation happens more frequently than one might expect. A client who signs an affidavit or answers interrogatories does so under oath. A lawyer who signs a pleading is verifying that the pleading is well grounded in fact. Before preparing any statement about the facts of the case, the legal professional must make sure the applicable witnesses and the client have been interviewed and appropriately quoted. Accuracy is a prerequisite for drafting any legal document.

SIDEBAR

The author has always stressed to his students how carelessly prepared pleadings can be used at trial against a party. In an early legal professional class, emphasis was placed on how important it is to draft accurately. Several years later the author was involved in a case in which a former student had prepared the pleadings. The cross-claim he had written for his client contradicted his client's position in the case. Improperly prepared pleadings can cause considerable harm in a case. Although this case was settled before a trial, this sloppy pleading compromised the client's position in that litigation.

Finally, a pleading reflects on the firm's integrity and reputation. If a legal professional prepares documents that do not track the truth, the court will give less than full credence to the professional and his or her firm in the future. The law firm's reputation is something that should be carefully guarded.

Develop the Facts

In the preparation of a pleading or motion, facts must be set forth that support the client's position. It is important to remember that the court does not know the facts about the dispute, so the drafter of the document needs to tell the problem to the court. When the drafting of the pleading or motion is finished, the document should be reviewed to determine whether the court will understand the client's reason for filing it.

Relate the Facts to a Law or Rule

There must be a legal basis for filing a paper with a court. Most litigation documents should specify a court rule or some other authority to justify the relief sought. If the complaint is based on a violation of a particular statute, the statute should be cited in a pleading paragraph of the complaint. If a motion to compel is based on a particular rule, the rule should be cited in the motion.

Describe the Injury to the Client

The manner in which the client has been damaged or will be affected must be described. In a complaint, the injuries or damages should be described. A motion should explain to the court why the client is seeking an order from the court.

Describe the Relief Sought

The court must always be told what relief the client is seeking. A pleading should specify whether the client wants money damages, an injunction, or a writ. A motion should describe the type of order the client is seeking from the court. A request or demand for relief places the opposing party on notice of what relief is sought by the pleading or the motion and also identifies for the court what action it should consider taking, if the party requesting the relief prevails. In opposing a motion, a party might request simply that the court overrule the motion, or in opposing a complaint, a party might demand that the matter be dismissed.

Remember the Client's Ultimate Objectives

Pleading and motion practice sometimes resembles a game of chess, especially when done by a litigation expert. There is much thought given to what is pled or not pled and to what motions are filed or not filed. There is even considerable thought given to the timing of the filing of motions.

Filing a motion may prompt the other side to file a retaliatory motion or pleading. When clients are billed hourly, the time spent on the motion or pleading is expected to produce results. As pleadings and motions are prepared, thought must be given to the client's aim in the litigation.

§ 7.7 Write Simply and Directly

Throughout this text, the need to abandon archaic expressions and to write clearly and understandably has been stressed. Pleading and motion practice is no exception. The rules specify "short and direct" court documents. Nevertheless, some lawyers continue to prepare pleadings in stilted legalese. This problem is a remnant of the practice of earlier generations of lawyers who were required to deal with the technical rules for litigation documents. Some lawyers who never practiced under the old rules use forms passed down from lawyers who did. Other lawyers use outdated form books.

In the *Conley v. Gibson* case mentioned earlier in this chapter, the Supreme Court told the lower courts that pleadings do not need to be technical to comply with the rules. This discussion should not lead to the conclusion that pleadings should be written informally. That conclusion would be wrong. Courts expect a professional product. A legal writer should write clearly, not informally.

Any professional writer understands the demands of the audience. The audience for a pleading or motion is a judge. That judge is highly educated. A pleading subtly educates that judge about the client and the client's case. The pleading should be read and reread with this principle in mind.

The facts must be stated in plain language and short sentences. Some lawyers have an annoying habit of beginning every pleading paragraph with the word "that." There is no reason to do this. Some lawyers draft pleadings using the abominable *and/or*. Certainly there is no reason to do that.

Legal professionals should avoid the temptation to write pleadings with legalese. If the pleading is written in a professional manner, the legal professional's supervisor should have no objection. Pleadings should be written so the writer can understand them. The rules require nothing more.

§ 7.8   Sample Pleadings and Motions

It is helpful to trace a lawsuit through its course from a drafting perspective. An examination of some actual court documents used in an important civil case will be instructive.

In 1965, Ralph Nader wrote a book entitled *Unsafe at Any Speed*. This book was about automobile design safety. During the 1960s, the courts began grappling with an issue of whether a car manufacturer could be held liable for producing enhanced injuries in motor vehicle accidents even if its motor vehicle did not cause the collision. In other words, if a vehicle was not safely designed to survive a crash, could its manufacturer be held responsible for the "secondary impact" (sometimes referred to as the "second accident")?

The pleadings (with minor editing) in this section are from *Evans v. General Motors*, 359 F.2d 822 (7th Cir.), *cert denied*, 385 U.S. 836 (1966), the first case to test this theory of liability in court. *Evans* was ultimately decided in favor of General Motors. Shortly thereafter, however, the

Eighth Circuit decided *Larsen v. General Motors Corp.*, 391 F.2d 495 (8th Cir. 1968), in favor of the plaintiff. Numerous states had to decide this question, which led to the following comment:

> *Evans* and *Larsen*, continuing their national battle for supremacy . . . have enunciated "second collision" principles precisely poles apart. Their clashing concept as to the appropriate legal principle controlling manufacturers' liability for design defects producing enhanced injuries in motor vehicle accidents but not causing or contributing to the initial collision, has led to a new "War between the States" unsurpassed since 1865.[2]

The facts of *Evans* are best recited by paraphrasing the facts from the appellate briefs filed by the parties with the Seventh Circuit:

> Roy L. Evans was driving a 1961 Chevrolet station wagon and was struck on the driver's side in an intersection collision. The complaint alleged the driver's side of the vehicle collapsed into Evans. He was killed as a result of the accident. The complaint alleged the 1961 Chevrolet vehicle did not have side rails but instead used an x-frame, which created an unreasonable risk of injury to the occupants of this vehicle. The complaint stated claims for negligence, strict liability in tort, and implied warranty. The complaint was brought by Barbara F. Evans, Evans' widow, on behalf of his surviving children.

The Complaint

A civil case is initiated by filing a complaint. It is not unusual for the litigation professional to prepare a complaint for the attorney's review. The amended complaint from *Evans* (found in the appendix) is a good example of a complaint.

Composition of the Complaint

Like other pleadings, a complaint has a caption. When the complaint is filed, the clerk assigns a number to the case, and this number is written on the complaint. The heading might simply say "Complaint." The first paragraph of the complaint, like the first paragraph of any pleading, typically begins by identifying the party filing the complaint.

There is no precise formula for the contents of a complaint. Usually the complaint recites the jurisdictional facts (the facts that give the court the power to resolve this particular controversy). The complaint also recites the facts that give rise to the alleged wrong, the legal theory of the claim, and the damages sought. The complaint closes with a "prayer" for relief. The prayer is simply a request for specific relief: money damages, an injunction, a declaratory judgment, or the like.

A complaint can be quite brief. Two or three short sentences can meet the legal minimum. Yet it is not usually in the plaintiff's interest to file such an abbreviated complaint. A complete statement of the claim will educate the court about the nature and extent of the plaintiff's claim. Setting out the theories in detail will save much effort later when the court requires a detailed statement of the claim as part of a pretrial order. Some courts even quote from the complaint when telling the jury about the case. So the manner in which the complaint is written can have significant ramifications throughout the lawsuit.

The defendant is required to answer the averments in the complaint. Writing short sentences can make it more difficult for the defense in good faith to deny the allegations of the complaint. So, how the complaint is drafted can have significant ramifications throughout the course of the lawsuit.

The Summons

The complaint is served with a summons. The summons is a form that tells the defendant that a response to the complaint must be filed, usually within twenty days of the receipt of the complaint. Defendants generally retain legal counsel shortly after they receive a summons.

A complaint tells the court what a lawsuit is about. It places the other party on notice of the lawsuit and provides some information about the claim that must be defended. Some court proceedings are commenced by the filing of a petition. Petitions are often used for divorce, adoption, guardianship, and estate proceedings. A petition is similar to a complaint.

After a lawsuit is filed, the party who is sued may want to file a counterclaim against the plaintiff or a claim against another party alleging that party is responsible for the wrongdoing. A sample counterclaim appears in the appendix. These documents are structured almost identically to a complaint.

Responding to the Complaint

Depending on the jurisdiction, a response to the complaint must be filed within twenty days of service of the complaint and summons. Parties can be defaulted and substantial damages taken against them if they ignore a pleading deadline. When a complaint is filed against a party, the party must respond either by filing a motion with the court to extend the time to file an answer to the complaint or by filing a responsive pleading. A responsive pleading is either a motion to dismiss or an answer. Before a motion to dismiss is prepared, the trial rules must be reviewed to see if the motion conforms to the rule. This is the attorney's ultimate responsibility.

Some important choices are made at this stage. If a defendant fails to file a timely motion to dismiss, the defendant waives certain of these defenses.

In answering the complaint, the legal professional goes through the complaint (preferably with the client) and makes an initial decision whether to admit or deny the allegations. The attorney must review the decisions to admit or deny. Admitting an allegation removes that issue from the controverted questions to be tried in the lawsuit. Denying an allegation in a complaint puts that allegation in dispute.

A party may also need to file certain affirmative defenses with the answer. Rule 8(c) of the Federal Rules of Civil Procedure provides the following:

> **Affirmative Defenses.** In pleading to a preceding pleading, a party shall set forth affirmatively accord and satisfaction, arbitration and award, assumption of risk, contributory negligence, discharge in bankruptcy, duress, estoppel, failure of consideration, fraud, illegality, injury by fellow servant, laches, license, payment, release, res judicata, statute of frauds, statute of limitations, waiver, and any other matter constituting an avoidance or affirmative defense. When a party has mistakenly designated a defense as a counterclaim or a counterclaim as a defense, the court on terms, if justice so requires, shall treat the pleading as if there had been a proper designation.

If these affirmative defenses are not claimed in the answer, they may be considered waived.

Often only a few sentences are needed to meet the minimum requirements for filing an answer. If the investigation of the case is thorough when the answer is filed, the answer can provide a map of the party's defense of the matter. A detailed answer can help educate the court about the merits of the defense, although at times a party might tactically decide to file a skeleton document to avoid educating the other party about its knowledge of the case. The answer filed in *Evans* is in the appendix.

§ 7.9 Discovery Practice

Lawyers typically do not like the day-to-day discovery practice. As noted earlier, a generation ago, trials were conducted by ambush, with neither side disclosing information to the opposition. Now, with the liberal rules of discovery, almost the reverse is true. Parties are required through the discovery process to disclose their entire case to the other side.

One method for conducting discovery is sending interrogatories to the adverse party. The legal professional may be asked to draft these questions. There are form books to help, but the questions should be tailored to the particular case. The party answering these interrogatories often answers these questions by providing as little information as possible while still complying with the rules. Interrogatories should be worded with this reality in mind.

In *Evans*, the plaintiff filed an extensive set of interrogatories. A few of these interrogatories have been included in the appendix.

In many cases, rules limit the number of interrogatories a party may file. Hence, the use of this scarce resource should be tailored to aid other discovery devices. Asking a party to itemize bills or other damages in a personal injury lawsuit may provide more information than simply asking the party to explain the accident. The legal professional who answers these interrogatories should remember that the client will be signing the answers. The client may be confronted with these answers at a trial. The answers should be prepared with this thought in mind.

The legal professional may be asked to prepare requests for production of documents to serve on the other party to the lawsuit. This is a request for the other side to produce exhibits and other documents that can be used in the lawsuit. In a substantial case that involves a major corporate client, months may be spent reviewing documents that must be produced pursuant to such a request. If a document is requested and there is no basis for objection, the document must be produced. Under no circumstances should it be concealed. The risk of concealment is that sanctions might be taken against the client. From a practical standpoint, it is not unusual for a disgruntled employee to leak this information to the other side of a case. If this happens, the effects on the lawsuit could be devastating to the client and to the law firm that cheated in the process.

In drafting discovery responses, it must be understood that even inadvertent failure to produce a document might be construed by a jury or the court as an attempt to subvert the process. A legal professional who is placed in charge of answering a request and has any questions about whether some item should be produced should ask for direction from a supervising attorney. It is best to always err on the side of caution.

§ 7.10 Other Pretrial Motions

Parties file numerous types of motions prior to a trial. Most of these motions are cataloged by the Federal Rules of Civil Procedure. A motion is simply a request to a court to take a particular action.

A commonly filed pretrial motion is a motion for summary judgment. It asks the court to rule for a particular party without a trial. Technically the motion claims there is no genuine issue of material fact that needs to be tried. Normally a summary judgment motion is filed with affidavits and other discovery information.

The legal writer may be asked to prepare the supporting affidavits. An affidavit is a sworn written statement. All legal professionals are asked sooner or later to prepare an affidavit. Usually the parties file a brief with the motion. How to prepare a brief is discussed in Chapter 11.

§ 7.11 Preparation for Trial

The court orders disclosure of witnesses' names and addresses as well as proposed exhibits. The legal professional often prepares these lists for trial. They are important. If a witness or exhibit is omitted, the court might not permit the witness to testify or might exclude the exhibit, so considerable care should be given to the preparation of these lists. Motions also are made at trial, such as a **motion in limine** (a motion to prevent a party from introducing prejudicial evidence during the trial).

At trial, written motions are usually prepared for a directed verdict (a request that the trial be terminated because the other party has not adduced sufficient evidence to warrant a finding) at the close of the adverse party's case and at the close of all the evidence.

Jury instructions need to be prepared. The writer should remember the audience. It is the jury. The instructions should be written so they can be understood by the jurors. Many states have developed pattern jury instructions to be used in various types of cases. These pattern jury instructions should be consulted before the drafting of instructions has begun.

Motion practice carries with it serious responsibilities. Courts expect ethical behavior. The lawyer is an officer of the court. Although it is the lawyer's ultimate responsibility to review pleadings for filing with a court, not all lawyers are as diligent as they should be. Lawyers sometimes are in a hurry or worried about another case. Therefore, the legal professional should prepare documents with great care and urge the supervising attorney to review the documents with equal care.

TERMS

motion in limine   A motion made before the commencement of a trial that requests the court to prohibit the adverse party from introducing prejudicial evidence at trial.

The best documents are written understandably but formally. The rules of drafting discussed in Chapters 3 through 6 should be applied, and the writer should be careful and accurate.

Writing Exercises

Complete the following exercises.

1. You represent Joe and Mary Roe who were injured in an automobile accident on January 1, 1991, at 8:00 A.M. Joe and Mary are husband and wife. You interviewed the Roes, who gave you the following information.

   They had eaten breakfast at the Pair of Eagles Restaurant. They had just gotten into their car and were exiting the Pair of Eagles parking lot and turning east on Highway 1. They looked both ways. A brick column partially obstructed their vision. When they exited onto Highway 1, their vehicle was struck by a vehicle driven by Sam A. Torney, seventeen years of age. In Sam's car were some open beer cans and two teenage friends of Sam, Bob Lawless and Sally Lawless.

   Your investigator obtained a statement from P. O. Stress, who was in a vehicle behind your clients. She said that it appeared to her that the Sam Torney vehicle was drag racing with another vehicle.

   A copy of the police department's accident report appears in Figure 7–5. The police officers on the scene, Bob N. Vester and D. A. Smith, issued no tickets, telling both drivers this was a civil matter. They noted damage to the Roe vehicle in the rear panel on the driver's side and damage to the middle of the front of the Torney vehicle.

   The damage to your client's vehicle was repaired at A-1 Body Shop at a total cost of $2,500.

   Both Roes were taken to Federal Hospital in Federal City, Indiana. Both were treated and released that day. Joe Roe sustained a cervical strain. He continues to have intermittent neck pain and headaches from the accident. His hospital bill was $1,150. His physician was Dr. W. P. Lash, an orthopedic surgeon, who treated him with conservative therapy and medication. Therapy bills totaled $1,500 from Federal Hospital, and prescriptions totaled $135.

   Mary Roe aggravated a low back injury she had sustained five years previously. She, too, was treated by Dr. W. P. Lash, who prescribed therapy and medication. Therapy bills totaled $1,350 from Federal Hospital, and prescriptions totaled $50.

FIGURE 7–5 Police Department Accident Report

Diagram: Not to scale

Indicate NORTH by an arrow

Highway #1

Pair of Eagles Restaurant

NARRATIVE (Refer to Vehicle by Number)

Vehicle No. 1 was leaving the Pair of Eagles Restaurant, making a right turn onto Highway No. 1,

Vehicle No. 2 struck Vehicle No. 1 in the left rear panel.

D1 Insured By Goode Ins. Co. 5 2.20/30 29   D2 Insured By Best Insurance Co. 812. 425. 2242

Other Participant(s) Name, Address (etc.)

Name of Witness No. 1 P. O. Stress   Address 801 Washington   Location at Time of Accident Behind Veh. No. 1

Name of Witness No. 2   Address   Location at Time of Accident

Name of Person Arrested   I.C. Code(s)   Name of Person Arrested   I.C. Code(s)

Time Notified 8:03 PM	Time Arrived 8:07 PM	Other Location of Investigation Federal City Hospital	Investigation Complete ☑Yes ☐No	Photos Taken ☐Yes ☑No
Assisting Officer D. D. Smith	I.D. No. 1015	Agency Federal City P.D.	Date of Report 1/01/91
Assisting Officer	I.D. No.	Agency	Driver Report Form Furnished ☑D1 ☑D2
Investigating Officer's Signature Bob N. Vester, Sgt.	I.D. No. 2684	Agency Federal City P.D.	

FIGURE 7–5 (continued)

Joe Roe missed seven days of work and Mary Roe missed fourteen. Joe lost wages of $500, and Mary lost wages of $1,000. The Roes want to sue Sam Torney.

Your supervisor tells you to prepare a draft of a complaint for filing in your local court. Start with a caption and prepare the remainder of the complaint. Request a jury trial.

2.   You represent Sam A. Torney. Sam has had a complaint filed against him for the accident described in the preceding exercise. Sam had a special model 1965 Chevrolet. He had spent months reconstructing this vehicle. He told you that he was traveling east on Highway 1 when suddenly the vehicle driven by the Roes pulled out in front of his vehicle. He said he might have been driving a little fast, but certainly not much over the speed limit. He said the Roe vehicle simply pulled out in front of him.

Sam was not injured in the accident, but he will need to special-order custom parts for his vehicle. His best estimate is that the cost to replace the damaged front end will cost about $3,000 to $3,500. He wants to file a counterclaim against the Roes. Your supervisor has requested that you prepare the counterclaim for filing with the court in which the complaint was filed. You should also file an answer to the complaint.

3.   Prepare a reply to the counterclaim filed by Sam Torney in exercise 2.

4.   Your supervisor wants you to file some interrogatories directed against the defendant in the *Roe v. Torney* litigation. She hands you a set of interrogatories (see Figure 7–6) and tells you the local court rule allows only thirty questions, counting subparts. Draft a set of interrogatories designed to elicit as much information as possible and still comply with the local rule.

5.   Your supervisor wants you to file some interrogatories directed against the plaintiff in the *Roe v. Torney* litigation. She hands you the set of interrogatories in Figure 7–6. She tells you the local court rule allows only thirty questions, counting subparts. Draft a set of interrogatories designed to elicit as much information as possible and still comply with the local rule.

6.   After interrogatories were filed, Sam Torney refused to answer a question about whether he had any previous driving convictions. Your supervisor met with Sam Torney's attorney on April 15, 1991, at your office, and Torney's attorney refused to produce any of the requested information. Assume the local rule reads as follows:

To curtail undue delay in the administration of justice, the court shall refuse to rule on any and all motions having to do with discovery under Rules 26 through 37 of the Rules of Civil Procedure unless moving counsel shall first advise the court in such motion that after personal consultation and a good faith effort to resolve differences, they are unable to reach an accord. This statement shall recite, in addition, the date, time, and place of such conference and the names of all parties participating therein. If counsel for any party advises the court in writing that opposing counsel has refused or delayed meeting and discussing the problems covered in this Rule, then the court may take such action as is appropriate to avoid delay.

FIGURE 7–6
Sample
Interrogatories

INTERROGATORIES OF PLAINTIFF TO DEFENDANT

The Plaintiff, pursuant to Rules 26 and 33 of the Rules of Civil Procedure, hereby propounds and serves the following written interrogatories to be answered under oath within thirty-three (33) days from the date of service thereof: (If any of the following interrogatories cannot be answered in full, please answer to the fullest extent possible.)

1. If you are an individual, please state:

   a. Your full name;
   b. Any other names by which you are or have been known or have used;
   c. Date of birth;
   d. Place of birth;
   e. Social Security number;
   f. Your present residence address;
   g. Your present business address;
   h. Your addresses for the past ten years, and the dates and duration of time you resided at each of the above addresses;
   i. Your address at the time of the occurrence.

2. If you are married, state:

   a. Your spouse's name and occupation;
   b. Date of marriage;
   c. Place of marriage;
   d. If you are male, your wife's maiden name.

3. If you have been married before, what are the present names and addresses of all prior spouses and the reason for the termination of said marriage?

4. What is the extent of your formal education?

5. What is your present occupation?

6. With respect to each of the positions of employment you have had in the past ten years, including your present employment, state:

   a. The name and address of your employer;
   b. The name and address of your supervisor;
   c. The dates of employment;
   d. The nature of your duties;
   e. The reason you left said employment.

7. If you are an association, please state:

   a. Your full and exact name;
   b. The present address of your principal office;

FIGURE 7–6
(continued)

    c. The names and addresses of your officers;

    d. The names and addresses of your members;

8. If you are a corporation, please state:

    a. The date of and state in which you were incorporated;

    b. The purposes for which you were incorporated;

    c. Whether you are now in good standing;

    d. If not, the date you ceased to be in good standing and the reasons therefor;

    e. The names and addresses of your principal officers;

    f. The name of the person in charge and the addresses of all places of business, if any, which you have in the state of Indiana.

9. State with as much detail as you can any conversation you or any of your employees or agents or representatives had with the plaintiff concerning the occurrence complained of, at any time just before, during, or after said occurrence.

10. Were any statements, written or otherwise, obtained from anyone, including plaintiff, witnesses, and you, concerning said occurrence complained of, by you or anyone acting on your behalf, including your insurance company?

11. If so, state:

    a. The names, addresses at the time, and present addresses of all persons giving such statements;

    b. The dates on which they were obtained;

    c. The names, addresses, and position or occupation of the persons who obtained same.

12. Have you or your attorneys, agents, or insurance company any pictures, moving or still, pertaining to this case?

13. If so, state:

    a. The names, addresses, and present whereabouts of all persons taking such photographs;

    b. The dates on which they were obtained;

    c. What objects, scenes, or views they depicted or will depict;

    d. The names, addresses, and occupations of all persons who have present custody or control thereof.

14. State the names and addresses known to you, your employees, your representatives, your attorneys, your insurance carriers, or their representatives, of any and all persons who have, or claim to have, any knowledge concerning any facts or records relating to any of the following:

    a. Persons who witnessed the occurrence complained of;

FIGURE 7–6
(continued)

b. Persons who were present at the scene of this occurrence immediately after its occurrence and at any time within the three hours following;

c. Persons who were within sight or hearing of this occurrence;

d. Persons who accompanied you up to the time of the occurrence;

e. Persons who were witnesses to any subsequent investigation;

f. The conduct, activity, physical condition, or statement of any person involved in the occurrence during the 24-hour period immediately preceding the occurrence;

g. The statement of any person relating to the occurrence, identifying the person or persons making such statement, the time and place of statement, and the persons then present;

h. The taking or existence of pictures, moving or still, relating to the occurrence or any of the issues in this case;

i. The condition of any equipment, machine, or vehicle involved in said occurrence, including its maintenance and repair or change prior to, at the time of, and subsequent to said occurrence;

j. Any other facts pertaining to the occurrence complained of, the injuries to plaintiff, and all other issues in this case.

15. Have you ever been a party to another lawsuit? If so, state:

a. The name and location of the suit;

b. The case number of the suit;

c. The date the suit was filed;

d. They type of action the suit involved;

e. Whether you were the plaintiff or defendant.

16. Have you been convicted of, or pled guilty to, any felony or misdemeanor at any time? If so, state:

a. The offense;

b. The date of such conviction or plea;

c. The court in which such conviction or plea occurred.

17. At the time of the occurrence complained of in plaintiff's complaint, were there any policy or policies of liability insurance or any indemnification agreement or insurance agreement in effect which covered or may cover any of the following:

a. The risk or claim upon which the complaint herein is based;

b. Any judgment that might be entered in this action;

c. Indemnification or reimbursement for any payments made to satisfy any judgement that may be entered in this action;

d. You;

e. Any equipment, machine, or motor vehicle that was involved in the occurrence complained of;

f. The operator, owner, lessor, and/or lessee of said equipment, machine, or motor vehicle, if other than yourself.

Prepare a motion to compel, with a one-page memorandum and a caption.

7.   Prepare jury instructions for the plaintiff in this litigation.

8.   Prepare jury instructions for the defendant in this litigation.

Enrichment Activities

1.   Go to your local courthouse or the nearest federal court. Ask the clerk for an indictment in a criminal case. Compare the function of an indictment with that of a complaint.

2.   Assume the complaint filed in writing exercise 1 was not filed in the right county. Your supervisor tells you that instead of filing an answer to the complaint, you should file a motion to dismiss.

   a.   Read Rule 12 of your state's rules of procedure.

   b.   Locate a form for a motion to dismiss.

   c.   Prepare a motion to dismiss the complaint with an accompanying brief based on the allegations of improper venue. Use your state's laws.

3.   Draft a divorce petition for filing in your county court.

Notes

[1]   Discovery is governed by rules 26–37 of the Federal Rules of Civil Procedure.

[2]   *Frericks v. General Motors Corp.*, 20 Md. App. 518, 317 A.2d 494, 495 (Ct. Spec. App. 1974) (footnotes omitted).

CHAPTER 8

LEGAL CORRESPONDENCE

Legal professionals generate a lot of correspondence—to clients, lawyers, opposing parties, and other professionals. Legal professionals may use correspondence to give opinions, gather or provide information, demand action, or settle cases. At times their letters are used to make important business decisions. For example, many insurance companies require the attorneys who represent them in a lawsuit to write monthly or quarterly reports concerning the progress of litigation. One insurance company might receive its attorney's progress report plus a settlement proposal concerning the same case from the opposing lawyer. Based on the monthly report, the settlement correspondence, and other independent information, the insurance company will decide to settle or not to settle the lawsuit.

§ 8.1 Functions of Legal Correspondence

In the general practice of law, a lawyer may use correspondence for various purposes. Correspondence is used to seek information, persuade, provide information, threaten, and make a record of a position. Often a letter combines several of these functions. A settlement letter, which is intended primarily to persuade, may also contain a threat. A letter demanding that a tenant surrender possession of an apartment may attempt to reason with the tenant to avoid litigation. A legal professional should be aware of the function of the letter before sending it.

To Seek Information

Legal professionals are always gathering information for their clients. In a personal injury case, for example, the legal professional may write to the client's physicians to request reports. The legal professional may also write to other persons to request weather information, engineering reports, police reports, or background information about the opposing party.

It is not unusual for a law firm to have a standard form for requesting information such as medical reports. It is important, however, to tailor letters to the facts of the case. In just a few minutes the form can be changed to fit the particular case, and the change will result in a more specific reply that may produce information the expert normally would not have provided.

Some professionals, such as engineers or physicians, may charge a fee for providing the requested information. Thus, it is certainly worthwhile to tailor the request for the particular situation rather than using a form request.

To Persuade

Legal professionals write letters to convince other parties to take action or refrain from taking action on a specific matter. For example, a legal professional might write a governmental agency on behalf of a client to convince the agency not to take some action against the client. Lawyers write other lawyers arguing the merits of a case. Lawyers also write letters to clients to convince them of the merits of a course of action.

Persuasive letters written by legal professionals emphasize the legal and factual merits of a client's position much as the argument section of a brief does. A settlement letter that has good facts but a tenuous legal argument showcases the facts and deemphasizes the legal problems. Tactical concerns often dictate the contents of persuasive letters. There may be a desire to keep from disclosing some information to the other side or to elicit a particular response.

Legal professionals can persuade by various techniques. At times, the logic of the position alone can be used to persuade. At other times, a threat of the consequences is necessary. Sympathy is sometimes used to persuade. The point is to identify the objective and select the best way to achieve that objective given the parties involved.

To Provide Information

Just as lawyers seek information, they are often asked to provide information to clients and others. At times this information is merely factual. A letter may report the status of a case, the result of an investigation, or the significance of a recently decided case or recently passed law. In many of these situations, accuracy is the paramount concern, and the letter should be read and edited with this concern in mind.

Providing accurate information means including all the relevant or material information. It may involve choosing whether to provide detailed information or to delete entirely any mention of a particular matter.

The legal professional may also render an opinion on a matter. The opinion may be a legal opinion, such as an assessment for a client as to whether a lawsuit is advisable. An opinion letter may address the advisability of pursuing a case that has economic, political, or practical implications. In writing opinion letters, the process is similar to that discussed in Chapter 10 for writing memoranda. In fact, in many cases, the processes are almost identical. In an opinion letter, as in a memorandum, the legal professional addresses all the pertinent facts and law and gives an objective assessment of the strengths and weaknesses of a legal position.

To Threaten

Some letters are intended merely to communicate a threat of action. A demand letter to a debtor is a good example of such a letter. These types of letters are used in a variety of situations. A client may want to start negotiations under a contract or over a custody arrangement in a divorce-related case. In such cases, a threat may open the negotiation process.

Many factors govern the content of demand letters. For example, federal, state, or local laws may prescribe what is appropriate and what must be included in letters to debtors. The same is true of letters to evict tenants. It is important to research any applicable laws before writing such letters.

As with other correspondence, the first concern should be to recognize the real objective of the letter. If a demand letter to collect a debt for a client is sent, payment of the debt is the obvious objective. Yet any experienced collection attorney knows there are often other objectives. For example, a letter may be sent only to remind the debtor of the obligation, as the debt simply may not be a high priority with the debtor until the letter is received. A gentle reminder rather than a threat may be all that is needed in these cases. In other cases, the letter may seek an acknowledgment of the debt or a response to the letter in order to learn more information about the debtor. For instance, employment information may be sought so that garnishment proceedings can be instituted. The letter may be intended solely as a record of a demand for payment to comply with a statutory prerequisite to an action.

The tone of the letter can vary from debtor to debtor. Hence, a demand letter can be written as a friendly reminder, a prodding letter, an appealing letter, or a threatening letter. There are many ways to write a demand letter.

To Record Information

At times, the sole purpose of a letter is to serve as a record of an event or transaction. In such cases, the letter may be intended for use in a future litigation between the parties or to ensure that the other party is aware that a paper trail has been made to document a situation. Examples of such letters may be the demand letter, a letter written to verify a meeting or phone conversation, or a letter written to record a deal made between the parties. In these cases, many of the rules and guidelines for drafting transaction documents (Chapters 3–6) will be helpful.

§ 8.2 Effective Letter Writing

The most important advice about letter writing is that the writer needs to recognize the objective of the letter. One helpful way to do this is to consider why a letter is being written rather than a telephone call being made. Once the objective of the letter is recognized, the writer should try to fulfill it as effectively as possible.

Often a client's main impression of a law firm is formed by reading letters from that firm. A misspelling, grammatical error, or typographical error in a letter detracts from the favorable impression the client may have formed from a personal conference. Such errors sometimes suggest that the client's case is not receiving proper care from the firm. Therefore, it is important to proofread each letter carefully before it is sent.

Letter writing involves more than careful proofreading. Style is the personalized way the writer writes. Too many legal professionals hide their style by using canned letters or language. There is no rule that says a letter must begin with "In reply to your letter of . . ." or end with "Thanking you for your attention in this matter, I remain . . ." There is no rule that says a letter from a legal professional must be crammed with legalese. A letter writer should strive to deliver the message in the best words possible, given the intended reader.

The author's former law partner uses contractions and colloquial expressions in his letters. He avoids all formality and legal terms. He is a writer when he is not practicing law. Some lawyers would never use any informality in their correspondence. This lawyer's letters, however, are readable, accurate, and reflect his personality. The reader seldom misses the message. The point is not necessarily to incorporate contractions—or even informality—into letters. The point is that the writer should use his or her own writing style.

Guidelines for Effective Letter Writing

What follows are some guidelines to use in writing effective legal correspondence.

1. Address the letter to a specific person, if possible   Legal professionals write letters to governmental entities and large corporations. If the name of the person responsible for taking the action sought is known, the letter should be written to that person. Otherwise, letters bounce from bureaucrat's desk to bureaucrat's desk. Even if a letter is addressed to the wrong person, that person will be responsible for handling it and channeling it to the right place.

2. Keep sentences and paragraphs short   A letter is not a treatise. Readability studies show that short sentences and paragraphs aid the reader in understanding the message. A letter will be more readable if the writer pays attention to sentence and paragraph length.

3. Write personally   The writer should not be afraid to use pronouns such as "I," "you," or "us" in correspondence. The letter should center attention not on the writer, but on the reader, so it should be written to that reader.

4. Simplify the language   Someone once asked a governmental agency if garbage trucks needed to have a certain permit and received this reply:

> Per your August 21, 1990 correspondence, received August 21, 1990, our agency has authorization to exercise discretion in the termination of policy, as well as the power to adopt applicable codes and statutes of other administrative/legislative bodies. In so doing, the Department uses as policy regarding the nonregulation of commodities with negative value (trash), 62.12 of the Federal Carrier Reports, where Administrative Rules No. 130, paragraph 25.130 is cited as authority for the non regulatory finding. If you have any further questions regarding this matter, please do not hesitate to call me.

The writer could have said, "No, our agency does not require a garbage truck owner to obtain a permit." The earth will not move and the National Guard will not be called out if a writer writes so that the reader can understand the letter.

5. Tell clients what they need to know   If the writer wants the client to take some course of action, he or she must not equivocate or give vague instructions. Instructions must be presented in a direct way.

Otherwise, the firm will only receive a phone call from the client asking for clarification.

6. Write what is meant So much miscommunication with clients occurs because legal professionals write letters to impress the client rather than to provide the pertinent information. The letter on the garbage truck permit issue is a good illustration of writing to impress the reader rather than to answer the question. A good means to accomplish a direct approach is by using active rather than passive voice.

7. Write to the reading level of the reader The vocabulary and reading ability of clients will vary incredibly. The same type of letter should not be written to all clients. In some ways, letter writing is easier than other forms of legal writing. The writer can visualize the targeted reader and consider the reader's level of education and background knowledge. Some clients expect formality, but formality does not mean a canned response. A writer can write formally but clearly. A writer can also write informally but clearly. The writer should choose the style that is most appropriate for the particular client.

8. Keep emotions out of letter writing Keeping this advice in mind almost always prevents letters written in anger or on impulse. It will prevent the writer from making insults and facetious comments in letters. Seldom will either a short-term or a long-term goal be accomplished by sending out a nonprofessional letter. A target of such a letter should put it away before responding. This may not ease the anger but should ensure a more appropriate response.

9. Proofread the letter Letters are often dictated in a hurry and signed with a glance. A few minutes should be spent on proofreading the letter before it is mailed.

10. Check for enclosures Probably the most common mistake made in connection with letters is to refer to an enclosure and then fail to enclose it. The letter should be checked for enclosures *before* it is sent out.

11. Mail the letter on time A mistake made repeatedly in the law office is neglecting to mail a letter on time. When a legal professional fails to make a deadline, the result can be costly to the client. The client's bail may be revoked, or the client may fail to attend a hearing or review a pleading on time. As a result of such mistakes, the client may lose the case and be required to pay damages he or she otherwise would not owe.

§ 8.3 The Format of Letters

The legal professional writes thousands of letters. This means the professional makes thousands of impressions. When a client shows a letter to friends and relatives, their judgment of the law firm's ability is influenced by the appearance of that correspondence. Every letter must be professional.

The Legal Business Letter

Legal correspondence tends to resemble other business letters, although the exact format may vary from law firm to law firm. The essential elements of a business letter include the date, address, salutation, body, and signature. Legal correspondence also may include a reference line, a complimentary close, identification notations, enclosure notations, and copy notations. In the following discussion, the important elements of a basic legal business letter, which are illustrated in Figure 8–1, are discussed.

Date

Usually the date is placed two to six lines (three is standard) below the printed letterhead. The date includes the month, day, and year.

Legal correspondence is often used to make a record of an event or transaction. In Chapter 7, the importance of complying with deadlines was emphasized. Dates are important in most phases of legal practice. Letters should never be predated or postdated and should always be mailed when they are supposed to be mailed.

Special Mailing and Handling Notations

If the correspondence is sent by other than regular mail (*e.g.*, certified, registered, express, or priority mail), this is noted about two lines below the date and two lines above the address. If the letter is addressed "Confidential" or "Personal," this information is also placed below the date and above the address.

Address

The inside address of a business letter is usually placed two lines below the date or two lines below the special notations, if there are any. The inside address follows this format:

FIGURE 8–1
The Basic
Format of a
Legal Business
Letter

Law Offices of
Cheng, Long and Fortini
506 Samson Blvd.
Evansville, Indiana 47708-1234

DATE   May 17, 1991

MAILING   CERTIFIED MAIL, RETURN
NOTATION   RECEIPT REQUESTED

ADDRESS   UNIVERSAL INSURANCE SOCIETY
                     One Bank Plaza
                     Suite 1187
                     P.O. Box 7007
                     Hartford, Connecticut 46240-7007

ATTENTION   Attn: Ms. Samantha Rice

SUBJECT   RE: Claim Number: 39625
                          Insured: Tommie Thomas
                          Claimant: Terri Hunt
                          Date of Loss: May 17, 1990

SALUTATION   Dear Ms. Rice:

                     As you know, I submitted a settlement demand to you on
                     February 6, 1991. You said that you would be contacting
                     me to see if this matter can be resolved without litigation.
                     Unless I hear from you before June 1, 1991, I will have no
                     choice but to recommend to my client that suit be filed.

COMPLIMENTARY   Yours very truly,
CLOSE
                     CHENG, LONG AND FORTINI

SIGNATURE   Jo Long

INITIALS   JL/jw

ENCLOSURE   Enc.: Copy of Feb. 6, 1991 Settlement Demand
COPIES   cc: Terri Hunt

For an individual: Name
                                Business or title
                                Full address

For a business: Name of entity
                                Department information if applicable
                                Full address

If the letter is addressed to a business but to the attention of a particular individual, this information is typed below the inside address.

It does not do much good to mail a letter properly dated to the wrong address. The address should be checked on all correspondence. The legal professional should not rely on others to do this. If possible, the letter should be addressed to a specific person rather than simply to a company or agency, especially if the letter is going to a large corporation or a governmental entity. Otherwise, the letter may be shuffled from person to person until it ends on the right desk. If it is addressed to a particular person, that person has the responsibility for seeing that it gets to the right desk.

Reference or Subject Information

Following the address, many business letters include a signal about the subject matter. The information reads like this:

Re: Sale of Smith Property

Some companies prefer to include a file reference, billing information, an insurance policy number, or other information. This information might read as follows:

Insured: John Doe
Date of Accident: April 13, 1990
Claim Number: XYZ-1334

In most legal correspondence, this information is placed two lines below the address or attention line and two lines above the salutation.

Body of Letter

The body of the letter contains the contents of the communication (the message). Since legal correspondence serves many purposes, the opening paragraph should identify the purpose of the letter, if possible. Often the lead sentence can state the purpose. If the message is quite lengthy, outlining the body of the letter may be helpful to both the writer and the reader. Such an outline will vary with the type and objective of the letter.

Complimentary Close and Signature

Most business letters end with a complimentary close such as "Very truly yours," "Yours truly," or "Sincerely." The complimentary close is followed by the signature, under which the name is typed.

The firm's letterhead should be used in the legal professional's correspondence. The professional's proper designation should always follow his or her name, especially if he or she does not have a license to practice law.

Enclosures

There is more than one way to indicate that the writer of a letter has included enclosures: "enc.," "Enclosure," and "Enclosures (2)" are all acceptable. Sometimes the enclosures are listed by typing "Enclosures:" and listing each item separately. When identification initials of the letter writer and typist are given, these are placed two lines below the last line of the signature block. The enclosure information follows one or two lines below the initials.

Copies of Letters

When indicating that copies of a letter were sent to other individuals, the most common notation is as follows:

c: John Doe

For more than one recipient, a "c" is added:

cc: John Doe
      Mary Roe
      Atlas Corporation

It is acceptable to type "Copies:" or "Copies to:" and list the individuals receiving the copies. This is typed two lines below any other notation. If the writer wants to send someone a copy of the letter but does not want to show that information on the original, a note is typed on the file copy indicating the blind copy: "bcc: John Smith."

§ 8.4 Examples of Legal Correspondence

A good way to learn how to write effective legal correspondence is to look at some examples of different forms of letters commonly written by attorneys. A settlement letter, a progress letter on a case, a demand letter, and an opinion letter can be found in the appendix.

Settlement Letters

A settlement letter or brochure is usually written to persuade an insurance company to settle a claim. Although the writer of letter naturally strives to make the strongest case possible, he or she must not oversell the case and tarnish the firm's credibility with the adjuster handling the claim. The letter should be realistic. If there is some information that the client is not ready to disclose—perhaps a witness or an exhibit—the writer must be careful not to misstate the case.

A settlement letter is a cross between a brief and a final argument. On the one hand, the letter may need to address the legal merits of the case. On the other hand, the letter also must be sensitive to the factual strengths and weaknesses of the claim.

The purpose of a settlement letter is to maximize the recovery in the lawsuit. The letter must use facts and law to convince the adjuster the case is worth settling with the demand. An insurance adjuster is a professional who investigates and adjusts claims. The adjuster and the adjuster's supervisor are the audience, so the letter should be tailored to them. An insurance adjuster is familiar with the insurance laws. Although the adjuster does not have the in-depth legal training of a lawyer, the adjuster has more insight in this area than many people.

The adjuster may have personally investigated the facts and should already have made an assessment of the insured's position. Adjusters know there are costs and risks associated with litigation. They usually are more sensitive to factual problems than to legal theories. Therefore, the writer should highlight the facts of the claim and should neutralize but not ignore unfavorable facts.

The facts of an accident usually can be categorized as the events of the accident (both before and after). These facts include the details of the accident as well as the injuries and damages incurred.

Descriptions of injuries should be reduced to understandable terms. A medical reference such as R. Gray, *Attorney's Textbook of Medicine* (Matthew Bender & Co., 1984) should be consulted if the writer does not understand the medical terms. The injuries should be explained graphically. Pain and suffering should be emphasized. Medical bills, lost wages, and hospital bills (so-called special damages) and the details of treatment and reports of treating medical experts should be itemized. Projected future medical care and lost wages should be included as well.

The physical limitations and emotional consequences of the injury should be related in detail. A typical day in the client's life should be described, stressing day-to-day activities that are no longer possible because of the injuries.

If there are unique legal questions raised by the case, these theories should be stated so the adjuster will understand the implication of the client's theory of the case. State the law so the adjuster understands the law. It is sometimes beneficial to show comparable verdicts in similar cases. *Verdicts, Settlements and Tactics* (Shepard's/McGraw Hill, monthly), for instance, reports this information to its subscribers.

A typical settlement letter without exhibits appears in the appendix.

Report Letters

Lawyers are typically asked by sophisticated clients to provide routine reports on the status of ongoing litigation. The main goal of report letters is to give an accurate accounting of the main points of the case. These reports are used by the client to assess the merits of a claim. The letter in the appendix is a good illustration of such a report.

Demand Letters

Some clients may consult the firm because they have a substantial number of delinquent accounts payable. Attorneys often do the collection work for these clients, who usually have tried to collect the debts themselves and hope the lawyers will be more successful. A similar situation arises when a landlord must evict a tenant from a rental property. In these situations, the legal professional is asked to prepare a demand letter.

Too often the legal professional reaches into a file and pulls out the first available form, but there are alternatives to this approach. First, the writer should find out the facts and try to figure out why the debt has not been paid. Are there extenuating circumstances? Second, the writer should find out the law. Many laws deal with this facet of a firm's practice. A demand letter may be subject to fair debt collection practice laws, and failure to obey these laws can be quite costly.

A typical demand letter is illustrated in the appendix.

Opinion Letters

The United States Attorney General is routinely asked to give legal opinions to various governmental agencies. These opinions are published in a set of books called the *Opinions of the Attorney General.* Most states also publish the opinions of their attorneys general. These opinions can be used as persuasive authority.

Attorneys are asked almost daily for their opinions on various legal matters: the marketability of real estate, for example, or how the antitrust laws apply to a particular transaction, or the validity of a noncompetition clause in a business contract. Often the opinions are given in writing.

An opinion letter is structured and written like a memorandum. In fact, the main difference between the two documents is that the client reads the letter, whereas most memoranda are read by other legal professionals.

On the basis of the legal opinion, the client may make significant business decisions. If there are doubts about the opinions, these doubts need to be clearly stated so that the client can reasonably appraise the business risks and benefits.

The sample legal opinion letter in the appendix concerns the marketability of a real estate title. This letter is included not so much for the way the opinion itself is written but to show the way in which the lawyer spells out all his reservations on matters on which he is not giving an opinion.

Writing Exercises

Complete the following exercises.

1. Write a letter to XYZ Insurance Company explaining that your law firm will be representing Sam Hunt in a claim against their insured, Sally Gunn, due to an automobile accident that occurred on May 30, 1991. The adjuster is Steve Settle, whose address is 555 Settle Street, Insuranceville, Indiana 46666. The XYZ policy number is 8263. Because you once had a bad experience with that company, send your letter by certified mail. Enclose a copy of the police report. Send a blind copy to your client.

2. Your firm is representing Griswold and Buxton shortly after they were indicted by the State of Connecticut. Using the sample memorandum in the appendix as a guide, write a letter to them explaining the merits of their constitutional challenge to that indictment.

3. You represent a client who sustained a cervical strain in an automobile accident. Draft a letter to a physician requesting a narrative report concerning the present and future medical problems of that client. The physician is Dr. Sarah Saw, an orthopedic surgeon. It has been a year since the accident, and your client is still complaining of pain.

4. Write a short letter to your client informing the client of a final hearing date in his divorce case.

Enrichment Activities

Complete the following activities.

1. Your firm represents Estelle Griswold *prior* to her indictment. You want to persuade the prosecutor not to file charges in that case. Write a letter attempting to persuade the prosecutor not to file charges. What, if any, information would you exclude from the letter? Discuss.

2. Suppose your firm represents Estelle Griswold *before* she and C. Lee Buxton set up their clinic. They have asked you the legal ramifications of setting up a birth control clinic. Using the memorandum in the appendix as a guide, write an opinion letter to Ms. Griswold answering her question. Then discuss whether you would vary the letter from the memorandum.

3. Critique the settlement letter used as an example in the appendix. What are the strengths and weaknesses of that letter?

4. Critique the progress letter used as an example in the appendix. What are the strengths and weaknesses of that letter?

CHAPTER 9

TRANSACTION DOCUMENTS

Legal professionals often refer to the preparation of transaction documents as **legal drafting.** Legal drafting of contracts, leases, and other transaction documents is unlike most other forms of writing, and some say there is no comparable form of writing. In preparing a transaction document, the legal professional is sometimes a mere scrivener reporting the transaction or the deal. At other times, the drafter is an architect of the transaction itself. One legal professional may be able to rely on a form to prepare a contract, while another may need to write an entirely unique document to complete a transaction. This chapter explores the process of preparing transaction documents.

§ 9.1 Putting Together Legal Relationships

Transaction documents describe and memorialize the agreement parties reach about how they will carry out a transaction. Adverse parties sometimes enter transactions with different perspectives. Parties look for opposite interpretations in documents governing a transaction. Writing under these circumstances is different from other forms of writing.

The role of the legal drafter is more than just that of a writer and observer of a transaction. The legal drafter is also an integral part of the negotiation process. When drafting a contract, for instance, the drafter has the opportunity to include or omit provisions to benefit a client. Particular words can be selected to favor one side over another.

The way in which documents are drafted can affect the outcome of the negotiations. It is not unusual for a legal professional to present to the opposing side a draft that sours the deal because the document arouses suspicion or distrust. Distrust of the legal drafter can cause harm to a client.

TERMS

---

legal drafting†   The preparation of transaction documents.

Parties negotiating a contract or lease may be far apart in their negotiating positions until a short time before the execution of the document, and after the execution of the document, the parties may never again reach amicable terms. In such cases, the document must be written flexibly enough to permit the parties to agree and soundly enough to prevent future controversies.

In putting together legal relationships, the drafter must be sensitive to the objectives of the parties, the function of the document, any legal or ethical constraints on the transaction, the details of the transaction, and various other practical considerations.

Objectives of the Parties

Parties enter into transactions with different assumptions. A person selling a business usually wants to ensure that the price will be paid. The seller wants security. The person purchasing the business may be taking a risk and may want some flexibility in the relationship. Accordingly, parties read agreements looking for opposite interpretations. The drafter must recognize the objectives of each of the parties to the transaction. As a drafter begins to put a transaction on paper, the drafter must be able to see how the objectives of the parties may conflict in the future. Understanding the objectives of the parties enables a legal professional to anticipate future problems with the relationship created by the document.

Functions of Transaction Documents

Legal drafting serves three functions. First, the writing may record an event (a **fulfilling document**, such as a deed). A fulfilling document is prepared merely to memorialize an event. It is intended to serve as evidence of a transaction. In preparing this type of document, the main objective is to ascertain the facts and record them in compliance with applicable legal requirements.

A fulfilling document is used as a receipt where property of value exchanges hands or as a memorial for an event that the parties want recorded. For example, at the supermarket, money is paid and a receipt is issued. The receipt is a record of the transaction. Similarly, upon graduation

───────────── **TERMS** ─────────────

fulfilling document† Document that records an event; *e.g.*, a deed.

from high school, a diploma is received. This is a record of the event. Many legal transaction documents serve the same function as a receipt or diploma—to record a transaction or event.

Second, the writing may anticipate and provide for future eventualities (an **achieving document,** such as a lease, option, or contract). An achieving document, like a fulfilling document, memorializes a transaction, but the achieving document also lays out a framework for a future relationship. In preparing this type of document, the drafter must not only ascertain facts and comply with legal requisites to the transaction but also anticipate various events that might occur during the transaction. Then the drafter must chart the response to those events.

An achieving document envisions an ongoing transaction. The parties have already agreed to the details of that relationship and have anticipated most of the situations that might occur during the relationship. For instance, the parties may be selling a house on contract with payments to be made over a period of time. This relationship may continue for years. The achieving document must anticipate the future problems of the parties and then accurately deal with these contingencies.

Third, the writing may provide for a means or method to resolve future problems (a **regulating document,** such as a collective bargaining agreement or the bylaws of a corporation). A regulating document develops procedures to resolve future problems without necessarily directing a particular result. A regulating document is prepared when there will be an ongoing relationship between parties. For example, the bylaws of a corporation provide a way for shareholders to hash out problems without necessarily telling how a particular problem will be resolved. A grievance procedure in a collective bargaining agreement is a means to resolve disputes between labor and management.

Legal and Ethical Considerations

Legal and ethical considerations impose constraints on all legal documents. The most cleverly drafted transaction document is useless if it violates legal or ethical constraints.

TERMS

achieving document† Document that records a transaction and provides a framework for a future relationship; *e.g.,* a lease, option, or contract.

regulating document† Document that provides for a means to resolve future problems; *e.g.,* a collective bargaining agreement or corporate bylaws.

Legal Considerations

An important concern of every legal drafter is compliance with any legal requisites. How competently a document is drafted is unimportant if the drafter ignores the applicable rules. A complaint using legal-size paper when the local rules mandate letter-size paper cannot be filed. A will that was not properly witnessed when drafted cannot be probated. A deed or mortgage that is not properly notarized cannot be recorded.

Some jurisdictions mandate certain "magic" language for some types of transactions. A statute may require that a warranty deed contain the words *convey and warrant.* An option may need to be *irrevocable.* The drafter must spend the time necessary to check the statutes and case law applicable to the transaction. The extra time taken to become educated makes the next effort easier.

The law permits a wide latitude to parties in structuring transactions and relationships. This latitude is referred to as **freedom of contract.** An unorthodox way of structuring a deal may become the way of doing business in the future. The drafter must recognize, however, that there are some limits on the right to freedom of contract. For example, a contract is not permitted to have an illegal purpose such as gambling or prostitution. Even if there is a legal purpose, a contract cannot violate the **doctrine of unconscionability** or the rule respecting contracts of adhesion. The basic test of unconscionability is whether the provisions at issue are so one-sided as to be oppressive and unfair.

A **contract of adhesion** is a standardized contract drafted by parties of superior bargaining strength who present the contract on a take-it-or-leave-it basis. Many insurance contracts and warranty agreements of major retailers fit this criteria. The lesson here is that the drafter has much flexibility in structuring relationships, yet this flexibility is not without limits. Obviously, no matter how skillfully the documents have been

---

TERMS

freedom of contract   A phrase relating to the contract clause of the Constitution, which provides that "no state shall . . . pass any . . . law impairing the obligation of contracts." This provision is a constitutional guaranty of the right to acquire and possess property and to dispose of it as one wishes.

doctrine of unconscionability   Doctrine prohibiting contracts in which a dominant party has taken unfair advantage of a weaker party, who has little or no bargaining power, and has imposed terms and conditions that are unreasonable and one-sided.

contract of adhesion   A contract prepared by the dominant party (usually a form contract) and presented on a take-it-or-leave-it basis to the weaker party, who has no real opportunity to bargain about its terms.

prepared, if the court decides that an unconscionable document or a contract of adhesion has been drafted, the drafter's efforts have been for naught.

Ethical Considerations

There are ethical constraints on the role of drafter. Generally, it is not ethical to represent conflicting interests to a transaction. A lawyer, for example, may not represent both the buyer and the seller to the same transaction.

Ethics rules require that attorneys supervise the work of nonlawyer assistants. Ethics rules and statutes forbid the unauthorized practice of law. For example, when legal professionals work with clients, they must make sure that the clients are aware that their work is being supervised by an attorney.

At times, one party to a transaction is unrepresented. If the other side is unrepresented, the legal drafter should be cautious not to overreach but, at the same time, should try to advance the best interests of the client.

SIDEBAR

A legal professional who is not a lawyer must identify himself or herself as a legal professional in communications with clients and others. In a telephone call, the identification should be made at the beginning of the conversation. In letters, the legal professional's designation should appear under his or her signature.

The Details of the Transaction

Perhaps the biggest mistake of the novice drafter is failing to gather sufficient factual information about the transaction. If factual information is not ascertained, the legal professional has little basis for predicting future complications. In any area of the legal practice, legal professionals must know as much about the applicable transaction as the parties (and their experts). Drafting requires the legal professional to spend as much time becoming acquainted with the details of the transaction and the applicable law as he or she spends writing.

When a transaction document is complete, it should embody the deal as accurately as possible. The highest compliment for a drafter is to be told that the document accurately reflects the transaction contemplated by the parties. The drafter is engineering a transaction, and the documents are the blueprint for that deal. To put a transaction together, the drafter must understand the dynamics of the relationship between the parties. The deal should be workable, but this does not mean that the documents will be ironclad. There are no ironclad documents. Nevertheless, the more the drafter knows about the details of the transaction, the more likely the transaction can be completed successfully.

Finally, the drafter must become familiar with the jargon and practices of the client's business. The draft should be written in language used in the client's business so that the client can help spot problems the drafter may have overlooked. If language the client can understand is used, the parties will be able to work out differences long after the execution of the documents, rather than resorting to attorneys or other third parties.

Practical Considerations

Legal professionals must take into account many practical considerations when they draft transaction documents. Practical considerations can impose constraints that the writer must consider from the outset of the drafting process.

Time and Money Constraints

It is important to understand that not every client can afford a fifty-page contract—nor is it always necessary. Some clients want to pay a minimal fee for a simple document. Other clients are not so concerned with cost but want the document to provide as much security as possible.

The legal professional has only so much time to satisfy clients' demands. Every client's demands cannot be satisfied if the professional focuses all his or her energy on one case or transaction. Law is a profession, but it is also a business.

The Parties' Personalities

A skilled legal professional will draft a simple one-page agreement for a wary client who distrusts lawyers and a fifty-page agreement for a nit-picking client who wants every detail spelled out. A legal professional can build trust with a difficult party by keeping the agreement simple and may solidify a difficult deal by producing comprehensive provisions.

Be Creative but Selective

A skilled drafter can patch together difficult negotiations with creative solutions. An imagination can solve drafting dilemmas when parties are working toward completion of an agreement. Language bridges many misunderstandings. At times, however, a skilled drafter will choose not to broach a subject, either knowing how the law will resolve the problem or fearing that the negotiations could be stalemated. The skill is in knowing when to take the appropriate course of action.

Anticipate Future Problems

The writer must anticipate future problems likely to be encountered in the parties' relationship. Every legal professional has been blamed for adding "legal complications" when the parties "had everything worked out." Sometimes the personality of the legal professional frustrates the process. More often problems arise because the transaction is more complicated than the client originally envisioned. Even in simple transactions parties fail to anticipate many potential problems. Few people worry about termites or water damage, for example, until these problems affect them personally. Experience, however, indicates that such problems are common enough that a contract for sale of real estate should contain provisions for them. Such are the typical situations confronted daily by drafters of transaction documents.

Avoid Making Business Judgments

Normally the drafter of transaction documents should avoid making business judgments. In an attempt to solve problems, the legal professional may suggest alternative courses of action, but making business decisions is not ordinarily within the scope of the legal professional's expertise. The drafter should usually allow the client to steer the course of the negotiations. The business client knows the economics of the transaction better than most legal professionals.

Avoid Overreaching Conduct

Although the drafter of documents is obliged to represent a client's "best interests," such representation does not include **overreaching conduct**—that is, outwitting the opponent through trickery or deceit. From a practical standpoint, overreaching may kill the deal. It may also lead to a tumultuous relationship between the parties. If the agreement is viewed as a treaty between the parties, a signed treaty may exist—but an unworkable relationship may be created.

TERMS

---

overreaching conduct   Taking unfair advantage in bargaining. Overreaching by one party might cause a contract to be voided.

§ 9.2 Volunteering to Draft the Document

An experienced drafter gains as much for the client through the drafting process as through the negotiation process. In fact, seldom is the negotiation process completed until the drafting process is completed.

Advantages of Drafting the Document

The skilled drafter, as a matter of strategy, frequently opts to prepare the first draft of the documents relating to a transaction. To appreciate the advantages of preparing the first draft, the legal professional should consider the fact that many issues are preempted by this process. Choices made by the drafter may not even be considered by opposing counsel who later reviews the documents on behalf of the opposing party. Rather than suggesting alternative courses of action, many reviewing attorneys overlook important options and suggest only cosmetic language changes. The party who drafts the documents has much control over how the transaction is structured.

Disadvantages of Drafting the Document

Writing the first draft of a transaction document has some disadvantages. Ambiguities are construed against the party who prepares the document under the so-called *contra proferentem* doctrine. Moreover, if not carefully written, the first draft can scuttle negotiations. When the other side reviews a twenty-page document and recalls that only thirty minutes were spent discussing the transaction, distrust can surface. This distrust may kill a project that the client has dreamed about for years.

All too often lawyers are blamed for losing a deal when the first draft fails to mirror the original understanding reached during negotiations. Clients fail to understand that in many of these cases, the parties had never reached any agreement on most of the basic provisions of a transaction. Furthermore, writing the first draft can be time-consuming and, therefore, expensive to the client.

§ 9.3 Consulting Checklists and Form Books

Many transactions, such as leasing an apartment, are executed over and over again. The legal professional asks certain standard questions when interviewing the client. There are various checklists that can be consulted before an interview is conducted, and many form books are available to help in starting the writing process.

Use of Checklists

On arrival in the office, many clients announce that they have "arrived at a deal" and that the attorney should "prepare the papers." More times than not, the "deal" is nothing more than an agreement about price. The plethora of other terms customarily included in the agreement have not been discussed, much less negotiated. The task of the legal professional is to put the entire transaction together.

Before meeting with any client concerning a drafting task, at least a cursory check of the applicable law should be made and a checklist prepared. Many form books contain sample checklists of areas to cover. The checklist should be reviewed just before the meeting even if it is not rigidly adhered to in the interview. No legal professional can draft a document properly unless he or she knows what the client knows and what the client wants. A drafter must listen to the client and rely on the checklist only to double-check that nothing was missed. Reed Dickerson summarizes what to do during client interviews:

> Find out what the client wants to accomplish and what specific problems it involves. Explore the detailed possibilities with him and help him think the problem through . . . At this stage, the draftsman pumps the client for information. He points out any substantive inconsistencies that he thinks he sees in the idea . . . He mentions any . . . practical problems, and any drafting problems, that he thinks the client ought to know about.[1]

A good legal professional asks questions carefully, listening and following up on the answers given. A checklist is used as a guide, not as an immutable agenda.

Use of Forms

Most students are introduced to the law library in sessions that are brief and sometimes rather spotty. Often their introduction to legal form books is completely ignored in their curriculum. Yet almost any transaction document a legal professional will need to draft has been written before and probably is in a form book. In fact, when inexperienced legal professionals begin to prepare transaction documents, they are likely to be overwhelmed by the number of available form books. Many legal writers—and many rookie attorneys—fail to recognize the unevenness of the available forms. Not all forms are well written or well designed.

Types of Form Books

Form books can be substantive, procedural, or a combination of the two. A **substantive form book** provides forms dealing with various legal transactions (wills, trusts, leases, contracts). A **procedural form book** deals with court-related documents (complaints, answers, motions, interrogatories, jury instructions). Form books may be combined with textbook materials explaining the applicable law, may cover the entire spectrum of legal instruments, or may cover only a single subject such as contracts or torts. Form books may include tax advice or may incorporate tax information directly into the forms. Form books may be premised on the law of a particular jurisdiction, which is the case with those found in many continuing legal education materials.

Other Sources of Forms

Lawyers and their secretaries often keep applicable forms from previous transactions, and the legal professional inevitably collects forms from other lawyers. Recently a significant market has developed in computer-based forms—documents that can be accessed through computer software.

The Importance of Modifying Forms

When the drafter first looks for a client checklist, he or she should scan alternative forms as well. A form is helpful as a checklist, a guide, and a means to begin the drafting project, but total reliance on one is seldom good practice. Too many legal professionals simply convert an existing document to fit the client's situation rather than create a new document for the transaction. While forms are an excellent starting point, forms should not dictate the substance of the transaction.

Some legal writers rely too heavily on "canned" documents, or so-called boilerplate. In some situations, a document that has evolved through several lawsuits may prove to be more accurate than a hastily drafted original document. Too frequently, however, the canned forms are infested with problems. Many of them are outdated or simply

---

TERMS

substantive form book† Book that provides forms for transaction-related documents such as wills, trusts, leases, and contracts.

procedural form book† Book that provides forms for court-related documents such as complaints, answers, motions, interrogatories, and jury instructions.

inappropriate. Seldom will a form fit a particular transaction perfectly. Every form can be improved.

The Use of Litigated Forms   Some form books are filled with forms copied from cases that have been litigated. One reason why the form may have ended up in litigation is because it was not well drafted. As one writer noted:

> An adjudicated form is a form that has attached to it a certificate that there is something terribly wrong with it. If there were not something terribly wrong with it, it would not have been adjudicated.[2]

Another commentator offered these words regarding the use of litigated forms:

> At this point we should like to inject a parenthesis on "annotated" forms. After examining and checking a vast number of footnotes, we are convinced of one fact: case citations for substantive forms consume valuable space for very little purpose. For one thing, it has been said with some justice that a good form would not have been litigated in the first place; if the issue was truly one of construction or interpretation, the fault usually lay in a missing or ambiguous clause. Why, therefore, perpetuate the omission or ambiguity, with the chance that some other court will reject the interpretation in the cited case? A clear English sentence is worth volumes of precedent. In the second place, it is rare that an entire agreement should be in issue in litigation. Perhaps the case has turned on a single phrase in paragraph 15; perhaps there are a dozen other latent ambiguities or contingencies which have not happened to arise. Nevertheless, the entire document is soberly reprinted as an "adjudicated" form. Moreover, even if the point has been in issue and if the interpretation is reasonably reliable as precedent, what about the time factor? Is a 1910 agreement adequate for 1948 problems? In most cases, the economic background is so different, the changes in common and statute law have been so great (e.g., the income tax!), that the cited form is frequently more misleading than helpful. Weighing these factors, we have so altered most of the usable forms in the reported cases that the product is unrecognizable; and we have therefore refrained from cloaking them in the mantle of "authority."[3]

In determining whether to use an adjudicated document, the drafter should question whether the selected provision expresses the intent of the parties better than one the drafter is able to draft. This test alone should determine whether any adjudicated form should be used—or for that matter, whether another's work should be substituted for the drafter's own.

A document should be designed to prevent litigation between the parties. Although this is not always possible, the drafter should hesitate before adopting a form that obviously has failed the litigation-avoidance test. Repeating the mistakes of others is not a skillful way to practice any craft.

The Fear of Modifying Forms It is the author's experience that most legal professionals modify a form only with trepidation. One day a sign was placed on the interstate announcing the closing of the State of Delaware,[4] and most drivers turned around. Why? Because anything that looks official is unlikely to be questioned. If a printed lease is handed to a tenant, usually it is signed with no change. If a typewritten lease is handed to a tenant, it is likely to be changed. If something is declared to be "standard policy," it is very seldom questioned:

> Twenty years ago I was involved in the legal end of real estate. People came to me to sign their leases and have them countersigned. Most paid their security deposits and moved along without reading the forms. On rare occasions someone would say, "I'd like to read this lease before signing it. I have a constitutional right to do so!"
>
> I'd always reply, "Of course you have a right to do so. Go right ahead and read it! "
>
> Halfway through the form the person would exclaim, "Wait a second! Hold it! This document practically makes me an indentured servant for the duration of the lease!"
>
> I'd reply, "I doubt that. This is a standard form. There's the form number in the lower left corner."
>
> The person usually responded, "Oh . . . a standard form. Well, in that case . . ." and he or she would sign, bullied into submission by several printed digits that apparently possessed some magical property.[5]

Legal professionals approach forms from form books the same way the tenant reads the standard contract—reluctant to make any modifications.

Any legal professional who picks up a form should immediately make a substantial change to it. Once a substantial change is made, the professional will have the confidence necessary to begin drafting the remainder of the transaction. Every competent drafter experiences "printer phobia"—the fear of changing anything that has been printed. The cure is to change the form just for the sake of change, and then start rewording the document.

Integrating a Variety of Forms

A variety of forms should be gathered for a project. One form may overlook some needed language, while another may more closely mimic the particular relationship being structured. A word of caution: whenever forms are integrated, they must be checked for consistency in the language. A surprising number of disputes arise because the language of one form conflicts with the language of another, or because the language used in one clause may suggest a different meaning when different language is used to express the same concept in another clause.

Maintaining Consistency   Too many disputes are generated by hand-written changes to a printed document. When one form contains part of the necessary information and another form contains the remaining necessary information, these forms are sometimes spliced together. The danger of inconsistency becomes a very real problem. A blank in a printed contract is an invitation to litigation. When inserting language into the blank, the drafter must make sure that the words are consistent with the printed language. Otherwise, he or she will be courting litigation. Consistency should be maintained among any forms that have been spliced together as well as in the language in the particular document. Inconsistencies created by handwritten changes to printed forms have occurred frequently enough for the courts to develop a rule: ambiguity is resolved in favor of the interpretation suggested by the handwritten provision.

In drafting a simple truck lease, for example, when students are told to provide that the lessee cannot assign the lease, they repeatedly make the mistake of ending the lease with a boilerplate clause that declares the lease to be "binding upon the heirs, successors and *assigns of the parties.*" Although a court might reach the intended result in this situation, the inconsistency is not worth the risk of litigation. Substitute provisions inserted into an existing form must be revised to read consistently with the other language of the document.

The following quotation best sums up the use of forms:

> Should lawyers refrain from using legal boilerplate? They cannot operate efficiently without it. Indeed, they cannot operate even inefficiently without it. The danger in prefabricated legal text is not that all forms are bad, but that even good forms can be bad if they are used indiscriminately or without a thorough grasp of the specific objectives that they are intended to serve in the particular case.[6]

But consider what one form-book editor wrote, "In short, a good form book is a good tool for a good lawyer; it never can be a good substitute for a good lawyer."[7]

A good drafter develops good forms. The best writers are always improving form books.

§ 9.4 The Components of the Document

Organizational principles are not difficult to apply in the early stages of drafting legal documents because no particular structure is required.

This point cannot be overemphasized. There is no "right" way that an agreement must be structured. A perfect document can be drafted without using a single "witnesseth," without a "whereas," and without beginning "Know all men by these presents . . ." or ending with "In witness whereof . . ." Nevertheless, agreements do tend to follow a certain pattern.

Preamble

Typically, a legal document begin with a **preamble** that recites the parties to the transaction and identifies the type of document being created. For example, a lease might begin this way:

> This lease is made this_____day of_____, 199___, by _____ ("lessor") and _____ ("lessee").

The same format is used to start a contract, option, or other multi-party document. While this approach is not mandated, it does tell the reader at the start the type of transaction contemplated and the parties to the agreement.

Recitals

Recitals usually follow the preamble and provide the purpose of the agreement for the reader. Recitals are intended to give some background information related to the formation of the agreement:

> Recitals which usually follow the description of the parties are designed to store the background or purposes of the agreement and often set forth matters of inducement or representation to create an estoppel. They are used to foreclose inquiring into the surrounding circumstances and previous negotiations. If the recitals are clear and the operative part is ambiguous, the recitals govern the construction. If the recitals are ambiguous, and the operative part is clear, the operative part must prevail. If both the recitals and the operative part are clear, but they are inconsistent with each other, the operative part is to be preferred. But recitals should be used with caution and a skillful draftsman will rarely resort to their use. A contract should explain itself and if a preamble or recital is

---

TERMS

preamble† Introductory part of a legal document, which identifies the parties and the type of document.

recitals† Statements that follow the preamble in a transaction document, outlining the purpose of the agreement and providing a brief background for the reader.

required to make it clear, it is generally a sign that the draft requires revision.[8]

In older documents (and in documents copied from older documents), the recitals may begin with the archaic expression "Witnesseth . . ." There is no reason to use this term or any other particular expression. A heading such as "Recitals" or "Background" may be chosen.

Courts vary as to whether they will interpret the recitals as part of the agreement, but if the drafter remembers that in preparing an agreement, he or she is writing part of the transcript of the trial involving the agreement, it cannot hurt to pad the recitals. Many defense firms, however, prepare lengthy recitals in release documents. Often these recitals greatly exaggerate the potential claims that are asserted. If the release is voided for some reason, these padded recitals may not be the actual script they want written for the jury.

In many cases, the drafter begins each new recital with a *whereas*. For example:

> Whereas the lessor is the owner of certain real estate described by Exhibit A hereto; Whereas the lessee is desirous of leasing this real estate;

There is no reason other than custom to begin the clauses with *whereas*, but many legal professionals do so.

Consideration

Usually the document then recites that there is **consideration** of some sort, in language such as the following:

> NOW, THEREFORE, in consideration of the mutual promises and agreements of the parties hereto, the parties now agree as follows:

Consideration is an act, forbearance, or promise that has an economic value and is used to create an enforceable contract. In some situations, the consideration must be recited in the body of the contract. Even where the

---

================ TERMS ================

consideration   The reason a person enters into a contract; that which is given in exchange for performance or the promise to perform; the price bargained and paid; the inducement. Consideration is an essential element of a valid and enforceable contract. A promise to *refrain* from doing something one is entitled to do also constitutes consideration.

consideration is not required to be stated, it is almost always good practice to do so.

Operative Provisions

The next section contains the operative provisions of the agreement. If there are definitions or preliminary terms, these usually are placed first. Boilerplate and housekeeping provisions, such as the provisions dealing with the assignability of the document, applicable law, notice provisions, and so on, usually are found at the end. Boilerplate provisions are the routine provisions found in all similar contracts.

The Parties' Signatures

Finally, the document typically ends with a sentence evidencing the signatures of the parties. For example:

> In witness whereof, the parties hereto have set their hands on the date first written.

A much simpler ending is also appropriate. Again, no particular form is usually required.

The Importance of Logical Structure

Although the drafter has considerable latitude in the design of legal documents, the experienced drafter soon discovers that the logic of an agreement can be tested by a study of its structure. Some writers cannot begin to write without a structured outline, and no writer should end the writing process without a careful concern for the elementary principles of arrangement.

§ 9.5 Examples of Transaction Documents

A legal professional is expected to be able to prepare many different types of transaction documents. This section examines some of the more commonly drafted documents.

Bills of Sale

A bill of sale is used when personal property is sold. The bill of sale is a simple receipt. Figure 9–1 is an example of a bill of sale.

THIS FORM HAS BEEN APPROVED BY THE INDIANA STATE BAR ASSOCIATION FOR USE BY LAWYERS ONLY. THE SELECTION OF A FORM OF INSTRUMENT, FILLING IN BLANK SPACES, STRIKING OUT PROVISIONS AND INSERTION OF SPECIAL CLAUSES, CONSTITUTES THE PRACTICE OF LAW AND MAY ONLY BE DONE BY A LAWYER.

BILL OF SALE

This Indenture Witnesseth, That

(''Transferor'') of _____ County, State of _____

in consideration of

Dollars ($ _____), the receipt of which is

acknowledged by Transferor, grants, sells, transfers and delivers to

(''Transferee'') of _____ County, State of _____

the following described personal property (''Property''):

SAMPLE

The Property is transferred to and for the benefit of Transferee and Transferee's successors, assigns and personal and legal representatives. Transferor makes the following representations under oath: (1) Transferor is the lawful owner of the Property; (2) the Property is free from all encumbrances and lawful claims for possession of others; (3) Transferor has the legal right to sell the Property; and (4) Transferor will warrant and defend the Property against the lawful claims and demands of all persons.

STATE OF   )
) SS:
COUNTY OF   )

Dated this _____ day of _____ , 19____

     Before me, the undersigned, a Notary Public, in and for said County and State, this _____ day of _____ , 19_____ , personally appeared:

and acknowledged the execution of the foregoing Bill of Sale. In witness whereof, I have subscribed my name and affixed my official seal.

My Commission Expires: _____ _____

_____
                NOTARY PUBLIC

Resident of _____ County

This instrument was prepared by _____ , Attorney at Law.

Reprinted with permission of Allen County Bar Association.

FIGURE 9–1   A Bill of Sale

Deeds

When real estate exchanges hands, the transaction is recorded by a deed. There are various types of deeds. A warranty deed is used when the party selling the real estate warrants title to the property. A quitclaim deed is used when the party sells whatever the party owns without a warranty. A corporate deed is used when a corporation conveys real estate. A sheriff's deed is used in cases such as foreclosures. An example of a warranty deed appears as Figure 9–2.

Corporate Documents

When a corporation is formed, **articles of incorporation** are prepared. The articles of incorporation serve as a record that the corporation is properly incorporated. An example of articles of incorporation is shown in Figure 9–3.

When a corporation is formed, the shareholders must set up rules for handling the affairs of the corporation. These rules are called **corporate bylaws**. The bylaws establish a board of directors, identify officers for the corporation and their duties, and set forth requirements regarding voting or shareholder issues and various other matters. Figure 9–4 shows an excerpt from a set of bylaws. The board of directors and the shareholders hold meetings. The records of these meetings are called minutes. An example of corporate minutes is found in the appendix.

Promissory Notes

One of the simpler achieving documents is a promissory note. A promissory note is a promise to pay a certain sum over a period of time. An example of a promissory note is included as Figure 9–5.

When preparing a promissory note, as when preparing bills of sale or deeds, the drafter usually starts with a form and fills in the blanks.

<hr>

TERMS

articles of incorporation The charter or basic rules that create a corporation and by which it functions.

corporate bylaws† Rules that establish a corporate board of directors, identify officers and their duties, and set forth requirements regarding voting or shareholder issues.

THIS FORM HAS BEEN APPROVED BY THE INDIANA STATE BAR ASSOCIATION FOR USE BY LAWYERS ONLY. THE SELECTION OF A FORM OF INSTRUMENT, FILLING IN BLANK SPACES, STRIKING OUT PROVISIONS AND INSERTION OF SPECIAL CLAUSES, CONSTITUTES THE PRACTICE OF LAW AND MAY ONLY BE DONE BY A LAWYER.

Mail tax bills to: Tax Key No.:_____

WARRANTY DEED

This indenture witnesseth that

of   *County in the State of*

Convey and warrant to

of   *County in the State of*
for and in consideration of
the receipt whereof is hereby acknowledged, the following Real Estate in   *County*
in the State of Indiana, to wit:

SAMPLE

State of Indiana,   **County, ss:** | **Dated this** _____ **Day of** _____ **19**____
Before me, the undersigned, a Notary Public in and for said
County and State, this   *day of*   _____
         19   *personally appeared:*

_____

_____

_____

An acknowledged the execution of the foregoing deed.   _____
In witness whereof, I have hereunto subscribed my name
and affixed my official seal. My commission expires   _____
_____ *19*

                                                          _____
_____
                              Notary Public   _____

Resident of _____ *County.*

This instrument prepared by _____ *Attorney at Law*

MAIL TO: COPYRIGHT THE ALLEN COUNTY INDIANA BAR ASSOCIATION, INC.   Rev. 8/87

Reprinted with permission of Allen County Bar Association.

FIGURE 9–2   A Warranty Deed

ARTICLES OF INCORPORATION
State Form 4159 (R6 / 3-88)

INSTRUCTIONS: *Use 8½ x 11 inch white paper for inserts.*
Filing requirements - Present original and
one copy to the address in the upper right
corner of this form.

Provided by: EVAN BAYH
Secretary of State
Room 155, State House
Indianapolis, Indiana 46204
(317) 232-6576
Indiana Code 23-1-21-2
FILING FEE $90.00

ARTICLES OF INCORPORATION OF

(Indicate the appropriate act)
The undersigned desiring to form a corporation (herein after referred to as "Corporation") pursuant to the provisions of:

☐ Indiana Business Corporation Law   ☐ Indiana Professional Corporation Act 1983

As amended, executes the following Articles of Incorporation:

ARTICLE I NAME

Name of Corporation

(The name must contain the word "Corporation," "Incorporated," "Limited," "Company" or an abbreviation of one of those words.)

ARTICLE II REGISTERED OFFICE AND AGENT

(The street address of the corporation's initial registered office in Indiana and the name of its initial registered agent at that office is:)
Name of Agent

Street Address of Registered Office   ZIP Code

ARTICLE III AUTHORIZED SHARES

Number of shares: _____
If there is more than one class of shares, shares with rights and preferences, list such information
on "Exhibit A."

ARTICLE IV INCORPORATORS
(The name(s) and address(es) of the incorporator(s) of the corporation:)

NAME	NUMBER and STREET OR BUILDING	CITY	STATE	ZIP CODE

In Witness Whereof, the undersigned being all the incorporators of said corporation execute these Articles of Incorporation and verify, subject to penalties of perjury, that the statements contained herein are true.

this _____ day of _____ 19 _____ .

Signature	Printed Name
Signature	Printed Name
Signature	Printed Name

This instrument was prepared by (Name)

Address (Street, Number, City and State)   ZIP Code

FIGURE 9–3   Articles of Incorporation

FIGURE 9–4
Corporate
Bylaws

BYLAWS
of
XYZ CORPORATION

ARTICLE I. OFFICE

SECTION 1.1. PRINCIPAL OFFICE. The principal office of the corporation shall be located in the City of Evansville, Vanderburgh County, State of Indiana. The corporation may have such other offices, either within or without the State of Indiana, as the Board of Directors may designate, or as the business of the corporation may from time to time require.

SECTION 1.2. REGISTERED AGENT AND OFFICE. The name of the first registered agent of the corporation is _____. The office of the resident agent of the corporation, required by the Indiana General Corporation Act to be maintained in the State of Indiana, may be, but need not be, identical with the principal office of the corporation, and the address of the registered office where the resident agent is located may be changed from time to time by the Board of Directors as provided by law.

ARTICLE II. MEETINGS OF SHAREHOLDERS

SECTION 2.1. ANNUAL MEETING. An annual meeting of the shareholders, for the purpose of electing directors and for the transaction of such other business as may come before the meeting, shall be held on the 31st day in the month of December in each year, beginning with the year _____ or on such other day within such month as shall be fixed by the Board of Directors. If the day fixed for the annual meeting shall be a legal holiday in the State of Indiana, such meeting shall be held on the next succeeding business day. If for any reason the annual meeting has not been called within six (6) months after the time designated for the meeting, any shareholder may call the annual meeting. If the election of directors shall not be held on the day designated herein for any annual meeting of the shareholders, or at any adjournment thereof, the Board of Directors shall cause the election to be held at a special meeting of the shareholders as soon thereafter as may be convenient.

SECTION 2.2. SPECIAL MEETINGS. Special meetings of the shareholders which may be held for any purpose or purposes, unless otherwise prescribed by law, may be called by the President, by a majority of the Board of Directors and must be called by the President or Secretary at the request of the holders of not less than twenty-five percent (25%) of all outstanding shares entitled to vote at such meeting.

FIGURE 9–5
A Promissory
Note

THIS FORM HAS BEEN APPROVED BY THE INDIANA STATE BAR ASSOCIATION FOR USE BY LAWYERS ONLY. THE SELECTION OF A FORM OF INSTRUMENT, FILLING IN BLANK SPACES, STRIKING OUT PROVISIONS AND INSERTION OF SPECIAL CLAUSES, CONSTITUTES THE PRACTICE OF LAW AND SHOULD BE DONE BY A LAWYER.

PROMISSORY NOTE

Indiana, _____ , 19__

I promise to pay to the order of

the sum of

as follows:

payable at

With interest at the rate of ___ percent per annum payable _____ from date during such period when there shall be no delinquency, but with interest at the rate of ___ percent per annum during such period of any delinquency, and with attorneys' fees, without any relief whatever from Valuation or Appraisement Laws. The drawers, sureties, guarantors and endorsers severally waive presentment for payment, protest, notice of protest and non-payment of this note and agree that on default in payment of this note or any part, principal or interest when due, the whole amount remaining unpaid shall, without notice of non-payment or demand of payment immediately become due and payable. The receipt of interest in advance or the extension of time shall not release or discharge any endorser, surety or guarantor on this note.

_____

_____

_____

This instrument prepared by _____ *Attorney at Law*

Leases

Many students are familiar with leases. A **lease** is a bilateral agreement that sets forth the terms for the rental of real estate. The lease is an excellent

TERMS

lease A contract for the possession of real estate in consideration of payment of rent, ordinarily for a term of years or months, but sometimes at will.

example of an achieving document. The lease maps out the rights of the tenant and the rights of the landlord. It structures a relationship that continues over time. It anticipates problems that might occur over the course of the relationship.

The lease usually includes basic information about the following:

- The parties
- Identification of the premises
- Term of the lease
- Amount of rent and when rent is to be paid
- Insurance
- Taxes
- Security deposit
- Parking
- Utilities

Some clients want a simple lease, while others want every contingency covered. The legal professional must determine whether the client wants a simple or detailed lease.

Contract for the Sale of Real Estate

Another commonly prepared achieving document is a contract for the sale of real estate. Like the lease, the real estate contract structures the terms of an ongoing real estate relationship, so many of the basic terms are similar to those of a lease. The principal difference between a real estate lease and a contract is that at the end of the term of the contract, the purchaser owns the property.

Writing Exercises

Complete the following exercises.

1. Your supervisor asks you to prepare a truck lease. The client is XYZ Company, which owns a 1958 dump truck that it wants to lease to Jane Smith. XYZ

Company realizes that Smith is not particularly creditworthy but feels that the risk is justified. However, it wants you to prepare a lease that protects XYZ as much as possible. The lease is for a term of two years and for a monthly rental of $500. Prepare a lease for this transaction. Make the lease nonassignable.

2. Your supervisor asks you to prepare a truck lease. The client is Jane Smith, who desires to lease a dump truck from the XYZ Company. The XYZ Company has submitted a lease to her, but it is totally unsatisfactory. The lease is for a term of two years and for a monthly rental of $500. Prepare a lease for the transaction. Prepare the lease to protect Jane Smith as much as possible. Make the lease assignable.

3. Jane Smith wants a truck lease that is assignable. XYZ Company wants a truck lease that is nonassignable. XYZ Company wants control over the person or entities who can use the truck. Jane Smith is not sure she wants to be a truck driver. Therefore, she wants to be able to assign the lease if she decides to get out of the truck-driving business. Discuss at least two provisions that might solve this situation.

4. Prepare a simple will. Your firm represents a young couple who want to leave their total estate to each other. If they both die at the same time, they want to leave their estate to their only child, who is a minor. The clients' names are Sam and Linda Washington. Their daughter is Yolinda. They want Sam's brother, Ralph Washington, and his wife Melinda to be the guardians for the person and estate of Yolinda. They will name each other as the personal representative for their respective estates, and they desire the personal representative to serve with no bond or with a minimal bond. Prepare the wills for Sam and Linda. The wills should comply with the laws of your state in all respects.

5. Make a copy of the apartment lease of a friend or classmate.

   a. List future problems that have been anticipated and solved by the lease.

   b. List at least five future problems that might occur but have not been anticipated by the lease.

6. Copy a fulfilling document not identified in the text.

Enrichment Activities

Complete the following activities.

1. Go to the office where real estate transactions for your county are recorded. Inspect documents from 1900, 1950, and the present. Make a report of the similarities and differences between how these documents have been prepared. Pay attention to length, wording, signature practices, and content.

2. Your supervisor tells you that a client who is selling her grocery business has made an appointment. Your supervisor wants you to conduct the interview.

The only details are that the client is renting the building and is selling the equipment and inventory. Payments will be made over time.

    a. Prepare a checklist of questions to ask the client during the interview.

    b. Name the different documents that might need to be prepared for the transaction.

    c. Prepare a contract for such a sale.

3. You desire to purchase a house on a two-acre lot. You will be paying a monthly amount to the seller over a period of five years, and then you will pay the balance of the contract. There is no realtor involved. You work for a law firm and the firm believes that it would be a good experience for you to prepare the contract.

    a. List problems that could go wrong during the term of the contract.

    b. What details should be taken care of in the contract?

    c. Review several forms. Are the forms more seller or purchaser oriented? Explain.

    d. Prepare the contract.

4. Form a corporation with a classmate for the purpose of providing legal professional services. Submit the articles of incorporation on a form used by your state. Then do the following:

    a. Negotiate a shareholders' agreement with the classmate. Prepare this agreement and a set of bylaws for the corporation.

    b. List future problems that might occur between you and your classmate after the corporation is functioning.

    c. Discuss how you solved these problems in the shareholders' agreement.

Notes

1 Reed Dickerson, *The Fundamentals of Legal Drafting* 36 (Boston: Little, Brown, 1965).

2 C. A. Beardsley, *Beware of, Eschew, and Avoid Pompous Prolixity and Platitudinous Epistles,* 16 Cal. S.B.J. 65, 66 (1941).

3 J. Rabkin and M. H. Johnson, 1 *Current Legal Forms with Tax Analysis* viii (New York: Matthew Bender, 1979).

4 Herb Cohen, *You Can Negotiate Anything* 59 (New York: Bantam Books, 1980).

5 *Id.* at 28.

6 Reed Dickerson, *Some Jurisprudential Implications of Electronic Data Processing,* 18 Law & Contemp. Probs. 61 (1963).

7 J. Rabkin and M. H. Johnson, 1 *Current Legal Forms with Tax Analysis* ix (New York: Matthew Bender, 1979).

8 J. G. Thomas, *Problems in Drafting Legal Instruments,* 39 Ill. B.J. 51, 55 (1950).

CHAPTER 10

LEGAL MEMORANDA

The law is only a memorandum.
Ralph Waldo Emerson,
"Politics," **Essay: Second Series**
(1844)

In England, there are two types of lawyers: **barristers** present oral arguments to the court, while **solicitors** advise clients and prepare written memoranda to assist barristers with their arguments. The memorandum that educates a British barrister on the legal points of a case serves essentially the same function in American law. Lawyers and other legal professionals prepare memoranda to educate other members of their firm about legal situations. The first writing experience of many law students is usually the preparation of a legal memorandum.

§ 10.1 What Is a Memorandum?

A memorandum is a written opinion on a legal matter that is usually prepared for intraoffice use. Rarely will a memorandum leave the law office. The memorandum is an informative and descriptive form of writing.

There are many reasons to write memoranda. A memorandum may be prepared to help with decision making: Should the firm accept a certain case? Should the client pursue or defend a claim? What action should a senior partner take in a problem case? A client may ask how a law applies to a given fact situation, and this query will be addressed by writing a memorandum.

Legal memorandum writing involves applying rules of law to fact problems. When a memorandum is prepared, the legal professional goes through the same thought process that a court may go through later to decide this particular problem. The difference is that the memorandum writer renders an opinion about what the result may be, whereas the judge actually decides the result. Most memorandum writers never recognize the similarity between what they do and what a court does.

§ 10.2 Preparing to Write a Memorandum— Some General Guidelines

Because most memoranda are read only by clients and other members of the law firm, the details of preparation vary from firm to firm. Nonetheless, several general guidelines are applicable to all facets of memorandum writing.

Give a Neutral Analysis

A memorandum should be written from a neutral point of view. A client may not appreciate abstract questions or theoretical answers. A good memorandum explores problems and finds acceptable solutions. The more the legal professional researches and thinks about a situation, the more likely he or she is to discover new approaches and favorable arguments for the client. Each argument and approach should be explored, and the memorandum should be used as a springboard for developing solutions.

The legal professional must not make the mistake of betraying his or her own feelings about whether a particular law is good or bad. Editorializing is not the mark of a professional. A legal professional asked to prepare a memorandum on an abortion question, for example, should describe the law, not what the individual feels the law ought to be.

Get Sufficient Instructions

Students like direction. If a teacher gives vague instructions, students typically complain. Most students want the comfort of structure, but in a law office, poor or inadequate instructions may be given. The lawyer assigning the memorandum may give vague instructions because the client's request is vague or because there is inadequate time to give a more detailed explanation. Unfortunately, sometimes poor instructions are all the instructions the professional receives. The legal professional who is assigned a memorandum to write, however, should try to find out as much information as possible.

Ascertain the Objectives of the Memorandum

The writer must first clarify the purpose of the memorandum—find out why the memorandum is necessary. Before writing, the writer should learn as much about the background of the memorandum as possible: the client objectives, the facts, the law, and the issues. Is it a preliminary assessment of the merits of a case? Will the contents be shown to the client or to other firm members? How much time should be devoted to the memorandum? Spending a few extra minutes at the preliminary stage to ascertain as much background information as possible saves hours of work later in the project.

Learn the Facts

The writer must find out the facts about the client's problem. Often the reason the writer becomes stymied in researching a problem is that he or she has an incomplete picture of the facts. When this happens, the subtleties of the problem are seldom appreciated. Extra time spent to learn about the facts saves many research hours.

Gather the Source Authority

The next step is to gather the relevant source materials as discussed in Chapter 2. If the problem is governed by a statute or regulation, a copy of this law should be made. Some firms prefer that the relevant authority be copied in the body of the memorandum. The writing process begins during research and does not end until the research is complete. In research, attention must be paid to the legal questions arising from the facts. If new issues are uncovered, these issues should be researched as well.

Organize the Issues

After gathering the source law and reviewing any secondary sources necessary to understanding the problem, the writer needs to organize the issues. In fact, it is usually a good idea to make an outline of the main points of a memorandum. Only then will the writer be ready to start the actual writing.

§ 10.3 Form of the Memorandum

Unlike the brief, which may have strict requirements as to form, there is no standard form that legal professionals must follow for a memorandum. The form of the memorandum differs from firm to firm and even from lawyer to lawyer. A memorandum should always contain pertinent client identification, a date, the legal professional's name, and a title. (See the sample memorandum in the appendix.) The memorandum also needs to contain the question or questions addressed by it, a statement of relevant facts, a discussion section, and a conclusion. In this regard, the structure of a memorandum is similar to that of a case brief, discussed in Chapter 2. The fact section of a case brief is the same as the statement of facts section in a memorandum. The questions addressed are the legal issues. The discussion section is similar to the legal reasoning section, and the conclusion is similar to the holding.

The reader must understand the scope of the memorandum. In all memoranda, any limitations should be explicitly stated. If certain issues have not been covered, the document should say so. If alternative arguments might lead to the same result, the alternatives should be described. In more complex memoranda, an introduction or summary section may be included to describe the main points of the memorandum. This section might include an outline of the memorandum or other background information.

Facts of the Memorandum

Clients come to lawyers with problems. The client tells the lawyer a story. The story may involve a dispute, or the story may only involve a potential dispute. On the other side of the dispute might be an individual, a company, or a governmental agency. The other party to the dispute may also be seeking legal advice. This is the peculiar work of the legal system: to prevent or resolve disputes, to plan around problems, and to structure relationships or to undo them.

The Importance of the Facts

The legal system resolves disputes by applying rules of law to them. There are hundreds of thousands of rules of law. The facts determine what rule of law applies. New facts may create new rules of law or may result in an old rule being applied in a new way. Consider the law as a catalog with hundreds of thousands of rules. As the legal professional is given the facts, he or she consults the catalog and selects the rule that best fits this problem. The right principle cannot be selected without knowledge of the factual dimensions of the problem. Sometimes the catalog does not have a rule that fits the facts, and then a new rule has to be created. This is how important facts are to the legal professional.

Legal problems are fact-sensitive—even a slight fact variation may change the rule or principle used to decide a case. Times change the facts as well. Consider, for example, *Roe v. Wade. Roe*, the case addressing the right to abortion, was decided in 1973. At that time, neonatal care was not as advanced as it is in the 1990s. Changes in modern medicine have advanced the date of viability, and this fact could affect a current analysis of *Roe*. As facts change, so does the analysis of issues. Fact analysis might change a result.

Too many legal professionals pay too little attention to the facts. The facts should be written as clearly and completely as a novelist tells a story. Some overemphasize the importance of legal principles when developing memoranda. Facts should receive as much attention as legal principles. Facts determine what principles apply to a dispute and may bend principles or reshape them. Facts determine the outcome of cases.

Legal professionals may be tempted to abbreviate the fact section of the memorandum under the assumption that their supervisors and the client already know the facts. There are several reasons why the facts should be thoroughly stated. First, the writer's opinion is based on a certain fact pattern. The fact pattern relied on should be clear to anyone who reads the memorandum. Second, the writer's supervisor should not have to reread the entire file to learn the key facts of the case.

Present the Facts in Narrative Form

The facts should be presented in a narrative form and should tell a story. The facts should be written in the third person and in the past tense unless the events are still occurring when the brief is written. As the story is narrated, the facts should be related in an organized manner. They can be developed by chronology or by cause and effect. For example, a cause-and-effect outline in a personal injury case might separate the accident details from the injury details. The most important facts may be put first and the least important facts later. Whatever method is used, the facts should not be presented haphazardly.

Present the Facts Objectively

The writer must not be judgmental of the facts. The facts in a memorandum should be presented neutrally. The fact section of the memorandum should not assess the merits of the facts. Any comment on how an assessment of the facts would change the analysis should be reserved for the discussion section of the memorandum. The writer should pay attention to facts that might cause a court to be sympathetic to the opponent's case as well as the client's case. It is not unusual for the result of a case to hinge on whose version of the facts is accepted by the court.

Suppose, for example, a client is bitten by a dog. In some states, it might be necessary to prove that the owner knew the dog had demonstrated dangerous propensities before this incident in order to establish that the owner of the dog is liable. One side might show an incident of the dog growling or nipping at another dog. Perhaps the dog's owner will bring in witnesses to show how lovable and peaceful this dog is. These neighbors might explain that the only time the dog was ever aggressive was when someone teased it. The facts may be evenly balanced, making it difficult to predict the outcome.

Develop All the Facts

Often the inability to make progress on researching or writing a memorandum stems from the lack of factual development of the case. Nothing is more crucial to the analysis than the development of the facts. On some occasions, the facts are given. On other occasions, the facts are hotly controverted. It may be difficult to know whether the client's version or the opposing party's version is correct. Both sides of the facts should be presented.

Issues in the Memorandum

Memoranda are much easier to write once the writer has focused the issues. As the research continues, what began as a one-issue problem may turn into a multiple-issue problem. Consider the dog-bite situation. As this case is prepared for trial, the lawyer might look to see if the client was a trespasser, licensee, or invitee. The owner of a dog may owe a different duty to a trespasser than to a guest. Another issue might be whether different standards of care apply to children and adults.

Issues can splinter as research continues. It is not unusual to begin researching one issue, only to discover several other important issues. Issues can also narrow. Research may reveal that the law is too settled to be contested and that it would be useless in the situation to pursue the issue any further. On the other hand, the situation may fit a narrow exception to a rule and, by phrasing the rule more specifically, the writer can better position the argument. Issues can also be combined. Several issues may really pertain to a broader question.

The Importance of the Issues

Nothing focuses and organizes a memorandum better than well-written issues. How issues are grouped or splintered and how they are ordered determines structure better than the most detailed outline. If the writer pays attention to the issues, structure will fall into place.

The presentation of the issues can even change the analysis of a problem. A good illustration of this point comes from Judge David Souter's testimony before the United States Senate during confirmation hearings prior to his appointment to the Supreme Court. Souter noted the tension between the right-to-exercise-religion clause and the establishment-of-religion clause of the First Amendment. On the one hand, the First Amendment to the United States Constitution guarantees the free exercise of religion. On the other hand, it ensures separation of church and state. A landmark Supreme Court case said Amish children could not be forced to attend high school against their religious beliefs. Judge Souter suggested this landmark case might have been decided differently had a state passed a law exempting the Amish child from attending high school. Then it might have been argued the state was favoring one religion over another.

How issues are framed determines the outcome of cases. Many experienced legal writers believe issue writing is crucial to the analysis. What questions are asked and how they are asked is determined by the writer, and often making this determination is the most important function of the legal writer.

The Format of the Issues

Issue writing is an art. Usually issues are written in a question form. An issue should emphasize the facts or law as appropriate. An issue should not be written as a sterile question but should incorporate the key facts of the problem. When the facts are incorporated into the statement of the issue, the issue becomes more concrete and less abstract. Consider the following statement of an issue, which does a good job of combining the facts with the legal problem:

> Was an indigent defendant charged with attempted robbery deprived of the assistance of counsel as protected by the due process clause of the Fourteenth Amendment when appointed counsel did not see or talk to the defendant until thirty minutes before trial, did not ask but one question at trial, did not interview or call witnesses, did not speak on the defendant's behalf at sentencing, and did not inform the defendant of his right to appeal?

The issues in memoranda, like the facts, should be neutrally written. The issue in a memorandum should not suggest the result. The statement of the issue above is from a brief rather than a memorandum and is written in a manner to suggest a result. A statement of the issue in a memorandum should be more neutrally written.

The Discussion Section of the Memorandum

The discussion section of a memorandum explains the reasoning process from the issue to the conclusion. Before preparing the discussion section, the writer should consider how a judge thinks.

A judge hears a story—often more than one version of it—and as the story unfolds, the judge is presented with issues or questions to resolve. The judge must select the legal principles (a statute or case law) applicable to the dispute and then apply these rules to the facts of the case in order to reach a conclusion or holding (the *ratio decidendi*). Most discussion sections in memoranda follow this same approach.

The Format of the Discussion Section

The discussion section can involve the analysis of very simple questions or very complex legal questions. The general approach, however, is the same.

Simple Issues   If the issue is simple and the rule of law to be applied to the dispute is fairly obvious, the discussion section of the memorandum can be structured as follows:

1. Issue
2. Rule of law
3. Application of rule
4. Conclusion

In law school, this approach is sometimes referred to by the acronym IRAC: issue, rule, application of rule, and conclusion.

Consider how these principles might be applied to the dog-bite case. The following is a sample memorandum in a case where the dog has never bitten anyone before, but the dog has snarled at the mail carrier and snapped at the ankles of several small children. The concern in this case is that the dog has never actually bitten anyone before. Your client has been seriously injured. Examine this short discussion:

Issue	The sole issue discussed is whether an owner of a dog that has demonstrated dangerous propensities can be held liable for damages caused by a dog bite even if the dog has not bitten anyone before

Rule	this incident. The law is settled in Indiana that owners are liable for a dog bite if the dog has dangerous propensities. A dog can demonstrate dangerous propensities without actually biting
Application of rule to facts	someone. Once an owner notices a pet may pose a threat to others, the owner is under a duty to prevent injury. When a dog has snarled and snapped at children and others, the owner is on
Conclusion	notice the dog poses a possible threat. In this case the owner was on notice of the dangerous propensities and should be held liable.

Notice how the issue, rule, analysis, and conclusion are developed. This format, which starts with the issue, identifies the rule, applies the rule of law to the facts, and arrives at the conclusion, is an effective format to follow.

This format need not be followed precisely in every case, however. At times the rule or principle, or even the conclusion, can be stated first. As the rules to be applied become more complex, some sections will need to be expanded more than others. For example, as the facts become more controverted, more of the memorandum must address the factual differences on the conclusion. The memorandum should describe how the result will change if the court believes one version of the story over the other version. At times, both the rule of law and the facts can be in doubt, and in such situations, the analysis can be quite lengthy.

Complex Issues   In many instances, memoranda will analyze more than one issue. Each issue should be discussed under a separate subhead. If three issues are developed in the memorandum, three subheadings should be inserted in the discussion section. Each subhead should be written in a declarative sentence and combine the key facts with the legal principle. Examine the subheads in the *Griswold* appellant brief in the appendix.

When legal issues become more complex, usually it is because the legal principles are more abstract. In many cases, the best advice is to recognize the likelihood that a more definite or concrete answer is not possible. Recognizing the fact that a clear-cut answer cannot possibly be provided takes considerable pressure off the writer in formulating the discussion section in the memorandum.

No matter how complicated the problem, the writer will be trying to apply the appropriate legal principle to the facts of the case. The manner in which the writer organizes and states the issues can help considerably in dealing with complex problems. Breaking the issues into narrower issues or subparts and trying to reduce general principles into narrower principles will aid the analysis process.

The Use of Logic in the Discussion Section

Legal principles should be developed and applied using deductive and inductive logic.

Deductive Logic A memorandum in the dog-bite situation could be developed like a syllogism in logic. The rule of law is the major premise. The facts are the minor premise. The conclusion flows from these statements. The dog-bite problem could be put into a syllogism form as follows:

Major Premise Owners of dog with vicious propensities are liable to dog-bite victims.

Minor Premise A dog who has snapped and snarled at children has vicious propensities.

Conclusion Owner of dog that bit client is liable to client.

This approach uses **deductive logic.**

Deductive logic is a form of reasoning by which specific conclusions are inferred from accepted general principles. Hence, if an accepted legal principle stated that a contract cannot be entered into in jest (major premise) and a court decided marriage is a contract (minor premise), a court could deductively conclude that a couple who married in jest did not enter into a valid contract. Legal rules are often deduced by such syllogisms.

Inductive Logic **Inductive logic,** on the other hand, is a form of reasoning by which general conclusions are drawn from particular situations. A good example of the use of the inductive approach is polling. A poll samples a few opinions and then draws a general conclusion. The inductive method is used in working jigsaw puzzles. After a few pieces are put together, the pattern is noticed. This method is often applied in case law situations.

Sometimes there are no rules for certain fact problems and the writer must look for trends in the law. Then a new rule can be made for the new fact pattern by following the trend of other jurisdictions. This is an inductive approach.

TERMS

deductive logic† A form of reasoning wherein specific conclusions are inferred from accepted general principles.

inductive logic† A form of reasoning wherein general conclusions are drawn from particular situations.

In *Griswold*, for example, the rule of law was not apparent. There was no right of marital privacy recognized in the case law. The appellant in *Griswold* had to construct the foundation of such a right of privacy from the pattern of rights protected by the United States Constitution. The lawyer in *Griswold* identified a pattern and convinced the court that the facts fit this pattern.

The student should look at the appendix and read the brief prepared on this issue by the appellant in *Griswold*. Much of the content of the brief is devoted to developing the legal principle. A rereading of Justice Douglas's opinion will show that much of his opinion was devoted to finding a right of privacy. This is a good example of the inductive approach.

Identifying the Legal Principle

Although there are four steps in the discussion section (identifying the issue, identifying the legal principle, applying the principle to the facts, and reaching the conclusion), most of the discussion section focuses on either identifying the legal principle or applying the principle to the facts, or both.

A memorandum is about law. The researcher researches the law and selects rules or principles from the research that pertain to the factual dispute. At times, such as in the dog-bite situation, the rules may be derived easily from good research techniques. Yet there are instances when no case or statute directly answers the question presented. Then the writer must explain why persuasive precedents from lower courts or precedents from other jurisdictions should be used or extrapolated.

At other times, persuasive authorities such as treatises, legal periodicals, or the *Restatements* must be used. These authorities, in the absence of binding authority, may suggest a cogent approach. Legal statements should always be buttressed with citations to the authorities on which they are based. Appropriate quotes should be used if they add to the presentation, but material should not be overquoted.

Lawyers use citations in the body of the memorandum rather than in footnotes. Use of correct citation form makes the memorandum look more professional. Use of incorrect citation form detracts from its professionalism. *The Bluebook: A Uniform System of Citation,* 15th ed. (The Harvard Law Review Association, 1991) tells how to cite all legal authority. This style guide should be used until the student learns how to cite cases, statutes, and other authority.

If the writer relies on *dicta*, he or she should say so. Cases both for and against the reasoning should be given, if applicable. Doubts should be explained and reasoning should be detailed. The discussion section takes a snapshot of the law at the time the memorandum is written and explains the snapshot to the reader. Sometimes the rule can be derived only by analogy. Sometimes other rules are used to illustrate the situation. The rule might be a mixture of several rules. Rules may conflict. In each of these cases, the writer not only must identify the rules but also must explain the reason why the rules have been selected.

How to Incorporate Case Law   The actual case, not a summary of the case, should be read and cited. Although summaries of cases in secondary sources such as encyclopedias or treatises will be read, these summaries should not be relied on in preparing a memorandum. Summaries may be inaccurate or incomplete. The summary of a case does not suggest factual similarities or differences. Only a careful reading of the case enables the writer to appreciate the legal implications of the source authority.

How to Incorporate Secondary Authority   In writing their first memorandum, many legal professionals make the same mistake many grade school students make in writing their first report: they copy from an encyclopedia or other secondary source. Worse yet, some legal professionals actually copy the West headnotes or summaries as original material in their memoranda. Source law, not secondary sources, should be read and cited. Secondary sources normally should not be cited (much less copied) in a brief or memorandum unless the citation is on a background issue over which there is no real dispute. West headnotes should never be cited or copied. Students are always amazed to be "caught" copying from West headnotes and wonder how the instructors knew. The answer is that only West headnotes are written in sentences like the following:

> Although decedent and man claiming to be her common-law husband and sole next of kin had lived together in one of homes maintained by decedent, and decedent had sometimes referred to him as her husband in city where that home was located, in view of absence of evidence of an express agreement to marry in praesenti, and in view of fact that decedent had been known as a single person in city where she had worked and where she had maintained another residence, and had held herself out as a single person in all of her business transactions, existence of a common-law marriage was not established. [*Borton v. Burns*, 11 Ohio Misc. 200, 230 N.E.2d 156 (1967).]

While this extended sentence structure is typical of West headnotes style, it is certainly not typical of the average student's writing style.

The legal professional can cite an A.L.R. annotation in a memorandum if it is especially relevant to the question presented. The professional should recognize that A.L.R. articles present cases on both sides of the question. The person who assigned the memorandum probably wants an answer, not a citation to an A.L.R. article. If an A.L.R. article is cited, the writer should take the time to explain any conflicts addressed by the annotation. The case must be applied to the facts of the particular situation.

How to Develop the Discussion   New legal professionals have a difficult time writing their first several memoranda. Most inexperienced writers develop the memorandum discussion as if they were writing a book report on each case they have read. They tend to summarize case after case in their discussion section. A memorandum, however, is about law. It is not about individual cases. Writers can describe tree after tree, or they can describe the forest. The legal professional must realize that cases are parts of larger principles or rules. The professional *must* write about the rules or principles, not just about the cases.

A good way to spot whether the discussion is being developed correctly is to look at the paragraphs. Does each paragraph begin with a different case? Does each paragraph discuss that case, then move on to the next case in the next paragraph? If so, the writer is writing about cases, not principles. When each paragraph in a memorandum discusses a different case, the writer is probably writing case summaries, and not deducing principles from the cases.

An easy way to overcome this thought process is by using "signals" in the memorandum. **Signals** are notations that tell the reader how legal authority supports the argument. The standard signals are described in *The Bluebook: A Uniform System of Citation* (Figure 10–1). Look at how these signals are used. If a case fully supports the statement made, the case is simply cited without any signal. If the case is merely an example of how a case supports the statement made, the signal *"See, e.g.,"* is used.

When signals are used in the discussion section, the reader looks at the cases as principles rather than as isolated cases. Using signals helps the writer begin synthesizing the cases. As cases are grouped, the writer begins to look for common threads or principles. The final product appears more professional. The first draft of the memorandum should be perused to see how signals are used, which reveals much about the extent to which the writer's thinking is developed on the subject. If the memorandum appears to discuss case after case, it should be rewritten using signals.

In summary, the discussion section initially identifies and justifies the legal principle used to reach the conclusion of the memorandum, then this rule is applied to the facts.

TERMS

signals†   Abbreviated notations that tell the reader how legal authority supports an argument.

FIGURE 10–1
Signals That
Indicate How
Legal
Authority
Supports the
Argument

INTRODUCTORY SIGNALS

[no signal]	The authority provided clearly states the proposition, identifies the source of a quotation, or identifies an authority that is referred to in text.
E.g.,	The cited authority states the proposition. It may be used in combination with other signals, for example, *But see, e.g.*
Accord	The authority that follows states or clearly supports the proposition, but the quotation or reference in text is from a different authority.
See	The cited authority clearly supports the proposition but does not directly state it.
See also	The authority that follows is additional source material that supports the proposition. It is often used to introduce additional sources once authorities that state or directly support a proposition have been given.
See generally	The cited authority presents helpful background material that is related to the proposition.
Cf.	Means "compare." The cited authority supports a proposition that is different from the main one but close enough to lend support.
Compare . . . with	A comparison of the authorities cited supports or illustrates the proposition.
Contra	The authority provided directly states the contrary of the proposition.
But see	The cited authority clearly supports a proposition contrary to the main proposition.
But cf.	The authority that follows supports a proposition analogous to the contrary of the main proposition.

Applying the Principle to the Facts

Law is not just abstract principles. Law is not just rules. Law is a way to solve problems. Memorandum writing involves the application of rules to problems. This means the writer must discuss how the facts affect the principle. The facts distinguish one case from another. Facts show how rules can conflict with one another.

Consider a parent who tells a child not to leave the house until the parent returns from work. This is a rule. Yet if a fire breaks out, the child must make a judgment. Facts can change rules. In some cases, the facts fit the rule. In such cases, the writer need only describe how the facts fit within the rule.

The point is that the memorandum writer must first deduce principles from the primary source law and then apply the principles to the facts of the problem. A major flaw in the writing of some legal professionals is their failure to address the facts of the case and relate the facts to the legal principles.

If the facts are unclear, the writer should say so. If more facts are needed, the writer should say so. If the facts are disputed, the writer should tell how believing one version over another version might affect the outcome. In a memorandum, the legal professional tries to do what a court will do: distinguish the facts, harmonize cases, and narrow or expand a rule.

Most general principles of law can be narrowed to more precise principles, and narrow principles can be expanded to general principles. A precedent may be expanded or limited in subsequent cases. The facts often are the reason why the court finds it necessary to change a rule or to change the scope of the rule. The writer needs to show why this situation is unique.

Applying the principles to the facts is the step most legal professionals forget in their discussion section.

Explaining the Reasoning

The conclusion is given in a separate section of the memorandum. The discussion section, however, explains how the writer reaches the conclusion. If facts are disputed, how the outcome of this dispute affects the analysis should be explained. If the principle applicable to the dispute is uncertain, the choices should be explained. Any reservations or doubts about the conclusion should be stated.

A memorandum predicts what happens when legal principles are applied to certain factual situations. The memorandum writer is simply doing what most professionals do: giving an informed opinion. An appraiser tells a homeowner what real estate is worth, and a physician makes a diagnosis. Legal professionals tell what the law is on a given subject.

The legal professional leads the reader to a conclusion in the discussion section. The conclusion may be full of doubt. If so, the legal professional tells the reader why there is so much doubt.

The Conclusion of the Memorandum

A memorandum must give an answer to the questions presented. This answer is given in a formal way in a section headed "Conclusion" or "Brief Answer."

Most students are accustomed to giving concrete answers rather than abstract answers. Students like concrete answers, yet the law does not always permit certainty The law does not always have ascertainable answers. Two judges who study the same legal problem may reach different conclusions. Legal professionals should approach legal problems as they approach other abstract problems. There will not always be a single solution or answer.

Legal conclusions cannot always be definite, but any legal conclusion should be made as definite as possible. If the conclusion can be stated definitely, the writer should answer it definitely. Experience in the legal process, however, teaches that the "sure winner" can be lost. There is room for judgment in making conclusions. Case law changes, judges retire, and an overlooked fact may become crucial to the outcome of a case. The composition of a court can change—a court may become more conservative or more liberal. A judge might change his or her mind.

The more memoranda the legal professional writes, the more both sides to a controversy will be seen and the more likely it is that the writer's opinion will be hedged and balanced. The writer, however, should never double-talk. The basis for any reservations should be explained. In short, a direct conclusion should be given, if possible, but if not, the reservations should be explained. The writer should remember that the supervisor or the client is asking for an opinion. The client is even paying a fee for the opinion. The supervisor may decide whether to try a case or settle it based on the conclusion given. A client may decide to appeal or not appeal on the basis of the conclusion. It is important, therefore, that the writer frame the conclusion in the most definitive or reasonable way possible, given the law and facts.

A memorandum writer has to balance probable results, given a new set of facts, given a law that might be modified or even changed by this case, and given the existing trends in the law. But a memorandum writer, unlike the court, does not have an advocate to argue the opposite side of the question. Although a memorandum writer cannot know whether the same judge or judges will be on the court when the researched problem is actually decided, the writer should be able to spot trends in the cases. Trends may develop because of societal pressures or because of changes in philosophy of judges. Thus the memorandum should develop both sides of the argument.

At times a memorandum may have to be written without all of the material facts. In such situations, it is difficult to give unequivocal opinions. Unless the law is certainly fixed and the facts have been carefully developed, the discussion section should be written flexibly to explore the legal and factual uncertainties. Even when the law is seemingly fixed, the memorandum might not anticipate an eroding precedent or a new trend.

Legal rules blur at the edges. Legal rules conflict. New facts change rules. Many variables affect case and statutory analysis. If precision is desired, another line of work may be necessary. The fuzziness of law is part of its intrigue. When a legal memorandum is prepared, the writer cannot pretend this fuzziness does not exist. The writer cannot pretend conflicting cases actually are consistent. Hard-and-fast rules must be stated where possible, but where uncertainty exists, it must be acknowledged. There is nothing wrong with saying that the result is unclear "because . . ." or that the principles of several cases are contradictory.

As the conclusion is stated, phrases such as "I believe," "I feel," or "I guess" should be avoided. As a professional, the writer should simply state the conclusion without injecting himself or herself into it. Some legal professionals forget they are representing the interests of clients. This text tells you to write the facts neutrally and make the conclusion as objective as possible, but in the real world, facts are not neutral. Parties see events from different perspectives. There is much room for judgment in making conclusions. Memorandum writing is not a theoretical exercise. The writer should use the memorandum as a springboard for developing theories and approaches for the client. The writer should always be scouting for an advantage for the client, given the factual situation. Yet, in the final analysis, the reasoning of the memorandum must constitute the best judgment of the writer.

§ 10.4 Style of the Memorandum

Style is the individualized way the writer writes. Look at a letter written to a friend. The personality shown in the letter is the writer's style. Because much legal writing is written impersonally, legal professionals sometimes think this means there is no room for style.

Consider the following passages:

Before: The Appellee's argument that appellee is not responsible under the dangerous propensity standard is specious because an animal which has nipped or growled at others has demonstrated a dangerous propensity.

After: Appellee is wrong. When a dog has previously snapped and snarled at other people, the dog has shown a dangerous propensity.

The first passage is dull, but the second passage is written so the reader appreciates the situation. Both make the same point, yet one is more direct and more readable. Legal writing does not have to bore the reader.

It is not unusual to see a clever courtroom attorney write a drab brief. This occurs when an attorney who is unafraid to use wits in the courtroom is afraid to use these same wits in a brief. Each writer has a different personality. Some writers are methodical, some are flamboyant, others are scholarly. The student needs to recognize his or her personality strengths and weaknesses. If points are best made with a scholarly development, that style should be used. If the writer is effective with a lighter style, that method should be used. But if the writer tends to be hurried or careless or to leave projects uncompleted, those personality traits must not be carried to the work.

Legal writing is a precise art. It must be practiced carefully. The writer's personality changes with the audience. People act differently among peers than they act with parents or employers. A person may be more formal with one person, less formal with another. Briefs and memoranda are written in a formal style, although some law firms permit less formality in memoranda than in briefs.

Formal style does not mean stuffy or filled with legalese. It does mean avoiding familiar or informal expressions. It means writing in third person (using *he, she,* or *it,* not *I, we,* or *you*) like most novels are written. The writer should write "The plaintiff argues . . .," "the petitioner asserts . . .," or "the appellee contends . . ." Even better, the parties' names can be used, for example, "the Bank argues . . ." "the Roes assert . . .," or "the X Corporation contends . . ."

The point is to use a style with which the writer is comfortable. That style should not interfere with the reasoning process but should enhance the way the reasoning process is presented to the reader.

§ 10.5   A Sample Memorandum

Suppose the year is 1963 and *Griswold v. Connecticut* has not yet been decided. The facts are that Estelle Griswold and Lee Buxton have just been indicted for selleing contraceptives in Connecticut. Remember, at this time, there is no authority for the right of privacy. Because there is no authority on the subject, legal professionals will have to prepare a memorandum using some creativity. A sample memorandum that could be written at this time is included in the appendix. Before reading this memorandum, however, the student may want to try his or her approach on this question.

Writing Exercises

1. Reread *Smith v. Lewis* and *Lucas v. Hamm* located in the appendix. Assume a physician has read about a theoretical treatment for a rare condition that has not yet been attempted on humans. Medical experts have questioned the benefits of the treatment on humans. A patient comes to the physician's office suffering from the rare condition. The physician says nothing to him about the theoretical treatment. The patient loses his hair as a result of the condition. Subsequent use of the treatment on humans shows that the hair loss would not have occurred if the treatment had been used. The patient now wants to sue the physician for malpractice. *Smith* and *Lucas* are the only two cases in your jurisdiction pertaining to this problem. Prepare a two-page typewritten memorandum regarding the correct application of the legal principles of these cases to this fact problem. Your memorandum should include the following sections: facts, issue, discussion, and conclusion.

2. In the hypothetical situation in question 1, what additional facts do you need? Explain.

3. Read the following statute and assume it is in effect in your state.

   P.L. 68 of the State of Ames

   Statute of Limitations:

   A product liability action must be commenced within two (2) years after the cause of action accrues or within ten (10) years after the delivery of the product to the initial user or consumer. However, if the cause of action accrues at least eight (8) years but less than ten (10) years after that initial delivery, the action may be commenced at any time within two (2) years after the cause of action accrues.

   Your supervisor has given you these facts:

   A punch press was manufactured and delivered to a wholesale distributor on March 1, 1980. The distributor shipped the punch press to a warehouse in Houston, Texas, on March 20, 1980. The press was then delivered to a customer on April 13, 1980. An employee of the customer was injured on the punch press on April 12, 1990. A lawsuit was brought on April 12, 1990.

   Your supervisor has researched this issue but does not have time to write a memorandum for the senior partner, who wants to know whether the statute of limitations has run. Prepare a two-page discussion section memorandum using the IRAC approach.

4. Read the following statute and assume it is the only statute in effect in the state of Ames.

    Public Law 158

    The owner, operator, or person responsible for the operation of a motor vehicle shall not be liable for loss or damage arising from injuries to or death of a guest, while being transported without payment thereof, in or upon such motor vehicle, resulting from the operation thereof, unless such injuries or death are caused by the wanton or willful misconduct of such operator, owner, or person responsible for the operation of such motor vehicle.

    Your research has uncovered one case pertaining to this statute: *Stillwell v. Adams*, 135 Ind. 495 (1963). There are no other cases on the subject. Turn to the appendix and read *Stillwell*.

    The facts of your client's case are as follows. Your client was injured when she was a passenger in a vehicle driven by X. X was drunk and was traveling at 120 mph on a curvy road. Your client was seriously injured. The attorney for whom you work wants to know whether to pursue the claim. Prepare the discussion section of a memorandum.

Enrichment Activity

1. Locate the nearest county or university law library. Go to that law library. Research the latest cases dealing with the right of privacy decided by lower courts (*i.e.*, courts other than the United States Supreme Court). Pick the most interesting case, and assume that case will be appealed to the United States Supreme Court. Write a memorandum using the facts of that case and any issues it raises relating to the right of privacy. Assume the United States Supreme Court has voted to grant certiorari or a writ of appeal in that case. Write a memorandum assessing the probable outcome of the case you picked.

CHAPTER 11

LEGAL BRIEFS

Lawyers: Persons who write a 10,000 word document and call it a brief.

————— Popular Saying

A lawsuit is society's way of resolving disputes between parties. A court resolves disputes by applying rules of law to the facts of the dispute. An adversary court system works best when both parties to a dispute are allowed an opportunity to fully argue their respective cases. Many legal arguments are presented to courts in written documents called briefs. A brief is written to persuade a court to rule favorably for a particular party. Many students who have never seen a brief may be misled by its name. In fact, briefs can be hundreds of pages in length. A brief does not mean a short document:

> Originally, the American legal brief was brief in fact; it was the lawyer's summary of the evidence offered and the legal position taken, something to inform the court of what was coming or remind it of what had passed. Today, the legal brief is hardly ever short and often terribly long; oral argument is ordinarily much briefer than the brief. This is partly because litigation has become more complicated. The procedure has in a sense been simplified, but the issues in litigation—both the facts and the law of the usual lawsuit—have become vastly more elaborate. (C. Rembar, *The Law of the Land* 179 [New York: Simon and Schuster, 1980].)

Sometimes lawyers refer to a brief as a memorandum when it is filed with a trial court. Such a memorandum should not be confused with the intraoffice memorandum discussed in Chapter 10.

SIDEBAR

Much of what has been discussed about memoranda writing is applicable to writing briefs. Briefs, like memoranda, are organized around issues. In a brief, as in a memorandum, issues are developed by identifying the legal principles applicable to the dispute and applying these legal principles to the facts of the case. However, instead of predicting a conclusion to a legal question, as the writer does in a memorandum, a brief writer *argues* for a particular conclusion. The brief writer uses both deductive and inductive logic in that argument.

Beyond the similarities lie significant differences between writing a brief and a memorandum. A memorandum is designed to give advice. In giving advice, the main concern is objectivity. Good advice weighs risks and benefits. A brief writer also gives advice to the court in the brief, but this is not the document's main function. The main function of a brief is to persuade. The writer attempts to persuade a court regardless of whether the advice is the best advice under the circumstances. Whereas the memorandum is characterized by objectivity and neutrality, neither characteristic is expected in a brief, although the brief writer owes an ethical duty not to misrepresent the law or facts of a case.

§ 11.1 Types of Briefs

Legal professionals file various types of briefs, depending on which court is hearing the case. A brief filed with a trial court differs in some respects from a brief filed with an appellate court or administrative agency.

Trial Briefs

An attorney may file a brief with a trial court to support a procedural motion or to argue the merits of the case. For example, a party who files a motion to dismiss a case in a trial court might be required to file a brief explaining the basis or reasoning for the motion. The opposing party will respond with a brief. If the motion to dismiss is overruled, the party might file a motion for summary judgment. Again, a brief may be filed with the motion. The opposing party will respond with its own brief in opposition to the motion. The same parties may later have a dispute over a discovery question. One party may then file a motion to compel discovery, and a brief may be filed with that motion. The other party may respond with another brief. The parties also may file briefs at trial or even after trial with a motion to amend the judgment or to correct errors made at trial.

Appellate Briefs

The idea of allowing parties to appeal the decision of a lower court dates to 700 B.C., when Athens set up the Court of Areopagus to review homicide and sacrilege cases. Now most decisions of a lower court can be reviewed by an appeals court. For example, decisions of the United States district courts (the federal trial courts) can be reviewed by federal circuit courts of appeal. The Supreme Court of the United States reviews the decisions of federal circuit courts of appeal. If an appeal is filed in a case, the parties file appellate briefs.

It is through the briefs filed with the court that an appellate judge becomes acquainted with the contentions of the parties to an appeal. An appellate brief is typically more formal in both form and content than a brief filed with a trial court. Most appellate courts have strict rules regarding the content and length of a brief, as well as the color of its cover, the width of its margins, and the length of each page, to name just a few typical requirements. If an appellant files a brief one day late, many appellate courts will simply dismiss the appeal. Appellate rules vary for each court, so the legal professional must become familiar with the relevant rules of the court before starting any briefing project.

Other Briefs

Briefs are not filed only with courts. A brief might be filed with a labor arbitrator in a labor-management arbitration proceeding. Briefs may be filed in a variety of administrative situations: a black-lung claim, a Social Security disability claim, a merit system proceeding. Although such briefs may be less formal in their structure and presentation, the writer uses the same thought process used to prepare a brief for filing with a court.

Briefs frame disputes. Briefs debate disputes. A good brief helps the court see the client's version of the case. A brief serves as a reminder to the court of the facts of the case if the case is taken under advisement. A good brief will be used by a court to write a good decision. This is how case law is made in the United States. The legal professional is a professional writer, and the brief is his or her work of art.

§ 11.2 Brief Writing Process

Brief writing is a fluid process. The first stage, like the first stage of writing a legal memorandum, begins with legal research. This is the time to gather the relevant primary authority (cases and statutes) as well as the various secondary sources (treatises, law review articles, encyclopedias) that support or contradict the client's position.

During the initial stage, an assessment of the strengths and weaknesses of the issues is made. As the writing process begins, the writer decides which issues are stronger than others, which issues can be ignored, and which issues should be grouped with other issues. Faced with one strong issue and one weak issue, a writer may elect to omit the weaker argument altogether, rather than lose credibility with the court by presenting it. The writing process continues until the brief is filed with the court.

§ 11.3 Form and Content of a Brief

The form of the brief differs from the form of a memorandum in some respects. The parts of a brief will vary from court to court. Some courts are quite strict about the format of a brief. Figure 11–1 illustrates the rules for the appendix portion of an appellate brief to one of the federal circuit courts. Requirements for a typical appellate brief include a table of contents, a table of authority, a jurisdictional statement, a statement of facts, a statement of the case (which is a review of the procedural steps in the case), the issues presented for review, an argument section (including perhaps an additional summary of this argument), and a conclusion section detailing the relief sought.

Table of Contents

Most appellate briefs contain a table of contents. Most trial briefs do not have such a section. The table of contents includes all the main headings to the brief (Jurisdictional Statement, Statement of Facts, Issues Presented for Review, and so on) with appropriate page references. For an example of a table of contents from an appellant's brief, refer to the *Griswold* brief in the appendix. The table of contents in a brief is quite similar to the table of contents in a textbook.

Table of Authority

The **table of authority** contains an alphabetical list of every case cited in the brief, noting the page on which each case appears. A separate list of every statute or regulation cited also indicates the page on which each appears in the brief. A section entitled "Other Authority" lists periodicals, restatements, and other secondary authorities cited in the brief along with a page reference for each. For an example of a table of authority, refer to the *Griswold* brief in the appendix. Most trial briefs do not have a table of authority.

The table of authority serves the same function as the index contained in the back of a textbook—namely, to refer the reader to an exact page for a particular reference. The table of authority, however, references legal sources cited in the brief, not general terms and subjects.

TERMS

table of authority† An alphabetical list of every case cited in a brief.

RULES OF APPELLATE PROCEDURE

Rule 30. Appendix to the Briefs

(a) **Duty of Appellant to Prepare and File; Content of Appendix; Time for Filing; Number of Copies.** The appellant must prepare and file an appendix to the briefs which must contain: (1) the relevant docket entries in the proceeding below; (2) any relevant portions of the pleadings, charge, findings, or opinion; (3) the judgment, order, or decision in question; and (4) any other parts of the record to which the parties wish to direct the particular attention of the court. Except where they have independent relevance, memoranda of law in the district court should not be included in the appendix. The fact that parts of the record are not included in the appendix shall not prevent the parties or the court from relying on such parts.

Unless filing is to be deferred pursuant to the provisions of subdivision (c) of this rule, the appellant must serve and file the appendix with the brief. Ten copies of the appendix must be filed with the clerk, and one copy must be served on counsel for each party separately represented, unless the court requires the filing or service of a different number by local rule or by order in a particular case.

(b) **Determination of Contents of Appendix; Cost of Producing.** The parties are encouraged to agree as to the contents of the appendix. In the absence of agreement, the appellant shall, not later than 10 days after the date on which the record is filed, serve on the appellee a designation of the parts of the record which the appellant intends to include in the appendix and a statement of the issues which the appellant intends to present for review. If the appellee deems it necessary to direct the particular attention of the

court to parts of the record not designated by the appellant, the appellee shall, within 10 days after receipt of the designation, serve upon the appellant a designation of those parts. The appellant shall include in the appendix the parts thus designated with respect to the appeal and any cross appeal. In designating parts of the record for inclusion in the appendix, the parties shall have regard for the fact that the entire record is always available to the court for reference and examination and shall not engage in unnecessary designation. The provisions of this paragraph shall apply to cross appellants and cross appellees.

Unless the parties otherwise agree, the cost of producing the appendix shall initially be paid by the appellant, but if the appellant considers that parts of the record designated by the appellee for inclusion are unnecessary for the determination of the issues presented the appellant may so advise the appellee and the appellee shall advance the cost of including such parts. The cost of producing the appendix shall be taxed as costs in the case, but if either party shall cause matters to be included in the appendix unnecessarily the court may impose the cost of producing such parts on the party. Each circuit shall provide by local rule for the imposition of sanctions against attorneys who unreasonably and vexatiously increase the costs of litigation through the inclusion of unnecessary material in the appendix.

(c) **Alternative Method of Designating Contents of the Appendix; How References to the Record May be Made in the Briefs When Alternative Method is Used.** If the court shall so provide by rule for classes of cases or by order in specific cases, preparation of the appendix

FIGURE 11–1
Requirements for an Appendix to a Brief to be Filed in a Federal Circuit Court

FIGURE 11–1
(continued)

may be deferred until after the briefs have been filed, and the appendix may be filed 21 days after service of the brief of the appellee. If the preparation and filing of the appendix is thus deferred, the provisions of subdivision (b) of this Rule 30 shall apply, except that the designations referred to therein shall be made by each party at the time each brief is served, and a statement of the issues presented shall be unnecessary.

If the deferred appendix authorized by this subdivision is employed, references in the briefs to the record may be to the pages of the parts of the record involved, in which event the original paging of each part of the record shall be indicated in the appendix by placing in brackets the number of each page at the place in the appendix where that page begins. Or if a party desires to refer in a brief directly to pages of the appendix, that party may serve and file typewritten or page proof copies of the brief within the time required by Rule 31(a), with appropriate references to the pages of the parts of the record involved. In that event, within 14 days after the appendix is filed the party shall serve and file copies of the brief in the form prescribed by Rule 32(a) containing references to the pages of the appendix in place of or in addition to the initial references to the pages of the parts of the record involved. No other changes may be made in the brief as initially served and filed, except that typographical errors may be corrected.

(d) Arrangement of the Appendix. At the beginning of the appendix there shall be inserted a list of the parts of the record which it contains, in the order in which the parts are set out therein, with references to the pages of the appendix at which each part be-

gins. The relevant docket entries shall be set out following the list of contents. Thereafter, other parts of the record shall be set out in chronological order. When matter contained in the reporter's transcript of proceedings is set out in the appendix, the page of the transcript at which such matter may be found shall be indicated in brackets immediately before the matter which is set out. Omissions in the text of papers or of the transcript must be indicated by asterisks. Immaterial formal matters (captions, subscriptions, acknowledgments, etc.) shall be omitted. A question and its answer may be contained in a single paragraph.

(e) Reproduction of Exhibits. Exhibits designated for inclusion in the appendix may be contained in a separate volume, or volumes, suitably indexed. Four copies thereof shall be filed with the appendix and one copy shall be served on counsel for each party separately represented. The transcript of a proceeding before an administrative agency, board, commission or officer used in an action in the district court shall be regarded as an exhibit for the purpose of this subdivision.

(f) Hearing of Appeals on the Original Record Without the Necessity of an Appendix. A court of appeals may by rule applicable to all cases, or to classes of cases, or by order in specific cases, dispense with the requirement of an appendix and permit appeals to be heard on the original record, with such copies of the record, or relevant parts thereof, as the court may require.

Jurisdictional Statement

Jurisdiction is the power of a court to hear and decide a case. The jurisdictional statement usually includes a statement of how the case was decided below, the type of appeal (interlocutory, emergency, or on the merits), and a citation to the statute or court rule giving the appellate court the right to hear the case. This section of the brief is usually routine and straightforward. In this section, the writer tells the court how the dispute arose and how the court has the power to resolve such a dispute. In most instances, briefs filed with a trial court will not include a jurisdictional statement unless a jurisdictional question is at issue.

Statement of the Facts

The facts of the case are the events that relate to the dispute between the parties. The party filing the initial brief is usually expected or required to recite the facts in that initial brief. In a trial court, the initial brief is usually filed by the moving party (the party making a request for the court to do something or not do something). In an appeals court, the initial brief is usually filed by the appellant. Usually the other party (the nonmoving party in the trial court and the appellee in an appeal) will be given an opportunity to file a response brief. Next, the moving party or appellant will file a reply brief. Although the party filing the initial brief writes the facts, the party filing the response brief restates any omitted or misrepresented facts in the response brief.

How the Facts Change in the Course of a Lawsuit

Between the initiation of a case and the time that case is decided by a court or a jury, the facts will change.

Begin with the filing of a lawsuit. One party files a complaint. The party being sued files a motion asking the court to dismiss the case. At this point, the court has no evidence before it. The only document the plaintiff has filed is a complaint. What are the facts in the situation? The facts on a motion to dismiss are the allegations in the complaint and anything that can reasonably be inferred from these allegations. The court will assume the facts of the complaint are true for purposes of ruling on such a motion. In preparing a brief in support of a motion to dismiss, the fact section would consist of the allegations made in the complaint.

Suppose the court overrules the motion to dismiss, and the opposing party then files a motion asking the court for summary judgment. Now the parties file affidavits with the court giving their versions of the dispute. The facts are set out in the affidavits. Usually at this point the court still has not heard any testimony. The court cannot tell from the affidavits which side is telling the truth. The facts on a motion for summary judgment are the statements made in the affidavits. In order to prevail on a motion for summary judgment, a party must convince a court that there is no genuine issue remaining in the case. In these situations, the party says to the court: "Even if the other side's facts are true, my client should win."

At trial the court hears testimony of witnesses to support the facts in the trial brief. In trial briefs, the parties frequently argue over which version of the facts is more credible. In deciding a case, the court or jury decides that one version of the facts is more credible. After such a decision or verdict, the prevailing party's version of the facts is usually accepted for purposes of an appeal. Thus the procedural posture of the case determines the facts.

In most appeals, the parties retell the facts to the court in the fact section of the appellate brief as the facts were narrated to the trial court. If the case was dismissed without a trial in the lower court, the facts are again the allegations in the complaint. If the lower court granted a motion for summary judgment, the facts on the appeal are the facts set out in the affidavits. If there was a trial, the facts are the testimony and exhibits presented at trial. A court reporter would have transcribed the testimony and attached the exhibits to a transcript to be used by the lawyers in preparing the case for the appeal.

How to Organize the Statement of Facts

A legal professional who is asked to prepare the fact section of an appellate brief will need to read the transcript and summarize in narrative form the testimony of the witnesses. A narrative statement presents the facts in a story form as opposed to presenting them in a witness-by-witness fashion.

At trial, witnesses are sometimes called ad hoc, as they are available. Their stories are not necessarily told in chronological or sequential order. In the brief, the story should not be told as the testimony was presented. The story should be told with a plan in mind.

In most cases, the writer needs to cite the page from the transcript to support each fact so the court and the adversary can check the statements if necessary. Thus, a page reference should be given for each factual statement. This is usually done by referring to a transcript page "(t.p.___)" or to a page of the record "(r.p.___)."

The facts are the events that relate to the dispute. If the case involves an automobile accident, the facts include the events leading up to the accident, the accident, and the postaccident investigation. Further facts have to do with the alleged injuries or damages, including treatment at a hospital, medical bills, and any resulting disability.

How to Present the Facts Objectively and Favorably

In a memorandum, the facts are recited neutrally. In a brief, the court expects the facts to be described fairly but knows the perspective is that of an advocate. The most effective factual statement will appear to have been written neutrally but actually will slant the facts favorably to the client's side. For example, a brief written on behalf of the wrongdoer might simply say this:

> As a result of this accident, John Roe sustained an injury to his right arm.

The person representing the injured party, however, might be more specific:

> As a result of this accident, John Roe's right arm was mangled in the punch press and is now nearly paralyzed. Despite extensive rehabilitative therapy, Mr. Roe has regained only 30 percent of the use of his right arm. Before the accident, the plaintiff was right-handed.

A rule common to writing both case briefs and memoranda is to include all relevant and material facts and to omit any facts not relevant or material to the dispute. This rule works well when the goal is to achieve neutrality or objectivity. The decision to include or exclude a marginally relevant fact is more subjective. Some facts naturally evoke sympathy with judges. Decisions to include or exclude facts in the fact section of the brief should be made from an adversarial perspective.

Less-experienced legal professionals frequently ignore facts that negatively impact their case. This is a mistake. If damaging facts are ignored in a brief, a good opponent highlights this "oversight" repeatedly in a response brief, stressing how important these facts are to the disposition of the case. A good opponent exploits any unfair presentation of the facts, and the court then wonders why facts were omitted. Bad facts should never be ignored.

Facts that do not affect the outcome of the issues being briefed should be omitted. The writer should include all facts relevant to the outcome, stressing the favorable ones and downplaying the unfavorable. Although this advice is inherently contradictory, the best way to write the facts in a brief is to write them fairly but slant them in favor of the client.

How to Downplay Unfavorable Facts

Different brief writers use different techniques to downplay unfavorable facts. Some writers like to bury unfavorable facts in the middle or at the end of a long paragraph. Others downplay unfavorable facts by the order in which the facts are presented, by sentence structure, by association with more favorable facts, or by word selection. For example, in the following passage, the plaintiff was drunk at the time of the accident. See how this fact is played down:

> *Facts of the Collision:* On April 1, 1990, Alex Martin was the owner and operator of a 1985 Buick Regal Sedan. He was traveling in a southerly direction on Pennsylvania Avenue. As he approached the parking lot of Duffy's Tavern in Evansville, Indiana, Juanita White pulled directly into the path of his vehicle, intending to execute a left turn. She completely blocked Mr. Martin's lane of travel and he had nowhere to go to avoid the collision.
>
> Immediately after the collision, Juanita White stated that she looked both ways but did not see Mr. Martin. She acknowledged that she pulled directly into his path and that the accident was her fault. Sometime later, when someone told her that Mr. Martin may have been drinking, was the first time she attributed any fault to him.

The Importance of the Statement of Facts

The fact statement of a brief is more important than the fact statement of a memorandum. The fact section tells the court what the dispute is about. If the brief is filed with a trial court, the fact statement may be used by the judge to refresh his or her recollection of the evidence in the case if a ruling is not made promptly. If the brief is filed with an appellate court, the fact statement explains to the appellate judges what the dispute is about. Remember that the appellate judges do not hear testimony of witnesses. The appellate judges learn about the case only from reading the briefs and perhaps by reviewing the transcript of the trial proceedings. In some cases, the only way the appellate court knows what happened in the lower court is by reading the factual statement of the brief. The factual statement should be written as favorably as possible for the client. The writer should spend some extra time with this section of the brief and reread the facts after the argument is finished. A little extra care with the facts can be very productive.

Statement of the Case

In a case brief, there is usually a section called **procedural posture.** The procedural posture reveals the stage of the case at which the dispute was decided. The case may have been decided by the lower court in

---

TERMS

procedural posture† The section of a case brief that tells at what stage of a case the dispute was decided.

dismissing a complaint or granting a motion for summary judgment. The lower court may have granted or denied an injunction. The case may have been decided after a trial or an appeal to various other courts.

The statement of the case serves a similar function. The statement of the case gives the history of what the parties did prior to filing the brief. It tells about the complaint, the answer, discovery disputes, and the trial. With this background, the statement of the case also sets the stage for the present brief. It tells how the parties have reached this particular juncture in the case.

But there is another important role for this section of a brief. This section determines how the issues will be defined. As noted in the discussion of the fact section of the brief, the facts of the case considered relevant differ at various stages of the case. The statement of the case pinpoints the way the court will look at the client's version of the facts.

Assume a traffic accident where vehicles heading in cross directions collide at an intersection and both parties claim a green light. One party files a lawsuit. If the other party files a motion to dismiss, the court must assume the truth of the plaintiff's allegations. If this case is dismissed and later appealed, the statement of the case will tell the appellate judges how the facts must be reviewed. The appellate court, like the trial court, must assume the truth of the allegations of the complaint.

The defendant might file a motion for summary judgment with an affidavit saying he had the green light. The plaintiff might then file an affidavit saying she had the green light. On a motion for summary judgment, the court cannot determine who is telling the truth, but only determines whether a genuine dispute exists as to the material facts of the controversy. In this hypothetical, there is a genuine issue of fact, so the court should deny this motion.

At trial, the court or jury might find for the plaintiff. Then, on appeal, the appellate court is required to accept the facts or version of the incident of the party who prevailed in the court below. So, if the plaintiff was the winning party in the court below, the appellate court would accept the plaintiff's version, and not the defendant's version, of the facts.

An example of a statement of the case might read as follows:

> This is a personal injury action brought by the plaintiffs, Steve Smith and Mary Ann Smith, for injuries they received in an automobile accident on May 17, 1975. The plaintiffs sued Lu Chang, the driver of the automobile they occupied. The suit against him was on the basis that he was guilty of wilful and wrongful misconduct as set forth in the Automobile Guest Statute as it exists in Indiana. The plaintiffs also sued the defendant, Hideaway Tavern, on the theory that it sold alcoholic beverages to minors (the plaintiffs and the defendant driver) and that the consumption of these beverages contributed to the automobile accident. The owners of Hideaway Tavern denied that any sale took place and

further contended that even if a sale took place, the consumption of alcoholic beverages did not contribute to the automobile accident.

The case was filed in Vanderburgh County on October 19, 1975, and was tried to a jury in the Vanderburgh Superior Court with the Honorable Wilbur Williams presiding. The trial commenced on October 7, 1977, and on October 8, 1977, the jury returned a verdict for the defendants. On October 8, 1977, the Court entered judgment on that verdict. The plaintiffs timely filed their Motion to Correct Errors, which was denied on February 1, 1978, and on March 1, 1978, the plaintiffs filed their transcript and proceeded with this appeal.

The Issues

Issues are the legal questions the court must answer. Issues arise in many different ways. A party who loses at trial may believe the case was not correctly decided. The party may claim errors were made in pretrial rulings. The party may claim errors were made in the discovery process. The party may believe the trial was not conducted fairly. The party may believe the court did not consider all the evidence in the case. In fact, the loser may believe the judge made repeated errors in the case.

If the appellate court agrees, it will either **remand** the case or reverse the case and enter judgment for the prevailing party. A plaintiff must identify the legal question presented to a trial court, and an appellant must identify the alleged errors presented to the appeals court. Legal questions and errors are identified by stating the issues. The issues define the questions that the parties are arguing about in a case.

The issue section usually appears early in the brief, although it may actually be prepared late in the writing process. Editors know that the preface of a book is often written last, although it appears in the front of the book. Issues and prefaces are written late in the process because both can be written better once the writer knows the strengths and weaknesses of the product.

The Importance of the Issues

The issue section is perhaps the most important section of the brief. Many times it is how the question is asked that suggests the answer to the

---

TERMS

remand   The return of a case by an appellate court to the trial court for further proceedings, for a new trial, or for entry of judgment in accordance with an order of the appellate court.

court. Framing the issue, however, requires substantial background in how legal precedent decides such questions. That is why this section is written only after much research and often much rewriting. In fact, that is why this section is frequently written last.

If an issue is not raised on appeal, the issue may be waived. In other words, if a party does not include an issue in the appeal, the court will not permit the party to raise the issue later. Consequently, a common error is to include an issue with little merit or to include two issues when one issue would suffice. Such a practice may compromise or detract from meritorious issues. A critical question, therefore, is whether a marginal issue should be presented in the brief.

How to Present the Issues

Issues are written in a question form. In *Griswold*, for example, the issues were written by the appellant as follows:

> 1. Whether Sections 53-32 and 54-196 of the General Statutes of Connecticut, on their face or as applied in this case, deprive these appellants of liberty or property without due process of law in violation of the Fourteenth Amendment to the Constitution of the United States.
> 2. Whether Sections 53-32 and 54-196 of the General Statutes of Connecticut, on their face or as applied in this case, deprive these appellants of their rights to freedom of speech in violation of the First and Fourteenth Amendments to the Constitution of the United States.

Some brief writers begin each issue with the word *whether*. The writer should never use the redundant phrase *whether or not*.

Issues that are related should be combined. Issues should be splintered if doing so will help the argument flow better. Parties are given wide latitude in determining how issues are grouped or divided, but a court does not want to reread the same argument stated three different ways, nor does it want to read an awkward brief in which issues have been combined unnaturally.

In preparing an issue, the question should be written by combining key facts with the legal principles. Inexperienced brief writers tend to ignore the facts in the statement of the issues. However, each case is different because of its unique facts. Both facts and law should be used in framing issues.

The writer should keep in mind that although the issues may be written late in the process, the judge may read them first. They should be written so the judge will want to rule in the client's favor before reading the argument section. Issues identify for the court the nature of the dispute. It cannot be overemphasized that how a dispute is framed often determines the way the dispute is resolved. Even if the issues are not written last, they should be read last to ensure that they are worded in the most favorable light possible, given the facts and procedural posture of the case.

In summary, the writer should incorporate the facts into the statement of the issues in a way that suggests a favorable answer for the client.

Argument

The argument section is the main part of the brief. Structurally, the argument section is divided into subsections that usually correspond with the number of issues, although at times several issues may be grouped under one subsection. Each subsection is given a subhead. These subheads serve the same function as headlines in a newspaper. A well-written subhead capsulizes the argument for that subsection. If written correctly, the subhead might be adopted as the rule of law or *ratio decidendi* of the case.

There is no rigid formula for structuring or ordering subtopics in an argument section. Sometimes the issues or subtopics are placed in the order they arose in the lower court, and sometimes the more important issues are placed before the less important ones. Sometimes issues are ordered so as to educate the court by presenting more basic issues before more complicated issues.

Under each subhead the writer presents the argument relating to the particular issue. Chapter 10 discusses how a writer develops the discussion section of a memorandum by identifying the issue, identifying the legal principle applicable to that issue, applying the legal principle to the facts of the case, and then reaching a conclusion. As in the discussion section of a memorandum, each subsection of the argument in a brief should address each of these steps of the legal thought process. As in memoranda, however, the process may not be developed in the same sequence in every brief.

The writer, in beginning to develop a subtopic, should remember that the judge deciding the case may not have extensive knowledge of the facts or law of the case. A brief must first educate and then persuade the court on the merits of the issues. The first sentence under a subtopic is sometimes the most difficult sentence to write, especially for an inexperienced brief writer. Sometimes writer's block occurs because the writer has not carefully thought out the argument before beginning the writing process, but even an experienced brief writer occasionally encounters writer's block. The first sentence should be written like the lead sentence of a news story: the legal writer, like the journalist, wants to capture the attention of the reader. This first sentence might begin with a recitation of certain key facts or a critical legal principle. It should lead with strength if possible.

There is an old adage among lawyers: "If the law is on your side, argue the law. If the facts are on your side, argue the facts. If neither the law nor the facts are on your side, then pound the table." In brief writing, there is some truth to this adage. If the facts enhance the argument, the facts should be emphasized. If the law favors the argument, the concentration should be on legal principles. If neither the law nor the facts advance the argument, however, the writer should consider not making it.

Arguing the Facts

The most common mistake of an inexperienced brief writer is to ignore the facts of a case in preparing the argument section of the brief. Many inexperienced writers concentrate too much of their argument on legal principles. Yet the facts caused the dispute. The facts are why the parties are in court. The key facts relating to each subtopic should be included in the discussion so the court can appreciate the relationship of the facts to the issue.

The court may not decide the case immediately after hearing the testimony. In fact, the case might be taken under advisement and decided months later. Then the trial brief will be used to refresh the judge's recollection of the case. Accurate factual accounts may be adopted by a court in its findings or decision.

In every brief, the facts set the stage for selecting the applicable legal principles. The argument section should create the most favorable picture possible of the relevant facts related to the issue being argued. Too often this picture is omitted.

In summary, the argument section of the brief should emphasize the factual strengths of the client's position while effectively minimizing the factual strengths of the opposing side. The argument section must explain how the facts impact the legal principles. The argument section also must explain how the different versions of the facts may affect the outcome of the case. An effective brief explains how facts are unique. Which set of facts is used by the court may determine what rules of law are selected to decide the case.

Arguing Legal Principles

In some cases, it may not be clear what legal principles will be used to decide the case. The common law is premised on the concept of evolving principles to meet changing situations. Legal principles change. There might not be a principle to deal with a new problem, or the existing principles might be contradictory. As new cases are decided, legal principles grow into general principles or splinter into narrower principles. Existing legal principles are rejected or approved. The function of a legal professional in preparing an argument is to demonstrate which rule of law ought to be applied to solve the dispute. Lawyers argue the applicability of one rule versus another rule.

An experienced attorney once told the author that if he had an old precedent supporting his position, he would argue, "This precedent has remained a settled principle for over a century." If the old precedent was against him, he would argue, "This antiquated principle has no validity in the twentieth century." If a recently decided case was favorable to his position, he would say, "This recently decided precedent has now settled this issue." If the recently decided case was unfavorable to his position, he would say, "This issue is still unsettled."

As the research phase is completed, the brief writer assesses what legal principles are applicable to the dispute and how those principles will likely affect the outcome of the case. Like the writer of a memorandum, the brief writer must first locate any binding authority. When there is binding authority, the issue is usually simple to argue. More commonly, though, there is uncertainty about the applicable legal principle or how that principle should be applied.

In some jurisdictions, courts may have already settled questions that are only now being litigated in a particular case. These courts may have found problems with expanding or narrowing the principle. Another jurisdiction may already have grappled with alternative approaches. These persuasive precedents may help a court decide on an approach in the case at hand.

On occasion, one case might contradict other cases in the same jurisdiction. This can happen when a court decides a case without completely researching the law. A court will then have to decide which case to follow.

As the legal professional identifies the principle applicable to a dispute, he or she must assess why a principle should be applied to the case. Are there sound logical or policy reasons justifying the use of the principle? For example, in the early 1900s, many states passed so-called **guest acts.** These laws prevented a guest (a passenger) in an automobile from suing the driver for negligence. At the time most of these laws were passed, there were few automobiles. Giving a passenger a ride was considered a treat. These guest laws were based on the belief that a person should not be allowed to sue someone who was doing them a favor. Today many families have two or three automobiles, and in most situations, damage claims are paid by insurance. The rationale for guest acts has eroded. There is little

---

TERMS

guest acts State statutes that govern the liability of the owner or operator of a motor vehicle for injury to an automobile guest. Under such statutes, the owner or driver is liable to a guest only for injury resulting from gross negligence.

justification for permitting someone to be careless with the modern automobile. Today it is not a special treat to ride in a car. It is something people do daily. As a result, many states have held their guest laws unconstitutional. Some states have not. In each situation, however, the courts have reassessed the rationale for these laws—the same as the legal professional should do in every brief.

When the Principle Is Ripe for Change Presented with facts that strongly suggest a change in the way a legal principle is applied, a court will sometimes be reluctant to change settled authority, no matter how sympathetic the facts. In such a case, the brief writer must provide an argument that explains the rationale for a change in the principle. The principle may be changed because other jurisdictions have confronted similar situations and have made the change. The principle may be changed because the logical extension of the rule leads to absurd results. The principle may need to be changed because of changes in society. When a court sees a distinction or a rationale for changing a principle, it will more readily conform the principle to the changed environment. This is how the common law system is intended to work.

When There Is No Decided Authority As in memorandum writing, legal professionals sometimes find there is no decided authority on a subject. The brief writer must then construct an argument telling the court what principles *ought* to be used by the court in deciding the case. In *Griswold*, there was no marital right of privacy before the decision of the Supreme Court in that case. See the brief filed by the appellant with the Supreme Court in *Griswold* (in the appendix). Notice how most of the argument section under Point III is spent developing the principle that Griswold felt was dispositive of the case.

When There Is Authority for and Against the Position At times there are cases both for and against the position. Although the brief writer will focus on the supportive precedent, the authority against the position must not be ignored. The writer should explain why these cases should not be followed. The cases should be harmonized if possible. If the cases cannot be harmonized, the result of the contrary cases should be criticized. When a writer ignores contrary authority, the court sometimes infers that those decisions are more harmful to the client's position than is actually so.

When the Law Is Contrary to the Position If the principle of law is clearly contrary to the position, the party must decide whether the argument should even be presented. A party is permitted to argue for a good faith change in authority. The writer, however, should make sure a good faith argument is possible. Otherwise sanctions can be taken against the client. No brief should ever present a frivolous argument. Although a brief writer is an advocate, the lawyer who signs the brief is an officer of the court. That lawyer has certain ethical duties that transcend the adversary relationship.

Arguing the Application of Law to Fact

Many brief writers quit after they discuss the facts and legal principles. Yet this is when most legal arguments begin. In appellate briefs, for example, the facts have already been decided. The parties may even have agreed on the legal principles applicable to the dispute. In many of these cases, the parties are arguing over the way rules are applied.

The issue in many cases is whether the rules fit the facts. Different facts may change the rules that will apply. So the parties argue over the significance of the facts. Suppose a statute reads as follows:

> Whoever steals, takes, or abstracts, or by fraud or deception obtains, or attempts so to obtain, from or out of any mail, post office, or station thereof, letter box, mail receptacle, or any mail route or other authorized depository for mail matter, or from a letter or mail carrier, any letter, postal card, package, bag, or mail, or abstracts or removes from any such letter, package, bag, or mail, any article or thing contained therein, or secretes, embezzles, or destroys any such letter, postal card, package, bag, or mail, or any article or thing contained therein. . . .

Suppose the client lives in an apartment with a roommate. The mail is placed through a slot in the door and then drops to the floor. The client opens her roommate's mail. Is there a violation of this statute? What facts are significant here? The student should try arguing both sides of this issue.

Brief writers develop an argument by the same inductive or deductive approaches used in developing the discussion section of a memorandum. The brief can use analysis or illustrations to argue the conclusion. The analysis should explore the rationale for the legal principle or rule. In the mail theft situation, the government might argue that the statute is meant to ensure the intended recipient receives the mail and that the statute should be broadly read to meet that objective. The defendant might argue that criminal statutes are narrowly construed and that once the mail is inside the apartment, it can no longer be considered within the realm of the post office authority.

The brief writer shows how facts of the case differ from those of other decided cases (distinguishing the case from other cases). The brief writer might describe how a favorable decision for the client would make other cases or statutes consistent (harmonizing the rules). In arguing the application of law to facts, the object is to convince a court that the most logical and wisest approach is to fit the rule to the client's position.

The facts of the case are usually unique in some way. New facts bend rules. The brief writer who can draw a word illustration of how facts are different or distinguishable from other decided cases or how facts are outside the scope of a statute starts the brief-writing process with a decided advantage.

The Conclusion Section

The conclusion section of the brief tells the court what the party wants. Does the writer want the court to grant an injunction, award damages, order a party to produce a document, or reverse a case? In short, this section tells the court what ruling the party is seeking. The language should be specific. It is useless to present a brilliant argument if the court is unsure after reading the argument what relief is appropriate.

§ 11.4 Style of a Brief

Style is the personalized way one writes. A brief is written in a formal style, but formal does not mean stuffy or boring. As in any form of writing, the writer should use a style consistent with his or her personality. A writer cannot educate or persuade a court by using stuffy language or convoluted principles a judge cannot comprehend.

The most important principle for a brief writer is to write so the court understands and appreciates the client's position. The brief must be readable. If the court consists of judges who are sophisticated students of the law, the argument can explain the subtleties of the law. If the court is less sophisticated, the argument must be written more to the point.

Chapter 5 of this text addresses how to develop a more readable style. Sentence or word length can be adjusted, depending on the audience. Shorter sentences are generally easier to understand, as are shorter words. The writer should not search for longer words to impress the court but should search for shorter words to make the brief more understandable. The most brilliant argument is useless if the court does not understand it. The goal is to develop an argument in readable language. Yet readability is just one concern of the brief writer. A brief must also persuade.

Law deals with human problems. Although brief writers cannot inject personal opinions into their arguments, they need to present briefs with their clients' interests in mind. The writer's style should not be detached from the client's position. A brief writer presents an argument as a novelist tells a story. The novel is a story about events that occur, not about the novelist's opinion of the events. A brief is an argument. A novel develops a story with a plot. A brief develops an argument by combining facts and law. This is the design of a brief. The way the legal professional tells these facts and law can affect the decision in a case.

Rules for Effective Brief Writing

Here are some rules that will help the writer present the facts and law in an effective way:

1. Do not simply rephrase legal authority   The study of law requires the ability to derive legal principles from primary source materials. Inexperienced legal professionals tend to read a case or secondary source and simply repeat or rehash the language in their brief without really understanding the material. The point is to read and understand the source law materials, and then explain the legal principle in a readable style without losing the meaning of the original principle.

2. Do not discuss case after case in paragraph after paragraph   Cases are precedents to be followed. It is the principle or holding in the case, however, and not the case itself, that is important. One of the best diagnostic clues for determining whether the principles are being handled correctly is to look at the paragraphs. If one paragraph begins with "In *Smith v. Jones* the court said . . .," and the next paragraph begins with "In *Doe v. Roe* the court said . . .," and the third paragraph begins with "In *Barber v. Martinez* . . .," it is likely the writer is only discussing the cases found, and not synthesizing those cases. The cure for this problem is to review the signals set out in Chapter 10 (especially Figure 10–1) to see whether the paragraphs can be combined into a single principle.

3. Do not inject your opinion   The court does not care how the *writer* feels on this issue. It cares about precedent, the merits of the case, and the logic of the position. The writer's opinion does not belong in a brief.

4. Do not write in first person   The brief is written formally. Phrases such as "I believe . . ." and "I think . . ." should not be used. A brief, like most novels, should be written in the third person.

5. Do not exaggerate or misrepresent your client's position   If the court feels the writer is not relating the client's position accurately, the result is usually unfavorable to the client.

6. Do not ignore the facts in the issue and argument sections   In their first efforts to write a brief, many students ignore the facts when they get to the issue and argument sections. But facts are what makes one case different from others. The writer who includes the facts only in the fact section and forgets the facts in the issue and argument sections of the brief is generally an inexperienced brief writer.

7. Do not ignore correct citation form   There are rules for citing cases and statutes, and a brief that fails to follow the correct citation form creates a poor impression on a court. Follow the citation form in *The Bluebook: A Uniform System of Citation* unless the rules of the court dictate otherwise.

8. Do not ignore precedents that obviously impact a decision in your case   An argument cannot omit relevant information. If certain precedents will obviously be relevant to a decision, these cases should be discussed.

9. Do not ignore the court rules   Even if the rules are read before the writer starts, it is good practice to reread the rules when the writer has finished. It is easier to see if the court rules have been complied with when the project is complete. The rules are different for each court, so the writer must become familiar with the relevant rules before starting a particular brief-writing project.

10. Do not neglect to proofread the brief carefully   A judge will read the brief. If there are grammatical or spelling errors, for instance, the court will be inclined to think that the writer did not feel the case was important enough to proofread. When a writer says, "My clients right's," a judge will cringe and wonder who is protecting that client.

11. Do not say "the law is clear . . ." or "it is obvious . . ."   Unless the law is "clear" or it is "obvious," the brief writer should avoid blanket conclusions. Most of the time these statements are red flags that the law is not clear or that it is not obvious. The writer loses credibility with the court when this happens.

Too much legal work is done under the pressure of a deadline. The brief writer should allow plenty of time for preparing the brief. If the writer rushes against a deadline, he or she will not have sufficient time to proofread carefully and check the rules.

 SIDEBAR

---

§ 11.5   Response or Reply Brief

Briefs argue disputes. Although there are instances where briefs are submitted simultaneously to a court, usually the parties take turns: One party (the moving party or the appellant) writes the first brief, and the opposing side (the nonmoving party or the appellee) then files a response brief. The party filing the first brief may have to file a reply brief to the response brief.

Before preparing a response or reply brief, the strengths of the client's case should be outlined. The writer should try to ascertain how the original brief handled these strengths. Did the other party omit facts or fail to discuss the facts in the argument section? Did the original brief omit a statement or case? Did the original brief minimize or exaggerate facts or the law? By identifying the strategy of the opponent, the writer should be able to refocus the dispute.

Some judges may read thousands of pages of briefs in a year. A judge soon learns whether a party is fairly stating the case. If the original brief omitted key facts, the writer should note the omission without saying the opposing side was less than honest. The court will draw the conclusion. If the original brief misstated a key legal principle, the exact quote from the court decision should be given. The quote should be compared with the misstatement. An effective technique is to quote the misrepresented material in the brief and then show why it is wrong. Again, the court can tell whether the party correctly stated the applicable principles. Seldom, if ever, should the brief attack the other brief writer.

At times a brief writer may personally attack the client. The writer should not respond to such an *ad hominen* argument but should simply point out that the other side prefers to avoid the legal and factual arguments in the case and would rather focus on nonlegal and personal issues.

At other times the original brief will have fairly stated the opponent's case. In those situations, the writer's duty is to state the client's position as forcefully and fairly as possible.

Briefs are intended to present disputes in a civilized manner. Both sides air their arguments, and then a court makes a decision. The decision becomes part of the common law tradition. Good decisions are made when good briefs are filed. In writing a brief, the writer should remember his or her importance to the process.

§ 11.6 A Sample Brief

Griswold v. Connecticut was decided by the United States Supreme Court. Before the decision in that case, both parties filed briefs with the Supreme Court. Both briefs are reprinted in the appendix. The student should read these briefs and see how the writers have applied the principles of effective brief writing.

Writing Exercises

1. Assume the same facts as in problem 4 of the writing exercises in Chapter 10 except there was no speeding involved on curvy roads. Instead, the driver had been driving normally but lost control of the vehicle for no explained reason and hit a viaduct. Assume that the driver was intoxicated and was arrested. The driver tested .16% on the Breathalyzer, and .10% is the minimum standard, so the driver pled guilty to a misdemeanor—driving while intoxicated—charge. You represent the passenger who sued the driver. In that lawsuit, the court granted a summary judgment for the driver and against your client. Prepare a two-page argument section for a brief arguing that *Stillwell v. Adams* (in the appendix) should be overruled.

2. Reread the facts of *Smith v. Lewis* (in the appendix). Rewrite these facts for a brief that would be favorable to the appellant.

3. Follow the instructions in problem 2 but rewrite the facts for a brief that would be favorable to the appellee.

4. Your firm is asked to file a petition to the California Supreme Court to reconsider its ruling in *Smith v. Lewis*. Describe the main theme or themes you would use in preparing a brief to be filed in connection with that petition.

Enrichment Activity

1. Reread *Griswold v. Connecticut* in the appendix. Trace the arguments made by the appellant and the appellee in their briefs to the rationales used by the different justices in their concurring and dissenting opinions. Comment on how much of their reasoning was adopted from the briefs of counsel and how much was their original thought.

APPENDICES

OUTLINE

**ROBERT LUCAS et al., Plaintiffs
and Appellants,**

v.

**L. S. HAMM, Defendant and Respondent.
S. F. 20269.**

Supreme Court of California,
In Bank.
Sept. 5, 1961.
Rehearing Denied Oct. 4, 1961.

GIBSON, Chief Justice.

Plaintiffs, who are some of the beneficiaries under the will of Eugene H. Emmick, deceased, brought this action for damages against defendant L. S. Hamm, an attorney at law who had been engaged by the testator to prepare the will. They have appealed from a judgment of dismissal entered after an order sustaining a general demurrer to the second amended complaint without leave to amend.

The allegations of the first and second causes of action are summarized as follows: Defendant agreed with the testator, for a consideration, to prepare a will and codicils thereto for him by which plaintiffs were to be designated as beneficiaries of a trust provided for by paragraph Eighth of the will and were to receive 15% of the residue as specified in that paragraph. Defendant, in violation of instructions and in breach of his contract, negligently prepared testamentary instruments containing phraseology that was invalid by virtue of section 715.2 and former sections 715.1 and 716 of the Civil Code relating to restraints on alienation and the rule against perpetuities.[1] Paragraph Eighth of these instruments "transmitted" the residual estate in trust and provided that the "trust shall cease and terminate at 12 o'clock noon on a day five years after the date upon which the order distributing the trust property to the trustee is made by the Court having jurisdiction over the probation of this will." After the death of the testator the instruments were admitted to probate. Subsequently defendant, as draftsman of the instruments and as counsel of record for the executors, advised plaintiffs in writing that the residual trust provision was invalid and that plaintiffs would be deprived of the entire amount to which they would have been entitled if the provision had been valid unless they made a settlement with the blood relatives of the testator under which plaintiffs would receive a lesser amount than that provided for them by the testator. As the direct and proximate result of the negligence of defendant and his breach of contract in preparing the testamentary instruments and the written advice referred to above, plaintiffs were compelled to enter into

---

1. Former section 715.1 of the Civil Code, as it read at the times involved here, provided: "The absolute power of alienation cannot be suspended, by any limitation or condition whatever, for a period longer than 21 years after some life in being at the creation of the interest and any period of gestation involved in the situation to which the limitation applies. The lives selected to govern the time of suspension must not be so numerous or so situated that evidence of their deaths is likely to be unreasonably difficult to obtain."

Section 715.2 reads as follows: "No interest in real or personal property shall be good unless it must vest, if at all, not later than 21 years after some life in being at the creation of the interest and any period of gestation involved in the situation to which the limitation applies. The lives selected to govern the time of vesting must not be so numerous or so situated that evidence of their deaths is likely to be unreasonably difficult to obtain. It is intended by the enactment of this section to make effective in this State the American common-law rule against perpetuities."

Former section 716, as it read at the times involved here, provided: "Every future interest is void in its creation which, by any possibility, may suspend the absolute power of alienation for a longer period than is prescribed in this chapter. Such power of alienation is suspended when there are no persons in being by whom an absolute interest in possession can be conveyed. The period of time during which an interest is destructible pursuant to the uncontrolled volition and for the exclusive personal benefit of the person having such a power of destruction is not to be included in determining the existence of a suspension of the absolute power of alienation or the permissible period for the vesting of an interest within the rule against perpetuities."

a settlement under which they received a share of the estate amounting to $75,000 less than the sum which they would have received pursuant to testamentary instruments drafted in accordance with the directions of the testator.

(The third cause of action will be discussed separately because it concerns matters not involved in the first two counts.)

It was held in Buckley v. Gray, 110 Cal. 339, 42 P. 900, 31 L.R.A. 862, that an attorney who made a mistake in drafting a will was not liable for negligence or breach of contract to a person named in the will who was deprived of benefits as a result of the error. The court stated that an attorney is liable to his client alone with respect to actions based on negligence in the conduct of his professional duties, and it was reasoned that there could be no recovery for mere negligence where there was no privity by contract or otherwise between the defendant and the person injured. 110 Cal. at pages 342-343, 42 P. 900. The court further concluded that there could be no recovery on the theory of a contract for the benefit of a third person, because the contract with the attorney was not expressly for the plaintiff's benefit and the testatrix only remotely intended the plaintiff to be benefited as a result of the contract. 110 Cal. at pages 346-347, 42 P. 900. For the reasons hereinafter stated the case is overruled.

The reasoning underlying the denial of tort liability in the Buckley case, i.e., the stringent privity test, was rejected in Biakanja v. Irving, 49 Cal.2d 647, 648-650, 320 P.2d 16, 65 A.L.R.2d 1358, where we held that a notary public who, although not authorized to practice law, prepared a will but negligently failed to direct proper attestation was liable in tort to an intended beneficiary who was damaged because of the invalidity of the instrument. It was pointed out that since 1895, when Buckley was decided, the rule that in the absence of privity there was no liability for negligence committed in the

performance of a contract had been greatly liberalized. 49 Cal.2d at page 649, 320 P.2d 16. In restating the rule it was said that the determination whether in a specific case the defendant will be held liable to a third person not in privity is a matter of policy and involves the balancing of various factors, among which are the extent to which the transaction was intended to affect the plaintiff, the foreseeability of harm to him, the degree of certainty that the plaintiff suffered injury, the closeness of the connection between the defendant's conduct and the injury, and the policy of preventing future harm. 49 Cal.2d at page 650, 320 P.2d 16. The same general principle must be applied in determining whether a beneficiary is entitled to bring an action for negligence in the drafting of a will when the instrument is drafted by an attorney rather than by a person not authorized to practice law.

Many of the factors which led to the conclusion that the notary public involved in Biakanja was liable are equally applicable here. As in Biakanja, one of the main purposes which the transaction between defendant and the testator intended to accomplish was to provide for the transfer of property to plaintiffs; the damage to plaintiffs in the event of invalidity of the bequest was clearly foreseeable; it became certain, upon the death of the testator without change of the will, that plaintiffs would have received the intended benefits but for the asserted negligence of defendant; and if persons such as plaintiffs are not permitted to recover for the loss resulting from negligence of the draftsman, no one would be able to do so, and the policy of preventing future harm would be impaired.

Since defendant was authorized to practice the profession of an attorney, we must consider an additional factor not present in Biakanja, namely, whether the recognition of liability to beneficiaries of wills negligently drawn by attorneys would impose an undue burden on the profession. Although in some situations liability could be large and unpredictable in amount, this is also true of an attorney's liability to his client. We are of the view that the extension of his liability to beneficiaries injured by a negligently drawn will does not place an undue burden on the profession, particularly when we take into consideration that a contrary conclusion would cause the innocent beneficiary to bear the loss. The fact that the notary public involved in Biakanja was guilty of unauthorized practice of the law was only a minor factor in determining that he was liable, and the absence of the factor in the present case does not justify reaching a different result.

It follows that the lack of privity between plaintiffs and defendant does not preclude plaintiffs from maintaining an action in tort against defendant.

Neither do we agree with the holding in Buckley that beneficiaries damaged by an error in the drafting of a will cannot recover from the draftsman on the theory that they are third-party beneficiaries of the contract between him and the testator.[2] Obviously the main purpose of a contract for the drafting of a will is to accomplish the future transfer of the estate of the testator to the beneficiaries named in the will, and therefore it seems improper to hold, as was done in Buckley, that the testator intended only "remotely" to benefit those persons. It is true that under a contract for the benefit of a third person performance is usually to be rendered directly to the beneficiary, but this is not necessarily the case. (See Rest., Contracts, § 133, com. d; 2 Williston on Contracts (3rd ed.1959) 829.) For example, where a life insurance policy lapsed because a bank failed to perform its agreement to pay the premiums out of the insured's bank account, it was held that after the insured's death the beneficiaries could recover against the bank as third-party beneficiaries. Walker Bank & Trust Co. v. First Security Corp., 9 Utah 2d 215, 341 P.2d 944, 945 et seq. Persons who had agreed to procure liability insurance for the protection of the promisees but did not do so were also held liable to injured persons who would have been covered by the insurance, the courts stating that all persons who might be injured were third-party beneficiaries of the contracts to procure insurance. Johnson v. Holmes Tuttle Lincoln-Merc., Inc., 160 Cal.App.2d 290, 296 et seq., 325 P.2d 193; James Stewart & Co. v. Law, 149 Tex. 392, 233 S.W.2d 558, 561-562, 22 A.L.R.2d 639. Since, in a situation like those presented here and in the Buckley case, the main purpose of the testator in making his agreement with the attorney is to benefit the persons named in his will and this intent can be effectuated, in the event of a breach by the attorney, only by giving the beneficiaries a right of action, we should recognize, as a matter of policy, that they are entitled to recover as third-party beneficiaries. See 2 Williston on Contracts (3rd ed. 1959) pp. 843-844; 4 Corbin on Contracts (1951) pp. 8, 20.

Section 1559 of the Civil Code, which provides for enforcement by a third person of a contract made "expressly" for his benefit, does not preclude this result. The effect of the section is

---

2. It has been recognized in other jurisdictions that the *client* may recover in a contract action for failure of the attorney to carry out his agreement. (See 5 Am.Jur. 331; 49 A.L.R.2d 1216, 1219-1221; Prosser, Selected Topics on the Law of Torts (1954) pp. 438, 442.) This is in accord with the general rule stated in Comunale v. Traders & General Ins. Co., 50 Cal.2d 654, 663, 328 P.2d 198, 68 A.L.R.2d 883, that where a case sounds in both tort and contract, the plaintiff will ordinarily have freedom of election between the two actions.

to exclude enforcement by persons who are only incidentally or remotely benefited. See Hartman Ranch Co. v. Associated Oil Co., 10 Cal.2d 232, 244, 73 P.2d 1163; cf. 4 Corbin on Contracts (1951) pp. 23-24. As we have seen, a contract for the drafting of a will unmistakably shows the intent of the testator to benefit the persons to be named in the will, and the attorney must necessarily understand this.

Defendant relies on language in Smith v. Anglo-California Trust Co., 205 Cal. 496, 502, 271 P. 898, and Fruitvale Canning Co. v. Cotton, 115 Cal.App.2d 622, 625, 252 P.2d 953, that to permit a third person to bring an action on a contract there must be "an intent clearly manifested by the promisor" to secure some benefit to the third person. This language, which was not necessary to the decision in either of the cases, is unfortunate. Insofar as intent to benefit a third person is important in determining his right to bring an action under a contract, it is sufficient that the promisor must have understood that the promisee had such intent. (Cf. Rest., Contracts, § 133, subds. 1(a) and 1(b); 4 Corbin on Contracts (1951) pp. 16-18; 2 Williston on Contracts (3rd ed. 1959) pp. 836-839.) No specific manifestation by the promisor of an intent to benefit the third person is required. The language relied on by defendant is disapproved to the extent that it is inconsistent with these views.

We conclude that intended beneficiaries of a will who lose their testamentary rights because of failure of the attorney who drew the will to properly fulfill his obligations under his contract with the testator may recover as third-party beneficiaries.

However, an attorney is not liable either to his client or to a beneficiary under a will for errors of the kind alleged in the first and second causes of action.

The general rule with respect to the liability of an attorney for failure to properly perform his duties to his client is that the attorney, by accepting employment to give legal advice or to render other legal services, impliedly agrees to use such skill, prudence, and diligence as lawyers of ordinary skill and capacity commonly possess and exercise in the performance of the tasks which they undertake. Estate of Kruger, 130 Cal. 621, 626, 63 P. 31; Moser v. Western Harness Racing Ass'n, 89 Cal. App.2d 1, 7, 200 P.2d 7; Armstrong v. Adams, 102 Cal.App. 677, 684, 283 P. 871; see Wade, The Attorney's Liability for Negligence (1959) 12 Vanderbilt Law Rev. 755, 762-765; 5 Am.Jur. 336. The attorney is not liable for every mistake he may make in his practice; he is not, in the absence of an express agreement, an insurer of the soundness of his opinions or of the validity of an instrument that he is engaged to draft; and he is not liable for being in error as to a question of law on which reasonable doubt may be entertained by well-informed lawyers. See Lally v. Kuster, 177 Cal. 783, 786, 171 P. 961; Savings Bank v. Ward, 100 U.S. 195, 198, 25 L.Ed. 621; 5 Am.Jur. 335; 7 C.J.S. Attorney and Client § 143, p. 980. These principles are equally applicable whether the plaintiff's claim is based on tort or breach of contract.

The complaint, as we have seen, alleges that defendant drafted the will in such a manner that the trust was invalid because it violated the rules relating to perpetuities and restraints on alienation. These closely akin subjects have long perplexed the courts and the bar. Professor Gray, a leading authority in the field, stated: "There is something in the subject which seems to facilitate error. Perhaps it is because the mode of reasoning is unlike that with which lawyers are most familiar. * * * A long list might be formed of the demonstrable blunders with regard to its questions made by eminent men, blunders which they themselves have been sometimes the first to acknowledge; and there are few lawyers of any practice in drawing wills and settlements who have not at some time either fallen into the net which the Rule spreads for the unwary, or at least shuddered to think how narrowly they have escaped it." Gray, The Rule Against Perpetuities (4th ed. 1942) p. xi; see also Leach, Perpetuities Legislation (1954) 67 Harv.L.Rev. 1349 [describing the rule as a "technicality-ridden legal nightmare" and a "dangerous instrumentality in the hands of most members of the bar"]. Of the California law on perpetuities and restraints it has been said that few, if any, areas of the law have been fraught with more confusion or concealed more traps for the unwary draftsman; that members of the bar, probate courts, and title insurance companies make errors in these matters; that the code provisions adopted in 1872 created a situation worse than if the matter had been left to the common law, and that the legislation adopted in 1951 (under which the will involved here was drawn), despite the best of intentions, added further complexities. (See 38 Cal.Jur.2d 443; Coil, Perpetuities and Restraints; A Needed Reform (1955) 30 State Bar J. 87, 88-90.)

In view of the state of the law relating to perpetuities and restraints on alienation and the nature of the error, if any, assertedly made by defendant in preparing the instrument, it would not be proper to hold that defendant failed to use such skill, prudence, and diligence as lawyers of ordinary skill and capacity commonly exercise. The provision of the will quoted in the complaint, namely, that the trust was to terminate five years after the order of the probate court distributing the property to the trustee, could cause the trust to be invalid only because of the remote possibility that the order of distribution would be delayed for a period longer than a life in being at the creation of the interest plus 16 years (the 21-year statutory period less the five

years specified in the will). Although it has been held that a possibility of this type could result in invalidity of a bequest (Estate of Johnston, 47 Cal.2d 265, 269-270, 303 P.2d 1; Estate of Campbell, 28 Cal.App.2d 102, 103 et seq., 82 P.2d 22), the possible occurrence of such a delay was so remote and unlikely that an attorney of ordinary skill acting under the same circumstances might well have "fallen into the net which the Rule spreads for the unwary" and failed to recognize the danger. We need not decide whether the trust provision of the will was actually invalid or whether, as defendant asserts, the complaint fails to allege facts necessary to enable such a determination,[3] because we have concluded that in any event an error of the type relied on by plaintiffs does not show negligence or breach of contract on the part of defendant. It is apparent that plaintiffs have not stated and cannot state causes of action with respect to the first two counts, and the trial court did not abuse its discretion in denying leave to amend as to these counts.

The third cause of action contains additional allegations as follows: After admission of the will and codicils to probate, Harold Houghton Emmick, Walton Russell Emmick, Cleta Inez Spelman, and Retha Newell, hereinafter called the contestants, instituted a will contest. The executors, defendant, and the contestants tentatively reached a settlement agreement, subject to court approval, under which $10,000 would be paid to the contestants from the assets of the estate in return for which each contestant would sign an "appropriate release." Defendant was negligent in the performance of his duties in that he caused to be executed on behalf of the estate and those interested therein, including plaintiffs, releases which did not preclude the contestants from a subsequent

---

3. Defendant asserts that a provision of a will like the one quoted in the complaint could not cause a trust to be invalid unless it also appeared that there were contingent interests which could not vest within the statutory time or that the trust could

not be terminated by the beneficiaries acting together within the statutory period. See Estate of Phelps, 182 Cal. 752, 759-760, 190 P. 17; Estate of Heberle, 155 Cal. 723, 726-727, 102 P. 935; Rest., Trusts, Second, § 337.

attack upon the validity of the testamentary instruments. After complete execution of the releases and their transmittal to escrow but before approval of the compromise by the court, defendant was advised by competent counsel that the residual clause of the will and codicils was invalid as a violation of the rule against perpetuities and that as a consequence the phraseology of the releases was inadequate to protect the estate and persons interested therein, and defendant was requested by competent counsel to modify the releases and insert appropriate language suggested by counsel under which the contestants would release the estate and persons interested in it from any claims of whatsoever kind or nature. Defendant refused to do so and also refused to call the court's attention to the recommendations. As a consequence of the failure to direct the matter to the attention of the court, the order approving the compromise was made on the assumption that the releases would give adequate protection. The sum of $10,000 was paid to the contestants from the assets of the estate, and the releases were filed in the proceedings. Subsequently the contestants joined in a legal attack upon the validity of the residual clause of the will and codicils and by virtue of the invalidity of the clause participated in the settlement referred to above concerning paragraph Eighth of the will. If the releases had been prepared in accord with good legal practice they would have precluded such participation, with the result that plaintiffs would have received an additional sum of $15,000 from the estate.

This cause of action, unlike the first two, does not concern defendant's conduct as attorney for the testator, but, rather, asserted negligence by him when acting as attorney for the executors with respect to the execution of releases in the settlement of a will contest based on lack of testamentary capacity. It is undisputed that the releases were adequate to preclude any further litigation of that contest, but plaintiffs assert that defendant had a duty to obtain releases which, in addition, would waive all other claims of the contestants against the estate and prevent them from subsequently attacking the validity of the trust provisions.

There are no allegations that the contestants, either at the time of the negotiations for the settlement or at the time of the signing of the releases, were willing to waive their rights to make other attacks upon the will after the settlement of that contest. In the absence of additional allegations we must assume that the agreed sum of $10,000 was intended solely for the settlement of the contest and the ground on which it was based, i.e., lack of testamentary capacity, and it would ordinarily be expected that the contestants would have demanded an additional sum for a more extensive waiver terminating their rights to attack the validity of the various provisions of the will. The written releases, of course, were required to conform to the settlement agreement. Under these circumstances it could well be argued that the attorneys for the contestants would have been derelict in their duty to their clients if they had approved broader releases. At most, under the allegations, defendant had a duty to request that the contestants sign broader releases, but there is no allegation that he failed to ask them to do so. The third count does not state a cause of action for negligence.

Although defendant pointed out in both the trial court and this court that there is no allegation that he could have secured releases different from the ones given, plaintiffs make no claim that they can amend their complaint so as to cure the deficiency, and we cannot properly hold that the trial court abused its discretion in denying leave to amend.

The judgment is affirmed.

TRAYNOR, SCHAUER, McCOMB, PETERS, WHITE and DOOLING, JJ., concur.

ROSEMARY E. SMITH, Plaintiff and
Respondent,
v.
JEROME R. LEWIS, Defendant
and Appellant.
Sac. 7981.
Supreme Court of California,
In Bank.
Jan. 20, 1975.

MOSK, Justice.

Defendant Jerome R. Lewis, an attorney, appeals from a judgment entered upon a jury verdict for plaintiff Rosemary E. Smith in an action for legal malpractice. The action arises as a result of legal services rendered by defendant to plaintiff in a prior divorce proceeding. The gist of plaintiff's complaint is that defendant negligently failed in the divorce action to assert her community interest in the retirement benefits of her husband.

Defendant principally contends, inter alia, that the law with regard to the characterization of retirement benefits was so unclear at the time he represented plaintiff as to insulate him from liability for failing to assert a claim therefor on behalf of his client.[1] We conclude defendant's appeal is without merit, and therefore affirm the judgment.

In 1943 plaintiff married General Clarence D. Smith. Between 1945 and his retirement in 1966 General Smith was employed by the California National Guard. As plaintiff testified, she informed defendant her husband "was paid by the state . . . it was a job just like anyone else goes to." For the first 16 years of that period the husband belonged to the State Employees' Retirement System, a contributory plan.[2] Between 1961 and the date of his retirement he belonged to the California National Guard retirement program, a noncontributory plan. In addition, by attending National Guard reserve drills he qualified for separate retirement benefits from the federal government, also through a noncontributory plan. The state and federal retirement programs each provide lifetime monthly benefits which terminate upon the death of the retiree. The programs make no allowance for the retiree's widow.

On January 1, 1967, the State of California began to pay General Smith gross retirement benefits of $796.26 per month. Payments under the federal program, however, will not begin until 1983, i.e., 17 years after his actual retirement, when General Smith reaches the age of 60. All benefits which General Smith is entitled to receive were earned during the time he was married to plaintiff.

On February 17, 1967, plaintiff retained defendant to represent her in a divorce action against General Smith. According to plaintiff's testimony, defendant advised her that her husband's retirement benefits were not community property. Three days later defendant filed plaintiff's complaint for divorce. General Smith's retirement benefits were not pleaded as items of community property, and therefore were not considered in the litigation or apportioned by

---

1. Defendant alternatively contends the state and federal military retirement benefits in question cannot properly be characterized as community property, and hence his advice to plaintiff was correct. As will appear, the contention is manifestly untenable in light of recent decisions by this court. (In re Marriage of Fithian (1974) 10 Cal.3d 592, 111 Cal.Rptr. 369, 517 P.2d 449; Waite v. Waite (1972) 6 Cal.3d 461, 99 Cal.Rptr. 325, 492 P.2d 13: Phillipson v. Board of Administration (1970) 3 Cal. 3d 32, 89 Cal.Rptr. 61, 473 P.2d 765.)

2. A contributory plan is one in which the member contributes to his retirement fund, normally through payroll deductions. A noncontributory plan is one in which no such contributions are made.

   The State Employees' Retirement System is now referred to as the Public Employees' Retirement System (Gov.Code, § 20000 et seq.).

the trial court. The divorce was uncontested and the interlocutory decree divided the minimal described community property and awarded Mrs. Smith $400 per month in alimony and child support. The final decree was entered on February 27, 1968.

On July 17, 1968, pursuant to a request by plaintiff, defendant filed on her behalf a motion to amend the decree, alleging under oath that because of his mistake, inadvertence, and excusable neglect (Code Civ. Proc., § 473) the retirement benefits of General Smith had been omitted from the list of community assets owned by the parties, and that such benefits were in fact community property. The motion was denied on the ground of untimeliness. Plaintiff consulted other counsel, and shortly thereafter filed this malpractice action against defendant.

Defendant admits in his testimony that he assumed General Smith's retirement benefits were separate property when he assessed plaintiff's community property rights. It is his position that as a matter of law an attorney is not liable for mistaken advice when well informed lawyers in the community entertain reasonable doubt as to the proper resolution of the particular legal question involved. Because, he asserts, the law defining the character of retirement benefits was uncertain at the time of his legal services to plaintiff, defendant contends the trial court committed error in refusing to grant his motions for nonsuit and judgment notwithstanding the verdict and in submitting the issue of negligence to the jury under appropriate instructions.[3]

The law is now settled in California that "retirement benefits which flow from the employment relationship, to the extent they have vested, are community property subject to equal division between the spouses in the event the marriage is dissolved." (In re Marriage of Fithian (1974) supra, 10 Cal.3d 592, 596, 111 Cal. Rptr. 369, 371, 517 P.2d 449, 451, citing Waite v. Waite (1972) supra, 6 Cal.3d 461, 99 Cal.Rptr. 325, 492 P.2d 13; Phillipson v. Board of Administration (1970) supra, 3 Cal.3d 32, 89 Cal.Rptr. 61, 473 P.2d 765; Benson v. City of Los Angeles (1963) 60 Cal.2d 355, 33 Cal.Rptr. 257, 384 P.2d 649; French v. French (1941) 17 Cal.2d 775, 112 P.2d 235; Crossan v. Crossan (1939) 35 Cal.App.2d 39, 94 P.2d 609.) Because such benefits are part of the consideration earned by the employee, they are accorded community treatment regardless of whether they derive from a state, federal, or private source, or from a contributory or noncontributory plan. (10 Cal.3d at p. 596, 111 Cal.Rptr. 369, 517 P.2d 449.) In light of these principles, it becomes apparent that General Smith's retirement pay must properly be characterized as community property.[4]

We cannot, however, evaluate the quality of defendant's professional services on the basis of the law as it appears today. In determining whether defendant exhibited the requisite degree of competence in his handling of plaintiff's divorce action, the crucial inquiry is whether his advice was so legally deficient when it was given that he may be found to have failed to use "such skill, prudence, and diligence as lawyers of ordinary skill and capacity commonly possess and

---

3. The jury was instructed as follows: "In performing legal services for a client in a divorce action an attorney has the duty to have that degree of learning and skill ordinarily possessed by attorneys of good standing, practicing in the same or similar locality and under similar circumstances."

"It is his further duty to use the care and skill ordinarily exercised in like cases by reputable members of his profession practicing in the same or a similar locality under similar circumstances, and to use reasonable diligence and his best judgment in the exercise of his skill and the accomplishment of his learning, in an effort to accomplish the best possible result for his client."

"A failure to perform any such duty is negligence."

"An attorney is not liable for every mistake he may make in his practice; he is not, in the absence of an express agreement, an insurer of the soundness of his opinions."

4. The fact General Smith will not receive any portion of the federal benefits until he reaches the age of 60 does not affect their community character. Though his right to the payments remained unmatured at the time of the divorce, it had fully vested. (In re Marriage of Fithian (1974) supra, 10 Cal.3d 592, 596, 111 Cal.Rptr. 369, 517 P.2d 449, fn. 2; Williamson v. Williamson (1962) 203 Cal.App.2d 8, 11, 21 Cal.Rptr. 164.)

exercise in the performance of the tasks which they undertake.'' (Lucas v. Hamm (1961) 56 Cal.2d 583, 591, 15 Cal.Rptr. 821, 825, 364 P.2d 685, 689.) We must, therefore examine the indicia of the law which were readily available to defendant at the time he performed the legal services in question.

The major authoritative reference works which attorneys routinely consult for a brief and reliable exposition of the law relevant to a specific problem uniformly indicated in 1967 that vested retirement benefits earned during marriage were generally subject to community treatment.[5] (See, e.g., Note, Pensions, and Reserve or Retired Pay, as Community Property, 134 A.L.R. 368; 15 Am.Jur.2d, Community Property, § 46, p. 859; 38 Cal.Jur.2d, Pensions, § 12, p. 325; 10 Cal.Jur.2d, Community Property, § 25, p. 692; 1 Cal.Family Lawyer (Cont. Ed.Bar 1962) p. 111; 4 Witkin, Summary of Cal.Law (1960) pp. 2723-2724; cf. 41 C.J.S. Husband and Wife § 475, p. 1010 & fn. 69 and 1967 Supp. p. 1011.) A typical statement appeared in The California Family Lawyer, a work with which defendant admitted general familiarity: ''Of increasing importance is the fact that pension or retirement benefits are community property, even though they are not paid or payable until after termination of the marriage by death or divorce.'' (1 Cal.Family Lawyer, supra, at p. 111.)

Although it is true this court had not foreclosed all conflicts on some aspects of the issue at that time, the community character of retirement benefits had been reported in a number of appellate opinions often cited in the literature and readily accessible to defendant. (Benson v. City of Los Angeles (1963) supra, 60 Cal.2d 355, 33 Cal.Rptr. 257, 384 P.2d 649;

French v. French (1941) supra, 17 Cal.2d 775, 112 P.2d 235; Cheney v. City & County of San Francisco (1936) 7 Cal.2d 565, 61 P.2d 754; Williamson v. Williamson (1962) supra, 203 Cal.App.2d 8, 21 Cal.Rptr. 164; Estate of Manley (1959) 169 Cal.App.2d 641, 337 P.2d 487; Estate of Perryman (1955) 133 Cal.App.2d 1, 283 P.2d 298; Crossan v. Crossan (1939) supra, 35 Cal. App.2d 39, 94 P.2d 609.) In *Benson*, decided four years before defendant was retained herein, we stated directly that ''pension rights which are earned during the course of a marriage are the community property of the employee and his wife.'' (60 Cal.2d at p. 359, 33 Cal.Rptr. at p. 259, 384 P.2d at p. 651.) In *French*, decided two decades earlier, we indicated that ''retire[ment] pay is community property because it is compensation for services rendered in the past.'' (17 Cal.2d at p. 778, 112 P.2d at p. 236.) The other cases contain equally unequivocal dicta.

We are aware, moreover, of no significant authority existing in 1967 which proposed a result contrary to that suggested by the cases and the literature, or which purported to rebut the general statutory presumption, as it applies to retirement benefits, that all property acquired by either spouse during marriage belongs to the community. (Civ.Code, § 5110, as amended Jan. 1, 1970; formerly Civ.Code, § 164.)

On the other hand, substantial uncertainty may have existed in 1967 with regard to the community character of General Smith's *federal* pension. The above-discussed treatises reveal a debate which lingered among members of the legal community at that time concerning the point at which retirement benefits actually vest.[6] (See also Kent, Pension Funds and Problems

---

5. In evaluating the competence of an attorney's services, we may justifiably consider his failure to consult familiar encyclopedias of the law. (People v. Ibarra (1963) 60 Cal. 2d 460, 465, 34 Cal.Rptr. 863, 386 P.2d 487.).

6. Indeed this debate may, to some extent, continue today. See, e.g., In re Marriage of Wilson (1974) 10 Cal.3d 851, 112 Cal.Rptr. 405, 519 P.2d 165.

Under California Community Property Laws (1950) 2 Stan.L.Rev. 447; Note, Community Property: Divison of Expectancies as Community Property at Time of Divorce (1942) 30 Cal. L.Rev. 469.) Because the federal payments were contingent upon General Smith's survival to age 60, 17 years subsequent to the divorce, it could have been argued with some force that plaintiff and General Smith shared a mere expectancy interest in the future benefits. (See French v. French (1941) supra, 17 Cal.2d 775, 778, 112 P.2d 235; but see fn. 4, *ante*.) Alternatively, a reasonable contention could have been advanced in 1967 that federal retirement benefits were the personal entitlement of the employee spouse and were not subject to community division upon divorce in the absence of express congressional approval. In fact, such was the conclusion reached in 1973 by Judge B. Abbott Goldberg in his scholarly article Is Armed Services Retired Pay Really Community Property? (1973) 48 State Bar Journal 12. Although we rejected Judge Goldberg's analysis in In re Marriage of Fithian (1974) supra, 10 Cal. 3d 592, 597, 111 Cal.Rptr. 369; 517 P.2d 449, footnote 2, the issue was clearly an arguable one upon which reasonable lawyers could differ. (See Sprague v. Morgan (1960) 185 Cal.App.2d 519, 523, 8 Cal.Rptr. 347; Annot., 45 A.L.R.2d 5, 15.)

Of course, the fact that in 1967 a reasonable argument could have been offered to support the characterization of General Smith's federal benefits as separate property does not indicate the trial court erred in submitting the issue of defendant's malpractice to the jury. The *state* benefits, the large majority of the payments at issue, were unquestionably community property according to all available authority and should have been claimed as such. As for the *federal* benefits, the record documents defendant's failure to conduct any reasonable research into their proper characterization under community property law.[7] Instead, he dogmatically asserted his theory, which he was unable to support with authority and later recanted, that all noncontributory military retirement benefits, whether state or federal, were immune from community treatment upon divorce. The jury could well have found defendant's refusal to educate himself to the applicable principles of law constituted negligence which prevented him from exercising informed discretion with regard to his client's rights.

As the jury was correctly instructed, an attorney does not ordinarily guarantee the soundness of his opinions and, accordingly, is not liable for every mistake he may make in his practice. He is expected, however, to possess knowledge of those plain and elementary principles of law which are commonly known by well informed attorneys, and to discover those additional rules of law which, although not commonly known, may readily be found by standard research techniques. (Lucas v. Hamm (1961) 56 Cal.2d 583, 591, 15 Cal.Rptr. 821, 364 P.2d 685; Lally v. Kuster (1918) 177 Cal. 783, 786, 171 P. 961;

---

7. At trial defendant testified that prior to the division of property in the divorce action, he had assumed the retirement benefits were not subject to community treatment, despite the fact General Smith had already begun to receive payments from the state; that he did not at that time undertake any research on the point nor did he discuss the matter with plaintiff; that subsequent to the divorce plaintiff asked defendant to research the question whereupon defendant discovered the *French* case which contained dictum in support of plaintiff's position; that the *French* decision caused him to change his opinion and conclude "that the Supreme Court, when it was confronted with this [the language in *French*] may hold that it [vested military reitrement pay] is community property." On the basis of *French* defendant filed his unsuccessful motion to amend the final decree of divorce to allow plaintiff an interest in the retirement benefits. Defendant admitted at trial, "I would have been very willing to assert it [a community interest] on her behalf had I known of the dictum in the *French* case at the time."

Floro v. Lawton (1960) 187 Cal.App.2d 657, 673, 10 Cal.Rptr. 98; Sprague v. Morgan (1960) supra, 185 Cal.App.2d 519, 523, 8 Cal.Rptr. 347; Armstrong v. Adams (1929) 102 Cal.App. 677, 684, 283 P. 871.) If the law on a particular subject is doubtful or debatable, an attorney will not be held responsible for failing to anticipate the manner in which the uncertainty will be resolved. (See e.g., Sprague v. Morgan (1960) supra.) But even with respect to an unsettled area of the law, we believe an attorney assumes an obligation to his client to undertake reasonable research in an effort to ascertain relevant legal principles and to make an informed decision as to a course of conduct based upon an intelligent assessment of the problem. In the instant case, ample evidence was introduced to support a jury finding that defendant failed to perform such adequate research into the question of the community character of retirement benefits and thus was unable to exercise the informed judgment to which his client was entitled. (See fn. 7, *ante.*)

We recognize, of course, that an attorney engaging in litigation may have occasion to choose among various alternative strategies available to his client, one of which may be to refrain from pressing a debatable point because potential benefit may not equal detriment in terms of expenditure at time and resources or because of calculated tactics to the advantage of his client. But, as the Ninth Circuit put it somewhat brutally in Pineda v. Craven (9th Cir. 1970) 424 F.2d 369, 372: "There is nothing strategic or tactical about ignorance. . . ." In the case before us it is difficult to conceive of tactical advantage which could have been served by neglecting to advance a claim so clearly in plaintiff's best interest, nor does defendant suggest any. The decision to forego litigation on the issue of plaintiff's community property right to a share of General Smith's retirement benefits was apparently the product of a culpable misconception of the relevant principles of law, and the jury could have so found.

Furthermore, no lawyer would suggest the property characterization of General Smith's retirement benefits to be so esoteric an issue that defendant could not reasonably have been expected to be aware of it or its probable resolution. (Lucas v. Hamm (1961) supra, 56 Cal.2d 583, 15 Cal.Rptr. 821, 364 P.2d 685.) In *Lucas* we held that the rule against perpetuities poses such complex and difficult problems for the draftsman that even careful and competent attorneys occasionally fall prey to its traps. The situation before us is not analogous. Certainly one of the central issues in any divorce proceeding is the extent and division of the community property. In this case the question reached monumental proportions, since General Smith's retirement benefits constituted the only significant asset available to the community.[8] In undertaking professional representation of plaintiff defendant assumed the duty to familiarize himself with the law defining the character of retirement benefits; instead, he rendered erroneous advice contrary to the best interests of his client without the guidance through research of readily available authority.

Regardless of his failure to undertake adequate research, defendant through personal experience in the domestic relations field had been exposed to community property aspects of pensions. Representing the wife of a reserve officer in the National Guard in 1965, defendant alleged as one of the items of community property "the retirement benefits from the Armed Forces and/or the California National Guard." On behalf of the husband in a 1967 divorce action,

8. It is undisputed that the only assets the parties had to show as community property after 24 years of marriage, aside from General Smith's retirement benefits, were an equity of $1,800 in a house, some furniture, shares of stock worth $2,800, and two automobiles on which money was owing.

defendant filed an answer admitting retirement benefits were community property, merely contesting the amount thereof. In 1965 a wife whom he was representing was so insistent on asserting a community interest in a pension, over defendant's contrary views, that she communicated with the state retirement system and brought to defendant correspondence from the state agency describing her interest in pension benefits. And representing an army colonel, defendant filed a cross-complaint for divorce specifically setting up as an item of community property "retirement benefits in the name of the defendant with the United States Government." It is difficult to understand why defendant deemed the community property claim to pensions of three of the foregoing clients to deserve presentation to the trial court, but not the similar claim of this plaintiff.

In any event, as indicated above, had defendant conducted minimal research into either hornbook or case law, he would have discovered with modest effort that General Smith's state retirement benefits were likely to be treated as community property and that his federal benefits at least arguably belonged to the community as well. Therefore, we hold that the trial court correctly denied the motions for nonsuit and judgment notwithstanding the verdict and properly submitted the question of defendant's negligence to the jury under the instructions given. (See fn. 3, *ante.*) For the same reasons, the trial court correctly refused to instruct the jury at defendant's request that "he is not liable for being in error as to a question of law on which reasonable doubt may be entertained by well informed lawyers." Even as to doubtful matters, an attorney is expected to perform sufficient research to enable him to make an informed and intelligent judgment on behalf of his client.[9]

Having concluded the issue of negligence was properly placed before the jury, we now consider defendant's claims that the verdict was excessive and unsupported by the evidence and that the trial court used an incorrect measure of damages in making a unitary award of $100,000. An economist appearing on plaintiff's behalf as an expert witness testified to the actuarial current value of the benefits payable under the state and federal retirement plans. His assessment was based upon General Smith's life expectancy of approximately 29 years, the total amount of future monthly payments from the pensions, including estimated cost of living increases, and an assumed average rate of interest. It was the witness' opinion that the state retirement benefits had a present value of $272,954 and the federal benefits were currently worth $49,078. Thus the estimated total value was $322,032, one-half of which is $161,016.

Defendant, on the other hand, presented no evidence on the issue of damages. His cross-examination of plaintiff's expert on questions

---

9. The principal thrust of the dissent is its conclusion (*post*, p. 637 of 118 Cal.Rptr. p. 605 of 530 P.2d) that "even assuming that defendant was negligent in failing to research the pension questions, the record does not furnish a balance of probabilities that his negligence—rather than the uncertain status of the law and the availability of uncontested alimony—caused plaintiff to lose a $100,000 pension award." Whether defendant's negligence was a cause in fact of plaintiff's damage—an element of proximate cause—is a factual question for the jury to resolve. (Valdez v. Clark (1959) 173 Cal.App.2d 476, 478-479, 343 P.2d 281; Land v. Gregory (1959) 168 Cal.App.2d 15, 19, 335 P.2d 141; Hill v. Matthews Paint Co. (1957) 149 Cal.App.2d 714, 723, 308 P.2d 865; Rest.2d Trusts § 434.) Here the jury was correctly instructed that plaintiff had the burden of proving, inter alia, that defendant's negligence was a proximate cause of the damage suffered, and proximate cause was defined as "a cause which, natural and continuous sequence, produces the damage, and *without which the damage would not have occurred.*" (Italics added.) Under the strict standards governing appellate review of dispute questions of fact (see, e.g., Nestle v. City of Santa Monica (1972) 6 Cal.3d 920, 925-926, 101 Cal.Rptr. 568, 496 P.2d 480; Land v. Gregory (1959) supra, 168 Cal.App.2d 15, 18-19, 335 P.2d 141), we see no reason on the present record to disturb the jury's implied finding of proximate cause.

such as General Smith's physical condition relative to his life expectancy and whether taxes were improperly omitted from his computation bears on the weight to be accorded the witness' conclusions, but does not prevent the testimony from supporting the verdict. Valuation is a question of fact for the jury, and its award of $100,000 in this case was well within the range of damages suggested by substantial evidence. (See Nestle v. City of Santa Monica (1972) 6 Cal. 3d 920, 925-926, 101 Cal.Rptr. 568, 496 P.2d 480; Primm v. Primm (1956) 46 Cal.2d 690, 693, 299 P.2d 231.)

Few cases have considered what constitutes the proper measure of damages in a legal malpractice action. The general rule is that a plaintiff is entitled only to be made whole: i.e., when the attorney's negligence lies in his failure to press a meritorious claim, the measure of damages is the value of the claim lost. (Lally v. Kuster (1918) supra 177 Cal. 783, 791, 171 P. 961.) Or, as stated by Justice Peters in Pete v. Henderson (1954) 124 Cal.App.2d 487, 489, 269 P.2d 78, 79, an attorney's "liability, as in other negligence cases, is for all damages directly and proximately caused by his negligence." Here, it is contended, the court's award of a gross sum permitted plaintiff to receive a windfall in excess of the loss occasioned by defendant's negligence.

It is true that if defendant had claimed General Smith's retirement benefits as community property in the original proceedings, as the jury found he should have done, the divorce court could not have awarded plaintiff her interest therein by a total sum calculated at present value. In Phillipson v. Board of Administration (1970) supra, 3 Cal.3d 32, 46, 89 Cal.Rptr. 61, 70, 473 P.2d 765, 774, we indicated that *"if the community musters sufficient assets to do so,* the preferable mode of division would be to award the pension rights to the employee and property of equal value to the spouse." (Italics added; accord, Waite v. Waite (1972) supra, 6 Cal.3d 461, 473-474, 99 Cal.Rptr. 325, 492 P.2d 13.) But such disposition presupposes the existence of other community assets equivalent in worth to the discounted value of the nonemployee spouse's interest in the retirement benefits. In the case at bar, the community possessed no such assets. (See fn. 8, *ante.*) The divorce court, therefor, would have been compelled to order General Smith to pay plaintiff her share of his retirement benefits on a monthly basis as he receives them. (See, e.g., In re Marriage of Fithian (1974) supra, 10 Cal.3d 592, 111 Cal.Rptr. 369, 517 P.2d 449; Waite v. Waite, supra; In re Marriage of Karlin (1972) 24 Cal.App.3d 25, 101 Cal.Rptr. 240; Bensing v. Bensing (1972) 25 Cal.App.3d 889, 102 Cal.Rptr. 255.)

A court of law, however, has no power to duplicate the variety of remedies available to a divorce court sitting in equity. In an action at law for malpractice, as in any negligence suit, the court is limited in its remedy to one award of money damages because it lacks the equitable power of contempt to enforce its judgment. Accordingly, the sum in this case was necessarily derived from an actuarial projection of the accumulated damage suffered by plaintiff now and in the future. By this method, the trial court was best able to approximate within its acknowledged powers the value of the claim lost to plaintiff through defendant's negligence.[10]

Defendant next contends that inadmissible character evidence was introduced against him in violation of Evidence Code section 1104.[11]

---

10. As with all actuarial projections, it is likely that General Smith will not live the precise number of years estimated in the calculation. However, the possibility he will live less than that number is no greater than the possibility he will live more. Thus, as is true of all tort awards computed on a lump-sum basis, the chances of windfall are equally distributed.

11. Evidence Code section 1104 states: "Except as provided in Sections 1102 and 1103, evidence of a trait of a person's character with respect to care or skill is inadmissible to prove the quality of his conduct on a specified occasion."

At trial plaintiff called a witness who had been represented previously by defendant in an unrelated divorce action. Her husband had belonged to the State Employees' Retirement System. The witness testified that she gave defendant certain documents furnished by the State of California to aid her in claiming her share of her husband's retirement benefits. Among other matters, the transmittal letter from the state described her community interest in the benefits and outlined procedures to preserve her rights. She further testified that defendant advised her that the retirement fund and its benefits were not community property despite their contributory nature. Although she disagreed and argued, defendant insisted upon his position in order to obtain the divorce without a lengthy or difficult trial. The witness stated that she finally acquiesced in the settlement.

Defendant conceded at trial that the testimony regarding his receipt of the documents was admissible on the issue of his awareness of the State of California's view of retirement benefits as community property. He objected to the balance, however, on the ground that evidence of prior conduct cannot be used to demonstrate subsequent negligence.

In response to plaintiff's questioning at trial, defendant testified that a contributory retirement fund and its benefits are properly classed as community property. He also stated that as an attorney he always attempted to achieve the best possible result for his client, no matter how tenuous he viewed a useful theory, and that if he personally entertained any doubt that an asset belonged to the community he would seek to assert his client's interest therein. Such testimony may legitimately be impeached by showing that defendant had made contradictory statements in the past and had conducted himself in an inconsistent manner, though the impeachment may relate to a collateral matter. (Evid.Code, §§ 776, 780; Law Revision Com. comment to Evid.Code, § 780; Laird v. T. W. Mather, Inc. (1958) 51 Cal.2d 210, 219, 331 P.2d 617; People v. Pierce (1969) 269 Cal.App.2d 193, 199, 75 Cal.Rptr. 257; Daggett v. Atchison, etc., Ry. Co. (1957) 48 Cal.2d 655, 662, 313 P.2d 557; Estate of Lances (1932) 216 Cal. 397, 404, 14 P.2d 768; Witkin, Cal.Evidence (2d ed. 1966) § 1187, pp. 1098-1099, § 1259, p. 1163.) Because the testimony in question was therefore admissible for the purpose of impeachment, we need not reach the issue whether the testimony was also admissible to prove facts other than subsequent conduct under Evidence Code section 1101, subdivision (b).[12]

Defendant also challenges the admission into evidence of a declaration which he filed in support of plaintiff's motion under section 473 of the Code of Civil Procedure[13] to amend the final divorce decree to include General Smith's retirement benefits as divisible community property. The declaration stated in essence that the benefits were in fact community property, but were not so pleaded because of defendant's mistake, inadvertence, and excusable neglect. The trial court allowed the declaration into evidence over objection as an admission of a party opponent. (Evid.Code, § 1220.)

While defendant's declaration was not rendered inadmissible by virtue of the hearsay rule, it properly should have been excluded from

---

12. Evidence Code section 1101, subdivision (b), states: "Nothing in this section prohibits the admission of evidence that a person committed a crime, civil wrong, or other act when relevant to prove some fact (such as motive, opportunity, intent, preparation, plan, knowledge, indentity, or absence of mistake or accident) other than his disposition to commit such acts."

13. Code of Civil Procedure section 473 provides in pertinent part: "The court may, upon such terms as may be just, relieve a party or his legal representative from a judgment, order, or other proceeding taken against him through his mistake, inadvertence, surprise or excusable neglect."

evidence on the ground that it had insubstantial probative value. (Evid.Code, § 352.) Although the trial judge is traditionally accorded wide discretion in these matters (Adkins v. Brett (1920) 184 Cal. 252, 258, 193 P. 251), the evidence here has dubious relevance to the issues in the lawsuit. Not only is the declaration conclusionary in form and nondescriptive of defendant's actual conduct, but it was filed on behalf of plaintiff at her request and represents merely an effort by defendant to advance his client's cause. In contrast to its probative value, the harmful effect of the declaration in the eyes of the jury was potentially significant. On its face the declaration, under oath, is manifestly a confession of error on the part of defendant. The jury possibly could have misunderstood its context or its purpose, or confused the quantum of asserted negligence necessary to permit the amendment of a judgment with that required to support a finding of malpractice.

Furthermore, as is the case with offers of compromise and subsequent remedial conduct, extrinsic policy reasons exist for excluding the declaration from evidence. (See Evid.Code, § 1150 et seq.) Were we to sanction the admissibility of such evidence, tension might develop between an attorney's duty to zealously represent his client (A.B.A. Code of Prof. Responsibility, Canon 7) and his instinct of self-protection. As a result, the attorney could become reluctant to seek an amended judgment under Code of Civil Procedure section 473, and the quality of legal representation in the state might suffer accordingly. In short, an attorney should be able to admit a mistake without subjecting himself to a malpractice suit.[14] Therefore, we conclude, the trial court erred in admitting the declaration into evidence.

Nevertheless, after review of the record in its entirety, it does not appear reasonably probable that a result more favorable to defendant would have been reached in the absence of the error. The section 473 declaration played a minor role in a lengthy and complex trial. Considerable independent evidence was presented upon which the jury could have based its finding of negligence, and at most the declaration had a cumulative effect. Furthermore, defendant's statements were merely read to the jury and not placed before it in evidence as an exhibit. He had ample opportunity at that time to rebut their effect and to explain the circumstances under which the declaration was filed. Thus, the admission of the declaration into evidence, though error, was not sufficiently prejudicial to warrant our reversing the judgment. (Cal.Const., art. VI, § 13; People v. Watson (1956) 46 Cal.2d 818, 836, 299 P.2d 243.)

Defendant's remaining contentions of error are without merit and require no further discussion.

The judgment is affirmed.

WRIGHT, C.J., and TOBRINER, SULLIVAN and BURKE,* JJ., concur.

CLARK, Justice (dissenting).
I dissent.

The evidence is insufficient to prove plaintiff lost $100,000 from her lawyer's negligence in 1967. There is no direct evidence a well-informed lawyer would have obtained an award of the husband's pensions in the wife's divorce, nor does the record provide such inference. Rather, the state of the law and the circumstances of the parties reveal lawyer Lewis reached a reasonable result for his client in 1967.

14. The court properly so instructed the jury. (See final paragraph of fn. 3, ante.)

*Retired Associate Justice of the Supreme Court sitting under assignment by the Chairman of the Judicial Council.

To establish liability for negligence, a plaintiff must show defendant's negligence contributed to injury so that "but for" the negligence the injury would not have been sustained. If the injury would have occurred anyway—whether or not the defendant was negligent—the negligence was not a cause in fact. (4 Witkin, Summary of Cal.Law (8th ed. 1970) § 622, pp. 2903-2904; Rest. 2d Torts (1966) § 432; Prosser, The Law of Torts (4th ed. 1971) p. 236 et seq.) "It is not enough merely to show that the probabilities were evenly divided. The evidence must be such that it could be found the balance of probabilities was in plaintiff's favor. (Prosser, 'Proximate Cause in California,' 38 Cal.L.Rev. 369, 378-379.)" (Singh v. Frye (1960) 177 Cal.App.2d 590, 593, 2 Cal.Rptr. 372, 374.)

This fundamental principle is reflected in legal malpractice cases. Prior to today's majority opinion, a lawyer was "not liable for being in error as to a question of law on which reasonable doubt may be entertained by well-informed lawyers. [Citations.]" (Lucas v. Hamm (1961) 56 Cal.2d 583, 591, 15 Cal.Rptr. 821, 825, 364 P.2d 685, 689.) The rule has been variously stated: "It has frequently been held that a lawyer is not liable for lack of knowledge as to the true state of the law where a doubtful or debatable point is involved." (Sprague v. Morgan (1960) 185 Cal.App.2d 519, 523, 8 Cal.Rptr. 347, 350.) Or, a lawyer "is not holden for errors in judgment nor in cases where well-informed attorneys entertain different views concerning a proposition of law which has not been settled." (Floro v. Lawton (1967) 187 Cal.App.2d 657, 673, 10 Cal.Rptr. 98, 108, quoting from 69 N.J.L.J. 265.) It should be noted the foregoing statements go

beyond lawyer *negligence*, going to the ultimate question of *liability*—he shall not be "liable" or "holden" for the errors.

The advice or services performed by the lawyer may be rendered erroneous by subsequent decisions, but if his contemporaries could reasonably have been expected to have performed in the same manner, it is illogical to assume the client would have gained more by having chosen another lawyer. The point is illustrated by the reasoning in Lucas v. Hamm, *supra*, 56 Cal.2d 583, 593, 15 Cal.Rptr. 821, 826, 364 P.2d 685, 690, involving a lawyer who prepared a will violating the rule against perpetuities. The court compared his position with that of a non-negligent lawyer, stating there was no liability because "an attorney of ordinary skill acting under the same circumstances might well have 'fallen into the net which the Rule spreads for the unwary' and failed to recognize the danger."

When we consider the law existing in 1967 and the circumstances of the parties, it cannot be concluded on the record before us that it was probable another lawyer would have obtained pension rights for plaintiff in addition to the award obtained for her by defendant.

As the majority opinion points out, when defendant was employed to procure the divorce in 1967, the law was clear that, other than military retirement payments, pension *payments* constituted community property. (E.g., Benson v. City of Los Angeles (1963) 60 Cal.2d 355, 359, 33 Cal.Rptr. 257, 384 P.2d 689; 4 Witkin, Summary of Cal. Law (7th ed. 1960) pp. 2733-2734.) However, *no reported California case prior to 1967 stated that a court was empowered to award an employee's future pension benefits to his spouse in a divorce action.* To the contrary, there were strong indications from statutory and case authorities that such an award could not be obtained. Further, in every reported case where a spouse sought award of the employee's pension, that spouse lost.[1]

Let us examine the hurdles faced by a 1967 lawyer seeking the pensions now claimed by plaintiff.[2]

INTEREST IS MERE EXPECTANCY

The first hurdle for a spouse seeking to recover an employee's pension in 1967 was the doctrine enunciated in Williamson v. Williamson (1962) 203 Cal.App.2d 8, 11, 21 Cal.Rptr. 164, 167, that in a divorce action pensions could be taken into account only to the extent that the employee had received benefits or was certain to receive benefits. The court stated: ''The principle established by these cases [French v. French (1941) 17 Cal.2d 775, 112 P.2d 235; Cheney v. City & County of San Francisco Employees Retirement System (1936) 7 Cal.2d 565, 61 P.2d 754; Crossan v. Crossan, *supra*, 35 Cal.App.2d 39, 94 P.2d 609] is that pensions become community property, subject to the division in a divorce, when and *to the extent* that the party is *certain* to receive some payment or recovery of funds. To the extent that payment is, at the time of the divorce, subject to conditions which may

or may not occur, the pension is an *expectancy*, not subject to division as community property.'' (Italics added.) In earlier discussion, the court quoted language in Cheney v. City & County of San Francisco, *supra*, 7 Cal.2d 565, 61 P.2d 754, referring to the contingent event of death. (203 Cal.App.2d at p. 10, 21 Cal.Rptr. 164.) Reading the two statements together, it appears the divorce court could not award future pension payments if they were conditioned on the employee's survival. In the instant case, such a rule would mean the divorce court could have awarded only an amount equal to the first two state pension payments received before the divorce decree.[3] Future payments were apparently subject to the contingency of survival. The first two payments were approximately $1,300, far less than the $100,000 award.

VESTED RIGHTS AND EMPLOYER's INTERESTS

The next hurdle facing counsel seeking a share of pension benefits in 1967 was authority indicating a spouse could not have a vested right in an employee's pension because it would interfere with the employer's interests in two respects. In Benson v. City of Los Angeles, *supra*, 60 Cal.2d 355, 361-362, 33 Cal.Rptr. 257, 260, 384 P.2d

---

1. Crossan v. Crossan (1939) 35 Cal.App.2d 39, 94 P.2d 609, did not involve an award of the employee's pension payments of benefits. In *Crossan* the employee's contributions to the pension fund were subject to withdrawal if his employment was terminated. The court held the divorce court could take into account the employee's interest in the fund and award his spouse more than one-half of the remaining community property to compensate for the contributions. There is no language in *Crossan* suggesting that an employee's pension *benefits* could be awarded to the spouse.

    Crossan is not helpful to plaintiff because the husband's contributions for retirement had been refunded several years prior to the divorce. Moreover, even if the contributions had not been previously withdrawn, *Crossan* would not have aided her significantly in an attempt to recover additional property because plaintiff received substantially all of the community property other than the pensions.

2. In doing so, we must assume that any claim by plaintiff would have been opposed by competent counsel. To assume otherwise in a malpractice action would place a burden on the lawyer to have made claims of such doubtful merit that the only hope of success would have been lack of opposition. Certainly, we should not encourage lawyers to make such claims, much less impose a duty to engage in the questionable practice.

3. The statements relied upon by the majority (*ante*, p. 626 of 118 Cal.Rptr., p. 594 of 530 P.2d) from Benson v. City of Los Angeles, *supra*, 60 Cal.2d 355, 359, 33 Cal.Rptr. 257, 384 P.2d 689 and French v. French, *supra*, 17 Cal.2d 775, 778, 112 P.2d 235, are consistent with the suggested interpretation of *Williamson*. I assume that the funds had not been spent.

689, 692, it was stated that the public policy permitting a governmental body to make reasonable modifications and changes to a retirement system "would be defeated by the vesting of rights in someone other than the employee." The court also stated: "No reason is suggested why we should depart from the foregoing decisions to the effect that a wife of a public employee acquires no vested interest in a pension until it becomes payable to her. On the other hand, to vest such an interest prior thereto 'would remove a considerable amount of the flexibility necessary for operation of pension systems, because it would mean that provisions benefiting any third person would be frozen into the law with respect to all employees then in service and that these interests could not be removed regardless of the consent of the employee and regardless of whether the employee was given other pension benefits which might be of greater value to him than the one sought to be eliminated.' (Packer v. Board of Retirement, *supra*, 35 Cal.2d 212, 217, 217 P.2d 660, 664.)"

The second reason in *Benson* for denying the spouse a vested right was that it would defeat the employer's purpose in providing a pension, namely, inducing competent persons to enter and remain in public service. (60 Cal.2d at p. 361, 33 Cal.Rptr. 257, 384 P.2d 689.)

In *Benson* the court concluded: "The vested interest which the wife may protect by her collateral control thus precludes an involuntary deprivation thereof in the case of the community interest in *insurance* on the husband's life. But the acquisition by a wife of a vested interest in her husband's public employment contract might defeat the public purpose in providing a retirement plan for public employees. The distinction lies in the nature of the control which the law permits the husband and wife to independently, lawfully exercise regardless of the community nature of the pension right, *and for policy reasons it is deemed necessary that the husband-employee alone exercise control unhampered by vested interests in any third party, including his community partner.*" (Italics added; 60 Cal.2d at p. 363, 33 Cal.Rptr. at p. 261, 384 P.2d at p. 653.)

EXEMPTION STATUTES

In 1967 there were numerous statutes exempting pensions from court process and prohibiting their assignment. A partial listing including nine such statutes is contained in Ogle v. Heim (1968) 69 Cal.2d 7, 9, 69 Cal.Rptr. 579, 442 P.2d 659, footnote 1. In *Ogle*, and the companion case of Miller v. Superior Court (1968) 69 Cal.2d 14, 16, 69 Cal.Rptr. 583, 442 P.2d 663, this court unanimously held that the exemption statutes were applicable to claims for child support and alimony, and refused to create a family obligation exception. (See also, Thomas v. Thomas (1961) 192 Cal.App.2d 771, 780-785, 13 Cal.Rptr. 872.) When in 1970 it was held that the exemption statutes would not preclude the divorce court awarding employee pension rights to a spouse, this court—although discussing the question for four pages—was unable to cite any California authority in favor of its position. (Phillipson v. Board of Administration, 3 Cal.3d 32, 43-47, 89 Cal.Rptr. 61, 473 P.2d 765.) It must be concluded that in 1967 the existing statutory and case law indicated that exemption statutes would preclude divorce court award of pension payments.

ALIMONY ADJUSTMENTS IN LIEU OF PENSION AWARDS

Two cases suggested that alimony award and modification, rather than a community property division, was the appropriate method to remedy imbalances arising from the husband's receipt of pension benefits. (Kinsey v. Kinsey (1964) 231 Cal.App.2d 219, 222, 41 Cal.Rptr. 802; Williamson v. Williamson, *supra*, 203 Cal.App.2d 8, 12, 21 Cal.Rptr. 164.) Further, because both cases had refused to award any part of an employee's pension to his spouse, the implication existed that award and modification of alimony was the *sole method* available to the divorce court.

FEDERAL LAW

The majority concedes that in 1967 there was substantial doubt whether federal military pensions constituted community property, awardable in a divorce action.

Aside from the questions discussed above, the principal argument that military pensions were not community property was based on the cases relating to National Service Life Insurance benefits. Wissner v. Wissner (1949) 89 Cal. App.2d 759, 764-771, 201 P.2d 837, had held that where the premiums were paid by community funds, the insurance proceeds became community property, and the widow would be entitled to half the benefits. (Petition for hearing denied with Schauer, J., voting for a hearing.) The United States Supreme Court reversed, holding that because federal statute specified the insured could designate and change the beneficiary, an award of a share of the policy proceeds to the widow, when another was designated as beneficiary, would frustrate the intention of Congress. (Wissner v. Wissner (1950) 338 U.S. 655, 658, 70 S.Ct. 398, 94 L.Ed. 424 et seq.; see Estate of Allie (1958) 50 Cal.2d 794, 798, 329 P.2d 903 et seq.)

The principle enunciated by the United States Supreme Court in *Wissner* of giving effect to the statutory provision governing the benefit at the expense of the community property system was applied under California law in Benson v. City of Los Angeles, *supra*, 60 Cal.2d 355, 33 Cal.Rptr. 257, 384 P.2d 689. This court held that the *widow's* benefit under a Los Angeles Charter provision, concededly community property of a first marriage, was payable in its entirety to the widowed second wife to the exclusion of the first wife.

In the light of *Wissner* and *Benson*, there existed strong reason to believe statutory provisions for payment to the retiree would be interpreted literally to effectuate congressional and legislative intent, thereby excluding community property claims. Additional legal problems inherent in an award of a military pension to a spouse, typical of those faced by counsel in 1967, are discussed in In re Marriage of Fithian (1974) 10 Cal.3d 592, 597-604, 111 Cal.Rptr. 369, 517 P.2d 449.

Although conceding this troubling federal question applied to the federal pension, the majority *incorrectly* implies the *Wissner* rule could not apply to the state pension. The majority opinion fails to recognize that the husband retired under section 228 of the Military and Veterans Code which is in accordance with "federal law, statutes, rules and regulations which . . . govern the retirement of commissioned officers and warrant officers of the reserve components of the Army of the United States on extended active duty; . . ." (Mil. & Vet.Code, § 228, see also §§ 100-104.) Certainly well-informed counsel in 1967 could reasonably have concluded that by appropriating federal law, the Legislature intended it determinative of the character of the pensions.

VICTORY?

Assuming defendant fully researched the question whether the pensions could be obtained and further assuming his analysis of the authorities led him to forecast this court's decisions in Phillipson v. Board of Administration, *supra*, 3 Cal.3d 32, 89 Cal.Rptr. 61, 473 P.2d 765, Waite v. Waite (1972) 6 Cal.3d 461, 99 Cal.Rptr. 325, 492 P.2d 13, and In re Marriage of Fithian, *supra*, 10 Cal.3d 592, 111 Cal.Rptr. 369, 517 P.2d 449, it does not follow that he should have pursued an award of the pensions. Although defendant by litigating the awardability of pensions would perhaps have performed a valuable service to the State of California by attempting to settle the law, the lawyer's first duty is to his client's best interest—not to the resolution of uncertain legal questions.

Considering the circumstances of this case, including the alimony obtained, expensive litigation by counsel to recover pensions would have gained the client little—if anything—above that obtained in the uncontested action. And, in view of the uncertainty in the law and the risk that the litigation might result in a net loss, pursuit of the pensions would have been an unrealistic alternative. After his retirement, the husband worked as an automobile salesman receiving commissions of approximately $300 per month. Plaintiff had been earning the same amount shortly before. Plaintiff informed defendant that her husband received $645 monthly pension from the National Guard. Under the divorce decree, plaintiff obtained substantially all of the community property for herself and her son, and was awarded $300 per month alimony and $100 per month child support for her son who was then 18. It is apparent that plaintiff would receive more than one-half of the expected joint incomes of the spouses from the pension payment and salaries.

Setting aside alimony awards because of error in the division of community property, this court has recognized the direct relationship between the two awards. (See v. See (1966) 64 Cal.2d 778, 786, 51 Cal.Rptr. 888, 415 P.2d 776; French v. French, *supra*, 17 Cal.2d 775, 778, 112 P.2d 235; cf. In re Marriage of Wilson (1974) 10 Cal.3d 851, 856, 112 Cal.Rptr. 405, 519 P.2d 165.) The relationship is emphasized in Kinsey v. Kinsey, *supra*, 231 Cal.App.2d 219, 222, 41 Cal.Rptr. 802, 805, in the pension context: "Manifestly, it would be grossly inequitable to permit plaintiff to retain the benefits of the property settlement and the alimony payments as provided by the terms of the interlocutory judgment entered after the default hearing that resulted from the stipulation of the parties, and also now to permit her to 'modify' this agreement in such fashion as to entitle her as a matter of right to one-half of defendant's future income in the event of his retirement. Plaintiff's present alimony award is subject to future modification and is ample protection for her future right to share in any income her husband may receive by reason of his pension payments."

Because of the relationship between community property and alimony awards, it was to be anticipated that had defendant succeeded through litigation in establishing a right to assignment of the pensions, the alimony award would have been *greatly reduced* or *eliminated altogether* and the award of the remaining community property possibly altered. Although an award of part of the pension would no doubt have been more valuable than an alimony award of equal amount, the benefit pales in significance when viewed in light of the uncertainty of the law and the large expense required to establish the right to assignment. Further, litigation would have created the risk that a court might conclude not only that pensions did not constitute awardable community property but also, based on the relative earning abilities of the spouses, alimony should be less than $300.

CONCLUSION

Given the uncertain status of the law, the circumstances of the parties, and the close relationship between property division and alimony payment, an ethical, diligent and careful lawyer would have avoided litigation over pension rights and instead would have sought a compensating alimony award for any inequity, as expressly suggested by Kinsey v. Kinsey, *supra*, 231 Cal.App.2d 219, 222, 41 Cal.Rptr. 802, and Williamson v. Williamson, *supra*, 203 Cal.App.2d

8, 12, 21 Cal.Rptr. 164.[4] So far as appears, defendant secured such compensating award.

Accordingly, even assuming that defendant was negligent in failing to research the pension questions, the record does not furnish a balance of probabilities that his negligence—rather than the uncertain status of the law and the availability of uncontested alimony—caused plaintiff to lose a $100,000 pension award.

I would adhere to the rule of Lucas v. Hamm, *supra*, 56 Cal.2d 583, 591, 15 Cal.Rptr. 821, 825, 364 P.2d 685, 689, that an attorney is not liable for errors on issues "on which reasonable doubt may be entertained by well-informed lawyers." As shown above, such an issue was presented Attorney Lewis in 1967 concerning recovery of unpaid pension benefits in a divorce action. Further, the law applicable to federal pension benefits also presented such an issue, applicable not only to the federal pension but also to the state pension by section 228 of the Military and Veterans Code.[5]

The majority limits *Lucas* to "esoteric" cases. (Ditto Op., p. 628 of 118 Cal.Rptr., p. 596 of 530 P.2d.) Even assuming *Lucas* to be so limited, the hurdles discussed above certainly make the instant case as "esoteric" as *Lucas*. As pointed out by Professor Leach in his classic 1938 article, Perpetuities in a Nutshell, 51 Harv. L.Rev. 638, 669-670, violation of the rule against perpetuities—the claimed malpractice in *Lucas*—may be avoided by use of a simple standard clause placed in every will. The 22 pages of legal discussion since 1967 by this court establishing awardability of pensions generally, of statutory pensions, and of military pensions (Phillipson v. Board of Administration, *supra*, 3 Cal.3d 32, 39-50, 89 Cal.Rptr. 61, 473 P.2d 765; Waite v. Waite (1972) 6 Cal.3d 461, 469-472, 99 Cal.Rptr. 325, 492 P.2d 13; In re Marriage of Fithian, *supra*, 10 Cal.3d 592, 596-604, 111 Cal.Rptr. 369, 517 P.2d 449) attest to the complexity of the pension issues.

I would reverse the judgment.

McCOMB, J., concurs.

4. The possibility of effectively dealing with the pension in this manner was apparently unavailable to counsel in Phillipson v. Board of Administration, *supra*, 3 Cal.3d 32, 89 Cal.Rptr. 61, 473 P.2d 765, the first case to recognize assignability of pensions. There the employee had fled the jurisdiction apparently taking all of the community property funds other than his contributions to the pension fund. (3 Cal.3d at p. 38, fn. 2, 89 Cal.Rptr. 61, 473 P.2d 765.)

5. Careful counsel confronted with a pension question would customarily start their research with the statutory basis, if any, of the pension. Certainly all careful counsel would eventually look for the statutory basis. It is regrettable that, in a case upholding an attorney malpractice judgment on a theory of failure to research, the majority fails to even mention the statute establishing one of the pensions and containing provisions contrary to part of the majority's analysis.

STILLWELL *v.* ADAMS.

From the St. Joseph Circuit Court, *Joseph W. Nyikos*, Judge.

Appellee, Kenneth Adams, incurred injuries from an automobile collision, and recovered $15,000.00 damages under the guest statute from appellant-driver, John Stillwell. Appellant appeals.

Reversed. By the Second Division.

Roland Obenchain, Jr., and *Douglas D. Seely, Jr.,* both of South Bend, for appellant.

David L. Matthews, of South Bend, for appellee.

MOTE, C. J.—This is an action for damages incurred by appellee in an automobile collision which occurred while appellee was riding as a guest passenger in appellant's car. A jury trial resulted in a verdict and judgment for appellee in the sum of fifteen thousand ($15,000.00) dollars.

It appears that appellant and appellee, prior to the accident, had visited several taverns in South Bend and each had consumed several bottles of beer. At approximately one o'clock in the morning, the two men decided to go to a restaurant to obtain some food. While en route to the restaurant, appellant attempted to make a left turn and crashed into a pillar of a viaduct.

The case was tried on appellee's amended complaint, which alleged that appellee suffered injury in the accident and that the accident was caused by the appellant's wanton and wilful misconduct.

The appellant assigns as error the trial court's overruling of his motion for new trial, and in support thereof, among other things, he contends that after the jury had been selected and sworn, and before the opening statements of the parties, the court erred in giving the following preliminary instruction:

"Negligence which renders one liable to another who is injured thereby is the doing of some act or thing which it is his duty to refrain from doing; or the failing to do some act or thing which it is his duty to do. Or, to put it in other words, the doing of something which a reasonably careful and prudent person would not have done under the same or like circumstances, or the failing to do something which a reasonably careful and prudent person would have done under the same or like circumstances, constitutes negligence; and where such negligent act is done or omitted, and by reason of it another suffers injury therefrom, such negligent person is liable to the injured person, he being without fault."

over appellant's objection, as follows:

"The Defendant objects and excepts to the giving of Instruction Number Four by the Court on its own motion for the reason that the instruction in its present form purports to define the word 'negligence,' and then states that where a negligent act is done or omitted, and that by reason of it, where another suffers injuries, such negligent person is liable to the person. This is a guest case under the Indiana Statutes relating to the liability of a host-driver to his guest passenger. There is no basis in law for the finding of liability on the part of a host on simple negligence. The instruction, therefore, tends to confuse the jury and indicate to them that upon a finding of negligence, liability can be predicated upon the defendant in this action."

1. In pursuance of Supreme Court Rule 1-7A, the trial court was required to give

preliminary instruction "as to the issues for trial," etc., and inasmuch as there were no issues tendered by the pleadings which concerned negligence, we think that the giving of such instruction constituted prejudicial error. *Hayes Freight Lines, Inc. et al.* v. *Wilson* (1948), 226 Ind. 1, 77 N.E. 2d 580; *Cleveland, Cincinnati, Chicago and St. Louis Railway Company* v. *Case* (1910), 174 Ind. 369, 91 N.E. 238; *Hoesel* v. *Cain et al.; Kahler* v. *Cain et al.* (1944), 222 Ind. 330, 53 N.E. 2d 165.

2. It has been asserted that this claimed error has not been properly presented, and if it is, then other instructions tendered by appellee and given by the court cured the harmful effect of said instruction. In view of the conclusion we have reached it is not necessary for us to, and we do not decide if such assertion is correct. It is enough to state, we think, that where the question is properly presented the giving of an instruction defining negligence as a preliminary instruction, when the action and issues are predicated upon the guest statute, so-called, hereinafter quoted, in and of itself is prejudicially harmful and erroneous.

However, we are not required to base our decision solely on the issue of the claimed erroneous instruction. The appellant also assigns as error, under the trial court's overruling of his motion for new trial, that the verdict of the jury is not sustained by sufficient evidence and is contrary to law.

The case is within the provisions of §47-1021, Burns' 1952 Replacement, which reads as follows:

"47-1021. Guest of Owners or Operators—Right to Damages.—The owner, operator, or person responsible for the operation of a motor vehicle shall not be liable for loss or damage arising from injuries to or death of a guest, while being transported without payment therefor, in or upon such motor vehicle, resulting from the operation thereof, unless such injuries or death are caused by the wanton or wilful misconduct of such operator, owner, or person responsible for the operation of such motor vehicle." [Acts 1929, ch. 201, §1, p. 679; 1937, ch. 259, §1, p. 1229.]

The definition of wanton or wilful misconduct is set forth in *Becker* v. *Strater* (1947), 117 Ind. App. 504, 72 N.E. 2d 580, as follows:

3. "Willful or wanton misconduct consists of the conscious and intentional doing of a wrongful act or omission of a duty, with reckless indifference to consequences, under circumstances which show that the doer has knowledge of existing conditions and that injury will probably result. *Bedwell* v. *Debolt* (1943), 221 Ind. 600, 50 N.E. 2d 875; *Hoesel* v. *Cain* (1943), 222 Ind. 330, 53 N.E. 2d 165; *Swinney* v. *Roler* (1943), 113 Ind. App. 367, 47 N.E. 2d 486; *Lee Brothers* v. *Jones* (1944), 114 Ind. App. 688, 54 N.E. 2d 108."

4. The burden was upon appellee, as plaintiff below, to show by a preponderance of the evidence that appellant was conscious of his conduct and, with knowledge of existing conditions that injury would probably result, he consciously and intentionally did some wrongful act or omitted some duty which produced the injury. *Brown* v. *Saucerman* (1958), 237 Ind. 598, 145 N.E. 2d 898; *Bedwell* v. *De Bolt* (1943), 221 Ind. 600, 50 N.E. 2d 875.

5. Under the new trial motion specification, we must examine the evidence to determine if there is any evidence or reasonable inference to be drawn therefrom which will support the verdict of the jury.

6. In determining whether a motorist has been guilty of wanton or wilful misconduct within the meaning of the guest statute, this court will consider the course of conduct involved and will not confine its inquiry to occurrences at the immediate time and place of the

accident. *Pierce* v. *Clemens* (1943), 113 Ind. App. 65, 46 N.E. 2d 836.

The evidence most favorable to the appellee tends to show the following facts:

Appellant, although he and appellee had been drinking beer, acted completely normal during the course of time leading to the accident, and his driving was normal. When approaching the intersection at which the collision occurred, appellant drove his vehicle in the lane nearest the curb and did not weave or straddle across the lanes. On the street, there were two driving lanes going north and two lanes going south. Appellant was driving at a speed of thirty (30) to forty (40) miles per hour while approaching the intersection. After moving his automobile to the inside lane, appellant slowed the automobile's speed to fifteen (15) or twenty (20) miles per hour. The traffic signal turned green when the vehicle was one-half (1/2) block from the intersection, and appellant accelerated to twenty (20) to twenty-five (25) miles per hour. Upon reaching the intersection, at that speed, appellant started to make a left turn just before reaching a viaduct through which the street ran. Appellee then observed lights of an oncoming car, which prior to the turn, had been obstructed from view by pillars supporting the viaduct. Appellee shouted, "Look out," and appellant accelerated the speed of the car and it collided with one of the pillars, resulting in appellee's alleged injuries.

A conditional examination of appellant was admitted into evidence. The examination contained the statement, "The beer could have affected my sight in driving."

7. We think that this evidence, most favorable to appellee, fails to support a verdict that appellant was guilty of wilful and wanton misconduct in the operation of the automobile. There is no evidence to support such a verdict from the course of conduct leading to the accident. On the contrary, the evidence affords no inference other than that appellant's actions and driving were normal. While the evidence may be such as to warrant an inference that appellant's action, in attempting the turn, was negligent, there is no showing of wilful and wanton misconduct as defined by our courts. There is no evidence or permissible inference therefrom to establish that appellant had knowledge of the existing conditions, including the approaching car, and that injury would probably result from his course of action.

A somewhat similar case wherein the driver of an automobile failed to see an approaching automobile and attempted to pass a line of traffic and thereby encountered disaster, was *Hoesel* v. *Cain et al.; Kahler* v. *Cain et al., supra.* The court in reversing a holding of wanton and wilful misconduct said:

"... But there is no evidence that he knew the car was approaching from the south until his car had crossed the center line. After the Hoesel car drew out of the right line of traffic Kahler proceeded into the vacated space but there is no evidence that Hoesel knew that fact. ... From this evidence the jury would have been warranted in concluding that Hoesel was negligent in not anticipating ... the possibility of encountering a car coming from the south, but without his actual knowledge of its approach we are unable to persuade ourselves that the evidence supports a reasonable inference of his wilful and wanton misconduct. ..."

See also *Sheets* v. *Stalcup* (1938), 105 Ind. App. 66, 13 N.E. 2d 346.

In the case of *Reynolds, Administratrix, etc.* v. *Langford* (1961), 241 Ind. 431, 172 N.E. 2d 867, the defendant, Langford, had driven his automobile through a stop sign into an intersection at a speed of fifty (50) to sixty (60) miles per hour and collided with a truck. There was evidence that Langford knew that there was a stop sign at the intersection, but none that he knew of the truck's presence until too late. Our Supreme Court said:

> "From the evidence in the record here we are unable to say that appellee consciously and with knowledge that the truck was approaching, intentionally and with reckless indifference to the consequences, drove into the intersection therein knowing that if he did so injury to his passenger would probably result."

8. In the instant case, there is no evidence to support an inference that appellant knew of the presence of the oncoming car, nor of the impending danger which the oncoming car precipitated. The evidence, including that pertaining to the course of events leading up to the collision, wholly fails to establish or furnish an inference that appellant exhibited an intentional and reckless indifference to consequences of his acts under circumstances which show that he had knowledge of existing conditions and that injury to his guest would probably result. Without such a showing, there is no support for a reasonable inference of wanton and wilful misconduct.

9. Since there is not sufficient evidence to support the verdict of the jury, the same is contrary to law. The judgment below is reversed and the trial court ordered to grant the motion for a new trial.

Hunter, Kelley and Pfaff, JJ., concur.

NOTE.—Reported in 193 N.E. 2d 74. Transfer denied 194 N.E. 2d 806.

In the
SUPREME COURT OF THE UNITED STATES

October Term, 1964

No. 496

ESTELLE T. GRISWOLD
AND
C. LEE BUXTON,
Appellants,

vs.

STATE OF CONNECTICUT
Appellee.

ON APPEAL FROM THE SUPREME COURT
OF ERRORS OF CONNECTICUT

BRIEF FOR APPELLANT

Thomas I. Emerson
127 Wall Street
New Haven, Connecticut

Catherine G. Rorabach
185 Church Street,
New Haven, Connecticut
Attorneys for Appellants

SUBJECT INDEX

* * *

• • •

In the
SUPREME COURT OF THE UNITED STATES

_____

October Term, 1964

_____

No. 496

_____

ESTELLE T. GRISWOLD
AND
C. LEE BUXTON,
Appellants,

v.

CONNECTICUT.

_____

Appeal From The Supreme Court Of Errors Of
Connecticut

_____

BRIEF FOR APPELLANTS[1]

_____

OPINION BELOW

The opinion of the Supreme Court of Errors of Connecticut is reported in 151 Conn. 544, 200 A.2d 479. It is reprinted in the record at pages 61-63.

_____

1. The authors of this brief wish to record their great and obvious debt to Professor Fowler V. Harper who worked on this matter up to the time of his death on January 8, 1965.

JURISDICTION

On November 19, 1961, appellants Estelle T. Griswold and C. Lee Buxton were arrested on informations filed by the Prosecuting Attorney for the Circuit Court of Connecticut, Sixth Circuit, alleging violations of Sections 53-32 and 54-196 of the General Statutes of Connecticut (R. 1, 7). Appellants filed demurrers on the grounds, *inter alia*, that said statutes were unconstitutional as being a denial of due process of law under the Fourteenth Amendment, and a denial of freedom of speech under the First and Fourteenth Amendments, of the Constitution of the United States (R. 2, 8). On December 20, 1961, the demurrers were overruled on both grounds (R. 3-6, 9-12).

Appellants were tried before the Circuit Court without a jury, found guilty and, on January 2, 1962, sentenced to pay fines of $100 each (R. 13-4). Appeals were taken from the judgments and, on order of the Circuit Court, the appeals were combined (R. 15). A statement of findings of fact, conclusions and rulings was made by the Circuit Court on June 12, 1962 (R. 16-30, 32-3).

Appellants filed an assignment of errors which, *inter alia*, again challenged the constitutionality of the Connecticut statutes on the grounds set forth above (R. 33-7). On January 7, 1963, the Appellate Division affirmed the convictions (R. 40-50).

The Appellate Division certified to the Supreme Court of Errors the two questions raised by the demurrers as to the constitutionality of the statutes (R. 49-50). The Supreme Court of Errors granted the petition of appellants to certify additional questions (R. 52-60). Thereafter, on April 28, 1964, the Supreme Court of Errors affirmed the judgment of the Appellate Division, holding that the Connecticut statutes under attack were not in conflict with the United States Constitution (R.

61-5). Stay of execution was ordered on May 20, 1964 (not printed in record).

Notice of appeal to the Supreme Court of the United States was filed with the Supreme Court of Errors of Connecticut on July 22, 1964 (R. 65-6). On December 7, 1964, this Court noted probable jurisdiction (R. 67).

This Court has jurisdiction under 28 U.S.C. 1257 (2). *Dahnke-Walker Milling Co.* vs. *Bondurant*, 257 U.S. 282 (1921).

STATUTES INVOLVED

The statutes involved in this case are Sections 53-32 and 54-196, General Statutes of Connecticut, Revision of 1958.

Section 53-32 provides:

> *"Use of drugs or instruments to prevent conception.* Any person who uses any drug, medicinal article or instrument for the purpose of preventing conception shall be fined not less than fifty dollars or imprisoned not less than sixty days nor more than one year or be both fined and imprisoned."

Section 54-196 provides:

> *"Accessories.* Any person who assists, abets, counsels, causes, hires or commands another to commit any offense may be prosecuted and punished as if he were the principal offender."

QUESTIONS PRESENTED

1. Whether Sections 53-32 and 54-196 of the General Statutes of Connecticut, on their face or as applied in this case, deprive these appellants of liberty or property without due process of law in violation of the Fourteenth Amendment to the Constitution of the United States.

2. Whether Sections 53-32 and 54-196 of the General Statutes of Connecticut, on their

face or as applied in this case, deprive these appellants of their rights to freedom of speech in violation of the First and Fourteenth Amendments to the Constitution of the United States.

STATEMENT OF THE CASE

Appellant C. Lee Buxton is a physician, licensed to practice in the State of Connecticut and Chairman of the Department of Obstetrics and Gynecology at the Yale Medical School (R. 17). He is an author in the field of his specialty and a leader in professional organizations concerned with that field (R. 17).

Appellant Estelle T. Griswold is Executive Director of the Planned Parenthood League of Connecticut (R. 17).

On November 1, 1961, following the decision of this Court in *Poe* vs. *Ullman*, 367 U.S. 497 (1961), the Planned Parenthood Center of New Haven was opened (R. 16-7). The purpose of the Center was to provide information, instruction and medical advice to married persons as to the means of preventing conception, and to educate married persons generally as to such means (R 17).

The Center occupied eight rooms of the building in which it was situated (R. 17). Dr. Buxton was Medical Director of the Center (R. 17). Mrs. Griswold was Acting Director of the Center in charge of its administration and its educational program (R. 17).

During the period of its operation, from November 1 to November 10, the Center made information, instruction, education and medical advice on birth control available to married persons who sought it (R. 17).

With respect to a woman who came to the Center seeking contraceptive advice the general procedure was to take her case history and explain to her various methods of contraception. She was then examined by a staff doctor, who prescribed the method of contraception selected

by her unless it was contraindicated. The patient was furnished with the contraceptive device or material prescribed by the doctor, and a doctor or nurse advised her how to use it. Fees were charged on a sliding scale, depending on family income, and ranged from nothing to $15. (R. 18-9).

Dr. Buxton, as Medical Director, made all medical decisions with respect to the facilities of the Center, the procedure to be followed, the types of contraceptive advice and methods available, and the selection of doctors to staff the Center (R. 18). In addition, on several occasions, as a physician he examined and gave contraceptive advice to patients at the Center (R. 18). Mrs. Griswold on several occasions interviewed persons coming to the Center, took case histories, conducted group orientation sessions describing the methods of contraception and, on one occasion, gave a patient a drug or medical article to prevent conception (R. 20).

Among those who went to the Center seeking contraceptive advice were three married women. They followed the procedure described above, were given contraceptive material prescribed by the doctor, and subsequently used the material for the purpose of preventing conception. (R. 20-2).

On November 10, 1961, after Dr. Buxton and Mrs. Griswold were arrested, the Center closed (R. 18).

The Prior Litigation And The State Court's Interpretation of Sections 53-32 And 54-196.

The Connecticut Supreme Court of Errors has passed upon the interpretation and validity of Sections 53-32 and 54-196 on four occasions prior to its decision in the case at bar:

In *State* vs. *Nelson*, 126 Conn. 412, 11 A.2d 856, decided in 1940, two physicians and a nurse were charged with assisting, abetting and counseling a married woman to use contraceptive devices under conditions where, in the opinion of the physician, "preservation of the general health" of the patient required such use to prevent conception. A demurrer to the information was sustained by the trial court on due process grounds. The Supreme Court of Errors, in a three to two decision, reversed the lower court and upheld the validity of the statutes. The Court construed the statutes as applying in all circumstances, regardless of health factors, but expressly did not decide whether an implied exception would be recognized where "pregnancy would jeopardize life" (126 Conn. at 418, 11 A.2d at 859).

The *Nelson* case involved the operation of a birth control clinic in Waterbury. At that time nine such clinics were functioning in Connecticut. Following the *Nelson* decision all the clinics in the State closed down. On remand to the trial court the Nelson prosecution was nolled.[2]

Shortly afterwards, Dr. Wilder Tileston, another Connecticut physician, brought a declaratory judgment action to determine whether Sections 53-32 and 54-196 made it unlawful for him to prescribe the use of contraceptive devices for married women, living with their husbands, in cases where in his professional judgment a pregnancy might result in death or serious injury to health. In *Tileston* vs. *Ullman*, 129 Conn. 84, 26 A.2d 582 (1942), the Supreme Court of Errors, again by a three to two vote, ruled that the statutes were to be construed as an absolute prohibition and permitted no exception under any circumstances. In the opinion of the majority the Legislature "was entitled to believe" that the alternative available

to the women, namely, abstinence from marital relations, "was reasonable and practical" (129 Conn. at 93, 26 A.2d at 587). The majority again sustained the statutes against the due process challenge. On appeal, this Court dismissed the case, without reaching the merits, on the ground that Dr. Tileston did not have standing to raise the constitutional rights of his patients. *Tileston* vs. *Ullman*, 318 U.S. 44 (1943).

The issues were raised again some years later in a group of declaratory judgment suits. Dr. C. Lee Buxton, appellant here, brought one of these suits, asserting his own rights to liberty and property in the practice of his profession and urging that such rights were infringed by legislation which prevented him from prescribing, in accordance with accepted medical practice, contraceptive devices to three married women who were plaintiffs in the other suits. In the case of one such plaintiff, a further pregnancy "would be exceedingly dangerous to her life." *Buxton* vs. *Ullman*, 147 Conn. 48, 52, 156 A.2d 508, 511 (1959). In another case a married couple had had three abnormal children, no one of whom lived more than ten weeks, the cause of these abnormalities was thought by the physicians to be genetic, and the prospect of another pregnancy was "extremely disturbing" to the couple (147 Conn. at 53, 156 A.2d at 511). In a further case, a married couple had had four children, none of whom had lived, and because of blood factor incompatibilities of the plaintiffs "the prospects that they can procreate a normal child is (*sic*) highly unlikely" (*ibid*). All the plaintiffs based their claims on due process. Demurrers to the complaints were sustained and the Supreme Court of Errors, this time unanimously, affirmed, considering the issues foreclosed by the prior decisions. On appeal, a majority of this Court held that the "fact that Connecticut has not chosen to press the enforcement of this statute deprives these controversies of the immediacy which is an indispensable

---

2. See 367 U.S. at 532. At the same time as it decided the *Nelson* case the Supreme Court of Errors, in a companion case, ruled that the Connecticut search and seizure laws did not authorize the seizure and destruction of the contraceptive materials in possession of the Waterbury clinic. *State* vs. *Certain Contraceptive Materials*, 126 Conn. 428, 11 A.2d 863 (1940).

condition of constitutional adjudication,'' *Poe* vs. *Ullman*, 367 U.S. 497, 508 (1961).

In the fourth case a young married couple brought a declaratory judgment action on the ground that the Connecticut statutes would deprive them of their rights, under the due process clause, to obtain medical advice on proper methods of contraception, ''thereby avoiding the possibility that children will be conceived before these plaintiffs are prepared psychologically or economically for the duties and obligations of parenthood.'' *Trubek* vs. *Ullman*, 147 Conn. 633, 165 A.2d 158 (1960). The Supreme Court of Errors, holding that the issues were concluded by previous decisions, affirmed the trial court's dismissal of the action. Appeal was dismissed and petition for certiorari denied by this Court. *Trubek* vs. *Ullman*, 367 U.S. 907 (1961).

As a result of these four decisions, together with the one rendered in the case at bar, it is clear that the Supreme Court of Errors has interpreted Sections 53-32 and 54-196 to mean that a physician is prohibited from advising or prescribing, and all persons are prohibited from using, contraceptive devices, regardless of whether:

(1) The persons involved are married and living together.

(2) The devices are prescribed by a licensed physician in accordance with ''generally accepted medical practice'' (126 Conn. at 419, 11 A.2d at 859).

(3) Contraceptive measures are ''necessary to protect and procure the best possible state of health and well being'' (126 Conn. at 415, 11 A.2d at 858).

(4) Pregnancy will seriously jeopardize life or health or result in defective or abnormal children or in still-births.

It is also clear, however, that Sections 53-32 and 54-196 do not prohibit the sale or use of contraceptive devices in Connecticut for the prevention of disease, as distinct from the prevention

of conception. The Supreme Court of Errors has not directly ruled on this question. But the conclusion is apparent from the following considerations:

(1) Section 53-32 applies only to the use of contraceptive devices ''for the purpose of preventing conception.'' It contains no reference to their use for other purposes, including the well-known practice of selling and using such devices for the prevention of disease.

(2) The Supreme Court of Errors has consistently cited with approval and relied upon the decisions of the Massachusetts Supreme Judicial Court interpreting the Massachusetts anti-contraceptive law (126 Conn. at 419, 421-2, 425, 11 A.2d at 859, 860, 862; 129 Conn. at 88, 89-91, 26 A.2d at 585, 585-6). That law does not forbid the use of contraceptive devices, but its prohibition does extend to any person who ''sells, lends, gives away, exhibits, or offers to sell, lend or give away . . . any drug, medicine, instrument or article whatever for the prevention of conception.'' Mass. G.L. (Ter. ed.) Chap. 272, § 21. In *State* vs. *Nelson* the Connecticut Supreme Court of Errors grouped the Massachusetts and Connecticut statutes in the same category of state anti-contraceptive laws, as ones that ''attempt complete suppression'' (126 Conn. at 420, 11 A.2d at 860). And in *Tileston* vs. *Ullman* it referred to the Massachusetts statute as a ''similar statutory prohibition'' (129 Conn. at 89, 26 A.2d at 585). In *Commonwealth* vs. *Corbett*, 307 Mass. 7, 29 N.E. 2d 151 (1940), it was held that the Massachusetts statute did not prevent the sale of contraceptive devices for the prevention of disease. And in *Tileston* the Connecticut Supreme Court of Errors expressly noted this interpretation and by clear implication accepted it (129 Conn. at 91, 26 A.2d at 586).

(3) This Court may take judicial notice of the statement of the Connecticut official charged with administration of State laws pertaining to the sale of drugs that certain contraceptive

devices may be prescribed by physicians for therapeutic purposes. In a letter dated September 15, 1954, which is a public record under Section 1-19 of the Connecticut General Statutes, the Commissioner of Food and Drugs wrote to the Secretary of the Bridgeport Pharmaceutical Association:

> "Since diaphragms have such therapeutic and other uses there is no reason why vaginal diaphragms may not be prescribed or ordered by a physician and such order filled by a pharmacist."

4. This Court may also take judicial notice that no prosecution has ever been brought in Connecticut charging violation of Section 53-32 by prescription, sale or use of contraceptive devices for the prevention of disease.

5. In *Poe* vs. *Ullman*, 367 U.S. 497, 502 (1961), the majority opinion noted: "We are advised by counsel for appellants that contraceptives are commonly and notoriously sold in Connecticut drug stores." And the Court relied upon this fact. In the trial of the case at bar the effort of appellants to introduce evidence to prove the statement made by counsel in *Poe* was excluded as irrelevant (R. 24-5). We repeat the statement of counsel in the *Poe* case.

In summary, then, Sections 53-32 and 54-196 do not apply to the use of contraceptive devices other than for prevention of conception, but for that purpose their use is precluded completely and without any exception.

SUMMARY OF ARGUMENT

I. Appellants, as defendants in a criminal prosecution, have standing to raise the constitutional issues presented here. Having this standing, they may raise all subsidiary questions bearing on the validity of the statutes, including the constitutional rights of their patients and potential patients.

II. The Connecticut anti-contraceptive statutes deny appellants the right to liberty and property without due process of law in violation of the Fourteenth Amendment:

A. The issues here are governed by the rules of due process as applied in cases where the governmental regulation touches upon fundamental individual and personal rights, not as applied in cases which involve commercial and property rights.

B. The legislative objectives sought by the Connecticut statutes have never been clearly enunciated, and hence the deference due the legislative judgment in this case is minimal.

C. The statutes, if designed as a health measure, are not reasonably related to the achievement of that objective, and are arbitrary and capricious.

D. The statutes were not intended as a device to maintain or increase the population of Connecticut and, if they were, would not constitute a reasonable method of achieving that objective.

E. If it were an objective of the statutes to restrict sexual intercourse to the propagation of children, that would not be a proper legislative purpose.

F. The statutes, considered as an effort to promote public morality by prohibiting the use of certain extrinsic aids to avoid conception, even within the marital relation, do not meet the applicable standards of due process. Where legislation is designed to promote public morality, due process requires that (1) the moral practices regulated by the statute be objectively related to the public welfare; or (2) if such is not the case (assuming this in itself is not sufficient to invalidate the statute), then the regulation must conform to the predominant view of morality prevailing in the community; in any event (3) the operation of the statute, weighing benefits against detriments, cannot be arbitrary or capricious. The statutes here fail to meet any of these tests.

G. The statutes, considered as an effort to protect public morals by discouraging sexual intercourse outside the marital relation, are not reasonably designed to achieve that end and impose restrictions on fundamental liberties far beyond what is necessary to accomplish such a purpose.

III. The Connecticut statutes violate due process in that they constitute an unwarranted invasion of privacy. Whether one derives the right of privacy from a composite of the Third, Fourth and Fifth Amendments, from the Ninth Amendment, or from the "liberty" clause of the Fourteenth Amendment, such a constitutional right has been specifically recognized by this Court. Although the boundaries of this constitutional right of privacy have not yet been spelled out, plainly the right extends to unwarranted governmental invasion of (1) the sanctity of the home, and (2) the intimacies of the sexual relationship in marriage. These core elements in the right to privacy are combined in this case. As Mr. Justice Douglas and Mr. Justice Harlan, the only Justices to reach the merits in *Poe* vs. *Ullman*, have pointed out, the Connecticut statutes constitute a shocking invasion of the protected private sector of life.

IV. The Connecticut statutes violate the First Amendment as incorporated in the Fourteenth:

A. The statutes are invalid on their face because they apply to "counseling" and other areas of speech.

B. The findings and conclusions of the trial court rested upon conduct within the area of protected speech. This failure of the courts below to separate speech from action renders the application of the statutes in this case invalid.

POINT I. Appellants Have Standing To Raise The Constitutional Issues Presented Here. Having This Standing They May Raise All Subsidiary Questions Bearing On The Validity Of The Statutes, Including The Constitutional Rights Of Their Patients And Potential Patients.

The question involved in *Poe* vs. *Ullman*, 367 U.S. 497 (1961)—that the Connecticut statutes have not been enforced—is no longer at issue here. By this prosecution Connecticut is attempting to enforce Sections 53-32 and 54-196 against these appellants. The fact that this prosecution, like the *Nelson* prosecution, is directed against the operation of a birth control center does not affect the issue. Plainly this case involves a real, not a hypothetical, controversy.

As defendants in a criminal prosecution, appellants have standing to assert that the Connecticut statutes applied to them deprive them of due process of law and the right to freedom of speech under the United States Constitution —issues consistently pressed by them throughout this litigation. Having standing to raise these issues, appellants may invoke in support of their position the rights of other persons affected by the operation of the statutes. These conclusions follow from the following considerations:

A.

Appellant Buxton, as a licensed physician, has a property right in the practice of his profession. Appellant Griswold, as Director of the Planned Parenthood League and as Acting Director of the Center, has a similar property right to engage in her occupation. Appellant Buxton also has the right to use assistants necessary to his practice. This Court has consistently held that these property rights may be restricted by State legislation only if such legislation meets the standards of due process of law under the Fourteenth

Amendment. *Dent* vs. *West Virginia*, 129 U.S. 114 (1889); *Pierce* vs. *Society of Sisters*, 268 U.S. 510 (1925); *Wieman* vs. *Updegraff*, 344 U.S. 183 (1952); see also *Truax* vs. *Raich*, 239 U.S. 33 (1915).

Since appellants are asserting their own constitutional rights to enjoy property they may also invoke the rights of persons with whom they have a professional relationship upon which their property rights depend. Thus, in *Truax* vs. *Raich, supra,* an employer was permitted to assert the rights of his employees; and in *Pierce* vs. *Society of Sisters, supra*, the owners of a private school were entitled to assert the rights of potential pupils and their parents. See also *Bantam Books, Inc.* vs. *Sullivan,* 372 U.S. 58, 64-5, footnote 6 (1963).

Furthermore, since the standards of due process require that the State legislation be not arbitrary, capricious or unreasonable, and since appellants challenge the statutes as invalid on their face, appellants may present to this Court all arguments touching upon the arbitrary character of the law, whether those features affect appellants directly or indirectly. *Aptheker* vs. *Secretary of State,* 378 U.S. 500 (1964); *Baggett* vs. *Bullitt,* 377 U.S. 360 (1964); *Cramp* vs. *Board of Public Instruction*, 368 U.S. 278 (1961); *Butler* vs. *Michigan*, 352 U.S. 380 (1957); *Thornhill* vs. *Alabama*, 310 U.S 88 (1940). Indeed, the very meaning of attacking a statute as void on its face is that the statute is invalid in all its applications, not merely in its application to the particular party bringing the challenge.[1]

---

1. Appellee, in its Motion to Dismiss Appeal, argued that appellants had raised below only the question whether the statutes were invalidly applied in this case, and not the question of whether they were invalid on their face (pp. 3-5). This is not correct. It is true that, in order to make clear the difference between this case and *Tileston* vs. *Ullman*, 318 U.S. 44, appellants asserted that the statutes ''as applied to'' them were unconstitutional (see, *e.g.*, R. 2, 8, 35-6, 54). But appellants consistently asserted that the statutes were void as a whole, not only in their application in this case (see *e.g.*, R. 27, 34). And the three courts below all dealt with the constitutional issues on this basis (see, *e.g.*, R. 9-11, 46-7, 47-8, 62-3).

B.

Appellants' liberties, also protected under the due process clause of the Fourteenth Amendment, are likewise restricted by the statutes involved here. Under our constitutional system appellants have the right to engage in activity, public or private, for the betterment of mankind or for the pleasure of themselves, as individuals or in association with others, and governmental restrictions upon such activities must conform to the standards of due process of law. As this Court said in *Meyer* vs. *Nebraska*, 262 U.S. 390, 399 (1923), ''Without doubt, [that liberty] denotes not merely freedom from bodily restraint but also the right of the individual to contract, to engage in any of the common occupations of life, to acquire useful knowledge, to marry, establish a home and bring up children, to worship God according to the dictates of his own conscience, and generally to enjoy those privileges long recognized at common law as essential to the orderly pursuit of happiness by free men.'' And the Court has recognized and protected against unconstitutional infringement not only the liberty of individuals to learn, as in *Meyer*, but the liberty to conduct a school (*Pierce* vs. *Society of Sisters, supra*); to form an association for advancement of civil rights (*N.A.A.C.P.* vs. *Alabama ex rel. Patterson*, 357 U.S. 449 (1958)); and to travel (*Aptheker* vs. *Secretary of State, supra*). The action of these appellants, in opening a center to deal with the human and social problems of parenthood and population, clearly falls within this category of protected liberty.

In addition appellant Buxton, at least, invokes another form of liberty: the right to intellectual freedom in the pursuit of knowledge in his chosen field of inquiry, and the right to practice his profession in accordance with scientifically accepted principles. Such liberties, also, have been given recognition by this Court. *Wieman* vs. *Updegraff*, 344 U.S. at 195-198 (concurring opinion); *Sweezy* vs. *New Hampshire,* 354 U.S. 234, 250-1, 261-4 (1957); *Barenblatt* vs. *U.S.,* 360 U.S. 109, 112 (1959); *Baggett* vs. *Bullitt,* 377 U.S. at 369-72. They are closely related to the fundamental right to freedom of expression, guaranteed by the First Amendment, but differ in that they may involve action as well as expression. Their protection against arbitrary or capricious government control demands special scrutiny.

Since appellants have standing to raise these issues, as in the case of their claims based on property rights, they may assert the rights of others which affect enjoyment of their own rights and, challenging the statutes on their face, may advance all considerations pertaining to the arbitrary character of the statutes as a whole. See cases cited *supra* in subsection A.

•••

POINT II. The Connecticut Anti-Contraceptive Statutes Deny Appellants The Right To Liberty And Property Without Due Process Of Law In That They Are Arbitrary And Capricious, And Have No Reasonable Relation To A Proper Legislative Purpose.

A. The Basic Standards Of Due Process. In *Meyer* vs. *Nebraska,* 262 U.S. 390 (1923), a State statute which prohibited the teaching of the German language to pupils who had not passed the eighth grade was attacked on due process grounds as violating the right of teachers to teach and parents to instruct their children. Holding the statute invalid, this Court laid down the requirements of the due process clause in the following terms:

> "The established doctrine is that this liberty may not be interfered with, under the guise of protecting the public interest, by legislative action which is arbitrary or without reasonable relation to some

purpose within the competency of the State to effect. Determination by the legislature of what constitutes proper exercise of police power is not final or conclusive but is subject to supervision by the courts." (pp. 399-400).

In *Nebbia* vs. *New York,* 291 U.S. 502 (1934), a State statute regulating the price of milk was attacked on due process grounds as violating the right of commercial enterprises to conduct their business without arbitrary governmental restrictions. Upholding the validity of the statute, the Court restated the requirements of the due process clause:

> "If the laws passed are seen to have a reasonable relation to a proper legislative purpose, and are neither arbitrary nor discriminatory, the requirements of due process are satisfied, and judicial determination to that effect renders a court *functus officio.*" (p. 537).

The standards imposed on State legislatures by the due process clause are thus well settled. In sum, they are that the legislation (1) must have a reasonable relation (2) to a proper legislative purpose, and (3) be not otherwise arbitrary or capricious.

In applying this doctrine, however, it is vital to emphasize the difference between the two situations typified by *Meyer* and *Nebbia.* In *Meyer* the legislation touched upon rights of a fundamental individual and personal character, essential to maintaining the independence, integrity and private development of a citizen in a highly organized, yet democratic, society. In *Nebbia* the legislation dealt with economic regulation of commercial and property rights, essential to maintaining the public interest in controlling a highly complex, industrialized society. The distinction is basic in striking the balance between public interest and private right in a modern, technologically developed nation.

And it follows that the function of this Court in reviewing legislation must be somewhat different in the two situations. The Court has, indeed, recognized this difference. Since *Nebbia* it has uniformly applied due process standards to allow Federal and State legislatures full leeway in their judgments as to the need and propriety of all types of economic regulation. See, *e.g., West Coast Hotel Co.* vs. *Parrish,* 300 U.S. 379 (1937); *Lincoln Federal Labor Union* vs. *Northwestern Iron & Metal Co.,* 335 U.S. 525 (1949); *Berman* vs. *Parker,* 348 U.S. 26 (1954); *Williamson* vs. *Lee Optical Co.,* 348 U.S. 483 (1955). At the same time it has subjected to much more intensive scrutiny under the due process clause legislation which impairs the freedom of the individual to live a fruitful life or to sustain his position as citizen rather than subject. *Pierce* vs. *Society of Sisters,* 268 U.S. 510 (1925); *Wieman* vs. *Updegraff,* 344 U.S. 183 (1952); *Slochower* vs. *Board of Education,* 350 U.S. 551 (1956); *Schware* vs. *Board of Bar Examiners,* 353 U.S. 232 (1957); *Aptheker* vs. *Secretary of State,* 378 U.S. 500 (1964).

The rights at stake in this litigation plainly fall within the latter category. Although regulation of the medical profession may at times involve restriction of commercial activities, or concern the needs of the public for safe and competent medical practices, that is not the thrust of the legislation here. Rather, the rights of appellants being abrogated are the right to practice medicine in accordance with scientifically accepted medical principles, the right to disseminate information, and the right to make available safe and effective medical services to those members of the community unable to afford or ignorant of the private facilities. And the rights of appellants' patients, also at stake here, are even more personal and equally fundamental. They concern the most intimate aspects of the marital relationship, the right to plan a family, the right to happiness, to health and even to life itself. State legislation impinging on these rights, we submit, should be subjected to the most careful inspection by this Court.

We are not, in short, asking here for reinstatement of the line of due process decisions exemplified by *Lochner* vs. *New York,* 198 U.S. 45 (1905). But we are asking the Court to adhere to the principles of the *Meyer* case:

> "That the State may do much, go very far, indeed, in order to improve the quality of its citizens, physically, mentally and morally, is clear; but the individual has certain fundamental rights which must be respected." (262 U.S. at 401).

B. The Objectives Of The Connecticut Statutes.

In order to apply the standards of due process to the Connecticut statutes here involved, it is first necessary to determine the precise objectives sought to be achieved by the legislature. Yet the purposes of the law are shrouded in obscurity. Section 53-32 was originally passed in 1879, as part of an amendment to the general obscenity statute, entitled "An Act to Amend an Act concerning Offenses against Decency, Morality, and Humanity."[1] It is a relic of Comstockery, a psychological attitude which, if it ever were, is no longer part of the mainstream of American life and thought.[2] It was modeled on the Federal law of 1873, 17 Stat. 598, and was comparable to legislation passed in a number of other States during the Comstock period.[3] But, with the exception of Connecticut and

1. Chapter 78 of the Public Acts of 1879. In a revision of the General Statutes in 1888, the obscenity law was broken up, and the part dealing with contraceptives was put in a separate section. Gen. Stats., 1888, § 1539. The 1879 amendment and the prior obscenity statute are quoted in the dissenting opinion of Judge Avery in *Tileston* vs. *Ullman,* 129 Conn. 84, 98-9, 26 A.2d 582, 589.

2. See Broun and Leech, *Anthony Comstock* (1927); Haney, *Comstockery in America* (1960), pp. 18-25.

3. See Dennett, *Birth Control Laws* (1926), pp. 19-29.

Massachusetts, those laws have not been construed as prohibiting the type of activities in which appellants here engaged.[4]

From the four decisions in which the Connecticut Supreme Court of Errors has dealt with the statutes (Statement of the Case, *supra*) we have endeavored to cull all the various objectives which have been suggested at one time or another. Apart from general, and unenlightening, references to public "health," "safety," "morals," and "welfare," the more specific possible legislative purposes may be listed as follows:

(1) To protect persons from the use of drugs or devices injurious to health or life. *State* vs. *Nelson*, 126 Conn. at 425, 11 A.2d at 862.

(2) To maintain and increase the population. *State* vs. *Nelson*, 126 Conn. at 425-6, 11 A.2d at 862.

(3) To restrict sexual intercourse to the propagation of (legitimate) children. *State* vs. *Nelson*, 126 Conn. at 425, 11 A.2d at 862; *Tileston* vs. *Ullman*, 129 Conn. at 90, 26 A.2d at 585.

(4) To promote public morals by prohibiting the use of particular methods of avoiding conception, *i.e.,* those employing extrinsic aids, even within the marital relation. *State* vs. *Nelson*, 126 Conn. at 424, 11 A.2d at 861.

(5) To protect public morals by discouraging sexual intercourse outside the marital relation. *State* vs. *Nelson*, 126 Conn. at 421, 424-5, 11 A.2d at 860, 861-2; *Tileston* vs. *Ullman*, 129 Conn. at 90, 26 A.2d at 585-6.

The Supreme Court of Errors has never clearly declared which one, or which combination, of these possible objectives the Connecticut legislature in 1879 sought to achieve. Indeed, in its last three decisions that Court seems to have abandoned the attempt to state the legislative purpose altogether. Under such circumstances the deference owed by this Court to the legislative judgment is surely minimal.

Of the possible objectives listed, most probably only the last two require serious consideration. Nevertheless we undertake in the following sections to apply the standards of the due process clause to each one, in the order given above.

It should be added that the issues must be decided here on the basis of current circumstances, not those existing in 1879 or earlier this century. *Block* vs. *Hirsh*, 256 U.S. 135, 155 (1921); *Chastleton Corp.* vs. *Sinclair*, 264 U.S. 543, 547-8 (1924); *Brown* vs. *Board of Education,* 347 U.S. 483, 492-3 (1954). Hence the material we present will deal with existing knowledge and conditions.

C. The Statutes, If Designed As A Health Measure, Are Not Reasonably Related To The Achievement Of That Objective, And Are Arbitrary And Capricious.

In *State* vs. *Nelson* the Connecticut Supreme Court of Errors somewhat casually remarks that, "Like an advertisement representing that and how venereal disease can be easily and cheaply cured, information and advice as to means, or furnishing materials intended for, contraception may be said to have 'a decided tendency to. . .' expose interested and uninformed persons to dangers from the use of drugs and devices injurious to health or even life." 126 Conn. at 424-5, 11 A.2d at 861-2.

It seems most unlikely, in view of the Comstockian background, that the Connecticut legislature had any such health purpose in mind. In any event, the legislation is not reasonably related to the achievement of that end. Contraceptive drugs or devices are not inherently

---

4. See, *e.g.,* *Bours* vs. *U.S.,* 229 F. 960 (C.A. 7, 1915); *Youngs Rubber Corp.* vs. *C.I. Lee & Co.,* 45 F.2d 103 (C.A. 2, 1930); *Davis* vs. *U.S.,* 62 F.2d 473 (C.A. 6, 1933); *U.S.* vs. *One Package,* 86 F.2d 737 (C.A. 2, 1936); *Consumers Union of U.S.* vs. *Walker,* 145 F.2d 33 (C.A. D.C., 1944). See Comment, *The History and Future of the Legal Battle Over Birth Control,* 49 Corn. L.Q. 275, 283-5, (1964).

harmful or dangerous. On the contrary, as will be shown later, their prescription is accepted medical practice; and in many cases they are the safest and most effective way to preserve health and life (see Section F, *infra*). Whatever threat to health they might possibly entail, if sold without restriction, can be met by conventional measures for licensing and supervision, as is done in the case of thousands of other medical products and as is done in the case of contraceptive devices in other States. Indeed, food and drug legislation designed to safeguard the public health has during the last few years reached a high point in extensive application and effective administration. To seek protection of the public health by prohibiting the use of contraceptive devices entirely, through a criminal statute, is absurd. And to seek that protection by prosecuting a noted specialist in the use of such devices, operating through carefully safeguarded procedures in their prescription and use, is doubly absurd.

It is, in short, impossible to conceive that the health objective was a significant factor in the passage of this legislation or has been a serious consideration in retaining the law on the statute books. And, even if it were, the law goes far beyond the requirements of a health regulation, and impinges so drastically upon basic individual rights, that it cannot stand upon any basis of reasonableness. See *Shelton* vs. *Tucker*, 364 U.S. 479 (1960); *Louisiana ex rel. Gremillion* vs. *N.A.A.C.P.*, 366 U.S. 293 (1961); *N.A.A.C.P.* vs. *Alabama ex rel. Flowers*, 377 U.S. 288 (1964); *Aptheker* vs. *Secretary of State*, 378 U.S. 500 (1964).

D. The Statutes Were Not Intended As A Device To Maintain Or Increase The Population Of Connecticut And, If They Were, Would Not Constitute A Reasonable Method Of Achieving That Objective.

The Supreme Court of Errors has never actually asserted that the anti-contraceptive statutes were passed by the Legislature for the purpose of maintaining or increasing the population of the State of Connecticut. In *State* vs. *Nelson* the Court did refer to this possible objective, introducing it as one that had been suggested by the defendants in that case, and saying: "If, as the defendants suggest, a purpose, either principal or incidental, was to promote a maintenance and increase of the population, that would not be an inadmissible motive and the efficacy, to that end, of the provision would be a legislative question." 126 Conn. at 425-6, 11 A.2d at 862. In no other decision has the Supreme Court of Errors ever mentioned the matter.[5]

There is no evidence that the Comstock laws in general, or Connecticut's in particular, were based upon any such notion of population control. Their motivation was entirely different (see Section B, *supra*). The Supreme Court of Errors clearly recognized this in twice so obviously declining to advance the argument itself. As one commentator has said, "This explanation of the statute strains credulity." Note, *Connecticut's Birth Control Law: Reviewing a State Statute Under the Fourteenth Amendment*, 70 Yale L.J. 322, 330 (1960).

Nor can the Court supply this as a current objective of the statutes, or a reason why the statutes have been left on the books. Virtually the whole world now recognizes that the current problems of population control—crucial as they are—involve limitations on, not expansion of, the population explosion (see Section F, *infra*). It cannot be assumed that the current policy of the Connecticut legislature would run so

---

5. The decision of the Appellate Division did refer to population control as a possible purpose of the statutes, saying:
   "It is not alone for the preservation of morality in the religious sense that the legislature may have been impelled to act, but also for the perpetuation of race and to avert those perils of extinction of which states and nations have been alertly aware since the beginning of recorded history. Each civilized society has a primordial right to its continued existence and to the discouragement of practices that tend to negate its survival." R. 49.
   But the Supreme Court of Errors did not refer to the point.

squarely counter to the entire direction of national and international developments in this field.

Furthermore, even if we presume that an increase in the population of Connecticut is an objective of the law, the measures adopted would not constitute a reasonable means of reaching that result. As already indicated, and as will be developed more fully later (see Section F, *infra*), the prohibitions of the law cut deeply into fundamental individual rights, including the right to protect life and health. On the other hand the factors determining the growth of population are so many and so complex,[6] that the measures prescribed by these statutes, especially if enforced only against birth control centers, would clearly not justify the human costs. Plainly other effective alternatives, far less serious in their abrogation of individual rights, are available to the Legislature, and due process requires that such "less drastic" means be employed. *Shelton* vs. *Tucker,* 364 U.S. 479, 488; *Aptheker* vs. *Secretary of State,* 378 U.S. 500, 508, 513-4; *cf. Dean Milk Co.* vs. *Madison,* 340 U.S. 349, 354-6 (1951).

Certainly this Court should not go out of its way to imply this purpose to the Connecticut legislature, when the Connecticut Supreme Court of Errors has not done so and when there is no suggestion that the Connecticut legislature has ever weighed or considered these difficult and disturbing judgments.

E. An Objective Of The Statutes To Restrict Sexual Intercourse To The Propagation Of Children Would Not Be A Proper Legislative Purpose.

That an objective of the Connecticut statutes is to restrict sexual intercourse to the propagation of (legitimate) children has never been explicitly stated by the Supreme Court of Errors. This idea

6. See, *e.g.*, Wyon, *Field Studies on Fertility of Human Populations,* in *Human Fertility and Population Problems* (Greep ed., 1962) at pp. 79-105; Symposium, *Population Control,* 25 Law and Contemp. Prob. 377 (1960).

seems to be implicit, however, in that Court's quotation with approval of the opinion of the Massachusetts Supreme Judicial Court, referring to laws of the Massachusetts and Connecticut variety: "Their plain purpose is to protect purity, to preserve chastity, to encourage continence and self-restraint, to defend the sanctity of the home, and thus engender. . .a virile and virtuous race of men and women." *State* vs. *Nelson,* 126 Conn. at 425, 11 A.2d at 862. The Connecticut Court added: "It is reasonable to assume that similar motives underlay the adoption of our own statute in 1879." *Ibid.*

In *Tileston* vs. *Ullman* the Supreme Court of Errors apparently reiterated these views, citing with approval a Massachusetts decision that the legislature "might take the view that the use of contraceptives would not only promote sexual immorality but would expose the commonwealth to other grave dangers." 129 Conn. at 90, 26 A.2d at 585.

If it be an objective of the law to restrict sexual intercourse to procreation—and such an aim would be consistent with the Comstock approach—then, we submit, this is not a proper legislative purpose under the requirements of the due process clause. However, since the matter has been left vague by the Supreme Court of Errors we do not feel it necessary to argue the question *in extenso* here. Much of what is said in the next section of this brief is equally applicable to this issue. Suffice it to say at this point, that such a legislative purpose would be so contrary to the basic drives of man, so far-reaching an invasion of individual liberty, and so disruptive of our marriage and family institutions as they exist today, that it cannot be conceived as falling within the police power of the State to promote morals or the general welfare. In any event, this Court, again, should not accept such a drastic view of the law without a much more clear-cut statement from the Connecticut legislature or courts that the statutes were designed to accomplish this end.

F. The Statutes, Considered As An Effort To Promote Public Morality By Prohibiting The Use Of Certain Extrinsic Aids To Avoid Conception, Even Within The Marital Relation, Are Arbitrary And Capricious And Not Reasonably Related To A Proper Legislative Purpose.

We come now to a more plausible objective of the statutes, though again one which has never been clearly articulated by the Connecticut legislature or courts. The closest approach to this position occurs in the *Nelson* decision of 1940, where the Supreme Court of Errors remarks, "...it is not for us to say that the Legislature might not reasonably hold that the artificial limitation of even legitimate child-bearing would be inimical to the public welfare and, as well, that use of contraceptives, and assistance therein or tending thereto, would be injurious to public morals." 126 Conn. at 424, 11 A.2d at 861. And later, "The legislature might regard the use of materials designed to prevent conception as prejudicial to public morals and inimical to the welfare and interests of the community, as the general dissemination of information as to how it could be accomplished, like distribution of obscene literature, plainly would be." *Ibid.*

We will assume that the Court was saying here, not that the use of all methods of avoiding conception was injurious to public morals (see Section E, *supra*), but that the use of "artificial" methods or "materials" would be. No similar statements are to be found in the other decisions of the Supreme Court of Errors, although general references to "public morality" may have been intended to encompass this idea. See *Tileston* vs. *Ullman*, 129 Conn. at 90, 94, 26 A.2d at 585, 587; *Buxton* vs. *Ullman*, 147 Conn. at 54-5, 156 A.2d at 512.

In order to appraise this position, it is first necessary to set forth some general medical information concerning various methods of avoiding conception. Then we examine the special

problem of the meaning of the due process clause in relation to legislation which has as its purpose the promotion of "public morality." Thereafter we undertake to apply these standards of due process to the precise issue of public morality raised here.

1. The Medical Background.

There are a number of methods of avoiding conception, some known and practiced for many years, others recently developed by medical science. These methods vary in the degree to which they are reliable in preventing conception. One of the most recent studies by a leading clinician includes the following table showing the results of tests of the effectiveness and reliability of some of these contraceptive methods.[7]

•••

In any event, allowing for these exceptions and ambiguities, the precise issue is whether the prohibition of those methods seleced by the Connecticut legislature, viewed as a regulation to promote the public morality, conforms to the standard of due process of law.

2. The Standards Of Due Process In Legislation Aimed At Promotion Of Public Morality.

When legislation is designed to promote health, safety, or the general welfare in a material sense, its validity under the due process clause can be tested by considerations that can be objectively determined and rationally weighed. Questions of whether the statute is arbitrary or capricious, or has a reasonable relation to a proper legislative purpose, turn in such cases upon factual material which can be discovered and presented to the court, and upon value judgments which

---

7. Garcia, *Clinical Studies on Human Fertility Control*, in Greep (ed.), *Human Fertility and Population Problems* (1963), p. 63.

are subject to exposition and debate. The Brandeis brief is, of course, a classic illustration of this approach to the due process clause.

When the legislation is designed to promote public morality, however, the problem of applying the standards of due process may take a different form. In some cases, such as a statute prohibiting prostitution, the moral purposes may be justified by reference to objective and rational factors relevant to the promotion of the general welfare. But in other cases the legislature may undertake to legislate purely on the basis of moral principles not subject to objective evaluation. In such a case, how are the customary criteria of due process to be applied?

Certainly the court cannot take the position that the simple claim of a moral aim by the legislature satisfies the requirements of due process. As Mr. Justice Harlan said in *Poe* vs. *Ullman*, "the mere assertion that the action of the State finds justification in the controversial realm of morals cannot justify alone any and every restriction it imposes," 367 U.S. at 545. Any such doctrine would immunize virtually all legislation from the mandate of the due process clause. It would allow the legislature to impose restraints upon individual liberties solely on the ground that some insignificant fraction of the community regarded the issue as a moral one. Thus, a law prohibiting women from appearing in public without veils, or forbidding women to use lipstick or cosmetics, even though some persons in the community might regard such practices as immoral, would surely be held an arbitrary infringement of personal liberty outlawed by the due process clause. What, then, should be the constitutional standards for applying the due process clause in cases where the legislature seeks to promote public morals?

We submit that the standard in such cases should at least be that (1) the moral practices regulated by the statute must be objectively related to the public welfare, or (2) in the event no such relationship can be demonstrated, the regulation must conform to the predominant view of morality prevailing in the community. In other words, if the legislature cannot establish that the law promotes the public welfare in a material sense, it cannot enforce the morality of a minority group in the community upon other members of the community.[14]

There is, so far as we are aware, no decision of the Supreme Court dealing with this exact problem. But the doctrine we urge here is fully supported by the obscenity cases. In *Roth* vs. *United States* a majority of the Court held that material alleged to be obscene could not be restricted unless it met the standard that "to the *average* person, *applying contemporary community standards*," the dominant theme appealed to prurient interests. 354 U.S. 476, 489 (1957). And it further adopted the provision in the A.L.I. Model Penal Code that material to be obscene must go "substantially beyond *customary* limits of candor." 345 U.S. at 487.

In subsequent cases a majority of the justices have reaffirmed this view that the test of obscenity must adhere to dominant community standards. Thus in *Manual Enterprises* vs. *Day*, Mr. Justice Harlan and Mr. Justice Stewart declared that, in order to sustain a conviction under Federal obscenity laws, the materials must be "deemed so offensive on their face as to affront *current community standards* of decency." 370 U.S. 478, 482 (1962). In *Jacobellis* vs. *Ohio*, Mr. Justice Brennan and Mr. Justice Goldberg, again referring to the A.L.I. Model Penal Code, repeated that obscenity must involve "a deviation from *society's* standards of decency." 378 U.S.

---

14. It may be argued that the first standard set forth above is sufficient in itself, without the second. That is, if the moral principles cannot be objectively related to the public welfare, the legislation does not, for that reason alone, meet the standards of due process. It is not necessary to take that position in order to decide this case, however, and we do not consider it further here.

184, 191-2 (1964). In the same case Mr. Chief Justice Warren and Mr. Justice Clark expressly affirmed their support for the *Roth* rule. 378 U.S. at 199-200. Mr. Justice Harlan stated he would apply the *Roth* rule only to the Federal Government. 378 U.S. at 204. Mr. Justice Stewart, although employing the "hard core pornography" test, did not alter his views on the subject of community standards. 378 U.S. at 197.[15]

The obscenity cases raise the same kind of problem as do the Connecticut statutes. In fact, as already pointed out, the Connecticut legislation had its origin in the Comstock laws, which were concerned primarily with matters of obscenity and decency. In both types of legislation the question is one of enforcing moral standards. It is true that the obscenity issues deal with rights under the First Amendment. The cases are not treated under traditional First Amendment doctrine, however, but rather in terms more appropriate to due process. And the individual rights infringed by the Connecticut statutes are fully as basic as the rights curtailed by obscenity laws.

We conclude, therefore, that in applying the standards of due process to the Connecticut statutes, taken as measures to promote public morality, the Court must consider (1) whether the law is objectively related to the public welfare; and (2) if it is not, whether it attempts to enforce on the entire community moral principles not conforming to the predominant view of morality held by the community. Furthermore, under the general standards of due process

15. The position that the community standards involved may be local rather than national standards is, as we read the cases, held by only three members of the Court: Mr. Chief Justice Warren, Mr. Justice Clark, and Mr. Justice Harlan.

Mr. Justice Black and Mr. Justice Douglas, of course, apply the standard that the First Amendment precludes any form of restriction upon expression alleged to be obscene. See *Roth* vs. *United States*, 354 U.S. at 508-14; *Jacobellis* vs. *Ohio*, 378 U.S. at 196-7. Hence their position does not employ the criterion of community standards.

(see Section B, *supra*), even if the law satisfies the two requirements just stated, it must still meet the traditional test that its general operation be not arbitrary or capricious. This requires the Court to consider (3) whether the advantages of the law are greatly outweighed by its disadvantages, taking into account that the legislation abrogates fundamental rights of the individual, including the right to health and life.

•••

5. **Any Possible Beneficial Aspects Of The Statute Are So Totally Outweighed By Their Cruel And Drastic Infraction Of Individual Rights, Their Inconsistencies And Irrationalities In Actual Operation, And Their Other Patent Defects, That They Must Be Held Arbitrary And Capricious And Hence In Violation Of Due Process Of Law.**

Our final point under the due process clause is that, even if the statutes were found to satisfy the due process requirements just discussed, they must still pass the basic test of being not arbitrary or capricious. This involves a general weighing of benefits against detriments. We realize that in this balancing process the burden is on appellants to show that the statutes are arbitrary. For reasons already mentioned, however, the burden is lighter in this case because fundamental rights of personal liberty are at stake, and hence the Court has a greater obligation to scrutinize the legislative judgment with skepticism and care. Moreover, there is here no clear-cut expression of statutory purpose which can serve as any solid foundation for a presumption in favor of the legislative judgment. In any event we believe the facts demonstrate that these Connecticut statutes cut so deeply into so many facets of individual liberty, and are so totally irrational in their social impact, that the burden of proving them arbitrary and capricious, even by the most exacting standard, is fully met.

The benefits accruing to the State of Connecticut from the statutes in question, being derived from governmentally enforced adherence to moral principles, and not being subject to objective measurement, are difficult to weigh in a due process balance. Our main attention, then, is focused on the other side of the scales.

Some of the detrimental effects of the statutes have already been pointed out. Others are apparent. We confine our treatment to a summary of the principal points.

(a) The Choice Between Ill-Health Or Death, And Abstinence.

For many women, as we have seen, pregnancy means serious illness or death. The methods of avoiding pregnancy barred by the Connecticut statutes, while not yet faultless, are in the opinion of the medical profession, the safest, the most effective, and the best, and provide a satisfactory solution to the problem. The methods allowed by the Connecticut statutes are ineffective and dangerous, and do not afford a satisfactory solution, medical or otherwise. The women suffering from such conditions are therefore placed in the position of risking serious injury or loss of life or, through abstinence, sacrificing the right to enjoy one of the most cherished aspects of the marriage relationship.

This cruel dilemma enforced by the Connecticut statutes cannot be justified. The right to protect one's own health and life is obviously fundamental. The power of the state to prohibit any person from taking medical measures to safeguard life and health, if it exists at all, is surely very narrowly circumscribed. It can be exercised only in the most extreme situations and upon the plainest showing of social necessity. Apart from the power to conscript men of arms under the war power, it is difficult to envisage the circumstances where such governmental measures could conceivably be warranted.

Certainly no instances come to mind where the state has prohibited an individual from preserving life and health through the use of medically accepted methods not harmful in themselves.

It is no answer to say that the individual has the alternative of abstinence. The conjugal right is itself fundamental, one of the most precious rights with which man is endowed. To condition the enjoyment of one elemental right upon the sacrifice of another, is not a choice the state may constitutionally impose. Whichever side of the coin one looks at, the lack of power in the state to deny liberty in this way remains.[72]

We know of no case where this Court has dealt with these precise questions. But in *Jacobson* vs. *Massachusetts*, 197 U.S. 11 (1905), this Court did at one point approach the problem. That case involved a Massachusetts statute providing for compulsory vaccination. The Court upheld the statute. In the course of his opinion, Justice Harlan addressed himself to the argument that there might be situations where it is "apparent or can be shown with reasonable certainty that [a person] is not at the time a fit subject of vaccination or that vaccination, by reason of his then condition, would seriously impair his health or probably cause his death." Justice Harlan was careful to make clear:

> "We are not to be understood as holding that the statute was intended to be applied to such a case, or, if it was so intended, that the judiciary would not be competent to interfere and protect the health and life of the individual concerned." 197 U.S. at 39.

The situation supposed by Justice Harlan, on a vastly augmented scale, is here presented by Connecticut's interpretation of its anti-

---

72. A third possibility, open in some circumstances, is sterilization or abortion. But these solutions, even if available, do not eliminate the dilemma but simply present it in a different form. See subsection g, *infra*.

contraceptive statutes. And this Court is now asked to ''protect the health and life'' of the many individuals concerned.

(b) Other Harms To The Individuals.

Even where actual life or grave and immediate impairment of health is not at stake, the Connecticut statutes impose serious deprivations upon many married couples. The fear of unwanted pregnancy is emotionally disturbing; indeed, ''it can produce the effect of a direct inhibition, particularly if it is obsessively exaggerated, as is often the case.''[73] The spacing of children is important to the health of the mother; in the Guttmacher poll of 3,381 physicians, well over two-thirds fixed the desirable interval between the termination of one pregnancy and the beginning of the next at from 10 to 24 months.[74] The bearing of defective children is tragedy for all concerned,—parents, children and society. Many other aspects of health and happiness turn on effective control of conception.[75]

Under the Connecticut statutes these problems can be solved only at the price of abstinence. Yet abstinence itself leads to unhappiness, tensions between husband and wife, extramarital relations, and divorce.[76] Again the statutes impose an intolerable choice which the state has no power to demand.

•••

73. Deutsch, *The Psychology of Women* (1945), p. 93.
74. Guttmacher, *Conception Control and the Medical Profession*, 12 Human Fertility 1, 6 (1947).
75. See subsection 3, *supra*, and brief of Planned Parenthood Federation, amicus curiae, Appendix B.
76. See subsection 3, *supra*, and brief of Planned Parenthood Federation, amicus curiae, Appendix B.

G. The Statutes, Considered As An Effort To Protect Public Morals By Discouraging Sexual Intercourse Outside The Marital Relation, Are Not Reasonably Designed To Achieve That End And Impose Restrictions On Fundamental Liberties Far Beyond What Is Necessary To Accomplish Such A Purpose.

We reach finally the last objective which has been advanced as a constitutional basis of the Connecticut statutes. The Supreme Court of Errors said in *State* vs. *Nelson* that ''it is not for us to say that the Legislature might not reasonably hold...that use of contraceptives, and assistance therein or tending thereto,' would be injurious to public morals; indeed, it is not precluded from considering that not all married people are immune from temptation or inclination to extramarital indulgence, as to which risk of illegitimate pregnancy is a recognized deterrent deemed desirable in the interests of morality.'' 126 Conn. at 424, 11 A.2d at 861. And twice it has quoted the Massachusetts decision in *Commonwealth* vs. *Gardner*, 300 Mass. 372, 15 N.E.2d 222 (1938), that the use of contraceptives would ''promote sexual immorality.'' 126 Conn. at 421, 11 A.2d at 860; *Tileston* vs. *Ullman*, 129 Conn. at 90, 26 A.2d at 585. We take it that the Supreme Court of Errors is saying that the statutes are constitutionally justified as measures to discourage extra-marital sexual relations of both married and unmarried persons.

Viewed in this way, the Connecticut statutes are designed to enforce moral principles. But in this situation the moral purpose may be objectively related to material public welfare and cannot be said to run clearly counter to the current moral standards of the community. Hence the objections founded on these grounds, as discussed in Section F, *supra*, are not applicable here.

Nevertheless, the statutes, scrutinized in light of the purpose now under consideration, violate due process in two major respects: (1) the means employed are not substantially and reasonably related to the objective sought; and (2) the statutes impose drastic restrictions upon individual rights far beyond what is necessary to achieve the stated purpose.

1. The Relation Of Means To End.

The means employed by the Connecticut statutes, ostensibly to discourage extra-marital relations, are to prohibit the *use* of contraceptive devices. The statutes do not regulate the sale, prescription, display, advertising or any other matters. Being directed solely at use, the statutes could accomplish their objective by simply prohibiting the use of such devices in extra-marital relations. Prohibition of use by married couples—the basis of this prosecution—has no relation whatever to the claimed objective. The situation is the same as if, in order to discourage adultery or fornication, Connecticut prohibited all sexual relations among its citizens.

Furthermore, in actual operation the statutes are enforceable *least of all* against those who use contraceptives in extra-marital relations. As already stated, contraceptive devices can be prescribed, sold and used in Connecticut for prevention of disease. And persons engaging in sexual relations outside the marriage status have a far better basis than married couples for asserting that the device was used for the prevention of disease. So too, those who engage in the sale and distribution of such items cannot be subjected to criminal penalties as accessories, since the State could not in any event prove that the person making the sale intended that the device be used for the prohibited purpose, prevention of conception, and not for the permissible purpose, the prevention of disease. With respect to the forbidden use of the articles in extra-marital relations, therefore, the task of the prosecutor is virtually impossible.

And, in fact, contraceptive devices are widely available for sale and use in Connecticut. The statutes, as this Court held in *Poe* vs. *Ullman*, have no effect upon individual users. Their only effect is on birth control clinics, whose services were not available to the unmarried.

In short, there is no substantial relation, in theory or in practice, between prohibiting the use of contraceptives within the marital relation and the discouragement of sexual relations outside the marriage bond.

2. The Breadth Of The Statutes.

Even if some relation were shown between means and end, the statutes are not narrowly drafted to accomplish their purpose, but sweep within their ambit much other conduct which is not appropriate to their purpose and which the State may not control. The manner in which the statutes infringe upon protected liberties has been discussed in Section F, *supra*, and need not be repeated here. The right to life and health, the right to make the fundamental decisions of married life, the right to privacy, the right to practice one's profession, are all drastically curtailed or denied. And the excessive breadth of the statutes is responsible for many of the inconsistencies and irrationalities that have been pointed out.

Nor is it necessary that the statutes sweep so broadly to achieve this aim of discouraging extra-marital relations. Alternatives are available. Connecticut has statutes against adultery, fornication and lascivious carriage. Conn. Gen. Stats., Sec. 53-218 and 53-219. Some regulation of sale or prescription of contraceptive devices, designed to keep them out of the hands of those seeking illicit sexual relations, is possible. Other States deal with the problem this way.

This case falls squarely within the doctrine of those decisions which have struck down legislation that was not narrowly drafted to meet the specific evil. *Wieman* vs. *Updegraff*, 344 U.S. 183 (1952); *Shelton* vs. *Tucker*, 364 U.S. 479 (1960); *Aptheker* vs. *Secretary of State*, 378 U.S. 500 (1964). What the Court said in *Butler* vs. *Michigan*, 352 U.S. 380 (1957)—a strikingly similar case—is fully applicable here:

> "The State insists that, by thus quarantining the general reading public against books not too rugged for grown men and women in order to shield juvenile innocence, it is exercising its power to promote the general welfare. Surely, this is to burn the house to roast the pig." 352 U.S. at 383.

H. CONCLUSION

Whatever we take to be the objective of the Connecticut statutes, they do not meet the standards of due process. Seldom has the Court had before it legislation for which the purposes were so obscure or the alleged benefits so ill-founded. And probably never has the Court had before it legislation which touched so drastically and so arbitrarily upon so many fundamental rights of the citizen. Fortunately the law is aberrational. Only Connecticut, and in part Massachusetts, have such legislation. We submit it cannot stand the test of due process of law.

POINT III. The Connecticut Anti-Contraceptive Statutes Violate Due Process Of Law In That They Constitute An Unwarranted Invasion of Privacy.

The concept of limited government has always included the idea that governmental powers stopped short of certain intrusions into the personal and intimate life of the citizen. This is indeed one of the basic distinctions between absolute and limited government. Ultimate and pervasive control of the individual, in all aspects of his life, is the hallmark of the absolute state. A system of limited government safeguards a private sector, which belongs to the individual, and firmly distinguishes it from the public sector, which the state can control.

Protection of this private sector—protection in other words of the dignity and integrity of the individual—has become increasingly important as modern society has developed. All the forces of a technological age—industrialization, urbanization, organization—operate to narrow the area of privacy and facilitate intrusions into it. In modern terms, the capacity to maintain and support this enclave of private life marks the difference between a democratic and a totalitarian society.

In our constitutional system, the principle of safeguarding the private sector of the citizen's life has always been a vital element. The Constitution nowhere refers to a right of privacy in express terms. But various provisions of the Constitution embody separate aspects of it. And the demands of modern life require that the composite of these specific protections be accorded the status of a recognized constitutional right.

The protected area of privacy is marked out in part by the First Amendment. Freedom of religion is a key element in any system for maintaining the independence and the dignity of the individual. So also is the right to hold beliefs and opinions without coercion from the state. This is the meaning of Justice Jackson's famous declaration that "no official, high or petty, can prescribe what shall be orthodox in politics, nationalism, religion or other matters of opinion or force citizens to confess by word or act their faith therein." *West Virginia State Board of Education* vs. *Barnette*, 319 U.S. 624, 642 (1943).

Another constitutional provision which recognizes the right of privacy is the Third Amendment. This forbids that any soldier "shall, in time of peace be quartered in any house, without the consent of the owner, nor in time of war, but in a manner to be prescribed by law." At the time the Constitution was framed, this invasion of privacy was one of the chief dangers threatening the personal life of the citizen.

Undoubtedly the most significant constitutional provision directed toward protection of privacy is the Fourth Amendment. This expressly guarantees the ''right of the people to be secure in their persons, houses, papers, and effects.'' The protection is phrased in terms of search and seizure, and arrest, because those were the chief manifestations of invasion of privacy under conditions existing when the Bill of Rights was adopted. But the concept which the Fourth Amendment undertakes to incorporate in our system of individual rights is certainly a much broader one. It embodies the ancient notion that ''a man's home is his castle.'' And applied to conditions of modern life, as Justice Bradley declared in *Boyd* vs. *United States:*

''The principles laid down in this opinion [*Entick* vs. *Carrington*] affect the very essence of constitutional liberty and security. They reach farther than the concrete form of the case then before the court, with its adventitious circumstances; they apply to all invasions on the part of the government and its employés of the sanctity of a man's home and the privacies of life. It is not the breaking of his doors, and the rummaging of his drawers, that constitutes the essence of the offence; but it is the invasion of his indefeasible right of personal security, personal liberty and private property, where that right has never been forfeited by his conviction of some public offence,—it is the invasion of this sacred right which underlies and constitutes the essence of Lord Camden's judgment.'' 116 U.S. 616, 630 (1855).

Another classic expression of this view that the Fourth Amendment incorporates a comprehensive protection of the right to privacy is that of Justice Brandeis, dissenting in *Olmstead* vs. *United States:*

''The protection guaranteed by the [Fourth and Fifth] Amendments is much broader in scope. The makers of our Constitution undertook to secure conditions favorable to the pursuit of happiness. They recognized the significance of man's spiritual nature, of his feelings and of his intellect. They knew that only a part of the pain, pleasure and satisfactions of life are to be found in material things. They sought to protect Americans in their beliefs, their thoughts, their emotions and their sensations. They conferred, as against the Government, the right to be let alone— the most comprehensive of rights and the right most valued by civilized men. To protect that right, every unjustifiable intrusion by the Government upon the privacy of the individual, whatever the means employed, must be deemed a violation of the Fourth Amendment. . . .'' 277 U.S. 438, 478 (1928).

And only recently this Court took occasion to refer to the ''right to privacy, no less important than any other right carefully and particularly reserved to the people.'' *Mapp* vs. *Ohio,* 367 U.S. 643, 656 (1961)[1]

Closely related to the Fourth Amendment is the Fifth Amendment. This established by constitutional mandate an accusatorial rather than an inquisitorial system of criminal prosecution. And in its broader reaches it protects the conscience and dignity of the individual from all outside forces, whether the government or the general public.[2]

1. See also *Monroe* vs. *Pape,* 365 U.S. 167 (1961). For a discussion of the significance of the Fourth Amendment cases, see Beaney, *The Constitutional Right to Privacy in the Supreme Court,* 1962 Sup. Ct. Rev. 212.
2. See, *e.g.,* Griswold, *The Right to be Let Alone,* 55 N.W.U.L. Rev. 216 (1960).

In short, just as the First Amendment, though referring concretely to speech, press, assembly and petition, protects a general right of expression and association (see *N.A.A.C.P.* vs. *Button*, 371 U.S. 415 (1963)), so the Third, Fourth and Fifth Amendments, while specifically mentioning only the major forms of invading privacy which were paramount at the time, embody a *general principle* which protects the private sector of life against "every unjustifiable intrusion by the Government."

It can be argued, further, that the right of privacy is protected by the Ninth Amendment. The framers there provided that "the enumeration in the Constitution, of certain rights, shall not be construed to deny or disparage others retained by the people." Professor Redlich in an important article has pointed out that in interpreting both the Ninth and Tenth Amendments, "the textual standard should be the entire Constitution." "The original Constitution," he wrote, "and its amendments project through the ages the image of a free and open society. The Ninth and Tenth Amendments recognized—at the very outset of our national experience—that it was impossible to fill in every detail of this image. For that reason certain rights were reserved to the people. The language and history of the two amendments indicate that the rights reserved were to be of a nature comparable to the rights enumerated." Redlich, *Are There "Certain Rights *** Retained by the People"?* 37 N.Y.U.L. Rev. 787, 810 (1962).

The Ninth Amendment was certainly intended to protect some rights of the people. As Dean Griswold has said, " 'The right to be let alone' is the underlying theme of the Bill of Rights."[3] It is submitted that the interest of married spouses in the sanctity and privacy of their marital relations, involves precisely the kind of right which the Ninth Amendment was intended to secure.

[3]*Id.* at 217.

Finally, protection against unwarranted intrusion by the government into private affairs is incorporated in the "liberty" guaranteed by the due process clause of the Fourteenth Amendment. That provision, as this Court has ruled, applies to the States the guarantees embodied in the First, Fourth and Fifth Amendments. *Gitlow* vs. *New York*, 268 U.S. 652 (1925); *Mapp* vs. *Ohio*, 367 U.S. 643 (1961); *Malloy* vs. *Hogan*, 378 U.S. 1 (1964). Further, the Court has specifically held that the due process clause of the Fourteenth Amendment embraces certain additional aspects of liberty not necessarily included in one of the specific provisions of the Bill of Rights. Such was the holding in *Rochin* vs. *California*, 342 U.S. 165 (1952). There police officers broke into defendant's bedroom where he was sitting partly dressed on his bed, upon which his wife was lying. They seized him and, by use of a stomach pump, extracted certain capsules which he had swallowed. This invasion of privacy was held, not a violation of the Fourth or Fifth Amendments, but a violation of due process in that it was inconsistent with the "respect for those personal immunities which . . . are 'so rooted in the traditions and conscience of our people as to be ranked as fundamental.' " 342 U.S. at 169.

It is true that the *Rochin* case involved intrusion upon privacy through physical violence. See *Irvine* vs. *California*, 347 U.S. 128 (1954). Yet the insistent development of the law has been to extend legal protection against harms to the person from physical to non-physical injuries. And there is no sound reason, especially under modern conditions of living, to withhold constitutional protection in those cases where the invasion of privacy, even though not achieved by physical means, is inconsistent with preserving the private sector of living against unwarranted infringement. As Mr. Justice Harlan said in *Poe* vs. *Ullman*, "It would surely be an extreme instance of sacrificing substance to form were it to be held that the Constitutional principle of privacy against arbitrary official intrusion comprehends only physical invasions by the police." 367 U.S. at 551. Indeed, in *Public Utilities Commission* vs. *Pollak*, 343 U.S. 451 (1952), although it did not there uphold the claim, the Court recognized that the liberty guaranteed by the due process clause embraced invasion of privacy by non-violent means.[4]

It should be noted that the development of the right of privacy in constitutional law has been paralleled by the growth of the right of privacy in tort law. Such a right is now recognized in most States, by judicial decision or legislation. As Harper and James have said: "Viewing this extraordinary development with the omniscience of hindsight, it appears that the inception of the doctrine was the almost inevitable development of the law under the pressure of great social need, produced by the technological developments and the vast extension of business which transformed American society into mass urbanization thus creating many new sensitivities."[5] The same needs which have led to the protection of privacy from non-governmental sources, even more urgently press for protection of that basic right from governmental invasion.

If, then, we accept the proposition that the Constitution affords protection to the right of privacy, the question becomes what standards are to be employed to delimit the area thus safeguarded. Such standards have not, of course, been fully worked out. Concededly the problem is a difficult one. Yet surely it is susceptible to resolution by normal judicial techniques, as the experience of the courts in the torts field attests. The issue must turn, as do other problems of intepreting the Bill of Rights, upon the fundamental ends sought by the constitutional guarantees, considered in the light of modern conditions and needs.

When we look at the legal development of the right of privacy, from earliest times to the present, two major elements stand out. What the law has most basically sought to protect, and what has in fact been brought within the concept, are (1) maintaining the sanctity of the home, and (2) preserving from outside intrusion the intimacies of the sexual relationship in marriage.

The reasons are not far to seek. The home is the ultimate refuge, of every person high or low, from the outside world. It is the one chief tangible base, especially now that geographical escape to the frontier is foreclosed, for seeking seclusion. And, of all relations with other people, marital relations are the most private, the most sought to be sheltered from the public gaze. In these two realms "the right to be let alone" becomes most meaningful and most precious.

Hence it is not surprising that the Third Amendment expressly deals with the quartering of outsiders "in any house," and that the Fourth Amendment protects the "right of the people to be secure in their. . .houses." At common law, and presently under legislation, invasion of the home is afforded greater protection than invasion of the person; search of a house requires a warrant whereas an arrest can be made on reasonable grounds to believe a crime has been committed. See Barrett, *Personal Rights, Property Rights, and the Fourth Amendment,* 1960 Sup. Ct. Rev. 46. Decisions of this Court under the Fourth Amendment have recognized the special significance attached to invasion of the home. Compare *Goldman* vs. *United States*, 316 U.S. 129 (1942), with *Silverman* vs. *United States,* 365 U.S. 505 (1961). In *Rochin* the "illegally breaking into

---

4. The case in which a constitutional right of privacy has so far been most explicitly recognized and sustained, is *York* vs. *Story*, 324 F.2d 450 (C.A. 9, 1963). In that case it was alleged that police officers took photographs of a woman complainant in the nude and distributed them among their fellow officers. The Court held that a cause of action was stated under 42 U.S.C.A. Sec. 1983 for depriving plaintiff of "rights. . . secured by the Constitution," specifically the right of privacy. See also Judge Washington, dissenting in *Silverman* vs. *U.S.*, 275 F.2d 173, 178 (C.A.D.C., 1960).

5. 1 Harper and James, *The Law of Torts* (1956), p. 683. See also Prosser, *Privacy*, 48 Calif. L. Rev. 383 (1960).

the privacy of petitioner'' in his bedroom was a major factor in finding a violation of due process. 342 U.S. at 172. See also *Monroe* vs. *Pape*, 365 U.S. 167 (1961); and compare *Public Utilities Commission* vs. *Pollak*, 343 U.S. 451 (1952); *Lanza* vs. *New York*, 370 U.S. 139 (1962). And the development of the right of privacy in tort law began with protecting the seclusion of the plaintiff in his house or on his land. See 1 Harper and James, *The Law of Torts* (1956), pp. 678-9.

The personal aspects of the marital relationship have likewise been consistently recognized as entitled to protection under the right of privacy. This factor was also present in *Rochin* vs. *California* and in *Monroe* vs. *Pape* (*supra*). Intrusion into this area, like invasion of the home, constituted the starting point in the growth of the right to privacy in tort law. See Harper and James, *supra*. Laws prohibiting the disclosure of the names of victims of sex crimes reflect the same concern. And at an earlier phase in the litigation over the statutes here at bar the Connecticut Supreme Court of Errors acknowledged the exceptional nature of this aspect of privacy by permitting the married couples involved to sue under fictitious names. *Buxton* vs. *Ullman*, 147 Conn. at 59-60, 156 A.2d at 514-5.

In reason, tradition and current practice, therefore, these two areas—the sanctity of the home and the wholly personal nature of marital relations—have been recognized as forming the inner core of the right of privacy. Whatever else that constitutional right may encompass, it surely includes protection for these aspects of the private sector of life.

The case now before the Court combines both of these critical elements in the right to privacy. The hand of the government reaches not only into the home but into the bedroom. The statutes are directed not at regulation of sale, prescription or advertising, but at *use*. Enforcement of the statute would entail search warrants to discover ''instruments'' of crime in the bathroom closet. Testimony of close friends or servants in the home would be required.

It is hardly necessary to detail these aspects of the case in this brief. Both Justices who reached the merits in *Poe* vs. *Ullman* were struck by the shocking invasion of privacy inherent in the Connecticut statutes, and said all that needs to be said on this score. Mr. Justice Douglas observed:

> ''The regulation as applied in this case touches the relationship between man and wife. It reaches into the intimacies of the marriage relationship. If we imagine a regime of full enforcement of the law in the manner of an Anthony Comstock, we would reach the point where search warrants issued and officers appeared in bedrooms to find out what went on. It is said that this is not the case. And so it is not. But when the State makes 'use' a crime and applies the criminal sanction to man and wife, the State has entered the innermost sanctum of the home. If it can make this law, it can enforce it. And proof of its violation necessarily involves an inquiry into the relations between man and wife.''
>
> ''That is an invasion of the privacy that is implicit in a free society.'' 367 U.S. at 519-21.

And Mr. Justice Harlan summed it up in the following terms:

> ''Precisely what is involved here is this: the State is asserting the right to enforce its moral judgment by intruding upon the most intimate details of the marital relation with the full power of the criminal law. Potentially, this could allow the deployment of all the incidental machinery of the criminal law, arrests, searches and seizures; inevitably, it must

mean at the very least the lodging of criminal charges, a public trial, and testimony as to the *corpus delicti*. Nor could any imaginable elaboration of presumptions, testimonial privileges, or other safeguards, alleviate the necessity for testimony as to the mode and manner of the married couples' sexual relations, or at least the opportunity for the accused to make denial of the charges. In sum, the statute allows the State to enquire into, prove and punish married people for the private use of their marital intimacy.'' 367 U.S. at 548.

It is no answer to say that the statutes have not been enforced in this way. The vice is that they can be. As long as the statutes are on the books the fundamental rights of privacy of married couples in Connecticut are threatened.

Nor is it an answer to say that other statutes, dealing with fornication, adultery, homosexuality and the like, raise the same issues of privacy. We are not concerned with those statutes here. In any event Mr. Justice Harlan disposed of the argument in *Poe* vs. *Ullman* when he said:

> "Adultery, homosexuality and the like are sexual intimacies which the State forbids altogether, but the intimacy of husband and wife is necessarily an essential and accepted feature of the institution of marriage, an institution which the State not only must allow, but which always and in every age it has fostered and protected. It is one thing when the State exerts its power either to forbid extra-marital sexuality altogether, or to say who may marry, but it is quite another when, having acknowledged a marriage and the intimacies inherent in it, it undertakes to regulate by means of the criminal law the details of that intimacy." 367 U.S. at 553.

We need only add that, as discussed in Point II, no compelling reasons of State policy justify the invasion of the constitutional right of privacy brought about by these statutes. Indeed, our analysis of the objectives sought by the legislation reveals that no material benefits whatever, but only positive harms, flow from this legislation. We submit that it would be hard to find a more far-reaching invasion of the private sector of life than this case discloses.

POINT IV. The Connecticut Statutes, On Their Face And As Applied In This Case, Violate The First And Fourteenth Amendments In That They Abridge Freedom Of Speech.

A.

Section 54-196 applies to any person "who assists, abets, *counsels*, causes, hires or commands another to commit any offense." As the statute is worded, and as the Connecticut Supreme Court of Errors has interpreted it, the mere "counselling" is sufficient to establish the offense. Thus in the leading case of *State* vs. *Scott*, 80 Conn. 317, 68 A. 258 (1907), the Court, in defining the rule for criminal liability of an accessory, stated:

> "Every one is a party to an offense who...does some act which forms part of the offense, or assists in the actual commission of the offense or of any act which forms a part thereof, or *directly or indirectly counsels* or procures any person to commit the offense or do any act forming a part thereof." 80 Conn. at 323, 68 A. at 260. (Italics added.)

The Supreme Court of Errors reiterated this position in a subsequent key decision on the statute, saying that the offense was established if "the defendant procured, *counseled or encouraged* [another] to do it," "... that she knowingly abetted, *counseled or encouraged* [the other] in his guilty purpose." *State* vs. *Wakefield*, 88 Conn. 164, 167, 173, 90 A. 230, 231, 233 (1914). (Italics added.)

Consequently Section 54-196, combined with Section 53-32 (the use statute), would apply to a mother who advises her newly married daughter to use contraceptives in order to avoid pregnancy during a period of ill-health. It would apply to a physician who, without making the materials available or taking other action, advises a patient on the harmless or deleterious qualities of a new contraceptive pill. It might apply to a faculty member of a medical school who instructs his students on the medical techniques of contraception. It might also make it a crime for an organization concerned with planned parenthood to publish a pamphlet urging the use of contraceptives for family planning. It would apply to a minister of the Congregational Church in Connecticut who counsels his parishioners that proper family planning is a religious obligation and that contraceptive devices are the best and most effective means of fulfilling this duty.[1]

These applications of the statute violate the First Amendment's guarantee against abridgement of freedom of speech. Such cases are clearly governed by the doctrine laid down by this Court in *Kingsley Pictures Corp.* vs. *Regents*, 360 U.S. 684 (1959). In that case the Court held unconstitutional under the First Amendment New York's ban on the film "Lady Chatterley's Lover." The State had argued that it could constitutionally forbid the advocacy of conduct—in this case, adultery—which it could validly make a crime. The Court, speaking through Mr. Justice Stewart, said:

"Its [the First Amendment's] guarantee is not confined to the expression of ideas that are conventional or shared by the majority. It protects advocacy of the opinion that adultery may sometimes be proper, no less than advocacy of socialism or the single tax." 360 U.S. at 689.[2]

It is no answer to say that the Connecticut courts would not attempt to apply the statutes to counseling of this nature. We do not know. Such an application of the statutes would be no more extreme than that sanctioned in *Tileston* vs. *Ullman*, 129 Conn. 84, 26 A.2d 582, or *Buxton* vs. *Ullman*, 147 Conn. 48, 156 A.2d 508.

In any event, the very breadth and ambiguity of the statutory prohibition against "counseling" operate to abridge freedom of speech. Persons apparently or possibly covered by its broad scope could not be certain what was prohibited and what was permitted. This kind of inhibiting effect upon the right to freedom of expression must fall under the repeated decisions of this Court in cases such as *Winters* vs. *New York*, 333 U.S. 507 (1948); *Burstyn* vs. *Wilson*, 343 U.S. 495 (1952); *Louisiana ex rel. Gremillion* vs. *N.A.A.C.P.*, 366 U.S. 293 (1961); *Cramp* vs. *Board of Public Instruction*, 368 U.S. 278 (1961); *N.A.A.C.P.* vs. *Alabama ex rel. Flowers*, 377 U.S. 288 (1964); *Baggett* vs. *Bullitt*, 377 U.S. 360 (1964).

We conclude, therefore, that the statute is invalid on its face.

B.

The application of the statutes to appellants in this case likewise abridged their rights to freedom of speech. In reaching its judgment that appellants were guilty of violating Sections 53-32 and 54-196 the trial court at many points relied

---

1. See the resolution of the Connecticut Conference of Congregational Churches approving the "proper use of medically approved contraceptives that may contribute to the spiritual, emotional and economic welfare of the family," quoted in Point II, Section F, subsection 4, *supra.*

2. Furthermore, in so far as the statutes operate to prevent the obtaining of medical advice, the case is similar to *N.A.A.C.P.* vs. *Button*, 371 U.S. 415 (1963), and *Brotherhood of R.R. Trainmen* vs. *Virginia ex rel. Virginia State Bar*, 377 U.S. 1 (1964).

upon conduct which was strictly speech and protected by the First Amendment. We do not contend that such conduct as examining patients, prescribing contraceptive devices, or furnishing patients with contraceptive materials constituted expression within the terms of the First Amendment. But other conduct, used as a basis for the finding of guilt, was exclusively speech.

The trial court included in its findings of fact, and hence as relevant to conviction, the following items of protected speech:

(1) The Center was opened "*to provide information, instruction and medical advice* to married persons as to the means of preventing conception and to *educate married persons* generally as to such means and methods." (R. 17).

(2) "The Center made such *information, instruction, education and medical advice available to married persons...*" (R. 17).

(3) Defendant Buxton gave "contraceptive *advice* to patients at the Center..." (R. 18).

(4) "... the patient attended a *group orientation session* with other patients at which all the methods of contraception available at the Center were described..." (R. 19).

(5) "... there were periods of time during which the patient...sat in the waiting room where there were *various pieces of literature*, including certain exhibits in evidence...available to her and which were *examined and read* by some of the patients of the Center." (R. 19).

(6) Defendant Griswold on several occasions "conducted the *group orientation session...*" (R. 20).

The trial court also included in its conclusions of law the following items:

(1) The three married women who testified concerning the use of contraceptives "sought and obtained instruction and *medical advice and counsel* as to methods of contraception ..." at the Center. (R. 23).

(2) "The actions of the defendants in supervising and participating in the operation of this Center...constituted assisting, abetting, *counselling,* causing and commanding these women to commit a violation of the Statute..." (R. 23).

(3) "The actions of the defendant Estelle T. Griswold...*in delivering orientation lectures* describing the various methods of contraception available at the Center...

• • •

CONCLUSION

Appellants contend that these Connecticut statutes, on their face and as applied, violate the due process clause of the Fourteenth Amendment in that they are not reasonably related to a legitimate legislative purpose, and are otherwise unreasonable, arbitrary and capricious; that they violate the same provision in that they constitute an unjustified invasion of privacy; and that they violate the First Amendment as incorporated in the Fourteenth Amendment. Appellants respectfully urge this Court to reverse the decision below.

Thomas I. Emerson,
127 Wall Street,
New Haven, Conn.

Catherine G. Rorabach,
185 Church Street,
New Haven, Conn.
Attorneys for Appellants.

In the
SUPREME COURT OF THE UNITED STATES

———

October Term, 1964

———

No. 496

———

ESTELLE T. GRISWOLD
AND
C. LEE BUXTON,

Appellants,

vs.

STATE OF CONNECTICUT.

Appellee.

ON APPEAL FROM THE SUPREME COURT
OF ERRORS OF CONNECTICUT

BRIEF FOR APPELLEE

Joseph B. Clark,
Ass't Prosecuting Attorney,
6th Circuit Court,
171 Church Street,
New Haven, Connecticut,
Attorney for Appellee.

Philip F. Mancini, Jr.,
Prosecuting Attorney,
Julius Maretz
Irwin P. Harrison
Of Counsel

THE HARTY PRESS, INC., NEW HAVEN, CONN.

SUBJECT INDEX

* * *

*Page references refer to original briefs, not text pages.

In the
SUPREME COURT OF THE UNITED STATES

———

OCTOBER TERM, 1964

———

No. 496

———

ESTELLE T. GRISWOLD
AND
C. LEE BUXTON,

Appellants,

vs.

STATE OF CONNECTICUT,

Appellee.

———

ON APPEAL FROM THE SUPREME COURT
OF ERRORS OF CONNECTICUT

———

BRIEF FOR APPELLEE

———

OPINIONS BELOW

The opinion of the Supreme Court of Errors of Connecticut is reported in 151 Conn. 544, 200 A.2d 479. It is reprinted in the record at pages 61-63.

The opinion of the Appellate Division of the Circuit Court of Connecticut is reported in 3 Conn. Cir. 6. It is reprinted in the record at pages 40-50.

JURISDICTION

On November 10, 1961 a warrant was issued charging that the appellant C. Lee Buxton, a duly qualified and licensed physician, and appellant Estelle T. Griswold "in violation of the provisions of Section 53-32 and 54-196 of the General Statutes of Connecticut, did assist, abet, counsel, cause and command certain married women to use a drug, medicinal article and instrument, for the purpose of preventing conception.'' (R. 1, 7) The appellants were arrested on the same date and on November 24, 1961 the appellants demurred to the informations on the grounds that as the cited statutes would be applied to the appellants they would be unconstitutional in that they would deny the appellants' rights to liberty and property without due process of law in violation of the 14th Amendment to the Constitution of the United States and that they would deny them their rights to freedom of speech and communication of ideas under the 1st and 14th Amendments to the Constitution of the United States. (R. 2, 8)

The demurrers were overruled. (R. 3-6, 9-12) On January 2, 1962, the appellants, after trial to the Court, were found guilty and sentenced to pay a fine of $100 each. (R. 13)

On January 10, 1962 after stipulation of the parties the Court entered an order for joint appeals. (R. 14-15)

Appellants filed an assignment of errors (R. 33-37) and an appeal was taken to the Appellate Division of the Circuit Court which affirmed the judgment of the Circuit Court, 6th Circuit in an opinion rendered January 7, 1963. (R. 40-50)

The Appellate Division certified two questions to the Supreme Court of Errors of Connecticut. (R. 49-50)

On January 31, 1963 appellants petitioned for certification of additional question which was granted on February 19, 1963. (R. 52-60). On April 28, 1964, the Supreme Court of Errors affirmed the judgment of the Circuit Court. (R. 61-65). Execution was ordered stayed on May 20, 1964 and on July 22, 1964 a motion of Appeal to the Supreme Court of the United States

was filed with the Supreme Court of Errors of Connecticut. (R. 65-66).

On December 7, 1964, this Court noted probable jurisdiction. (R. 67).

This Court has jurisdiction under 28 U.S.C. 1257 (3). *Mergenthaler Linotype Co.* v. *Davis*, 251 U.S. 256, 259 (1919)

STATUTES INVOLVED

Statutes involved in this case are Sections 53-32 and 54-196, General Statutes of Connecticut, Revision of 1958.

Said statutes are quoted in Brief for Appellants, page 3. They will also be found set out in the Record, page 50.

QUESTIONS PRESENTED

Where the appellants served as director (Estelle T. Griswold) and medical director (C. Lee Buxton) of a center to which married women came to obtain contraceptives and instructions as to their use to prevent pregnancy and where such married women received such contraceptive articles and instructions (in some cases from the appellants themselves) did Section 53-32, General Statutes of Connecticut, Revision of 1958 in connection with Section 54-196 of said statutes: 1) deny the appellants their rights to liberty and property in violation of the Fourteenth Amendment to the Constitution of the United States? 2) deny these appellants their rights to freedom of speech and communication of ideas under the First and Fourteenth Amendments to the Constitution of the United States?

STATEMENT OF THE CASE

The Planned Parenthood Center of New Haven, hereinafter referred to as the Center, was opened on November 1, 1961 to provide information, instruction and medical advice to married persons as to the means and methods of preventing conception and to educate married persons generally as to such means and methods (Finding, Par. 1, R. p. 16, 17). The Center was located at 79 Trumbull Street in New Haven (Finding, Par. 2, R. p. 17). The Center operated from November 1, 1961 to November 10, 1961. (Finding, Par. 3, R. p. 17). The Planned Parenthood League of Connecticut also occupied an office on the second floor of the same building (Finding, Par. 4, R. p. 17).

The defendant Estelle T. Griswold held the salaried office of executive director of the League (Finding, Par. 5, R. p. 17). She was also the Acting Director of the Center and in charge of the Administration and the educational program both before the Center opened and during its time of operation (Finding, Pars. 6, 11, R. pp. 17, 18).

The defendant C. Lee Buxton is a physician licensed to practice in the State of Connecticut (Finding, Par. 7, R. p. 17). He was the medical director of the Center both before its opening and while it was in operation. (Finding, Par. 8, R. p. 17). As such medical director and after consultation with the Medical Advisory Committee of the Center which committee was appointed by him, the defendant C. Lee Buxton made all medical decisions as to the facilities of the Center, including the types of contraceptive advice available and provided at the Center, the types of contraceptive articles and materials available at the Center for distribution to patients, and the methods of providing the same (Finding, Par. 9, R. p. 18). In addition, the defendant C. Lee Buxton on several occasions examined and gave contraceptive advice to patients at the Center, while it was in operation from November 1 to November 10, 1961 (Finding, Par. 10, R. p. 18).

The defendant Estelle T. Griswold on several occasions between November 1 and November 10, 1961, while the Center was in operation, interviewed persons prior to giving them appointments at the Center; took case histories; conducted the group orientation session, describing the various methods of contraception available at the Center; and gave a woman a drug or medicinal article to prevent conception (Finding, Par. 13, R. p. 20).

Joan B. Forsberg, a housewife and mother of three children living with her family in New Haven, Connecticut, upon learning of the existence of the Center, arranged for an appointment at the Center which was made for November 8, 1961, and on that date she went to the Center seeking contraceptive advice (Finding, Par. 14, R. p. 20). She gave a history to a receptionist, attended an orientation session at which the defendant Estelle T. Griswold instructed her and other women as to the various methods of contraception available at the Center, and told her and the other women that they could choose the method they would individually prefer and be furnished with the necessary materials if the doctor approved, was given a pelvic examination by a staff doctor, was told by the staff doctor that the anti-ovulation pill method of contraception which she had chosen was all right for her to use, was instructed by the doctor in its use, was thereafter given a supply of sixty anti-ovulation pills (State's Exhibit K) by the person on duty at the registration desk at the direction of the defendant Estelle T. Griswold, and before leaving paid a fee to the Center and was told to return to the Center in two months (Finding, Par. 14, R. p. 20). After her visit to the Center, Mrs. Forsberg used approximately thirty of these pills (State's Exhibit K) furnished her at the Center for the purpose of preventing conception and the use thereof did prevent conception (Finding, Par. 15, R. p. 20).

On November 7, 1961, Marie Wilson Tindall, a housewife and mother, living in New Haven, Connecticut, having made an appointment, went to the Center seeking contraceptive advice (Finding, Par. 16, R. pp. 20, 21). She had a history taken by the receptionist, attended an orientation session with other women at which time were described the various types of contraceptives available at the Center, was given a pelvic examination by a staff doctor, told the doctor that she had chosen a diaphragm as the type of contraceptive she wished to use, was fitted and given by the doctor a diaphragm and accompanying articles (State's Exhibits M through P), and thereafter was instructed in how to use them, and before leaving paid a fee of $7.50 to the Center (Finding, Par. 16, R. pp. 20, 21). After her visit to the Center, Mrs. Tindall used the diaphragm and other articles (State's Exhibits M through P) furnished to her at the Center for the purpose of preventing conception (Finding, Par. 17, R. p. 21).

On November 9, 1961, Rosemary Anne Stevens, married almost a year and living with her husband in New Haven, Connecticut, having made an appointment, went to the Center seeking to obtain contraceptive advice additional to that previously attained (Finding, Par. 18, R. p. 21). While at the Center Mrs. Stevens had her history taken by the defendant Estelle T. Griswold, attended an orientation session at which the defendant Estelle T. Griswold described the methods of contraception available at the Center, was given a pelvic examination by the defendant C. Lee Buxton acting as staff doctor on that day at the Center, was advised by the defendant C. Lee Buxton that the method of contraception (ortho-gynol contraceptive jelly) which she had chosen was satisfactory to her, was given instruction by him as to its use, and before leaving the Center was given a tube of orthogynol vaginal jelly (State's Exhibit L) by the defendant Estelle T. Griswold and paid a fee of $15.00 to the Center (Finding, Par. 18, R. p. 21). After her visit to the Center, Mrs. Stevens used this jelly (State's Exhibit L) for the purpose of preventing conception (Finding, Par. 19, R. p. 21). Mrs. Stevens' decision to continue the method of contraception she had been using was based on advice received by her from the defendants Estelle T. Griswold and C. Lee Buxton (Finding, Par. 20, R. p. 22).

HISTORY OF STATUTE

The Connecticut statute relating to contraceptives stems from the Comstock Act of 1873 (17 Stat. 598) currently 18 U.S.C. Sec. 1461, 18 U.S.C. Sec. 1462 and 19 U.S.C. Sec. 1305.

As originally introduced the Federal Bill contained an exemption for physicians from the portion of the bill which prohibited the possession, sale, or mailing of contraceptives. The Bill was amended on the floor of the Senate by Senator Buckingham of Connecticut by striking out the exemption in favor of physicians. The bill as amended passed and became 17 Stat. 598 (1873). In 1878 an attempt to amend the statute failed. From 1924 to 1936 twelve bills were introduced without success.[1]

In 1881 New York became the first state to pass a statute regulating contraceptive devices modeling the Comstock Act, N.Y. Penal Code of 1881, Sec. 318-19.

On March 28, 1879 after legislative battle Connecticut amended Conn. Gen. Stat. Rev. 1875. Title 20, Ch. 8, Sec. 4, p. 513—which concerned introduction of obscene matter into the family or school—By adopting Public Act (of 1879) Chapter LXXVIII which added to the then existing statute provisions on possession of obscene material, the use of any drug, medicinal article, or instrument for the prevention of conception, or causing unlawful abortion. The text of this public act and the statute it amended are set out in Appendix A to this Brief. For a history

---

1. An excellent presentation of the history of the Comstock Act as well as statutes on contraceptives and cases reported under the federal and state statutes is found in Smith, *The History and Future of the Legal Battle Over Birth Control*, 49 Cornell Law Quarterly 275 (Winter, 1965).

of the legislative action on this act see Appendix B to this Brief. The part of the above statute dealing with the use of any drug, medicinal article, or instrument for the purpose of preventing conception was made a separate statute in the statutory revision of 1885 (Section 1539) and placed in Chapter 99 Offenses Against Humanity and Morality. From 1885 to the present day there have been five revisions of the General Statutes of Connecticut. The statute was reprinted each time, Conn. Gen. Stat. Rev. 1902, Section 1327; Rev. 1918, Section 6399; Rev. 1930, Section 6246; Rev. 1949, Sec. 8568; and Rev. 1958, Section 53-32. The statute in 1958 was taken out of the chapter on Offenses Against Humanity and Morality and placed in Chapter 939, Offenses Against the Person.

From 1879 to 1916 no attempt was made to either repeal or amend the contraceptive statute. In 1917 a bill was introduced which sought outright repeal of the statute. It failed. From 1923 to 1935 bills were introduced at each session of the General Assembly attempting to amend or repeal the statute all without success. There was no legislative activity in this area from 1935 to 1941. From 1941 to the present there have been attempts to amend or repeal the contraceptive statutes at each session of the legislature. All these bills have failed. Appendix C of this Brief is a history of the unsuccessful attempts to alter what is now Conn. Gen. Stat. 53-32. It is interesting to note that most of these attempted amendments sought to insert an exception into the statute for physicians to prescribe contraceptives for health purposes.

Connecticut and New York are not alone in having statutes based on the Comstock Act, as of December 31, 1964, thirty states of the Union still have some statute specifically applicable to the prevention of conception.[2]

2. Citation of the various statutes will be found in the Appendix A at pages 23a to 27a of the Brief Amicus Curia filed by the Planned Parenthood Federation of America, Inc. in this case.

Although no attempt has been made to check the charters and/or ordinances of the municipalities in the states with no statutes on contraceptives, there is at least one city having such a law which can be noted from the case of *McConnell* v. *Knoxville*, 172 Tenn. 190, 110 S.W. 2d 478 (1937) upholding the power of the City of Knoxville, Tennessee to regulate the sale of contraceptives within its city limits.

Of the thirty states which have statutes regarding contraceptives, law of Massachusetts, Minnesota, Mississippi, Missouri, Nebraska, and New York, would be violated by the facts in the case at bar.[3]

SUMMARY OF ARGUMENT

The decision of the General Assembly of Connecticut that the use of contraceptives should be banned is a proper exercise of the police power of the state.

ARGUMENT

I

Appellants Do Not Have Standing To Raise Constitutional Claims Of Persons Not Parties To These Actions

The appellants were convicted as accessories (Sec. 54-196) to violations of Connecticut's Anti-Contraceptive Statute (Sec. 53-32). The basis of their conviction was that they provided women with contraceptive devices and instructed them as to their use as contraceptives. Since the appellants are asking this Court to upset their convictions, it logically follows that the issues raised here should be confined to the question of whether or not the Anti-Contraceptive Statute violates the appellants' constitutional rights.

3. Mass. Ann. Laws (1956) tit. 1, Sec. 21; Minn. Stat. (1961) Secs. 617.25, Laws 1963, ch. 753; Miss. Code Ann. (1956), Secs. 2289; Mo. Rev. Stat. (1959), Secs. 563.300; Neb. Rev. Stat. (Reissue 1956), ch. 28 Secs 423, N.Y. Pen. Law art. 106. Secs. 1142, 1143.

The Court has on numerous occasions laid down the rule that one cannot attack a statute on the ground that it violates the rights of third parties. *New York ex rel Hatch* v. *Reardon* 204 U.S. 152 (1907); *Yazoo M.V.R.R.* v. *Jackson Vinegar Co.,* 226 U.S. 217 (1912); *Standard Stock Food Co.* v. *Wright,* 225 U.S. 540 (1912); *Collins* v. *Texas,* 223 U.S. 288 (1912); *Rosenthal* v. *New York,* 226 U.S. 260 (1912); *Tileston* v. *Ullman,* 318 U.S. 44 (1943).

In *Collins* v. *Texas,* supra, the holding was that an osteopath convicted for practicing medicine without a license did not have standing to contend that the statute in question infringed on the religious freedoms of certain religious groups.

The *Tileston* case, supra, is even more directly in point and should be considered as *stare decisis* on the issue of whether the appellants can raise the constitutional claims of their patients or potential patients. The *Tileston* case was a previous challenge of Connecticut's Anti-Contraceptive Statute by a physician who attempted to raise the constitutional rights of his patients. This Court held that Tileston did not have standing to litigate his patients' claims.

The appellants attempt to distinguish the *Tileston* case from the case at bar on the basis that the physician in that case did not raise any constitutional issues of his own. However, the appellants have not cited any cases or offered reasoning that would indicate that this distinction has any legal significance. One wonders if the appellants in making this distinction between *Tileston* and the instant case have just cynically thrown in a few constitutional issues on behalf of the physician in the hopes of coming out from under the umbrella of *Tileston.* To allow the appellants to raise the claims of patients of the physician is particularly ludicrous in the light of the fact that it was a group of patients who testified against the physician and made possible the conviction.

Appellants further contend that the patients' constitutional claims can be raised because the Anti-Contraceptive Statute is "void on its face." Admittedly, this Court has permitted the assertion of a third person's constitutional rights in a group of cases, terming the statutes in question to be void on their face. However, this doctrine has been limited to cases where a statute by its terms prohibits the exercise of expression. In cases where a statute by its terms does not prohibit expression, but which is applied to expression situations this Court has not applied the doctrine. *United States* v. *Petrillo,* 332 U.S. 1 (1947); Sedler, *Standing to Assert Constitutional Jus Tertii in the Supreme Court,* 71 Yale L.J. 599 at page 616 (1962). Connecticut Anti-Contraceptive Statute deals with the use of contraceptive devices and only in a very secondary way through the accessory statute can it at all be considered to touch upon the rights of expression.

Nowhere in the record of this case prior to the notice of appeal to this court from the Supreme Court of Errors of Connecticut (R. p. 66) is there a claim 1) that these statutes are void on their face, 2) invade the privacy and liberty of women contrary to the Fourth, Ninth, and Fourteenth Amendments to the Constitution of the United States.

The Connecticut practice is that in order to be considered by the appellate Courts error must be specifically assigned and must "directly assert that the trial court committed error in the respects specified." (Connecticut Practice Book, (1963) Section 990). Further the claims of error must be briefed to be considered by the appellate court. (Conn. Practice Book, Section (1963) Section 1019). *Leo Foundation* v. *Cabelus,* 151 Conn. 655, 201 A2d 654, 655 (1964).

"As is always the case, however, state procedural requirements governing assertions and pursuance of direct and collateral constitutional challenges to criminal prosecutions must be respected." *Mapp* v. *Ohio*, 367 U.S. 643, 659, 6 L. Ed 2d 1081, 1092, 81 S. Ct. 1684, 1693, (1961) Note 9.

To say that the statutes are void on their face is a shocking claim. For then they could be used by the single and the married.

That contraceptives could be used by the married in relations with their spouses is a decision for legislative determination. But that single people should be allowed to use a contraceptive device is so contra to American experience, thought, and family law that it does not merit further discussion. That the appellant Griswold would supply contraceptives to the single element of society at the Center is only a conjecture. However, the appellants at the trial did introduce as defendants exhibit 4 a pamphlet entitled "Modern Methods of Birth Control" on the back inside cover of which was stamped the following: "This publication was prepared under medical auspices for the use of persons 21 years of age or older, or married. . . ."

The appellants in their claims of error below and in their Brief before the Supreme Court of Errors, it is supposed, to avoid the ruling of *Tileston* v. *Ullman*, 318 U.S. 44, 46, 87 L. Ed 603, 604 (1942) that a physician could not litigate the rights of patients not parties to the action, put great emphasis on the proposition even to the point of putting it in italics that the issue was "a denial of defendants' " rights and not that of the patients. Brief of Defendants-Appellants (page 59) A-427 Connecticut Records and Briefs 615. Also the appellants in their Jurisdictional statement, p. 12, state that they are asserting rights personal to them. Manifestly since this has been the issue argued by them and considered by the courts below, they cannot now be permitted to change their grounds of appeal. It would certainly be a novel rule if defendants in a criminal case were allowed to set up as a defense rights personal to a state's witness who testified against the defendants.

II

The Decision Of The Appellate Division (R. 40-50) And The Supreme Court Of Errors (R. 61-63) That Section 53-32 And 54-196 Of The General Statutes Of Connecticut, Revision Of 1958, Should Be Sustained On The Ground That Said Statutes Constitute A Proper Exercise Of The Police Power Of The State.

Of the few jurisdictions that have ruled on the constitutionality of contraceptive statutes all seem to be in agreement with the Connecticut Court that the regulation of contraceptives is a legitimate exercise of the state's police power to regulate public morals. Harrison, *Connecticut's Contraceptive Statute: A Recurring Problem in Constitutional Law*, 35 Connecticut Bar Journal 315 (September, 1960)

See *Commonwealth* v. *Allison*, 227 Mass. 57, 116 N.E. 265 (1917); *Commonwealth* v. *Gardner*, 300 Mass. 372, 15 N.E. 2d 222 (1938); *People* v. *Pennock*, 294 Mich. 578, 293 N.W. 759 (1940); *People* v. *Byrne,* 99 Misc. 1, 163 N.Y.S. 682 (917); *People* v. *Sanger,* 222 N.Y. 192, 118 N.E. 637 (1918), appeal dismissed for want of jurisdiction, 251 U.S. 537, 64 L.Ed. 403, 40 S. Ct. 55 (1919); *State* v. *Arnold,* 217 Wisc. 340, 258, N.W. 843 (1935); *State* v. *Kohn,* 42 N.J. Super. 578, 127 A.2d 451 (1956); *Sanitary Vendors, Inc.,* v. *Byrne,* 40 N.J. 157, 190 A.2d 876 (1963); *Cavalier Vending Corp.* v. *State Bd. of Pharmacy,* 195 Va. 626, 79 S.E.2d 636 (1954), appeal denied, 347 U.S. 995, 98 L. Ed. 1127, 74 S. Ct. 871 (1954); *Lanteen Laboratories* v. *Clark,* 294 Ill. App. 81, 13 N.E. 2d 678 (1938). Also see 1 C.J.S.—Abortion Section 44, page 341, 12 Am. Jr. 2d.—Birth Control, Section 4, page 370, and 96 A.L.R. 2d 948.

The fact that Connecticut's substantive statute (General Statutes, Section 53-32) is directed to the use of contraceptives and not to the dissemination of contraceptives—as are the statutes of some other states—is of no moment.

For the Connecticut accessor statute (Gen. Stat. 54-196) when used in conjunction with the substantive statute bars the dissemination of contraceptives. In light of the Federal statutes (18 U.S.C. Section 1461, 18 U.S.C. Section 1462 and 19 U.S.C. Section 1305)—which contain prohibitions against mailing shipping or importing contraceptives or information about them—Connecticut's treatment of the contraceptive problem seems to be the most logical.

New York has a statute which prohibits the sale of contraceptives. There is an exception to that statute providing that physicians might use or prescribe such articles or drugs for the cure and prevention of disease. But in interpreting that section the New York Court, Cropsey, J. stated: "If it (New York Statute) did in terms prevent the use of the articles, and make their use a crime, it would nevertheless be constitutional; and this would be so, even if there were no exception made to the provision." *People* v. *Byrne,* 163 N.Y.S. 682, 684 (1917).

The present action presents the same fact situation as was before this court in the cases of *Sanger* v. *People of the State of New York*, 251 U.S. 537, 64 L. Ed 403, 40 S. Ct. 55 (1919) and *Gardner* v. *Commonwealth*, 305 U.S. 559, 83 L. Ed. 353, 59 S. Ct. 90 (1938)—criminal convictions arising out of the operation of a birth control center where contraceptives were disseminated. This Court dismissed the appeals from the New York and Massachusetts Courts for want of a substantial federal question. It is submitted that the same should be done in the instant case.

As this Court has stated: "The possession and enjoyment of all rights are subject to such reasonable conditions as may be deemed by the governing authority . . . essential to the safety, health, peace, good order, and morals of the community." *Jacobson* v. *Massachusetts*, 197 U.S. 11, 26, 49 L. Ed. 643, 650, 25 S. Ct. 358, 361 (1905).

Connecticut has statutes restricting several relations to the married with their spouses (Gen. Stat. Section 53-218. Adultery and Gen. Stat. 53-219—Fornication.) "[I]t (the Legislature) is not precluded from considering that not all married people are immune from temptation or inclination to extra-marital indulgence, as to which risk of illegitimate pregnancy is a recognized deterrent. . . ." *State* v. *Nelson*, 126 Conn. 412, 424, 11 A 2d 856, 861 (1940).

The appellants and their friends in their attempt to assert that the Connecticut Statutes as herein used are an unreasonable use of the police power have equated the use of contraceptives and the practice of birth control.

While it is true that to use contraceptives is to practice birth control; it is not correct to say that to practice birth control one must use contraceptives.

In Connecticut no one may use an article as a contraceptive. That does not mean that married people may not practice birth control. Abstinence, withdrawal and the rhythm method are available to the married in Connecticut. There can be no doubt that abstinence from sexual intercourse will prevent pregnancy. The appellants seem to think withdrawal is effective, for they introduced into evidence at the trial over the objection of the appellee Defendants' Exhibit No. 6, a book in which is contained the following:

> However, withdrawal has had a very poor reputation among doctors for generation, and some physicians still attribute many male and female ills to this technique. One gets the impression that such medical charges are more emotional than authoritive. In recent years, when some of us have been led to reexamine this method, we have been surprised to discover that there is virtually nothing of substance in medical literature to provide a scientific foundation for the charge. Guttmacher, *The Complete Book of Birth Control*, Ballantine Books, p. 64.

The rhythm system has been receiving more scientific attention of late. That the time of being able to pinpoint the time that ovulation occurs may be here may be seen from a recent gynecological report. Groden, *Ovulation Regulation*, 32 The Linacre Quarterly (February, 1965) pp. 66-72.

"Moreover, although it is somewhat dangerous to argue from statistics, at least one comparative study between those who practiced contraception and those who practiced rhythm showed that the rate of infidelity was much higher among those who practiced contraception (*Supplément de la Vie Spirituelle*, 1958, No. 1, pp. 60-61), Connery, *The Sign,* October 1960.

III

Appellant's Constitutional Rights Are Not Violated By These Statutes

A

Appellant Buxton

It is argued by the appellant Buxton that his right to practice medicine is impaired. The state denies this. It is the opinion of the appellee that the practice of medicine is directed to the treatment, cure, and/or prevention of disease. Nowhere in either the testimony, findings, or claims of error is there any claim that the women who testified in this case were in other than perfect health.

Therefore, the operation of the Planned Parenthood Center by the Planned Parenthood League in New Haven was not the practice of medicine. Nor could it be, for in Connecticut a corporation cannot practice medicine. The exceptions to the foregoing restrictions in the practice of medicine are hospitals and clinics formed by three or more physicians. The Planned Parenthood Center of New Haven cannot fit either exception, nor can the appellant, Griswold, hide her conduct under the protective cover of the appellant Buxton's medical coat. Dr. Buxton's conviction rested on his behavior as staff doctor on the day of Mrs. Steven's visit to the Center, not on his being the medical director of the Center. That when Mrs. Stevens was given a pelvic examination by Dr. Buxton, he was practicing medicine cannot be disputed by the state. But when he decided that Mrs. Stevens could use the contraceptive jelly (State's Exhibit L) and it must be remembered that the decision as to the type of contraceptive to be used was in the final analysis the decision of the staff doctor who examined the "patient"—(Finding Par. 12e R. p. 19) it cannot be said that it was a medical decision. Mrs. Stevens is a young woman. She was married less than a year. There is no indication in the record that she was in other than perfect health. There is no legitimate medical reason in the record of this case why Dr. Buxton instructed Mrs. Stevens to use the contraceptive jelly and instructed her in its use. That Mrs. Stevens did in fact use the jelly as a contraceptive upon the advice of the appellants Buxton and Griswold who supplied Mrs. Stevens with the jelly and extracted a fee of $15.00 from Mrs. Stevens—was the undisputed testimony of Mrs. Stevens and was found as a fact by the trial court (Finding Par. 20 R. p. 22). Therefore the only reason for that can be advanced for Dr. Buxton's actions enabling Mrs. Stevens to use this jelly as a contraceptive was that it was in line with his social philosophy. It is the position of the appellee, the State of Connecticut, that this social philosophy must fall before the police power of the state.

"Besides, there is no right to practice medicine which is not subordinate to the police power of the states." *Lambert* v. *Yellowley,* 272 U.S. 581, 596, 71 L. Ed. 422, 429, 47 S. Ct. 210, 214, 49 A.L.R. 575, 583 (1926).

B

Appellant Griswold

The appellant Estelle T. Griswold was the Executive Director of the Planned Parenthood League of Connecticut, a salaried position (Finding Par. 5, R. p. 17). In addition she was Acting Director of the Planned Parenthood Center of New Haven both before its opening and while it was in operation and was in charge of administration of the Center (Finding Par. 6, R. p. 17, Finding Par. 11, R. p. 18). From the Brief of the appellants (pp. 14-15) one might be led to the conclusion that the appellant Griswold was merely assisting the appellant Buxton. The converse is more accurate. "The policy of open defiance of the Connecticut Statute had been considered by the League as a possible response to an unfavorable decision of the Court (*Poe* v. *Ullman*, 3567 U.S. 497, 81 S. Ct. 1752, 6 L. ed 2d 989 (1961)). Mrs. Richard Griswold, Executive Director of the League, had urged this approach, but not all of her colleagues agreed with her. But the League's Board of Directors unanimously endorsed Mrs. Griswold's position in a meeting one week after the decision was rendered." Smith, *The History And Future of the Legal Battle Over Birth Control,* 49 Cornell Law Quarterly 295-296 (1964). The appellant Griswold at all times was in charge of the Center. Her claim of a right to earn a living is entitled to the same consideration as would be a similar claim made by one charged with being a supplier of burglar tools.

"[I]t is entirely true—that no person in any business has such an interest in possible customers as to enable him to restrain exercise of proper power of the State upon the ground that he will be deprived of patronage." *Pierce* v. *Society of Sisters*, 268 U.S. 510, 535-536, 45 S. Ct. 571, 69 L. Ed. 1070 (1925). In that case it was held that the State could not make public schools the only schools for children from eight to sixteen years of age. This Court stated: "These parties (private schools) are engaged in a kind of undertaking not inherently harmful, but long regarded as useful and meritorious." *Pierce* v. *Society of Sisters,* supra p. 534. This cannot be said of the use of contraceptives or indeed even of birth control. "Birth control is a highly controversial subject. Social thinking is divergent. It finds frequent expression at legislative hearing." *Tileston* v. *Ullman*, 129 Conn. 84, 94, 26 A 2d 582, 587 (1942).

"Certainly, Connecticut's judgment (on contraception) is no more demonstrably correct or incorrect than are the varieties of judgment, expressed in law, on marriage and divorce, on adult consensual homosexuality, abortion and sterilization, or euthanasia and suicide." Mr. Justice Harlan, dissenting in *Poe* v. *Ullman,* 367 U.S. 497, 547, 6 L. Ed. 2d 989, 1021; 81 S. Ct. 1752, 1779 (1961).

C

Appellant's Freedom of Speech Has Not Been Violated

The appellant's claim of freedom of speech is without merit. It was not the speech of the appellants that caused their conviction. It was their actions. When they furnished contraceptive material to women to be used as contraceptives and instructed the women as to their use to prevent pregnancy, then the appellants have, under Connecticut law, committed a crime and have no more right to justify their conduct as being protected by the constitutional right of freedom of speech than a man yelling fire in a crowded theater, or a person placing a wager over the phone, or a purveyor of implements to one whom the purveyor knows intends to use them as burglar tools. To accept the appellants' claim of freedom of speech would be to change a right into a license.

IV

Comments As To Certain Claims Made By Appellants In Their Brief

There has been no invasion of anyone's privacy in this case. "The necessary proof of the offense was supplied by the voluntary testimony of three married women. This evidence was not coerced nor was it illegally or surreptitiously obtained." Opinion of Appellate Division R. p. 47.

The legislative hearings concerning the repeal and/or amending of the Connecticut statutes banning the use of contraceptives (Conn. Gen. Stat. Rev. 1958 §§ 53-32 and 54-196) have shown that there is a dispute (to give the appellants the benefit of any doubt) as to the medical reasons for repealing the statutes or for amending them to allow doctors to prescribe contraceptives. At the hearings on House Bill (H.B.) 1177 to repeal what is now § 53-32 and H.B. 1182 exempting from the statutes a) physicians in the case where a danger to life or impairment of health of a married woman, b) married persons using method so proscribed, c) pharmacists filling such prescription, held by the Public Health and Safety Committee on April 20, 1955 several prominent physicians testified in opposition to the bills. John M. Paget, M.D., Neurologist and Neurological Surgeon, Diplomat of American Board of Neurological Surgery and a Fellow of the American College of Surgery stated: "As a specialist of the diseases of the nervous system, it is my considered opinion that the practice of birth control is frequently responsible for nervous disorders." page 268. Transcript of Testimony at Public Hearings. Several obstetricians and Gynecologists also spoke in opposition to the proposed bills: Jules Terry, M.D. page 269, Katherine Quinn Nolan, M.D. p. 270 and Frederick C. LeBrett, M.D. pp. 272-274. Dr. LeBrett, who was the Chief, Department of Obstetrics and Gynecology at St. Mary's

Hospital at Waterbury ended his testimony: "In conclusion, I object to these bills because, one, they will in no way reduce the incidence of hemorrhage, or toxemia in pregnancy, two all authorities agree that hemorrhage is best prevented by good pregnancy control not birth control, and three, all authorities including our own committee of the Connecticut State Medical Society agree that toxemia is best prevented by good pregnancy control. No article on birth control or pregnancy prevention has been deemed worthy of print in the Year Book of Obstetrics and Gynecology for many years. It definitely has no place in our modern obstetrics practice." pp. 273-274.

Similarly at the hearing on H.B. 572, whoch would have permitted physicians to prescribe contraceptives to meet the health needs of married women and married women to use contraceptives so prescribed before the Public Health and Safety Committee of the Connecticut General Assembly on March 21, 1957, physicians spoke in opposition to the proposed legislation. Thomas J. Tarasovic, M.D., Obstetrician and Counselor of the Bridgeport Medical Society stated: "Modern medicine in recent years has made such important strides in affording new relief and treatment for conditions which previously seriously complicated pregnancy that it becomes almost a farce to need a measure allowing physicians to give contraceptive advice to married women patients whose health or life would be endangered by pregnancy." p. 297.

"Because of the new many successful procedures in the treatment of conditions complicating pregnancy, because our maternal mortality is now, as a result, at an almost irreducible minimum this bill becomes unnecessary." p. 298.

John F. Knowland, M.D. Surgeon, former president of the Bridgeport Medical Society testified in part: "I am here to oppose the proposed legislation, primarily because I am a physician. I will limit all my remarks to the medical aspects of this controversial subject." p. 299.

"Furthermore, I would have to appear before you today in opposition to this proposed legislation, because I feel that no doctor in the light of modern medicine and obstetrics can justifiably say to the cardiac, to the tuberculosis patient, to the hypertensive that they could not have a baby." p. 300. The transcripts of testimony of the public hearings on bills before the Connecticut General Assembly—in the instances cited above before the Public Health and Safety Committees in 1955 and 1957, are official records of the State of Connecticut and may be found in the State Library at Hartford as well as in the Office of the Secretary of State. The above testimony is cited not as being an extensive treatment of the testimony before the General Assembly on the subject of contraceptives, but as an example of the medical testimony before the General Assembly in support of the retention of the contraceptive statutes in their present form.

From the foregoing it would appear—and giving the appellants the benefit of any doubts—that the situation before the General Assembly is quite similar to that faced by Congress when it restricted the prescription of liquor. In both the *Lambert* v. *Yellowley,* 272 U.S. 581, 71 L. Ed. 442, 47 S. Ct. 210, 49 A.L.R. 575, (1926) and the case at bar it can be said that "High medical authority being in conflict as to the medicinal value," in the *Lambert,* supra, case liquor as medicine and in the situation presently before the Court the medical need for contraceptives, that the legislature acted within the scope of its police power. Nor can the *Lambert* case (supra) be distinguished from the case at bar on the grounds that Congress limited the amount of liquor a physician could prescribe while Connecticut by the use of its contraceptive statute (Sec. 53-32) and its accessory statute (Sec.

54-196) bars the physician prescribing contraceptives at all, for it is clear that had Congress banned physicians from prescribing liquor at all, the decision of *Lambert* v. *Yellowley,* supra, would have been the same.

One would think that if there was a medical necessity for the repeal or amendment of Connecticut's contraceptive statute, the Connecticut Medical Society would have taken a position that the statute be so repealed or amended. In an editorial comment to an article by the appellant Buxton entitled *Birth Control Problems in Connecticut—Medical Necessity, Political Cowardice and Legal Procrastination* in 28 Connecticut Medicine—Connecticut State Medical Journal (August, 1964) page 581, the editor notes: "The Connecticut State Medical Society has taken no official position on this problem."

The appellee emphasizes the opinions filed by the Courts below in the consideration of these cases—(Memorandum on Demurrer to Information (R. pp. 3-6, 9-12) filed by Lacy, J., the opinion of the Appellate Division of the Circuit Court (R. pp. 40-50), and the opinion of the Supreme Court of Errors of Connecticut (R. pp. 61-63). This is not the first time that the constitutionality of these two statutes has been under attack in the courts of Connecticut under various factual situations. *State* v. *Nelson* (and companion cases) 126 Conn. 412, 11 A. 2d 856 (1940), like the present case, was a criminal prosecution of two physicians and a nurse (no such occupation is claimed for the appellant Griswold) who were participants in the operation of a birth control center in Waterbury. The issue before the Supreme Court of Errors raised by demurrer was the constitutionality of the State's charge that Dr. Nelson, Dr. Goodrich, and nurse McTernan assisted, abetted and counseled married women to use a drug and contraceptive device for the purpose of preventing conception because in the opinion of the defendants the preservation of the general health of the women required it. The Supreme Court of Errors citing *People* v. *Byrne,* 163 N.Y.S. (Supreme Court Term (1917) 682 and *Commonwealth* v. *Gardner,* 300 Mass. 372, 15 N.E. 2d 222 (1938), 305 U.S. 559, 59 S. Ct. 90, 83 L. Ed 353 (1938) (appeal dismissed for want of a substantial federal question) held the statutes good against the constitutional attack as a proper exercise of the police power of the State.

From 1940 to the time of the instant case the Supreme Court of Errors of Connecticut has held the statutes here were a proper exercise of the police power of the State on three occasions. These were all actions for declaratory judgments. *Tileston* v. *Ullman,* 129 Conn. 84, 26 A 2d 582 (1942) held that these statutes prohibited a physician from prescribing contraceptives for married women in cases where pregnancy would endanger the life or health of the married women. This court dismissed an appeal on the grounds that a physician had no standing to litigate the rights of patients not parties to the action. *Tileston* v. *Ullman,* 318 U.S. 44, 46, 87 L. Ed. 603, 604 (1942). In 1959 the Supreme Court of Errors again held these statutes good against a claim of unconstitutionality in cases where a physician, the same Dr. Buxton who is one of the appellants in the present case, and his patients claimed an exception for a physician to prescribe the use of contraceptives to married women in cases where pregnancy would endanger the life or health of married women. The difference between *Tileston,* supra, and the 1959 case was that in 1959 the married women and the physician were both parties to the action, *Buxton* v. *Ullman* (and companion cases), 147 Conn. 48, 156 A. 2d 508 (1959). This Court dismissed the appeals from the Supreme Court of Errors of Connecticut for an absence of a justiciable controversy. *Poe* v. *Ullman* (and companion cases), 367 U.S. 497, 6 L. Ed 2d 989, 81 S. Ct. 1752 (1961). The last case considered by the Courts of Connecticut prior to the present

cases, was *Trubek* v. *Ullman,* 147 Conn. 633, 165 A 2d 158 (1960), 367 U.S. 907, 6 L. Ed 2d 1249, 81 S. Ct. 1917 (1961) appeal dismissed, certiorari denied. The issue is does a married couple have a right to use contraceptives, no medical reasons being advanced. In the record of the present case there is no reason advanced such as in the previous cases that the statutes should not be applied. The closest fact situation would seem to be the *Trubek* case, supra, yet the appellants arguments and authority are directed more at a fact situation as in *Tileston,* supra, or the earlier *Buxton,* supra—urgent medical reasons to avoid pregnancy. The only reasons that the appellants can legitimately raise in the present case for their participation in the Center which distributed contraceptives was that it was in accord with their social philosophy.

Again the appellants make the claim in their brief (page 11, 77) and in their Petition, p. 18, state that contraceptive devices may be obtained in Connecticut. There is no foundation in the record for this statement. In fact the opposite is true. In their assignment of errors to the Appellate Division of the Circuit Court, R. p. 37, and their Petition For Certification By the Supreme Court of Errors, R. p. 54, 58-59, the appellants cited as error the sustaining of objection made by the appellee to a question posed on cross-examination: ''Now in the course of your investigation, Detective Berg, did you ascertain whether these products were available anywhere else in the City of New Haven?'' This is the only place in the record where availability of contraceptives is mentioned. The appellants have not claimed this ruling on evidence in their Notice of Appeal to This court nor in Questions to be reviewed in the Jurisdictional Statement. Manifestly they cannot make that claim now. In any case, it is Hornbook law that it cannot be set up as a defense to a prosecution of a crime that another who has committed the same offense has not been indicted. 1

Whartons Criminal Law, 12th Ed. Section 392. Further even if the appellants had introduced evidence at the trial that contraceptives were readily available, they did not, or requested the trier to take judicial notice of the supposed availability and use of contraceptives, they made no such request, it still would not help the appellants in this case. A custom and usage prevailing in a community cannot be set up as a defense to a prosecution for a crime, because such custom and usage cannot operate to supersede a criminal statute, or to overthrow the rules of evidence by which the commission of an offense is proved, even though such custom and usage may have been for a long time acquiesced in by the community in which it prevails. 1. Whartons Criminal Law, 12th Ed. Section 388. If such were not the rule, no one would be convicted of gambling offenses.

At page 10 of the appellant's Brief a portion of a letter by the then State Commissioner of Food and Drugs is quoted to substantiate their claim regarding the sale of contraceptive devices. The letter referred to is not based upon any legal authority, and, at most, represents the personal views of the then Commissioner.

As is evidenced by the following, the present Commissioner does not share the views quoted by the appellants: "Please be advised that this officer is not responsible for or agreed with what might have been the opinion of the Commissioner of Food and Drugs of that date." Letter of Commissioner Frassinelli, dated June 30, 1960, to Fowler V. Harper. Further an article in the August 28, 1962 edition of the Hartford Courant indicates that the State Consumer Protection Commissioner persuaded a pharmacy chain in the Hartford area to stop the sale of foam contraceptive.

Again the appellants in their brief pp. 72-74 cite the so-called population explosion. It is interesting to note that in both the nation and in the State of Connecticut the birth rate is on the decline. An Associated Press release emanating in Washington, D.C. as reported in the New Haven Register of September 21, 1964 states that "[t]he population reference bureau says the birth rate in the United States is declining." "In a report the bureau said the decline cannot be attributed either to a change in childbearing potential of American women or the development of new contraceptives." The Connecticut statistics on births are even more informative. According to the State Department of Health as reported in the New Haven Register of December 29, 1864 there were ten fewer births in Connecticut in the first ten months of 1964 as compared to the previous year. The complete figures for 1964 as reported in the New Haven Register of February 21, 1965 shows that the birth rate dropped from 20.6 to 20.2 per 1,000 population, making the seventh successive year that the rate has decreased.

The arguments of the appellants in essence attack the desirability of these statutes. It has been held that the Supreme Court may not decide the desirability of legislation in determining its constitutionality; the forum for correction of ill-considered legislation being a responsive legislature. *Daniel v. Family Sec. Life Ins. Co.,* 336 U.S. 220, 69 S. Ct. 550 (1949)

CONCLUSION

The judgment of the Supreme Court of Errors of Connecticut should be affirmed.

Respectfully submitted,

JOSEPH B. CLARK
Counsel for Appellee

171 Church Street
New Haven, Connecticut
March 8, 1965

GRISWOLD *v.* CONNECTICUT.

APPEAL FROM THE SUPREME COURT OF ERRORS OF CONNECTICUT.

No. 496. Argued March 29–30, 1965.— Decided June 7, 1965.*
*[381 U.S. 480]

Mr. Justice Douglas delivered the opinion of the Court.

Appellant Griswold is Executive Director of the Planned Parenthood League of Connecticut. Appellant Buxton is a licensed physician and a professor at the Yale Medical School who served as Medical Director for the League at its Center in New Haven—a center open and operating from November 1 to November 10, 1961, when appellants were arrested.

They gave information, instruction, and medical advice to *married persons* as to the means of preventing conception. They examined the wife and prescribed the best contraceptive device or material for her use. Fees were usually charged, although some couples were serviced free.

The statutes whose constitutionality is involved in this appeal are §§ 53–32 and 54–196 of the General Statutes of Connecticut (1958 rev.). The former provides:

"Any person who uses any drug, medicinal article or instrument for the purpose of preventing conception shall be fined not less than fifty dollars or imprisoned not less than sixty days nor more than one year or be both fined and imprisoned."

Section 54–196 provides:

"Any person who assists, abets, counsels, causes, hires or commands another to commit any offense may be prosecuted and punished as if he were the principal offender."

The appellants were found guilty as accessories and fined $100 each, against the claim that the accessory statute as so applied violated the Fourteenth Amendment. The Appellate Division of the Circuit Court affirmed. The Supreme Court of Errors affirmed that judgment 151 Conn. 544, 200 A. 2d 479. We noted probable jurisdiction. 379 U.S. 926.*
*[381 U.S. 481]

We think that appellants have standing to raise the constitutional rights of the married people with whom they had a professional relationship. *Tileston* v. *Ullman*, 318 U.S. 44, is different, for there the plaintiff seeking to represent others asked for a declaratory judgment. In that situation we thought that the requirements of standing should be strict, lest the standards of "case or controversy" in Article III of the Constitution become blurred. Here those doubts are removed by reason of a criminal conviction for serving married couples in violation of an aiding-and-abetting statute. Certainly the accessory should have standing to assert that the offense which he is charged with assisting is not, or cannot constitutionally be, a crime.

This case is more akin to *Truax* v. *Raich*, 239 U.S. 33, where an employee was permitted to assert the rights of his employer; to *Pierce* v. *Society of Sisters*, 268 U.S. 510, where the owners of private schools were entitled to assert the rights of potential pupils and their parents; and to *Barrows* v. *Jackson*, 346 U.S. 249, where a white defendant, party to a racially restrictive covenant, who was being sued for damages by the covenantors because she had conveyed her property to Negroes, was allowed to raise the issue that enforcement of the covenant violated the rights of prospective Negro purchasers to equal protection, although no Negro was a party to the suit. . . .

Coming to the merits, we are met with a wide range of questions that implicate the Due Process Clause of the Fourteenth Amendment.

Overtones of some arguments* suggest that
*[381 U.S. 482]
Lochner v. *New York*, 198 U.S. 45, should be our
guide. But we decline that invitation... We do
not sit as a super-legislature to determine the
wisdom, need, and propriety of laws that touch
economic problems, business affairs, or social
conditions. This law, however, operates directly
on an intimate relation of husband and wife and
their physician's role in one aspect of that
relation.

The association of people is not mentioned
in the Constitution nor in the Bill of Rights. The
right to educate a child in a school of the parent's
choice—whether public or private or paro-
chial—is also not mentioned. Nor is the right
to study any particular subject or any foreign
language. Yet the First Amendment has been
construed to include certain of those rights.

By *Pierce* v. *Society of Sisters, supra,* the right
to educate one's children as one chooses is made
applicable to the States by the force of the First
and Fourteenth Amendments. By *Meyer* v.
Nebraska, supra, the same dignity is given the right
to study the German language in a private
school. In other words, the State may not, consistently with the spirit of the First Amendment,
contract the spectrum of available knowledge.
The right of freedom of speech and press includes not only the right to utter or to print, but
the right to distribute, the right to receive, the
right to read (*Martin* v. *Struthers,* 319 U.S. 141, 143)
and freedom of inquiry, freedom of thought, and
freedom to teach (see *Wieman* v. *Updegraff,* 344
U.S. 183, 195)—indeed the freedom of the entire university community. Without* those peri-
*[381 U.S. 483]
pheral rights the specific rights would be less
secure. And so we reaffirm the principle of the
Pierce and the *Meyer* cases.

In *NAACP* v. *Alabama,* 357 U.S. 449, 462,
we protected the "freedom to associate and
privacy in one's associations,"... In other words,

the First Amendment has a penumbra where
privacy is protected from governmental intrusion. In like context, we have protected forms
of "association" that are not political in the
customary sense but pertain to the social, legal,
and economic benefit of the members. *NAACP*
v. *Button,* 371 U.S. 415, 430–431. In *Schware* v.
Board of Bar Examiners, 353 U.S. 232, we held it
not permissible to bar a lawyer from practice,
because he had once been a member of the
Communist Party. The man's "association with
that Party" was not shown to be "anything more
than a political faith in a political party" (*id.,*
at 244) and was not action of a kind proving bad
moral character. *Id.,* 245–246.

Those cases involved more than the "right
of assembly"—a right that extends to all irrespective of their race or ideology. *De Jonge* v.
Oregon, 299 U.S. 353. The right of "association,"
like the right of belief (*Board of Education* v. *Barnette,*
319 U.S. 624), is more than the right to attend
a meeting; it includes the right to express one's
attitudes or philosophies by membership in a
group or by affiliation with it or by other lawful
means. Association in that context is a form of
expression of opinion; and while it is not expressly included in the First Amendment its existence is necessary in making the express
guarantees fully meaningful.*
*[381 U.S. 484]
The foregoing cases suggest that specific
guarantees in the Bill of Rights have penumbras,
formed by emanations from those guarantees
that help give them life and substance. See *Poe*
v. *Ullman,* 367 U.S. 497, 516–522 (dissenting
opinion). Various guarantees create zones of
privacy. The right of association contained in
the penumbra of the First Amendment is one,
as we have seen. The Third Amendment in its
prohibition against the quartering of soldiers "in
any house" in time of peace without the consent of the owner is another facet of that privacy.
The Fourth Amendment explicitly affirms the

"right of the people to be secure in their persons, houses, papers, and effects, against unreasonable searches and seizures." The Fifth Amendment in its Self-Incrimination Clause enables the citizen to create a zone of privacy which government may not force him to surrender to his detriment. The Ninth Amendment provides: "The enumeration in the Constitution, of certain rights, shall not be construed to deny or disparage others retained by the people."

The Fourth and Fifth Amendments were described in *Boyd* v. *United States*, 116 U.S. 616, 630, as protection against all governmental invasions "of the sanctity of a man's home and the privacies of life." † We recently referred*
*[381 U.S. 485]
in *Mapp* v. *Ohio*, 367 U.S. 643, 656, to the Fourth Amendment as creating a "right to privacy, no less important than any other right carefully and particularly reserved to the people. See Beaney, The Constitutional Right to Privacy, 1962 Sup. Ct. Rev. 212; Griswold, The Right to be Let Alone, 55 Nw. U.L. Rev. 216 (1960).

We have had many controversies over these penumbral rights of "privacy and repose." See, *e.g., Breard* v. *Alexandria*, 341 U.S. 622, 626, 644; *Public Utilities Comm'n* v. *Pollak*, 343 U.S. 451; *Monroe* v. *Pape*, 365 U.S. 167; *Lanza* v. *New York*, 370 U.S. 139; *Frank* v. *Maryland*, 359 U.S. 360; *Skinner* v. *Oklahoma*, 316 U.S. 535, 541. These cases bear witness that the right of privacy which presses for recognition here is a legitimate one.

The present case, then, concerns a relationship lying within the zone of privacy created by several fundamental constitutional guarantees. And it concerns a law which, in forbidding the *use* of contraceptives rather than regulating their manufacture or sale, seeks to achieve its goals by means having a maximum destructive impact upon that relationship. Such a law cannot stand in light of the familiar principle, so often applied by this Court, that a "governmental purpose to control or prevent activities constitutionally subject to state regulation may not be achieved by means which sweep unnecessarily broadly and thereby invade the area of protected freedoms." *NAACP* v. *Alabama*, 377 U.S. 288, 307. Would we allow the police to search the sacred precincts of marital bedrooms for telltale signs of the use of contraceptives? The* very idea is
*[381 U.S. 486]
repulsive to the notions of privacy surrounding the marriage relationship.

We deal with a right of privacy older than the Bill of Rights—older than our political parties, older than our school system. Marriage is a coming together for better or for worse, hopefully enduring, and intimate to the degree of being sacred. It is an association that promotes a way of life, not causes; a harmony in living, not political faiths; a bilateral loyalty, not commercial or social projects. Yet it is an association for as noble a purpose as any involved in our prior decisions.

Reversed.

†The Court said in full about this right of privacy:
"The principles laid down in this opinion [by Lord Camden in *Entick* v. *Carrington*, 19 How. St. Tr. 1029] affect the very essence of constitutional liberty and security. They reach farther than the concrete form of the case then before the court, with its adventitious circumstances; they apply to all invasions on the part of the government and its employees of the sanctity of a man's home and the privacies of life. It is not the breaking of his doors, and the rummaging of his drawers, that constitutes the essence of the offence; but it is the invasion of his indefeasible right of personal security, personal liberty and private property, where that right has never been forfeited by his conviction of some public offence,—it is the invasion of this sacred right which underlies and constitutes the essence of Lord Camden's judgment. Breaking into a house and opening boxes and drawers are circumstances of aggravation; but any forcible and compulsory extortion of a man's own testimony or of his private papers to be used as evidence to convict him of crime or to forfeit his goods, is within the condemnation of that judgment. In this regard the Fourth and Fifth Amendments run almost into each other." 116 U.S., at 630.

Mr. Justice Goldberg, whom The Chief Justice and Mr. Justice Brennan join, concurring.

I agree with the Court that Connecticut's birth-control law unconstitutionally intrudes upon the right of marital privacy, and I join in its opinion and judgment. Although I have not accepted the view that "due process" as used in the Fourteenth Amendment incorporates all of the first eight Amendments (see my concurring opinion in *Pointer* v. *Texas*, 380 U.S. 400, 410, and the dissenting opinion of Mr. Justice Brennan in *Cohen* v. *Hurley*, 366 U.S. 117, 154), I do agree that the concept of liberty protects those personal rights that are fundamental, and is not confined to the specific terms of the Bill of Rights. My conclusion that the concept of liberty is not so restricted and that it embraces the right of marital privacy though that right is not mentioned explicitly in the Constitution[1] is supported both by numerous* decisions of this Court,

*[381 U.S. 487]

referred to in the Court's opinion, and by the language and history of the Ninth Amendment. In reaching the conclusion that the right of marital privacy is protected, as being within the protected penumbra of specific guarantees of the Bill of Rights, the Court refers to the Ninth Amendment, *ante*, at 484. I add these words to emphasize the relevance of that Amendment to the Court's holding.

The Court stated many years ago that the Due Process Clause protects those liberties that are "so rooted in the traditions and conscience of our people as to be ranked as fundamental.". . .*

*[381 U.S. 488]

This Court, in a series of decisions, has held that the Fourteenth Amendment absorbs and applies to the States those specifics of the first eight amendments which express fundamental personal rights.[2] The language and history of the Ninth Amendment reveal that the Framers of the Constitution believed that there are additional fundamental rights, protected from governmental infringement, which exist alongside those fundamental rights specifically mentioned in the first eight constitutional amendments.

The Ninth Amendment reads, "The enumeration in the Constitution, of certain rights, shall not be construed to deny or disparage others retained by the people." The Amendment is almost entirely the work of James Madison. It was introduced in Congress by him and passed the House and Senate with little or no debate and virtually no change in language. It was proffered to quiet expressed fears that a bill of specifically enumerated rights[3] could not be sufficiently broad to cover all essential*

*[381 U.S. 489]

rights and that the specific mention of certain rights would be interpreted as a denial that others were protected.[4]

In presenting the proposed Amendment, Madison said:

"It has been objected also against a bill of rights, that, by enumerating

---

1. My Brother Stewart dissents on the ground that he "can find no . . . general right of privacy in the Bill of Rights, in any other part of the Constitution, or in any case ever before decided by this Court." *Post*, at 530. He would require a more explicit guarantee than the one which the Court derives from several constitutional amendments. This Court, however, has never held that the Bill of Rights or the Fourteenth Amendment protects only those rights that the Constitution specifically mentions by name.

2. See, *e.g., Chicago, B. & Q. R. Co.* v. *Chicago*, 166 U.S. 226; *Gitlow* v. *New York, supra; Cantwell* v. *Connecticut*, 310 U.S 296; *Wolf* v. *Colorado*, 338 U.S. 25; *Robinson* v. *California*, 370 U.S. 660; *Gideon* v. *Wainwright*, 372 U.S. 335; *Malloy* v. *Hogan*, 378 U.S. 1; *Pointer* v. *Texas, supra; Griffin* v. *California*, 380 U.S. 609.

3. Madison himself had previously pointed out the dangers of inaccuracy resulting from the fact that "no language is so copious as to supply words and phrases for every complex idea." The Federalist, No. 37 (Cooke ed. 1961), at 236.

4. Alexander Hamilton was opposed to a bill of rights on the ground that it was unnecessary because the Federal Government was a government of delegated powers and it was not granted the power to intrude upon fundamental personal rights. The Federalist, No. 84 (Cooke ed. 1961), at 578-579.

particular exceptions to the grant of power, it would disparage those rights which were not placed in that enumeration; and it might follow by implication, that those rights which were not singled out, were intended to be assigned into the hands of the General Government, and were consequently insecure. This is one of the most plausible arguments I have ever heard urged against the admission of a bill of rights into this system; but, I conceive, that it may be guarded against. I have attempted it, as gentlemen may see by turning to the* last clause of the fourth

*[381 U.S. 490]

resolution [the Ninth Amendment]." I Annals of Congress 439 (Gales and Seaton ed. 1834).

Mr. Justice Story wrote of this argument against a bill of rights and the meaning of the Ninth Amendment:

"In regard to . . . [a] suggestion, that the affirmance of certain rights might disparage others, or might lead to argumentative implications in favor of other powers, it might be sufficient to say that such a course of reasoning could never be sustained upon any solid basis. . . . But a conclusive answer is, that such an attempt may be interdicted (as it has been) by a positive declaration in such a bill of rights that the enumeration of certain rights shall not be construed to deny or disparage others retained by the people." II Story, Commentaries on the Constitution of the United States 626–627 (5th ed. 1891). . . . These statements of Madison and Story make clear that the Framers did not intend that the first eight amendments be construed to exhaust the basic and fundamental rights which the Constitution guaranteed to the people.

While this Court has had little occasion to interpret the Ninth Amendment,[6] "[i]t cannot be presumed that any* clause in the constitution is intended to be without effect." *Marbury* v.

[381, U.S. 491]

Madison, 1 Cranch 137, 174. In interpreting the Constitution, "real effect should be given to all the words it uses." *Myers* v. *United States,* 272 U.S. 52, 151. The Ninth Amendment to the Constitution may be regarded by some as a recent discovery and may be forgotten by others, but since 1791 it has been a basic part of the Constitution which we are sworn to uphold. To hold that a right so basic and fundamental and so deep-rooted in our society as the right of privacy in marriage may be infringed because that right is not guaranteed in so many words by the first eight amendments to the Constitution is to ignore the Ninth Amendment and to give it no effect whatsoever. Moreover, a judicial construction that this fundamental right is not protected by the Constitution because it is not mentioned in explicit terms by one of the first eight amendments or elsewhere in the Constitution would violate the Ninth Amendment, which specifically states that* "[t]he enumeration in the Constitu-

*[381 U.S. 492]

tion, of certain rights, shall not be *construed* to deny or disparage others retained by the people." (Emphasis added.)

A dissenting opinion suggests that my interpretation of the Ninth Amendment somehow "broaden[s] the powers of this Court." *Post,* at 520. With all due respect, I believe that it misses the import of what I am saying. I do not take the position of my Brother BLACK in his dissent in *Adamson* v. *California,* 332 U.S. 46, 68, that the entire Bill of Rights is incorporated in the Fourteenth Amendment, and I do not mean to imply that the Ninth Amendment is applied

---

6. This Amendment has been referred to as "The Forgotten Ninth Amendment," . . .

against the States by the Fourteenth. Nor do I mean to state that the Ninth Amendment constitutes an independent source of rights protected from infringement by either the States or the Federal Government. Rather, the Ninth Amendment shows a belief of the Constitution's authors that fundamental rights exist that are not expressly enumerated in the first eight amendments and an intent that the list of rights included there not be deemed exhaustive. As any student of this Court's opinions knows, this Court has held, often unanimously, that the Fifth and Fourteenth Amendments protect certain fundamental personal liberties from abridgment by the Federal Government or the States. See, *e.g.*, *Bolling* v. *Sharpe*, 347 U.S 497; *Aptheker* v. *Secretary of State*, 378 U.S. 500; *Kent* v. *Dulles*, 357 U.S. 116; *Cantwell* v. *Connecticut*, 310 U.S. 296; *NAACP* v. *Alabama*, 357 U.S. 449; *Gideon* v. *Wainwright*, 372 U.S. 335; *New York Times Co.* v. *Sullivan*, 376 U.S. 254. The Ninth Amendment simply shows the intent of the Constitution's authors that other fundamental personal rights should not be denied such protection or disparaged in any other way simply because they are not specifically listed in the first eight constitutional amendments. I do not see how this broadens the authority* of the Court; rather it serves to
*[381 U.S. 493]
support what this Court has been doing in protecting fundamental rights.

Nor am I turning somersaults with history in arguing that the Ninth Amendment is relevant in a case dealing with a *State's* infringement of a fundamental right. While the Ninth Amendment—and indeed the entire Bill of Rights—originally concerned restrictions upon *federal* power, the subsequently enacted Fourteenth Amendment prohibits the States as well from abridging fundamental personal liberties. And, the Ninth Amendment, in indicating that not all such liberties are specifically mentioned in the first eight amendments, is surely relevant in showing the existence of other fundamental personal rights, now protected from state, as well as federal, infringement. In sum, the Ninth Amendment simply lends strong support to the view that the ''liberty'' protected by the Fifth and Fourteenth Amendments from infringement by the Federal Government or the States is not restricted to rights specifically mentioned in the first eight amendments. Cf. *United Public Workers* v. *Mitchell*, 330 U.S. 75, 94–95.

In determining which rights are fundamental, judges are not left at large to decide cases in light of their personal and private notions. Rather, they must look to the ''traditions and [collective] conscience of our people'' to determine whether a principle is ''so rooted [there] . . . as to be ranked as fundamental.'' *Snyder* v. *Massachusetts*, 291 U.S. 97, 105. The inquiry is whether a right involved ''is of such a character that it cannot be denied without violating those 'fundamental principles of liberty and justice which lie at the base of all our civil and political institutions.'. . .'' *Powell* v. *Alabama*, 287 U.S. 45, 67. ''Liberty'' also ''gains content from the emanations of . . . specific [constitutional] guarantees'' and ''from experience with the requirements of a free society.'' *Poe** v.
*[381 U.S. 493]
Ullman, 367 U.S. 497, 517 (dissenting opinion of Mr. Justice Douglas).[7]

I agree fully with the Court that, applying these tests, the right of privacy is a fundamental personal right, emanating ''from the totality of the constitutional scheme under which we live.'' *Id.*, at 521. Mr. Justice Brandeis, dissenting in *Olmstead* v. *United States*, 277 U.S. 438, 478, comprehensively summarized the principles underlying the Constitution's guarantees of privacy:

7. In light of the tests enunciated in these cases it cannot be said that a judge's responsibility to determine whether a right is basic and fundamental in this sense vests him with unrestricted personal discretion. . . .

"The protection guaranteed by the [Fourth and Fifth] Amendments is much broader in scope. The makers of our Constitution undertook to secure conditions favorable to the pursuit of happiness. They recognized the significance of man's spiritual nature, of his feelings and of his intellect. They knew that only a part of the pain, pleasure and satisfactions of life are to be found in material things. They sought to protect Americans in their beliefs, their thoughts, their emotions and their sensations. They conferred, as against the Government, the right to be let alone—the most comprehensive of rights and the right most valued by civilized men.' "*

*[381 U.S. 495]

The Connecticut statutes here involved deal with a particularly important and sensitive area of privacy—that of the marital relation and the marital home. This Court recognized in *Meyer* v. *Nebraska, supra,* that the right "to marry, establish a home and bring up children" was an essential part of the liberty guaranteed by the Fourteenth Amendment. 262 U.S., at 399. In *Pierce* v. *Society of Sisters*, 268 U.S. 510, the Court held unconstitutional an Oregon Act which forbade parents from sending their children to private schools because such an act "unreasonably interferes with the liberty of parents and guardians to direct the upbringing and education of children under their control." 268 U.S., at 534-535. As this Court said in *Prince* v. *Massachusetts*, 321 U.S. 158, at 166, the *Meyer* and *Pierce* decisions "have respected the private realm of family life which the state cannot enter."

I agree with Mr. Justice Harlan's statement in his dissenting opinion in *Poe* v. *Ullman*, 367 U.S. 497 551-552: "Certainly the safeguarding of the home does not follow merely from the sanctity of property rights. The home derives its pre-eminence as the seat of family life. And the integrity of that life is something so fundamental that it has been found to draw to its protection the principles of more than one explicitly granted Constitutional right.... Of this whole 'private realm of family life' it is difficult to imagine what is more private or more intimate than a husband and wife's marital relations."

The entire fabric of the Constitution and the purposes that clearly underlie its specific guarantees demonstrate that the rights to marital privacy and to marry and raise a family are of similar order and magnitude as the fundamental rights specifically protected.

Although the Constitution does not speak in so many words of the right of privacy in marriage, I cannot believe that it offers these fundamental rights no protection. The fact that no particular provision of the Constitution*

*[381 U.S. 496]

explicitly forbids the State from disrupting the traditional relation of the family—a relation as old and as fundamental as our entire civilization—surely does not show that the Government was meant to have the power to do so. Rather, as the Ninth Amendment expressly recognizes, there are fundamental personal rights such as this one, which are protected from abridgment by the Government though not specifically mentioned in the Constitution.

My Brother STEWART, while characterizing the Connecticut birth control law as "an uncommonly silly law," *post*, at 527, would nevertheless let it stand on the ground that it is not for the courts to " 'substitute their social and economic beliefs for the judgment of legislative bodies, who are elected to pass laws.' " *Post*, at 528. Elsewhere, I have stated that "[w]hile I quite agree with Mr. Justice Brandeis that . . . 'a . . . State may . . . serve as a laboratory; and try novel social and economic experiments,' *New State Ice Co.* v. *Liebmann*, 285 U.S. 262, 280, 311 (dissenting opinion), I do not believe that this includes the power to experiment with the fundamental liberties of citizens. . . ."[8] The vice of the dissenters' views is that it would permit such experimentation by the States in the area of the fundamental personal rights of its citizens. I cannot agree that the Constitution grants such power either to the States or to the Federal Government.

The logic of the dissents would sanction federal or state legislation that seems to me even more plainly unconstitutional than the statute before us. Surely the Government, absent a showing of a compelling subordinating state interest, could not decree that all husbands and wives must be sterilized after two children have been born* to them. Yet by their reasoning such
*[381 U.S. 497]
an invasion of marital privacy would not be subject to constitutional challenge because, while it might be "silly," no provision of the Constitution specifically prevents the Government from curtailing the marital right to bear children and raise a family. While it may shock some of my Brethren that the Court today holds that the Constitution protects the right of marital privacy, in my view it is far more shocking to believe that the personal liberty guaranteed by the Constitution does not include protection against such totalitarian limitation of family size, which is at complete variance with our constitutional concepts. Yet, if upon a showing of a slender basis of rationality, a law outlawing voluntary birth control by married persons is valid, then, by the same reasoning, a law requiring compulsory birth control also would seem to be valid. In my view, however, both types of law would unjustifiably intrude upon rights of marital privacy which are constitutionally protected.

8. *Pointer* v. *Texas, supra,* at 413. See also the discussion of my Brother DOUGLAS, *Poe* v. *Ullman, supra,* at 517–518 (dissenting opinion).

In a long series of cases this Court has held that where fundamental personal liberties are involved, they may not be abridged by the States simply on a showing that a regulatory statute has some rational relationship to the effectuation of a proper state purpose. . . .

Although the Connecticut birth-control law obviously encroaches upon a fundamental personal liberty, the State does not show that the law serves any "subordinating [state] interest which is compelling" or that it is "necessary . . . *
*[381 U.S. 498]
to the accomplishment of a permissible state policy." The State, at most, argues that there is some rational relation between this statute and what is admittedly a legitimate subject of state concern—the discouraging of extra-marital relations. It says that preventing the use of birth-control devices by married persons helps prevent the indulgence by some in such extra-marital relations. The rationality of this justification is dubious, particularly in light of the admitted widespread availability to all persons in the State of Connecticut, unmarried as well as married, of birth-control devices for the prevention of disease, as distinguished from the prevention of conception, see *Tileston* v. *Ullman*, 129 Conn. 84, 26 A. 2d 582. But, in any event, it is clear that the state interest in safeguarding marital fidelity can be served by a more discriminately tailored statute, which does not, like the present one, sweep unnecessarily broadly, reaching far beyond the evil sought to be dealt with and intruding upon the privacy of all married couples. See *Aptheker* v. *Secretary of State,* 378 U.S. 500, 514; *NAACP* v. *Alabama,* 377 U.S. 288, 307–308; *McLaughlin* v. *Florida, supra,* at 196. Here, as elsewhere, "[p]recision of regulation must be the touchstone in an area so closely touching our most precious freedoms." *NAACP* v. *Button,* 371 U.S. 415, 438. The State of Connecticut does have statutes, the constitutionality of which is beyond doubt, which prohibit adultery and

fornication. See Conn. Gen. Stat. §§ 53-218, 53-219 *et seq.* These statutes demonstrate that means for achieving the same basic purpose of protecting marital fidelity are available to Connecticut without the need to "invade the area of protected freedoms." *NAACP* v. *Alabama, supra,* at 307. See *McLaughlin* v. *Florida, supra,* at 196.

Finally, it should be said of the Court's holding today that it in no way interferes with a State's proper regulation* of sexual promis-
*[381 U.S. 499]
cuity or misconduct. As my Brother HARLAN so well stated in his dissenting opinion in *Poe* v. *Ullman, supra,* at 553.

> "Adultery, homosexuality and the like are sexual intimacies which the State forbids . . . but the intimacy of husband and wife is necessarily an essential and accepted feature of the institution of marriage, an institution which the State not only must allow, but which always and in every age it has fostered and protected. It is one thing when the State exerts its power either to forbid extra-marital sexuality . . . or to say who may marry, but it is quite another when, having acknowledged a marriage and the intimacies inherent in it, it undertakes to regulate by means of the criminal law the details of that intimacy."

In sum, I believe that the right of privacy in the marital relation is fundamental and basic—a personal right "retained by the people" within the meaning of the Ninth Amendment. Connecticut cannot constitutionally abridge this fundamental right, which is protected by the Fourteenth Amendment from infringement by the States. I agree with the Court that petitioners' convictions must therefore be reversed.

Mr. Justice Harlan, concurring in the judgment.

I fully agree with the judgment of reversal, but find myself unable to join the Court's opinion. The reason is that it seems to me to evince an approach to this case very much like that taken by my Brothers BLACK and STEWART in dissent, namely: the Due Process Clause of the Fourteenth Amendment does not touch this Connecticut statute unless the enactment is found to violate some right assured by the letter or penumbra of the Bill of Rights.*
*[381 U.S. 500]
In other words, what I find implicit in the Court's opinion is that the "incorporation" doctrine may be used to *restrict* the reach of Fourteenth Amendment Due Process. For me this is just as unacceptable constitutional doctrine as is the use of the "incorporation" approach to *impose* upon the States all the requirements of the Bill of Rights as found in the provisions of the first eight amendments and in the decisions of this Court interpreting them. See, *e.g.,* my concurring opinions in *Pointer* v. *Texas,* 380 U.S. 400, 408, and *Griffin* v. *California,* 380 U.S. 609, 615, and my dissenting opinion in *Poe* v. *Ullman,* 367 U.S. 497, 522, at pp. 539-545.

In my view, the proper constitutional inquiry in this case is whether this Connecticut statute infringes the Due Process Clause of the Fourteenth Amendment because the enactment violates basic values "implicit in the concept of ordered liberty," *Palko* v. *Connecticut,* 302 U.S. 319, 325. For reasons stated at length in my dissenting opinion in *Poe* v. *Ullman, supra,* I believe that it does. While the relevant inquiry may be aided by resort to one or more of the provisions of the Bill of Rights, it is not dependent on them or any of their radiations. The Due Process Clause of the Fourteenth Amendment stands, in my opinion, on its own bottom.

A further observation seems in order respecting the justification of my Brothers BLACK and STEWART for their "incorporation" approach to this case. Their approach does not rest on historical reasons, which are of course wholly lacking (see Fairman, Does the Fourteenth Amendment Incorporate the Bill of Rights? The Original Understanding, 2 Stan. L. Rev. 5 (1949)), but on the thesis that by limiting the content of the Due Process Clause of the Fourteenth Amendment to the protection of rights which can be found elsewhere in the Constitution, in this instance in the Bill of Rights, judges will thus be confined to "interpretation" of specific constitutional* provisions,
    *[381 U.S. 501]
and will thereby be restrained from introducing their own notions of constitutional right and wrong into the "vague contours of the Due Process Clause." *Rochin* v. *California*, 342 U.S. 165, 170.

While I could not more heartily agree that judicial "self restraint" is an indispensable ingredient of sound constitutional adjudication, I do submit that the formula suggested for achieving it is more hollow than real. . . .

Judicial self-restraint will not, I suggest, be brought about in the "due process' area by the historically unfounded incorporation formula long advanced by my Brother BLACK, and now in part espoused by my Brother STEWART. It will be achieved in this area, as in other constitutional areas, only by continual insistence upon respect for the teachings of history, solid recognition of the basic values that underlie our soceiety, and wise appreciation of the great roles that the doctrines of federalism and separation of powers have played in establishing and preserving American freedoms. See *Adamson* v. *California*, 332 U.S. 46, 59 (Mr. Justice Frankfurter, concurring). Adherence to these principles will not, of course, obviate all constitutional differences of opinion among judges,

nor should it. Their continued recognition*
    *[381 U.S. 502]
will, however, go farther toward keeping most judges from roaming at large in the constitutional field than will the interpolation into the Constitution of an artificial and largely illusory restriction on the content of the Due Process Clause.†

Mr. Justice White, concurring in the judgment.

In my view this Connecticut law as applied to married couples deprives them of "liberty" without due process of law, as that concept is used in the Fourteenth Amendment. I therefore concur in the judgment of the Court reversing these convictions under Connecticut's aiding and abetting statute.

It would be unduly repetitious, and belaboring the obvious, to expound on the impact of this statute on the liberty guaranteed by the Fourteenth Amendment against arbitrary or capricious denials or on the nature of this liberty. Suffice it to say that this is not the first time this Court has had occasion to articulate that the liberty entitled to protection under the Fourteenth Amendment includes the right "to marry, establish a home and bring up children," *Meyer* v. *Nebraska*, 262 U.S. 390, 399, and "the liberty . . . to direct the upbringing and education of children," *Pierce* v. *Society of Sisters*, 268 U.S. 510, 534–535, and that these are among "the basic civil rights of man." *Skinner* v. *Oklahoma*, 316 U.S. 535, 541. These decisions affirm that there is a "realm of family life which the

---

†Indeed, my Brother BLACK, in arguing his thesis, is forced to lay aside a host of cases in which the Court has recognized fundamental rights in the Fourteenth Amendment without specific reliance upon the Bill of Rights. *Post*, p. 512, n. 4.

state cannot enter" without substantial justification. *Prince* v. *Massachusetts*, 321 U.S. 158, 166. Surely the right invoked in this case, to be free of regulation of the intimacies of* the
*[381 U.S. 503]
marriage relationship, "come[s] to this Court with a momentum for respect lacking when appeal is made to liberties which derive merely from shifting economic arrangements." *Kovacs* v. *Cooper*, 336 U.S. 77, 95 (opinion of Frankfurter, J.).

The Connecticut anti-contraceptive statute deals rather substantially with this relationship. For it forbids all married persons the right to use birth-control devices, regardless of whether their use is dictated by considerations of family planning, *Trubek* v. *Ullman*, 147 Conn. 633, 165 A. 2d 158, health, or indeed even of life itself. *Buxton* v. *Ullman*, 147 Conn. 48, 156 A. 2d 508. The anti-use statute, together with the general aiding and abetting statute, prohibits doctors from affording advice to married persons on proper and effective methods of birth control. *Tileston* v. *Ullman*, 129 Conn. 84, 26 A. 2d 582. And the clear effect of these statutes, as enforced, is to deny disadvantaged citizens of Connecticut, those without either adequate knowledge or resources to obtain private counseling, access to medical assistance and up-to-date information in respect to proper methods of birth control. *State* v. *Nelson*, 126 Conn. 412, 11 A. 2d 856; *State* v. *Griswold*, 151 Conn. 544, 200 A. 2d 479. In my view, a statute with these effects bears a substantial burden of justification when attacked under the Fourteenth Amendment. *Yick Wo* v. *Hopkins*, 118 U.S. 356; *Skinner* v. *Oklahoma*, 316 U.S. 535; *Schware* v. *Board of Bar Examiners*, 353 U.S. 232; *McLaughlin* v. *Florida*, 379 U.S. 184, 192.

An examination of the justification offered, however, cannot be avoided by saying that the Connecticut anti-use statute invades a protected area of privacy and association or that it demeans the marriage relationship. The nature of the right invaded is pertinent, to be sure, for statutes regulating sensitive areas of liberty do, under*
*[381 U.S. 504]
the cases of this Court, require "strict scrutiny," *Skinner* v. *Oklahoma*, 316 U.S. 535, 541, and "must be viewed in the light of less drastic means for achieving the same basic purpose." *Shelton* v. *Tucker*, 364 U.S. 479, 488. "Where there is a significant encroachment upon personal liberty, the State may prevail only upon showing a subordinating interest which is compelling." *Bates* v. *Little Rock*, 361 U.S. 516, 524. See also *McLaughlin* v. *Florida*, 379 U.S. 184. But such statutes, if reasonably necessary for the effectuation of a legitimate and substantial state interest, and not arbitrary or capricious in application, are not invalid under the Due Process Clause. *Zemel* v. *Rusk*, 381 U.S. 1.†*
*[381 U.S. 505]
As I read the opinions of the Connecticut courts and the argument of Connecticut in this Court, the State claims but one justification for its anti-use statute. Cf. *Allied Stores of Ohio* v. *Bowers*, 358 U.S. 522, 530; *Martin* v. *Walton*, 368 U.S. 25, 28 (Douglas, J., dissenting). There is no serious contention that Connecticut thinks the use of artificial or external methods of contraception immoral or unwise in itself, or that the anti-use statute is founded upon any policy of promoting

---

†Dissenting opinions assert that the liberty guaranteed by the Due Process Clause is limited to a guarantee against unduly vague statutes and against procedural unfairness at trial. Under this view the Court is without authority to ascertain whether a challenged statute, or its application, has a permissible purpose and whether the manner of regulation bears a rational or justifying relationship to this purpose. A long line of cases makes very clear that this has not been the view of this Court. *Dent* v. *West Virginia*, 129 U.S. 114; *Jacobson* v. *Massachusetts*, 197 U.S. 11; *Douglas* v. *Noble*, 261 U.S. 165; *Meyer* v. *Nebraska*, 262 U.S. 390; *Pierce* v. *Society of Sisters*, 268 U.S. 510; *Schware* v. *Board of Bar Examiners*, 353 U.S. 232; *Aptheker* v. *Secretary of State*, 378 U.S. 500; *Zemel* v. *Rusk*, 381 U.S. 1.

The traditional due process test was well articulated, and applied, in *Schware* v. *Board of Bar Examiners*, *supra*, a case which placed no reliance on the specific guarantees of the Bill of Rights. . . .

population expansion. Rather, the statute is said to serve the State's policy against all forms of promiscuous or illicity sexual relationships, be they premarital or extramarital, concededly a permissible and legitimate legislative goal.

Without taking issue with the premise that the fear of conception operates as a deterrent to such relationships in addition to the criminal proscriptions Connecticut has against such conduct, I wholly fail to see how the ban on the use of contraceptives by married couples in any way reinforces the State's ban on illicit sexual relationships. See *Schware* v. *Board of Bar Examiners*, 353 U.S. 232, 239. Connecticut does not bar the importation or possession of contraceptive devices; they are not considered contraband material under state law, *State* v. *Certain Contraceptive Materials*, 126 Conn. 428, 11 A. 2d 863, and their availability in that State is not seriously disputed. The only way Connecticut seeks to limit or control the availability of such devices is through its general aiding and abetting statute whose operation in this context has* been quite

*[381 U.S. 506]

obviously ineffective and whose most serious use has been against birth-control clinics rendering advice to married, rather than unmarried, persons. Cf. *Yick Wo* v. *Hopkins*, 118 U.S. 356. Indeed, after over 80 years of the State's proscription of use, the legality of the sale of such devices to prevent disease has never been expressly passed upon, although it appears that sales have long occurred and have only infrequently been challenged. This "undeviating policy . . . throughout all the long years . . . bespeaks more than prosecutorial paralysis." *Poe* v. *Ullman*, 367 U.S. 497, 502. Moreover, it would appear that the sale of contraceptives to prevent disease is plainly legal under Connecticut law.

In these circumstances one is rather hard pressed to explain how the ban on use by married persons in any way prevents use of such devices by persons engaging in illicit sexual rela-

tions and thereby contributes to the State's policy against such relationships. Neither the state courts nor the State before the bar of this Court has tendered such an explanation. It is purely fanciful to believe that the broad proscription on use facilitates discovery of use by persons engaging in a prohibited relationship or for some other reason makes such use more unlikely and thus can be supported by any sort of administrative consideration. Perhaps the theory is that the flat ban on use prevents married people from possessing contraceptives and without the ready availability of such devices for use in the marital relationship, there will be no or less temptation to use them in extramarital ones. This reasoning rests on the premise that married people will comply with the ban in regard to their marital relationship, notwithstanding total nonenforcement in this context and apparent nonenforcibility, but will not comply with criminal statutes prohibiting extramarital affairs and the anti-use statute in respect to illicit sexual relationships, a premise whose validity has not been* demonstrated and whose intrinsic

*[381 U.S. 507]

validity is not very evident. At most the broad ban is of marginal utility to the declared objective. A statute limiting its prohibition on use to persons engaging in the prohibited relationship would serve the end posited by Connecticut in the same way, and with the same effectiveness, or ineffectiveness, as the broad anti-use statute under attack in this case. I find nothing in this record justifying the sweeping scope of this statute, with its telling effect on the freedoms of married persons, and therefore conclude that it deprives such persons of liberty without due process of law.

Mr. Justice Black, with whom Mr. Justice Stewart joins, dissenting.

I agree with my Brother STEWART's dissenting opinion. And like him I do not to any extent whatever base my view that this Connecticut law is constitutional on a belief that the law is wise or that its policy is a good one. In order that there may be no room at all to doubt why I vote as I do, I feel constrained to add that the law is every bit as offensive to me as it is to my Brethren of the majority and my Brothers HARLAN, WHITE and GOLDBERG who, reciting reasons why it is offensive to them, hold it unconstitutional. There is no single one of the graphic and eloquent strictures and criticisms fired at the policy of this Connecticut law either by the Court's opinion or by those of my concurring Brethren to which I cannot subscribe— except their conclusion that the evil qualities they see in the law make it unconstitutional.

Had the doctor defendant here, or even the nondoctor defendant, been convicted for doing nothing more than expressing opinions to persons coming to the clinic that certain contraceptive devices, medicines or practices would do them good and would be desirable, or for telling people how devices could be used, I can think of no reasons at this time why their expressions of views would not be* protected by the First
*[381 U.S. 508]
and Fourteenth Amendments, which guarantee freedom of speech. Cf. *Brotherhood of Railroad Trainmen* v. *Virginia ex rel. Virginia State Bar*, 377 U.S. 1; *NAACP* v. *Button*, 371 U.S. 415. But speech is one thing; conduct and physical activities are quite another. See, *e.g.*, *Cox* v. *Louisiana*, 379 U.S. 536, 554–555; *Cox* v. *Louisiana*, 379 U.S. 559, 563–564; *id.*, 575–584 (concurring opinion); *Giboney* v. *Empire Storage & Ice Co.*, 336 U.S. 490; cf. *Reynolds* v. *United States*, 98 U.S. 145, 163–164. The two defendants here were active participants in an organization which gave physical examinations to women, advised them what kind of contraceptive devices or medicines would most likely be satisfactory for them, and then supplied the devices themselves, all for a graduated scale of fees, based on the family income. Thus these defendants admittedly engaged with others in

a planned course of conduct to help people violate the Connecticut law. Merely because some speech was used in carrying on that conduct—just as in ordinary life some speech accompanies most kinds of conduct—we are not in my view justified in holding that the First Amendment forbids the State to punish their conduct. Strongly as I desire to protect all First Amendment freedoms, I am unable to stretch the Amendment so as to afford protection to the conduct of these defendants in violating the Connecticut law. What would be the constitutional fate of the law if hereafter applied to punish nothing but speech is, as I have said, quite another matter.

The Court talks about a constitutional "right of privacy" as though there is some constitutional provision or provisions forbidding any law ever to be passed which might abridge the "privacy" of individuals. But there is not. There are, of course, guarantees in certain specific constitutional provisions which are designed in part to protect privacy at certain times and places with respect to certain activities. Such, for example, is the Fourth* Amendment's guarantee
*[381 U.S. 509]
against "unreasonable searches and seizures." But I think it belittles that Amendment to talk about it as though it protects nothing but "privacy". To treat it that way is to give it a niggardly interpretation, not the kind of liberal reading I think any Bill of Rights provision should be given. The average man would very likely not have his feelings soothed any more by having his property seized openly than by having it seized privately and by stealth. He simply wants his property left alone. And a person can be just as much, if not more, irritated, annoyed and injured by an unceremonious public arrest by a policeman as he is by a seizure in the privacy of his office or home.

One of the most effective ways of diluting or expanding a constitutionally guaranteed right is to substitute for the crucial word or words of a constitutional guarantee another word or words, more or less flexible and more or less restricted in meaning. This fact is well illustrated by the use of the term "right of privacy" as a comprehensive substitute for the Fourth Amendment's guarantee against "unreasonable searches and seizures." "Privacy" is a broad, abstract and ambiguous concept which can easily be shrunken in meaning but which can also, on the other hand, easily be interpreted as a constitutional ban against many things other than searches and seizures. I have expressed the view many times that First Amendment freedoms, for example, have suffered from a failure of the courts to stick to the simple language of the First Amendment in construing it, instead of invoking multitudes of words substituted for those the Framers used. . . . For these reasons I get nowhere in this case by talk about a constitutional "right of privacy" as an emanation from* one or more constitutional provisions.[1] I

*[381 U.S. 510]

like my privacy as well as the next one, but I am nevertheless compelled to admit that government has a right to invade it unless prohibited by some specific constitutional provision. For these reasons I cannot agree with the Court's judgment and the reasons it gives for holding this Connecticut law unconstitutional.

This brings me to the arguments made by my Brothers HARLAN, WHITE and GOLDBERG for invalidating the Connecticut law. Brothers HARLAN[2] and WHITE would invalidate it by reliance on the Due Process Clause

1. The phrase "right to privacy" appears first to have gained currency from an article written by Messrs. Warren and (later Mr. Justice) Brandeis in 1890 which urged that States should give some form of tort relief to persons whose private affairs were exploited by others. The Right to Privacy, 4 Harv. L. Rev. 193. Largely as a result of this article, some States have passed statutes creating such a cause of action, and in others state courts have done the same thing by exercising their powers as courts of common law.

2. Brother HARLAN's views are spelled out at greater length in his dissenting opinion in *Poe v. Ullman*, 367 U.S. 497, 539-555.

of the Fourteenth Amendment, but Brother GOLDBERG, while agreeing with Brother HARLAN, relies also on the Ninth Amendment. I have no doubt that the Connecticut law could be applied in such a way as to abridge freedom of* speech and press and therefore

*[381 U.S. 511]

violate the First and Fourteenth Amendments. My disagreement with the Court's opinion holding that there is such a violation here is a narrow one, relating to the application of the First Amendment to the facts and circumstances of this particular case. But my disagreement with Brothers HARLAN, WHITE and GOLDBERG is more basic. I think that if properly construed neither the Due Process Clause nor the Ninth Amendment, nor both together, could under any circumstances be a proper basis for invalidating the Connecticut law. I discuss the due process and Ninth Amendment arguments together because on analysis they turn out to be the same thing—merely using different words to claim for this Court and the federal judiciary power to invalidate any legislative act which the judges find irrational, unreasonable or offensive.

The due process argument which my Brothers HARLAN and WHITE adopt here is based, as their opinions indicate, on the premise that this Court is vested with power to invalidate all state laws that it considers to be arbitrary, capricious, unreasonable, or oppressive, or on this Court's belief that a particular state law under scrutiny has no "rational or justifying" purpose, or is offensive to a "sense of fairness and justice."[3] If these formulas based on "natural justice," or others which mean the

3. Indeed, Brother WHITE appears to have gone beyond past pronouncements of the natural law due process theory, which at least said that the Court should exercise this unlimited power to declare state acts unconstitutional with "restraint." He now says that, instead of being presumed constitutional (see *Munn v. Illinois*, 94 U.S. 113, 123; compare *Adkins v. Children's Hospital*, 261 U.S. 525, 544), the statute here "bears a substantial burden of justification when attacked under the Fourteenth Amendment."

same thing,[4] are to prevail, they require judges to determine* what is or is not constitutional
*[381 U.S. 512]
on the basis of their own appraisal of what laws are unwise or unnecessary. The power to make such decisions is of course that of a legislative body. Surely it has to be admitted that no provision of the Constitution specifically gives such blanket power to courts to exercise such a supervisory veto over the wisdom and value of legislative policies and to hold unconstitutional those laws which they believe unwise or dangerous. I readily admit that no legislative body, state or national, should pass laws that can justly be given any* of the invidious labels invoked as
*[381 U.S. 513]
constitutional excuses to strike down state laws. But perhaps it is not too much to say that no legislative body ever does pass laws without believing that they will accomplish a sane, rational, wise and justifiable purpose. While I completely subscribe to the holding of *Marbury* v. *Madison*, 1 Cranch 137, and subsequent cases, that our Court has constitutional power to strike down statutes, state or federal, that violate commands of the Federal Constitution, I do not believe that we are granted power by the Due Process Clause or any other constitutional provision or provisions to measure constitutionality by our belief that legislation is arbitrary, capricious or unreasonable, or accomplishes no justifiable purpose, or is offensive to our own notions of "civilized standards of conduct."[5] Such an appraisal of the wisdom of legislation is an attribute of the power to make laws, not of the power to interpret them. The use by

federal courts of such a formula or doctrine or whatnot to veto federal or state laws simply takes away from Congress and States the power to make laws based on their own judgment of fairness and wisdom and transfers that power to this Court for ultimate determination—a power which was specifically denied to federal courts by the convention that framed the Constitution.[6]*
*[381 U.S. 514]
Of the cases on which my Brothers WHITE and GOLDBERG rely so heavily, undoubtedly the reasoning of two of them suports their result here—as would that of a number of others which they do not bother to name, e.g.,*
*[381 U.S. 515]
Lochner v. *New York*, 198 U.S. 45, *Coppage* v. *Kansas*, 236 U.S. 1, *Jay Burns Baking Co.* v. *Bryan*, 264 U.S. 504, and *Adkins* v. *Children's Hospital*, 261 U.S. 525. The two they do cite and quote from, *Meyer* v. *Nebraska*, 262 U.S. 390, and *Pierce* v. *Society of Sisters*, 268 U.S. 510, were both decided in opinions by Mr. Justice McReynolds which elaborated the same natural law due process philosophy found in *Lochner* v. *New York, supra,* one of the cases on which he relied in *Meyer,* along with such other long-discredited decisions, as, *e.g., Adams* v. *Tanner*, 244 U.S. 590, and *Adkins* v. *Children's Hospital, supra. Meyer* held unconstitutional, as an "arbitrary" and unreasonable interference with the right of a teacher to carry on his occupation and of parents to hire him, a*
*[381 U.S. 516]
state law forbidding the teaching of modern foreign languages to young children in the schools.[7]

---

4. A collection of the catchwords and catch phrases invoked by judges who would strike down under the Fourteenth Amendment laws which offend their notions of natural justice would fill many pages....

5. See Hand, The Bill of Rights (1958) 70:
"[J]udges are seldom content merely to annul the particular solution before them; they do not, indeed they may not, say that taking all things into consideration, the legislators' solution is too strong for the judicial stomach...."

6. This Court held in *Marbury* v. *Madison*, 1 Cranch 137, that this Court has power to invalidate laws on the ground that they exceed the constitutional power of Congress or violate some specific prohibition of the Constitution....

7. In *Meyer*, in the very same sentence quoted in part by my brethren in which he asserted that the Due Process Clause gave an abstract and inviolable right "to marry, establish a home and bring up children," Mr. Justice McReynolds also asserted the heretofore discredited doctrine that the Due Process Clause prevented States from interfering with "the right of the individual to contract." 262 U.S., at 399.

And in *Pierce*, relying principally on *Meyer*, Mr. Justice McReynolds said that a state law requiring that all children attend public schools interfered unconstitutionally with the property rights of private school corporations because it was an "arbitrary, unreasonable and unlawful interference" which threatened "destruction of their business and property." 268 U.S., at 536. Without expressing an opinion as to whether either of those cases reached a correct result in light of our later decisions applying the First Amendment to the States through the Fourteenth,[8] I merely point out that the reasoning stated in *Meyer* and *Pierce* was the same natural law due process philosophy which many later opinions repudiated, and which I cannot accept. Brothers WHITE and GOLDBERG also cite other cases, such as *NAACP* v. *Button*, 371 U.S. 415, *Shelton* v. *Tucker*, 364 U.S. 479, and *Schneider* v. *State*, 308 U.S. 147, which held that States in regulating conduct could not, consistently with the First Amendment as applied to them by the Fourteenth, pass unnecessarily broad laws which might indirectly infringe on First Amendment freedoms.[9] See *Brotherhood of Railroad Trainmen* v. *Virginia ex rel.** *Virginia State Bar*, 377 U.S. 1, 7–8.[10]

*[381 U.S. 517]

Brothers WHITE and GOLDBERG now apparently would start from this requirement that laws be narrowly drafted so as not to curtail free speech and assembly, and extend it limitlessly to require States to justify any law restricting "liberty" as my Brethren define "liberty." This

would mean at the* very least, I suppose, that

*[381 U.S. 518]

every state criminal statute—since it must inevitably curtail "liberty" to some extent—would be suspect, and would have to be justified to this Court.[11]

My Brother GOLDBERG has adopted the recent discovery[12] that the Ninth Amendment as well as the Due Process Clause can be used by this Court as authority to strike down all state legislation which this Court thinks* violates

*[381 U.S. 519]

"fundamental principles of liberty and justice," or is contrary to the "traditions and [collective] conscience of our people." He also states, without proof satisfactory to me, that in making decisions on this basis judges will not consider "their personal and private notions." One may ask how they can avoid considering them. Our Court certainly has no machinery with which to take a Gallup Poll.[13] And the scientific miracles of this age have not yet produced a gadget which the Court can use to determine

---

8. Compare *Poe* v. *Ullman*, 367 U.S., at 543–544 (Harlan, J., dissenting).

9. The Court has also said that in view of the Fourteenth Amendment's major purpose of eliminating state-enforced racial discrimination, this Court will scrutinize carefully any law embodying a racial classification to make sure that it does not deny equal protection of the laws. See *McLaughlin* v. *Florida*, 379 U.S. 184.

10. None of the other cases decided in the past 25 years which Brothers WHITE and GOLDBERG cite can justly be read as holding that judges have power to use a natural law due process formula to strike down all state laws which they think are unwise, dangerous, or irrational. . . .

---

11. Compare *Adkins* v. *Children's Hospital*, 261 U.S. 525, 568 (Holmes, J., dissenting). . .

12. See Patterson, The Forgotten Ninth Amendment (1955). Mr. Patterson urges that the Ninth Amendment be used to protect unspecified "natural and inalienable rights." P. 4. The Introduction by Roscoe Pound states that "there is a marked revival of natural law ideas throughout the world. Interest in the Ninth Amendment is a symptom of that revival." P. iii.

    In Redlich, Are There "Certain Rights. . . Retained by the People"?, 37 N.Y.U.L. Rev. 787, Professor Redlich, in advocating reliance on the Ninth and Tenth Amendments to invalidate the Connecticut law before us, frankly states:

    "But for one who feels that the marriage relationship should be beyond the reach of a state law forbidding the use of contraceptives, the birth control case poses a troublesome and challenging problem of constitutional interpretation. He may find himself saying, 'The law is unconstitutional—but why?' There are two possible paths to travel in finding the answer. One is to revert to a frankly flexible due process concept even on matters that do not involve specific constitutional prohibitions. The other is to attempt to evolve a new constitutional framework within which to meet this and similar problems which are likely to arise." *Id.*, at 798.

what traditions are rooted in the "[collective] conscience of our people." Moreover, one would certainly have to look far beyond the language of the Ninth Amendment[14] to find that the Framers vested in this Court any such awesome veto powers over lawmaking, either by the States or by the Congress. Nor does anything in the history of the Amendment offer any support for such a shocking doctrine. The whole history of the adoption of the Constitution and Bill of Rights points the other way, and the very material quoted by my Brother GOLDBERG shows that the Ninth Amendment was intended to protect against the idea that "by enumerating particular exceptions to the grant of power" to the Federal Government, "those rights which were not singled out, were intended to be assigned into the hands of the General Government [the United States], and were consequently* inse-

*[381 U.S. 520]

cure."[15] That Amendment was passed, not to broaden the powers of this Court or any other department of "the General Government," but, as every student of history knows, to assure the people that the Constitution in all its provisions was intended to limit the Federal Government to the powers granted expressly or by necessary implication. If any broad, unlimited power to hold laws unconstitutional because they offend what this Court conceives to be the "[collective]

conscience of our people" is vested in this Court by the Ninth Amendment, the Fourteenth Amendment, or any other provision of the Constitution, it was not given by the Framers, but rather has been bestowed on the Court by the Court. This fact is perhaps responsible for the peculiar phenomenon that for a period of a century and a half no serious suggestion was ever made that the Ninth Amendment, enacted to protect state powers against federal invasion, could be used as a weapon of federal power to prevent state legislatures from passing laws they consider appropriate to govern local affairs. Use of any such broad, unbounded judicial authority would make of this Court's members a day-to-day constitutional convention.

I repeat so as not to be misunderstood that this Court does have power, which it should exercise, to hold laws unconstitutional where they are forbidden by the Federal Constitution. My point is that there is no provision* of the Con-

*[381 U.S. 521]

stitution which either expressly or impliedly vests power in this Court to sit as a supervisory agency over acts of duly constituted legislative bodies and set aside their laws because of the Court's belief that the legislative policies adopted are unreasonable, unwise, arbitrary, capricious or irrational. The adoption of such a loose, flexible, uncontrolled standard for holding laws unconstitutional, if ever it is finally achieved, will amount to a great unconstitutional shift of power to the courts which I believe and am constrained to say will be bad for the courts and worse for the country. Subjecting federal and state laws to such an unrestrained and unrestrainable judicial control as to the wisdom of legislative enactments would, I fear, jeopardize the separation of governmental powers that the Framers set up and at the same time threaten to take away much of the power of States to govern themselves

---

13. Of course one cannot be oblivious to the fact that Mr. Gallup has already published the results of a poll which he says show that 46% of the people in this country believe schools should teach about birth control. Washington Post, May 21, 1965, p. 2, col. 1. I can hardly believe, however, that Brother GOLDBERG would view 46% of the persons polled as so overwhelming a proportion that this Court may now rely on it to declare that the Connecticut law infringes "fundamental" rights, and overrule the long-standing view of the people of Connecticut expressed through their elected representatives.

14. U.S. Const., Amend. IX, provides:
    "The enumeration in the Constitution, of certain rights, shall not be construed to deny or disparage others retained by the people."

15. 1 Annals of Congress 439.

which the Constitution plainly intended them to have.[16]*

*[381 U.S. 522]

I realize that many good and able men have eloquently spoken and written, sometimes in rhapsodical strains, about the duty of this Court to keep the Constitution in tune with the times. The idea is that the Constitution must be changed from time to time and that this Court is charged with a duty to make those changes. For myself, I must with all deference reject that philosophy. The Constitution makers knew the need for change and provided for it. Amendments suggested by the people's elected representatives can be submitted to the people or their selected agents for ratification. That method of change was good for our Fathers, and being somewhat old-fashioned I must add it is good enough for me. And so, I cannot rely on the Due Process Clause or the Ninth Amendment or any mysterious and uncertain natural law concept as a reason for striking down this state law. The

Due Process Clause with an "arbitrary and capricious" or "shocking to the conscience" formula was liberally used by this Court to strike down economic legislation in the early decades of this century, threatening, many people thought, the tranquility and stability of the Nation. See, *e.g., Lochner* v. *New York*, 198 U.S. 45. That formula, based on subjective considerations of "natural justice," is no less dangerous when used to enforce this Court's views about personal rights than those about economic rights. I had thought that we had laid that formula, as a means for striking down state legislation, to rest once and for all in cases like *West Coast Hotel Co.* v. *Parrish*, 300 U.S. 379; *Olsen* v. *Nebraska ex rel. Western Reference & Bond Assn.*, 313 U.S. 236, and many other* opinions.[17] See also

*[381 U.S. 523]

Lochner v. *New York*, 198 U.S. 45, 74 (Holmes, J., dissenting).

In *Ferguson* v. *Skrupa*, 372 U.S. 726, 730, this Court two years ago said in an opinion joined by all the Justices but one[18] that

> "The doctrine that prevailed in *Lochner, Coppage, Adkins, Burns,* and like cases—that due process authorizes courts to hold laws unconstitutional when they believe the legislature has acted unwisely—has long since been discarded. We have returned to the original constitutional proposition that courts do not substitute their social and economic beliefs for the judgment of legislative bodies, who are elected to pass laws."

16. Justice Holmes in one of his last dissents, written in reply to Mr. Justice McReynolds' opinion for the Court in *Baldwin* v. *Missouri*, 281 U.S. 586, solemnly warned against a due process formula apparently approved by my concurring Brethren today. He said:

"I have not yet adequately expressed the more than anxiety that I feel at the ever increasing scope given to the Fourteenth Amendment in cutting down what I believe to be the constitutional rights of the States. As the decisions now stand, I see hardly any limit but the sky to the invalidating of those rights if they happen to strike a majority of this Court as for any reason undesirable. I cannot believe that the Amendment was intended to give us *carte blanche* to embody our economic or moral beliefs in its prohibitions. Yet I can think of no narrower reason that seems to me to justify the present and the earlier decisions to which I have referred. Of course the words 'due process of law,' if taken in their literal meaning, have no application to this case; and while it is too late to deny that they have been given a much more extended and artificial signification, still we ought to remember the great caution shown by the Constitution in limiting the power of the States, and should be slow to construe the clause in the Fourteenth Amendment as committing to the Court, with no guide but the Court's own discretion, the validity of whatever laws the States may pass." 281 U.S., at 595. See 2 Holmes-Pollock Letters (Howe ed. 1941) 267-268.

17. *E.g.,* in *Day-Brite Lighting, Inc.,* v. *Missouri*, 342 U.S. 421, 423, this Court held that "Our recent decisions make plain that we do not sit as a superlegislature to weigh the wisdom of legislation nor to decide whether the policy which it expresses offends the public welfare.". . .

18. Brother HARLAN, who has consistently stated his belief in the power of courts to strike down laws which they consider arbitrary or unreasonable, see, *e.g., Poe* v. *Ullman*, 367 U.S. 497, 539-555 (dissenting opinion), did not join the Court's opinion in *Ferguson* v. *Skrupa*.

And only six weeks ago, without even bothering to hear argument, this Court overruled *Tyson & Brother* v. *Banton*, 273 U.S. 418, which had held state laws regulating ticket brokers to be a denial of due process of law.[19] *Gold** v. *DiCarlo*, 380 U.S.
*[381 U.S. 524]
520. I find April's holding hard to square with what my concurring Brethren urge today. They would reinstate the *Lochner, Coppage, Adkins, Burns* line of cases, cases from which this Court recoiled after the 1930's, and which had been I thought totally discredited until now. Apparently my Brethren have less quarrel with state economic regulations than former Justices of their persuasion had. But any limitation upon their using the natural law due process philosophy to strike down any state law, dealing with any activity whatever, will obviously be only self-imposed.[20]

In 1798, when this Court was asked to hold another Connecticut law unconstitutional, Justice Iredell said:

> "[I]t has been the policy of all the *American* states, which have, individually, framed their state constitutions since the revolution, and of the people of the *United States*, when they framed the Federal Constitution, to define with precision the objects

19. Justice Holmes, dissenting in *Tyson*, said:
"I think the proper course is to recognize that a state legislature can do whatever it sees fit to do unless it is restrained by some express prohibition in the Constitution of the United States or of the State, and that Courts should be careful not to extend such prohibitions beyond their obvious meaning by reading into them conceptions of public policy that the particular Court may happen to entertain." 273 U.S., at 446.
20. Compare *Nicchia* v. *New York*, 254 U.S. 228, 231, upholding a New York dog-licensing statute on the ground that it did not "deprive dog owners of liberty without due process of law." And as I said concurring in *Rochin* v. *California*, 342 U.S. 165, 175, "I believe that faithful adherence to the specific guarantees in the Bill of Rights insures a more permanent protection of individual liberty than that which can be afforded by the nebulous standards" urged by my concurring Brethren today.

of the legislative power, and to restrain its exercise within marked and settled boundaries. If any act of Congress, or of the Legislature of a state, violates those constitutional provisions, it is unquestionably void; though, I admit, that as the authority to declare it void is of a delicate and awful nature, the Court will never resort to that authority, but in a clear and urgent case. If, on the other hand, the Legislature of the Union, or the Legislature of any member of the Union, shall pass a law, within the* general scope of
*[381 U.S. 525]
their constitutional power, the Court cannot pronounce it to be void, merely because it is, in their judgment, contrary to the principles of natural justice. The ideas of natural justice are regulated by no fixed standard: the ablest and the purest men have differed upon the subject; and all that the Court could properly say, in such an event, would be, that the Legislature (possessed of an equal right of opinion) had passed an act which, in the opinion of the judges, was inconsistent with the abstract principles of natural justice." *Calder* v. *Bull*, 3 Dall. 386, 399 (emphasis in original).

I would adhere to that constitutional philosophy in passing on this Connecticut law today. I am not persuaded to deviate from the view which I stated in 1947 in *Adamson* v. *California*, 332 U.S. .46, 90-92 (dissenting opinion):

> "Since *Marbury* v. *Madison*, 1 Cranch 137, was decided, the practice has been firmly established, for better or worse, that courts can strike down legislative enactments which violate the Constitution. This process, of course, involves interpretation, and since words can have many meanings, interpretation obviously may result in contraction or extension of the original

purpose of a constitutional provision, thereby affecting policy. But to pass upon the constitutionality of statutes by looking to the particular standards enumerated in the Bill of Rights and other parts of the Constitution is one thing; to invalidate statutes because of application of 'natural law' deemed to be above and undefined by the Constitution is another. 'In the one instance, courts proceeding within clearly marked constitutional boundaries seek to execute policies written into the Constitution: in the other, they roam at will in the limitless* area of their own beliefs as to
*[381 U.S. 526]
reasonableness and actually select policies, a responsibility which the Constitution entrusts to the legislative representatives of the people.' *Federal Power Commission* v. *Pipeline Co.,* 315 U.S. 575, 599, 601, n. 4.''[21] (Footnotes omitted.)

The late Judge Learned Hand, after emphasizing his view that judges should not use the due process formula suggested in the concurring opinions today or any other formula like it to invalidate legislation offensive to their ''personal preferences,''[22] made the statement, with which I fully agree, that:

> ''For myself it would be most irksome to be ruled by a bevy of Platonic Guardians, even if I* knew how to choose them, which
> *(381 U.S. 527]

I assuredly do not.''[23]

So far as I am concerned, Connecticut's law as applied here is not forbidden by any provision of the Federal Constitution as that Constitution was written, and I would therefore affirm.

Mr. Justice Stewart, whom Mr. Justice Black joins, dissenting.

Since 1879 Connecticut has had on its books a law which forbids the use of contraceptives by anyone. I think this is an uncommonly silly law. As a practical matter, the law is obviously unenforceable, except in the oblique context of the present case. As a philosophical matter, I believe the use of contraceptives in the relationship of marriage should be left to personal and private choice, based upon each individual's moral, ethical, and religious beliefs. As a matter of social policy, I think professional counsel about methods of birth control should be available to all, so that each individual's choice can be meaningfully made. But we are not asked in this case to say whether we think this law is unwise, or even asinine. We are asked to hold that it violates the United States Constitution. And that I cannot do.

In the course of its opinion the Court refers to no less than six Amendments to the Constitution: the First, the Third, the Fourth, the Fifth, the Ninth, and the Fourteenth.* But the Court
*[381 U.S. 528]

---

21. *Gideon* v. *Wainwright,* 372 U.S. 335, and similar cases applying specific Bill of Rights provisions to the States do not in my view stand for the proposition that this Court can rely on its own concept of ''ordered liberty'' or ''shocking the conscience'' or natural law to decide what laws it will permit state legislatures to enact. . . .

22. Hand, The Bill of Rights (1958) 70. See note 5, *supra.* See generally *id.,* at 35-45.

23. *Id.,* at 73. While Judge Hand condemned as unjustified the invalidation of state laws under the natural law due process formula, see *id.,* at 35-45, he also expressed the view that this Court in a number of cases had gone too far in holding legislation to be in violation of specific guarantees of the Bill of Rights. Although I agree with his criticism of use of the due process formula, I do not agree with all the views he expressed about construing the specific guarantees of the Bill of Rights. Although I agree with his criticism of use of the due process formula, I do not agree with all the views he expressed about construing the specific guarantees of the Bill of Rights.

does not say which of these Amendments, if any, it thinks is infringed by this Connecticut law.

We *are* told that the Due Process Clause of the Fourteenth Amendment is not, as such, the "guide" in this case. With that much I agree. There is no claim that this law, duly enacted by the Connecticut Legislature, is unconstitutionally vague. There is no claim that the appellants were denied any of the elements of procedural due process at their trial, so as to make their convictions constitutionally invalid. And, as the Court says, the day has long passed since the Due Process Clause was regarded as a proper instrument for determining "the wisdom, need, and propriety" of state laws. Compare *Lochner* v. *New York*, 198 U.S. 45, with *Ferguson* v. *Skrupa*, 372 U.S. 726. My Brothers HARLAN and WHITE to the contrary, "[w]e have returned to the original constitutional proposition that courts do not substitute their social and economic beliefs for the judgment of legislative bodies, who are elected to pass laws." *Ferguson* v. *Skrupa, supra,* at 730.

As to the First, Third, Fourth, and Fifth Amendments, I can find nothing in any of them to invalidate this Connecticut law, even assuming that all those Amendments are fully applicable against the States.[1] It has* not even been

*[381 U.S. 529]

argued that this is a law "respecting an establishment of religion, or prohibiting the free exercise thereof."[2] And surely, unless the solemn process of constitutional adjudication is to descend to the level of a play on words, there is not involved here any abridgment of "the freedom of speech, or of the press; or the right of the people peaceably to assemble, and to petition the Government for a redress of grievances."[3] No soldier has been quartered in any house.[4] There has been no search, and no seizure.[5] Nobody has been compelled to be a witness against himself.[6]

The Court also quotes the Ninth Amendment, and my Brother GOLDBERG's concurring opinion relies heavily upon it. But to say that the Ninth Amendment has anything to do with this case is to turn somersaults with history. The Ninth Amendment, like its companion the Tenth, which this Court held "states but a truism that all is retained which has not been surrendered," *United States* v. *Darby*, 312 U.S. 100, 124, was framed by James Madison and adopted by the States simply to make clear that the adoption of the Bill of Rights did not alter the plan that* the *Federal* Government was to be a govern-

*[381 U.S. 530]

ment of express and limited powers, and that all rights and powers not delegated to it were retained by the people and the individual States. Until today no member of this Court has ever suggested that the Ninth Amendment meant anything else, and the idea that a federal court could ever use the Ninth Amendment to annul a law passed by the elected representatives of

1. The Amendments in question were, as everyone knows, originally adopted as limitations upon the power of the newly created Federal Government, not as limitations upon the powers of the individual States. But the Court has held that many of the provisions of the first eight amendments are fully embraced by the Fourteenth Amendment as limitations upon state action, and some members of the Court have held the view that the adoption of the Fourteenth Amendment made every provision of the first eight amendments fully applicable against the States. See *Adamson* v. *California*, 332 U.S. 46, 68 (dissenting opinion of Mr. Justice Black).

2. U.S. Constitution, Amendment I. To be sure, the injunction contained in the Connecticut statute coincides with the doctrine of certain religious faiths. But if that were enough to invalidate a law under the provisions of the First Amendment relating to religion, then most criminal laws would be invalidated. See, *e.g.*, the Ten Commandments. The Bible, Exodus 20:2-17 (King James).

3. U.S. Constitution, Amendment I. If all the appellants had done was to advise people that they thought the use of contraceptives was desirable, or even to counsel their use, the appellants would, of course, have a substantial First Amendment claim. But their activities went far beyond mere advocacy. They prescribed specific contraceptive devices and furnished patients with the prescribed contraceptive materials.

4. U.S. Constitution, Amendment III.

5. U.S. Constitution, Amendment IV.

6. U.S. Constitution, Amendment V.

the people of the State of Connecticut would have caused James Madison no little wonder.

What provision of the Constitution, then, does make this state law invalid? The Court says it is the right of privacy "created by several fundamental constitutional guarantees." With all deference, I can find no such general right of privacy in the Bill of Rights, in any other part of the Constitution, or in any case ever before decided by this Court.[7]

At the oral argument in this case we were told that the Connecticut law does not "conform to current community standards." But it is not the function of this Court to decide cases on the basis of community standards. We are here to decide cases "agreeably to the Constitution and laws of the United States." It is the essence of judicial* duty to subordinate our own personal

*[381 U.S. 531]

views, our own ideas of what legislation is wise and what is not. If, as I should surely hope, the law before us does not reflect the standards of the people of Connecticut, the people of Connecticut can freely exercise their true Ninth and Tenth Amendment rights to persuade their elected representatives to repeal it. That is the constitutional way to take this law off the books.[8]

---

7. Cases like *Shelton* v. *Tucker*, 364 U.S. 479 and *Bates* v. *Little Rock*, 361 U.S. 516, relied upon in the concurring opinions today, dealt with true First Amendment rights of association and are wholly inapposite here. See also, *e.g.*, *NAACP* v. *Alabama*, 357 U.S. 449; *Edwards* v. *South Carolina*, 372 U.S. 229. Our decision in *McLaughlin* v. *Florida*, 379 U.S. 184, is equally far afield. That case held invalid under the Equal Protection Clause, a state criminal law which discriminated against Negroes.

  The Court does not say how far the new constitutional right of privacy announced today extends. See, *e.g.*, Mueller, Legal Regulation of Sexual Conduct, at 127; Ploscowe, Sex and the Law, at 189. I suppose, however, that even after today a State can constitutionally still punish at least some offenses which are not committed in public.

8. See *Reynolds* v. *Sims*, 377 U.S. 533, 562. The Connecticut House of Representatives recently passed a bill (House Bill No. 2462) repealing the birth control law. The State Senate has apparently not yet acted on the measure, and today is relieved of that responsibility by the Court. New Haven Journal-Courier, Wed., May 19, 1965, p. 1, col. 4, and p. 13, col. 7.

**Monte MAULLER and Carol Mauller,
Appellants-Plaintiffs,**

v.

**CITY OF COLUMBUS, Board of
Commissioners of Bartholomew
County, Appellees-Defendants.
No. 73A01-8910-CV-418.**

Court of Appeals of Indiana,
First District.
April 4, 1990.
Transfer Denied July 6, 1990.
RATLIFF, Chief Judge.

STATEMENT OF THE CASE

Carol and Monte Mauller appeal a summary judgment entered against them in their action against the City of Columbus, Indiana (City), and the Board of Commissioners of Bartholomew County, Indiana (County Board). We affirm.

FACTS

On August 12, 1986, Carol Mauller (Carol) was playing left field in an organized softball game at the Bartholomew County Stadium, where she had previously played more than two dozen games. Prior to the game, Carol observed that dirt was removed from the area surrounding home plate and into the batter's box areas and that as a result there was a depression around home plate.

During the course of the game, after Carol had batted, she attempted to score from second base when one of her teammates hit the ball to the outfield. When she rounded third base, her coach instructed her to slide into home plate. When she slid into home plate, the rubber cleats on Carol's softball shoes caught under the edge of home plate and she suffered a double fracture and dislocation of her right lower leg and ankle.

Carol and her husband, Monte Mauller, sued the City and the County Board for negligence in failing to properly maintain the playing field in a safe condition. Bartholomew County was the owner of the property and had contracted with the City for the City's services in properly maintaining the playing field at the Bartholomew County Stadium.

The City and the County Board filed motions for summary judgment, contending there was no issue as to any material fact regarding liability and Carol had incurred the risk of injury. The trial court examined pleadings, briefs, and depositions and held the City and the County Board should be granted judgment as a matter of law because there was no genuine issue of material fact.[1] Further facts will be provided as necessary.

ISSUE

Whether the trial court erred in entering summary judgment against Carol and Monte when Carol's deposition established she was aware of the specific conditions of the home plate area, and the potential for injury, yet she intentionally slid into home plate?

DISCUSSION AND DECISION

Carol contends the trial court erred in granting summary judgment to the City and to the County Board because there was a genuine issue of material fact as to whether Carol incurred the

---

1. The City's and County Board's motions for summary judgment contained several afffirmative defenses, but their supporting memorandums, and Carol's response argued only about the defense of incurred risk. The Record before us does not contain the oral argument made to the trial court on the motions for summary judgment and the judgment contains no indication on what theory the grant of summary judgment was based. However, all parties on appeal assume the trial court granted the motions because it determined Carol had incurred the risk of injury.

risk of injury. When reviewing a grant of summary judgment, we use the same standard of review as the trial court: summary judgment is proper only when there is no issue of material fact and the moving party is entitled to judgment as a matter of law. Ind. Trial Rule 56(c); *Seiler v. Grow* (1987), Ind.App., 507 N.E.2d 628, 630, *trans. denied.* In determining whether a genuine issue of material fact exists, we consider all matters in a light most favorable to the nonmovant. *Watson Rural Water Co. v. Indiana Cities Water Corp.* (1989), Ind.App., 540 N.E.2d 131, 132, *trans. denied; Jackson v. Warrum* (1989), Ind.App., 535 N.E.2d 1207, 1210. Generally, incurred risk is a question of fact for the jury. *Kroger Co. v. Haun* (1978), 177 Ind.App. 403, 407, 379 N.E.2d 1004, 1007. "Incurred risk can be found as a matter of law *only* if the evidence is without conflict and the sole inference to be drawn is that the plaintiff (a) had actual knowledge of the specific risk, and (b) understood and appreciated the risk." *Stainko v. Tri-State Coach Lines, Inc.* (1987), Ind.App., 508 N.E.2d 1362, 1364, *trans. denied.*

The incurred risk defense requires not "merely a general awareness of a potential for mishap, but . . . demands a subjective analysis focusing on the plaintiff's actual knowledge and appreciation of the specific risk involved and voluntary acceptance of that risk." *Get-N-Go, Inc. v. Markins* (1989), Ind., 544 N.E.2d 484, 486 (citing *Beckett v. Clinton Prairie School Corp.* (1987), Ind., 504 N.E.2d 552, 554). "By definition . . . the very essence of incurred risk is the conscious, deliberate and intentional embarkation upon a course of conduct with knowledge of the circumstances." *Power v. Brodie* (1984), Ind.App., 460 N.E.2d 1241, 1243, *trans. denied* (quoting *Gerrish v. Brewer* (1979), Ind.App., 398 N.E.2d 1298, 1301).[2] Thus, we may affirm summary judgment only if the evidence, viewed in a light most favorable to Carol and Monte, supports the sole inference that she had actual knowledge of, and voluntarily intended to expose herself to, the risk of sliding into home plate when dirt was displaced creating a depression near the plate.[3]

Carol's deposition testimony establishes her team prohibited softball players from wearing metal cleats, shoes designed and recommended for playing softball are rubber soled and contain rubber cleats, and she wore such softball shoes. Carol's deposition testimony also establishes she was aware of the general risk of sliding in a softball game, she had been provided training by her coach on the proper way to slide in order to avoid an injury, and she knew a woman softball player who had injured herself sliding into a base during a previous summer. Carol's deposition also establishes she was aware, before the game of August 12, 1988, that dirt was dug out around home plate and the batter's box areas on both sides of home plate. Carol also saw during her first time at bat on August 12, 1988, that the holes around home plate had not been filled in. She had encountered similar conditions at the playing field on about five out of the thirteen occasions when she had played softball that summer. Carol stated she did not consider not playing the game due to the condition

2. Carol and Monte argue Carol must have had actual knowledge of the condition of the ground around home plate at the time she was rounding third base and attempting to score. Carol and Monte argue Carol had forgotten about the ground conditions around home plate and they cite *Gerrish* for the proposition that Carol could not intentionally incur a risk she had forgotten about. We note *Gerrish* held that, by definition, the doctrine of momentary forgetfulness is not a part of the doctrine of incurred risk. *Id.* at 1301.

3. Carol and Monte contend the specific risk of which Carol must have had actual knowledge in order to have voluntarily exposed herself to it was the risk that she could catch her rubber cleats under home plate because the dirt surrounding home plate was removed. We disagree. Knowledge of specific risk does not "connote that the victim had prescience that the particular accident and injury which in fact occurred was going to occur." *Tavernier v. Maes* (1966), 242 Cal.App.2d 532, 543, 51 Cal. Rptr. 575, 582 (action by participant in softball game for injuries sustained when sliding).

of the field around home plate. Carol's deposition establishes she knew home plate was implanted solidly in the ground and would not "give" as first, second, and third bases would when she slid into them. Finally, Carol's deposition establishes she decided to slide into home as soon as her coach instructed her when she was rounding third base. She stated she never considered not sliding when he instructed her to do so that day.

Carol's deposition thus shows that she had actual knowledge and appreciation of the specific conditions around home plate and of the general danger of sliding into home plate, and that she consciously, deliberately and intentionally slid into home plate with knowledge of those circumstances. Therefore, her deposition establishes she voluntarily accepted the risk of injury when sliding into home plate under those conditions.[4]

The only evidence before the trial court was Carol's deposition and the affidavit she presented with her response to the City's and County Board's motions for summary judgment. There was no conflict in the evidence. Conflict existed only upon the parties' interpretation of the evidence. Therefore, the trial court did not err in stating that as a matter of law Carol had incurred the specific risk of injury and that summary judgment against her was appropriate as a matter of law.[5] We affirm the trial court's grant of summary judgment in favor of the City and the County Board as against Carol and Monte.

Affirmed.

SHIELDS, P.J., and ROBERTSON, J., concur.

---

4. We agree with well-established law that "[a] person who voluntarily participates in a lawful sport, game, or contest assumes the ordinary risks of such activity." 57A Am.Jr.2d *Negligence* § 835 (1989). *See also* 4 Am.Jur.2d *Amusements and Exhibitions* § 98 (1962); and Annotation, *Liability for Injury to or Death of Participant in Game or Contest*. 7 A.L.R.2d 704(II)(a) (§ 3) (1949).

5. As the County Board notes, incurred risk is a complete defense in a negligence action involving a governmental entity because Indiana's Comparative Fault law does not apply to tort claims against governmental entities. *See* IND. CODE § 34-4-33-8.

TITLE: Right of Privacy — Griswold

REQUESTED BY: Sara Supervisor

SUBMITTED BY: Clark Robinson

DATE SUBMITTED: December 5, 1961

Memorandum

Statement of Facts:

On November 1, 1961, the Planned Parenthood League of New Haven opened a center to provide advice to married couples as to the means to prevent conception. Estelle T. Griswold was the executive director of the league. Her husband, Lee Buxton, was a physician licensed to practice medicine in the State of Connecticut and a professor at the Yale Medical School. The defendants gave information, instruction and medical advice to married couples as to the means of preventing conception. Buxton made all medical decisions as to the type of contraceptive advice that should be given. He also examined several patients. Estelle Griswold interviewed patients, took case histories, conducted group orientation sessions and described to patients the various methods of contraception.

On November 10, 1961, a warrant was issued charging C. Lee Buxton and Estelle T. Griswold with violating Sections 53-32 and 54-196 of the General Statutes of Connecticut. This indictment charged the Griswolds with "assist(ing), abet(ting), counsel(ing), cause(ing) and command(ing) certain named women to use a drug, medicinal article and instrument, for the purpose of preventing conception."

Statutes Involved

Section 53-32 provides:

> "Any person who causes any drug, medicinal article or instrument for the purpose of preventing conception shall be fined not less than fifty dollars or imprisoned not less than sixty days nor more than one year or be fined and imprisoned."

Section 54-196 provides:

> "Any person who assists, abets, counsels, causes, hires or commands another to commit any offense may be prosecuted and punished as if he were the principal offender."

Issues Presented

I.   Whether Sections 52-32 and 54-196 of the General Statutes of Connecticut constitute an unwarranted invasion of privacy in contravention of the Third, Fourth, Fifth, Ninth, and Fourteenth Amendments to the U.S. Constitution.

II.   Whether Sections 52-32 and 54-196 of the General Statutes of Connecticut deprive married couples of their ''liberty'' without due process of law as defined by the Fourteenth Amendment.

Discussion

Issue I: There is no express right of privacy in the Constitution nor have the courts yet recognized an implicit right of privacy sufficiently broad to shelter our clients' activities.

Nowhere in the Constitution -- and in particular the Bill of Rights -- is there mention of ''privacy.'' Nor is any one of the protections set forth in the Bill of Rights or elsewhere sufficiently broad to shelter, by itself, the activities of Buxton and Griswold from government interference. Nevertheless, several provisions of the Bill of Rights, read together, imply the existence of a right of privacy, at least in the views of certain constitutional commentators. Justice Brandeis, dissenting in a prohibition-era search-and-seizure case, used the phrase ''the right to be let alone'' to describe a fundamental right implicit in many provisions of the Constitution. Olmstead v. United States, 277 U.S. 438, 478 (1928). Dean Erwin Griswold of the Harvard Law School recently stated that '''[t]he right to be let alone' is the underlying theme of the Bill of Rights.'' The Right to Let Alone, 55 Nw. U. L. Rev. 216, 217 (1960).

The Bill of Rights Manifests a Concern for Privacy

A review of various provisions of the Bill of Rights supports the view that protection of personal privacy was foremost in the minds of the drafters. The First Amendment, protecting as it does religion and free expression, marks out a man's faith and thought -- the private workings of the mind -- as an area into which the state shall not intrude. The Third Amendment recognizes the sanctity of the home; no soldier may be quartered in a house without the consent of the owner or process of law.

The most resounding guarantee of privacy is that of the Fourth Amendment: there is a ''right of the people to be secure in their persons, houses, papers and effects." The Supreme Court has considered the intent and breadth of this provision in the area of police searches, and has been willing at times to read it broadly. Discussing the reach of the Fourth Amendment in 1886, the Court stated: "It is not the breaking of [the citizen's] doors, and the rummaging of his drawers, that constitutes the essence of the offense; but it is the invasion of his indefeasible right of personal security, personal liberty and private property . . ." Boyd v. United States, 116 U.S. 616, 630. And more recently, the Court has described a "right to privacy, no less important than any other right carefully and particularly reserved to the people." Mapp v. Ohio, 367 U. S. 643, 656 (1961). See also: Weeks v. United States, 232 U.S. 383 (1914); Ex Parte Jackson, 727 (1878). But see: Frank v. Maryland, 359 U.S. 360 (1959) (claim of privacy outweighed by need to protect public health); Marron v. United States, 275 U.S. 192 (1927). See generally: Beaney, The Constitutional Right to Privacy, 1962 Sup. Ct. Rev. 212. The Fifth Amendment privilege against self-incrimination likewise illustrates the concern of the drafters of the Bill of Rights for the sanctity of the individual, implicitly recognizing a private sphere that the state shall not invade.

In addition to these enumerated protections, the Bill of Rights contains a general provision that "the enumeration in the Constitution, of certain rights, shall not be construed to deny or disparage others retained by the people." U.S. Const. Amend. 9. In a recent article on the Ninth and Tenth Amendments, Professor Redlich states: "The language and history of the two amendments indicate that the rights reserved were to be of a nature comparable to the rights enumerated." Are There "Certain Rights . . . Retained by the People"?, 37 N.Y.U. L. Rev. 787, 810 (1962). Thus, the specific provisions of the Third, Fourth and Fifth Amendments, which appear to contemplate invasion, search and coercion by military and law enforcement officials were not intended to be an exclusive list of personal liberties protected by the Bill of Rights.

> The U. S. Supreme Court has given little recognition to a right of privacy outside of Fourth Amendment search and seizure cases.

In fact, review of Supreme Courts cases dealing with these protections shows only an occasional willingness of that body to extend the realm of protection beyond specific situations described in the Third and Fourth Amendments. In 1886 the Court struck down a law requiring the production of private papers, failing which the government's allegations were deemed valid. No search or seizure was actually involved, but the Court found the Fourth Amendment broad enough to cover this invasion of privacy. Boyd v. United States, 116 U.S. 616. In Siverman v. United States the Court found that driving a "spike microphone" into the wall of a suspect's house violated the Fourth Amendment, even though the actual invasion of the home was only a few inches. 365 U.S. 505 (1961). Justice Douglas, concurring, emphasized that the real evil was the invasion of privacy, not the technical trespass. Id. at 512-513.

There are also Supreme Court decisions refusing to take an expansive view of the Fourth Amendment. In a prohibition-era case, Carroll v. United States, the Court held that the warrant requirement of the Fourth Amendment did not extend to a search of an automobile, where there was probable cause, even though a search of a house based on the same information would require a warrant. 267 U.S. 132 (1925). In a 1928 wiretapping case the scope of the Fourth Amendment was fully explored by the Court. The majority opinion, authored by Chief Justice Taft, concluded that the searches referred to in the Fourth Amendment must be of physical things: papers, houses, people or property. Olmstead v. United States, 277 U.S. 438, 464. Justice Brandeis, dissenting, emphasized that constitutional provisions protecting individuals against specific government abuses must be capable of adaptation as the world changes. The Fourth and Fifth Amendments, according to Brandeis, apply to "every unjustifiable intrusion by the government upon the privacy of the individual." Id. at 478-79.

> There is no precedent that would protect the activities of our clients, but these activities fall within a "right of privacy" that some students of the Constitution have urged the courts to recognize.

The Supreme Court has not recognized a broad right of privacy implicit in the Bill of Rights, despite learned commentary and thoughtful dissenting opinions to the effect that such a right exists. Although the Connecticut statues at issue intrude into what have been traditionally the most private areas of personal life -- intimate decisions of married couples affecting procreation -- they do not offend any specific provision of the Constitution. However, because Buxton and Griswold provided contraceptive information and devices only to married couples, the facts of this case raise strong privacy concerns, more so than had counseling been provided to the public in general. Thus, if we are to urge on the courts the view that there is implicit in the Constitution a right of privacy, Buxton's and Griswold's claims would appear to fall within the zone of protection described by the constitutional scholars and dissenting Justices who believe in a constitutional "right of privacy."

Issue II: The due process clause of the Fourteenth Amendment
             provides protection of "personal liberties."

The due process clause of the Fourteenth Amendment provides that no State shall "deprive any person of life, liberty or property without due process of law . . ." The Supreme Court has held that the Fourteenth Amendment extends the protections of the First, Fourth and Fifth Amendments to the States, not merely the Federal government. Gitlow v. New York, 268 U.S. 652 (1925); Mapp v. Ohio, 367 U.S. 643 (1961). Moreover, the "liberty" interests so protected go beyond those specifically set out in the First, Fourth and Fifth Amendments. In 1952 the Court considered a case in which police entered a dwelling, seized a suspect in his bedroom and forcibly pumped his stomach to retrieve contraband he had swallowed. This bodily invasion was found by the Court to violate the due process clause -- rather than the Fourth or Fifth Amendment -- because it offended "personal immunities . . . rooted in the tradition and conscience of our people." Rochin v. California, 342 U.S. 165, 169. The rule that emerges from Rochin appears to be that some invasions of personal privacy are too shocking to be permitted under a process of law.

There is also a well-established line of cases holding that infringements of personal "liberty" by the states must meet certain requirements to be upheld under the due process clause: state laws must not be arbitrary and capricious, and must have a reasonable relationship to a legitimate legislative purpose. In 1923 the Court struck down a Nebraska law forbidding the teaching of German to pupils below the eighth grade level. The Court held that the statute impinged upon choices of parents, students and teachers so fundamental that the state could not justify this limitation. Thus, the "liberty" interest identified in the due process clause was implicated. Meyer v. Nebraska, 262 U.S. 390. In contrast, in 1934 the Court upheld a New York law setting milk prices -- arbitrarily, it was complained -- on the grounds that economic regulation is a proper legislative concern of the state. Nebbia v. New York, 291 U.S. 502. The rule that emerges from Meyer and Nebbia is that laws infringing on personal liberties require a higher degree of justification under the due process clause than laws pertaining to traditional state functions such as economic regulations.

> The state statutes restricting the activities of our clients will not meet the tests applied by the U.S. Supreme Court to laws infringing personal liberties under the "due process" clause.

The Connecticut statutes used to restrict the activities of Buxton and Griswold have serious implications for personal liberty: Buxton, a physician, is restricted in practicing his profession; his patients are deprived of information and services affecting their marital well-being and even health; Griswold, a public health counselor, is prevented from counseling her clients according to her conscience and her perception of their needs; her clients -- married couples -- are foreclosed from certain procreative decisions by action of the state. The facts in this case would require the courts to subject it to a due process analysis of the type applied in Meyer. Regulation of the sexual and procreative decisions of married couples must be neither arbitrary nor capricious and must have a demonstrable relation to a proper legislative objective.

Conclusions

> The courts have not recognized a broad right of privacy, but it is possible that they may do so.

The courts have never recognized a constitutional right to privacy broad enough to protect the activities of our clients, Buxton and Griswold. There is, however, scholarly commentary to the effect that such a right exists. More importantly, there have been and continue to be justices on the highest court who believe that such a right is implicit in the Bill of Rights. These justices have always been a minority.

> Fundamental personal liberties are protected under the due process clause.

The meaning and scope of the due process clause of the Fourteenth Amendment has been considered by the Supreme Court and the contours of due process law are well established. It would appear that the Connecticut statutes in question cannot meet the tests applied under the due process clause to laws restricting fundamental personal liberties.

Litigation strategy: we should advocate (1) due process protection of our clients' activities and (2) recognition of a right of privacy implicit in the U.S. Constitution.

We should urge, as the primary theory of our case, that the statutes in question deprive married couples of fundamental personal liberties without due process of law, as defined in the Fourteenth Amendment and the cases construing it. As a secondary matter, we should urge the court to recognize a constitutional right of privacy protecting the activities of married couples and those who assist them in intimate decisions. Success on this latter theory is not likely, however.

UNITED STATES DISTRICT COURT
SOUTHERN DISTRICT OF INDIANA
EVANSVILLE DIVISION

BARBARA F. EVANS, Personal)
Representative of the Estate of)
Roy Evans, Deceased)
)   CAUSE No. EV 64-C-85
vs.)
)
GENERAL MOTORS CORP.)

FIRST AMENDED COMPLAINT

Count I.

Plaintiff complains of the defendant and for her cause of action, alleges and says:

1. The plaintiff is a citizen and resident of the State of Indiana residing on Wortman Road in Vanderburgh County, Indiana.

2. The defendant is a corporation duly organized under and by virtue of the laws of the State of Delaware and is therefore a citizen of said state. The defendant maintains its principal place of business in Detroit, Michigan, and is therefore also a citizen of said state.

3. This controversy, exclusive of interest and costs, exceeds the sum of Ten-thousand Dollars ($10,000.00). By reason of the above and foregoing facts this court has jurisdiction of the within controversy.

4. The plaintiff is the duly appointed and acting Personal Representative of the Estate of Roy Evans, deceased, having been duly appointed and qualified by the Probate Court of Vanderburgh County, Indiana.

5. The defendant is a corporation engaged in the design, manufacture, sale, and distribution of many products including automobiles, and trucks designated and identified by the trade name "Chevrolet."

6. On the 25th day of January, 1964, Roy Evans was the owner of a certain 1961 Chevrolet Station Wagon automobile which had been designed, constructed, manufactured and assembled by the defendant, General Motors Corp.

The defendant had negligently and carelessly designed, constructed, manufactured, and assembled this automobile by incorporating in the automobile a frame known as an "X frame" which frame was weak in the middle and did not have side rails to protect drivers involved in side impact collisions. Because of this design, construction, manufacture and assembly of the "X frame" Roy Evans, as the driver of the automobile, was seated outside of the "X frame" and had no outer frame protection from side impact collisions.

7. On the 25th day of January, 1964, while Roy Evans was driving this 1961 Chevrolet Sation Wagon automobile, and as a direct and proximate result of the negligence of the defendant in designing, constructing, manufacturing and assembling of this automobile in such a manner as to render its use dangerous to life and limb, Roy Evans received fatal injuries when the left

side of said automobile collapsed into and against his person inflicting upon his body and person fatal injuries. The collapse occurred when an automobile was struck from the left side by another automobile at the intersection of St. Joseph Avenue and Schenk Roads in Vanderburgh County, Indiana, and there was no outer frame protecting him from such a side impact collision.

8. Roy Evans's automobile by reason of the "X frame" and the absence of any side guardrail type frame, perimeter type frame or any other type of outer frame protection failed to afford him protecton from side impact collision. The "X frame" did permit the collapse of the body of the Chevrolet automobile against the body and person of Roy Evans.

9. In the design, construction, manufacture, assembly and inspection of said Chevrolet automobile the defendant, General Motors Corp., knew or in the exercise of reasonable care and caution should have known that it was reasonably foreseeable that persons driving the automobile could be involved in side impact collisions such as described above and that drivers in the automobiles would be seriously injured or killed because of the absence of outer frame protection.

10. In the design, construction, manufacture, assembly, and inspection of the Chevrolet Station Wagon automobile the defendant knew or in the exercise of reasonable care and caution should have known that it was creating an unreasonable risk of causing substantial bodily harm and/or death to persons driving the automobile, including plaintiff's decedent, by not having reasonable and adequate side guardrail protection from side impact collisions.

11. This occurrence and Roy Evans's death occurred directly and proximately by reason of each one of the following negligent and careless acts or omissions to act upon the part of the defendant, General Motors Corp.:

(a) The defendant negligently made the automobile under a design which made it dangerous for persons seated in the driver's seat of the automobile, including plaintiff's decedent, when involved in side impact collisions, such as described above, because of the absence of a side guardrail type frame, perimeter type frame, or *any* other type of outer frame protection.

(b) The defendant negligently failed to exercise reasonable care in the manufacture of the automobile when it knew that its manufacture was creating an unreasonable risk of bodily harm to persons seated in the driver's seat of the automobile, including plaintiff's decedent, when involved in side impact collisions such as above described, because of the absence of a side guardrail type frame, perimeter type frame, or any other type of outer frame protection.

(c) The defendant negligently assembled the automobile with an "X frame" when it knew or in the exercise of reasonable care and caution should have known that it was assembling an unsafe automobile and was creating an unreasonable risk of bodily harm to persons seated in the driver's seat of the automobile, including plaintiff's decedent, when involved in side impact collisions because of the absence of a side guardrail type frame, perimeter type frame, or any other type of outer frame protection.

(d) The defendant negligently and carelessly failed to test and subject the design of the automobile to the effect of side impact collisions on drivers seated in the front seat of its 1961 Chevrolet Station Wagons.

(e) The defendant failed to make a test or safety check of models on the 1961 Chevrolet Station Wagon automobiles when subjected to side impact collisions, when the defendant knew or in the exercise of reasonable care and caution should have known that such tests and safety checks would have revealed the weakness of said "X frame" from side impact collisions.

(f) The defendant negligently failed to warn drivers of 1961 Chevrolet Station Wagon automobiles, including Roy Evans, that said automobile did not have a side guardrail type frame, perimeter type frame, or any other type of outer frame protection, and was weak in the middle and had no strong side frame protection to protect drivers when involved in side impact collisions.

(g) The defendant negligently and carelessly failed to install adequate safety devices in the automobile to protect drivers of the automobiles, including plaintiff's decedent, from side impact collisions.

(h) The defendant failed in the design of the automobile to plan for safety frame protection for drivers of the automobile seated in the front seat when said defendant knew or in the exercise of reasonable care and caution should have known that the automobiles could and would be subjected to side impact collisions.

(i) The defendant in the manufacture of said automobile failed to measure up to the automobile idustry's standards and to keep abreast of current scientific knowledge by using the "X frame," when the defendant knew or in the exercise of reasonable care, and caution should have known, that the auto industry was affording protection to drivers of automobiles from side impact collisions by the use of a side guardrail type frame, perimeter type frame, or any other type of outer frame protection.

12. At the time of his death, Roy Evans left surviving his wife, Barbara F. Evans, and four (4) minor children, namely, Kerry, Jeffery, Linda, and Lisa, all of whom were completely dependent upon him.

13. By reason of the above and foregoing, the plaintiff has been damaged in the sum of Four-hundred-eighty thousand Dollars ($480,000.00).

Wherefore, plaintiff demands judgment of and from the defendant in the sum of Four-hundred-eighty thousand Dollars ($480,000.00), for her costs herein, and for all further just and proper relief in the premises.

Count II.

Plaintiff for Count II of her amended complaint against the defendant states the following facts:

1. Plaintiff restates and repeats the allegations contained in Rhetorical paragraphs numbered 1, 2, 3, 4, and 5, inclusive of her Count I of her amended complaint, as is fully set forth herein.

2. Prior to the 25th day of January 1964, plaintiff purchased a 1961 Chevrolet Station Wagon automobile. That at said time said automobile was purchased there was implied warranties from the defendant, General Motors Corp., that the automobile was of merchantable quality and was reasonably fit for use as an automobile.

3. These implied warranties were breached in that the automobile was not reasonably fit for use as an automobile nor was it of merchantable quality for the following reasons:

(a) The automobile was unsafe because it had an "X frame."

(b) The automobile did not have reasonable and adequate side guardrail type frame, perimeter type frame, or any other type of outer frame protection.

4. On the 25th day of January, 1964, while Roy Evans was driving the automobile, he received fatal injuries when the left side of his said automobile collapsed into and against his body and person inflicting upon his body and person fatal injuries. The collapse occurred when said automobile was struck from the left side by another automobile at the intersection of St. Joseph Avenue and Schenk Roads in Vanderburgh County, Indiana. That his death resulted from said automobile not being reasonably fit for use as an automobile nor of merchantable quality for the reasons set forth above.

5. At the time of his death, Roy Evans left surviving his wife, Barbara F. Evans, and four (4) minor children, namely, Kerry, Jeffery, Linda, and Lisa, all of whom were completely dependent upon him.

6. By reason of the above and foregoing, the plaintiff has been damaged in the sum of Four-hundred-eighty thousand Dollars ($480,000.00).

Wherefore, plaintiff demands judgment of and from the defendant in the sum of Four-hundred-eighty thousand Dollars ($480,000.00), for her costs herein, and for all further just and proper relief in the premises.

Count III.

Plaintiff further complains of the defendant and for her Third Count of complaint herein alleges and says:

1. Plaintiff restates and repeats the allegations contained in rhetorical paragraphs 1, 2, 3, 4, and 5 inclusive of Count 1 of her Amended Complaint, as if fully set forth herein.

2. Prior to the 25th day of January, 1964, defendant had engaged in the business of manufacturing and selling a certain 1961 Chevrolet Station Wagon automobile, which automobile was then and there in a defective condition, unreasonably dangerous to the users thereof. At the time of defendant's manufacture and sale of this automobile it was expected that such automobile would reach the users thereof without substantial change from the condition in which it was sold.

3. This automobile was dangerous to users thereof in that it was then and there equipped with an "X frame" which did not have any side frame protection located outside the drivers and passengers. That the automobile reached the plaintiff's decedent, Roy Evans, the user thereof, without substantial change in the condition in which it was originally sold by the defendant with the "X frame" still incorporated in the automobile and there still being no side frame protection located outside the driver.

4. On the 25th day of January, 1964, while Roy Evans was driving the automobile, he received fatal injuries when the left side of the automobile collapsed into and against his body and person inflicting upon his body and person fatal injuries. This collapse occurred when the automobile was struck from the left side by another automobile at the intersection of St. Joseph Avenue and Schenk Road in Vanderburgh County, Indiana, and there was no frame outside his left side.

5. The defendant's placing of the automobile into the stream of commerce without frame protection located outside the driver was the reason for the same to collapse and proximately causing the injuries and death of plaintiff's decedent. By reason thereof, defendant is strictly liable to plaintiff.

6. At the time the defendant manufactured this automobile the defendant General Motors knew that it was reasonably foreseeable that users of the automobile could be involved in side impact collisions, and would be subject to more serious injuries and/or death because of the absence of outer frame protection.

Wherefore, plaintiff prays judgment of and from the defendant in the sum of $480,000.00.

(Signed)_____
Attorney for the Plaintiff
[Address]
[Telephone Number]

STATE OF INDIANA   )
) SS:
COUNT OF VANDERBURGH   )

IN THE VANDERBURGH SUPERIOR COURT

XYZ CORP., an Indiana   )
corporation,   )
                    Plaintiff,)

        v.   )   CAUSE No. 82CO2-9001-CP-0123
)
JOHN C. WASHINGTON,   )
)
        Defendant and   )
        Counterclaimant,   )
)
        v.   )
)
XYZ CORP., an Indiana   )
corporation,   )
)
        Counterclaim   )
        Defendant.   )

COUNTERCLAIM

Counterclaimant, for his cause of relief against the counterclaim defendant, states:

1. Counterclaimant and counterclaim defendant are residents of _____ County, Indiana [or incorporate allegations from plaintiff's complaint].

2. At the commencement of this suit, the counterclaim defendant was and still is indebted to counterclaimant upon a promissory note which was executed by counterclaim defendant on [date] in the sum of $_____. A true and accurate copy of the note is attached hereto as Exhibit A.

3. Counterclaimant is willing and entitled to set off against any sum found to be due and owing to the counterclaim defendant by counterclaimant in this action.

WHEREFORE, counterclaimant requests judgment against the counterclaim defendant in the sum of $_____, for setoff of this amount against counterclaim defendant's claim if he prevails, for the costs of this action, and for all other appropriate relief.

(Signed)_____
Attorney for Counterclaimant
[Address]
[Telephone Number]

UNITED STATES DISTRICT COURT
SOUTHERN DISTRICT OF INDIANA
EVANSVILLE DIVISION

BARBARA F. EVANS, Personal)
Representative of the Estate of)
Roy Evans, Deceased)
)
)   CAUSE No. EV 64-C-85
         vs.   )
)
GENERAL MOTORS CORP.)

Defendant's Answer to First Amended Complaint.

In response to the allegations of Count I of Plaintiff's Amended Complaint, defendant states:

1. Defendant admits the allegations contained in rhetorical paragraph 1 of Plaintiff's Amended Complaint.

2. Defendant admits the allegations contained in rhetorical paragraph 2 of Plaintiff's Amended Complaint.

3. Defendant admits plaintiff is demanding defendant pay to her an amount in excess of $10,000, exclusive of interest and costs, which defendant denies, and by reason of these facts this Count has jurisdiction of this case.

4. Defendant is without information sufficient to form a belief as to the truth of the allegations contained in rhetorical paragraph 4 of Plaintiff's Amended Complaint.

5. Defendant admits the allegations contained in rhetorical paragraph 5 of Plaintiff's Amended Complaint.

6. Defendant admits that on January 25, 1964, Roy L. Evans was the owner of a 1961 Chevrolet Station Wagon automobile that had been designed, constructed, manufactured and assembled by defendant, and that the automobile had an ''X frame,'' but denies allegations of rhetorical paragraph 6 not specifically admitted.

7. Defendant denies the allegations contained in rhetorical paragraph 7 of Plaintiff's Amended Complaint.

8. Defendant denies the allegations contained in rhetorical paragraph 8 of Plaintiff's Amended Complaint.

9. Defendant denies the allegations contained in rhetorical paragraph 9 of Plaintiff's Amended Complaint.

10. Defendant denies the allegations contained in rhetorical paragraph 10 of Plaintiff's Amended Complaint.

11. Defendant denies the allegations contained in rhetorical paragraph 11 of Plaintiff's Amended Complaint.

12. Defendant is without information sufficient to form a belief as to the truth of the allegations contained in rhetorical paragraph 12 of Plaintiff's Amended Complaint.

In response to the allegations of Count II of Plaintiff's Amended Complaint, defendant states:

1. Defendant incorporates by reference its answers to rhetorical paragraphs 1, 2, 3, 4 and 5 of its answer to Count I of Plaintiff's Amended Complaint.

2. Defendant admits that prior to the 25th day of January, 1964, plaintiff or plaintiff's husband, Roy L. Evans, purchased a 1961 Chevrolet Station Wagon automobile, but not from the defendant or any authorized dealer of defendant, and denies that there was any implied warranty from defendant to plaintiff of any character.

3. Defendant denies the allegations contained in rhetorical paragraph 3 of Plaintiff's Amended Complaint.

4. Defendant denies the allegations contained in rhetorical paragraph 4 of Plaintiff's Amended Complaint.

5. Defendant is without information sufficient to form a belief as to the truth of the allegations contained in rhetorical paragraph 5 of Plaintiff's Amended Complaint.

6. Defendant denies the allegations contained in rhetorical paragraph 6 of Plaintiff's Amended Complaint.

First Affirmative Defense.

Defendant, for its first affirmative defense to Plaintiff's Amended Complaint, and to each Count thereof, states that neither Count of Plaintiff's Amended Complaint states a claim against defendant on which relief can be granted.

Second Affirmative Defense.

1. Within Vanderburgh County, Indiana, there is a wide, paved, public highway of the county running in a general direction of north and south, which is commonly known and designated as St. Joseph Avenue. St. Joseph Avenue is intersected at right angles by a county road, which is commonly known and designated as Schenk Road. Schenk Road forms a ''T'' intersection with St. Joseph Avenue.

2. On the 25th day of January, 1964, at approximately 4:15 p.m., Roy L. Evans was driving his 1961 Chevrolet Station Wagon in a southwesterly direction on St. Joseph Avenue and was in the process of making a left-hand turn off Schenk Road toward the south on St. Joseph Avenue, at which time Alan Ray Tolley, a 17-year-old youth, was driving a 1957 Ford Tudor Sedan automobile in a northerly direction on St. Joseph Avenue at a high rate of speed.

3. At that time and place Roy L. Evans was negligent in the operation of his 1961 Chevrolet Station Wagon, as a result of which negligence, or combined with the negligence of Alan Ray Tolley, while such 1961 Chevrolet Station Wagon was in the process of entering St. Joseph Avenue and in the process of turning to the south it was struck in the left side by the 1957 Ford with such force that the 1961 Chevrolet Station Wagon was driven fifty (50) feet in a northwesterly direction from the point of the collision and the 1957 Ford Tudor was driven one hundred (100) feet in a northerly direction from the point of impact.

4. The death of Roy L. Evans was the direct result of:
   a. His negligent failure to look for other vehicles using St. Joseph Avenue as he approached and drove onto that through highway;
   b. His negligent entering onto St. Joseph Avenue at a time when in the exercise of reasonable care it would have been obvious that it was unsafe to have done so, and his negligent failure to take any steps to avoid being struck by the automobile of Alan Ray Tolley;
   c. His negligent failure to yield the right of way to the automobile driven by Alan Ray Tolley;
   d. His negligent failure to stop and exercise reasonable care before and on entering St. Joseph Avenue as required by law.

5. The death of Roy L. Evans was the direct result of the negligence of Alan Ray Tolley, to wit:
   a. That Alan Ray Tolley at said time and place negligently drove the Ford automobile, which he was then and there driving at a high and dangerous rate of speed of seventy (70) to seventy-five (75) miles per hour, which rate of speed was greater than was reasonable and prudent at the time and place.

    b. That Alan Ray Tolley negligently and carelessly failed to keep a proper lookout for traffic at the intersection and on St. Joseph Avenue including the automobile in which plaintiff's decedent was driving.

    c. That Alan Ray Tolley negligently and carelessly failed and neglected to keep the Ford automobile under his reasonable and proper control at the time and place so as to have avoided the collision.

6. The only proximate cause of the collision and death of Roy L. Evans was such negligence on the part of Roy L. Evans or Alan Ray Tolley or both of them.

Third Affirmative Defense.

1. On February 21, 1964 the plaintiff, Barbara F. Evans, as the personal representative of the estate of Roy L. Evans, deceased, filed a complaint for the same damages sued for here in the amount of $600,000 against such Alan Ray Tolley and Wilburn D. Tolley, the father of Alan Ray Tolley, in the Vanderburgh Circuit Court, alleging that the collision in question and the death of Roy L. Evans was the direct and proximate result of negligence on the part of Alan Ray Tolley, a certified copy of which "Complaint for Damages" is attached hereto marked Exhibit A.

2. Some time after February 21, 1964, the exact date being unknown to defendant, a complete settlement of the claim of this plaintiff for the alleged wrongful death of Roy L. Evans against Alan Ray Tolley and Wilburn D. Tolley was finally and completely settled by the payment of $20,000 by Alan Ray Tolley and Wilburn D. Tolley to the plaintiff, and plaintiff Barbara F. Evans executed at such time, in consideration for such $20,000, settlement papers constituting a complete release of Alan Ray Tolley and Wilburn D. Tolley. Barbara F. Evans, having already recovered for the wrongful death of her husband Roy L. Evans, is now barred from seeking a second recovery or additional recovery from this defendant.

Wherefore, defendant prays for judgment and for all other proper relief.

Fourth Affirmative Defense.
(To All Paragraphs of Complaint.)

1. For a long number of years prior to January 25, 1964, thousands of drivers and passengers in automobiles of all kinds, makes and models, with all kinds of frames and body constructions, have been injured or killed each year in automobile accidents in the State of Indiana and throughout the United States.

2. Such accidents, injuries, and deaths have been well publicized in newspapers, on the radio and television and elsewhere, and the fact of their occurrence has been common knowledge. Plaintiff's husband, therefore, had knowledge that drivers and passengers were being so injured and killed in such accidents involving all kinds of automobiles.

3. In operating his 1961 Chevrolet Station Wagon on the public streets and highways, plaintiff's husband necessarily assumed the risks of being involved in such accidents including the risk of being struck by another automobile, such as the Ford that actually struck him, traveling at a high rate of speed and with force sufficient to cause death.

UNITED STATES DISTRICT COURT
SOUTHERN DISTRICT OF INDIANA
EVANSVILLE DIVISION

BARBARA F. EVANS, Personal)
Representative of the Estate of)
Roy Evans, Deceased)
)   NO. EV 64-C-85
)
vs.)
)
)
GENERAL MOTORS CORP.)

Written Interrogatories to be Answered by the Defendant, General Motors Corp.

You are hereby notified to answer under oath the next numbered interrogatories from 1 to 99, inclusive, as set out below, within fifteen days from the time service is made upon you, in accordance with Rule 33 of the Federal Rules of Civil Procedure:

Interrogatory No. 1.

Do you maintain production records that indicate the date that a 1961 Chevrolet Station Wagon Model No. 1835 bearing Manufacturer's Identification Number 11835F138206 was manufactured and distributed? If so, state:

    (a) The date that you began manufacturing models of this type.
    (b) The location of the plants where models of this type were produced.
    (c) The location of the plant where this particular automobile was manufactured.
    (d) The date that this particular automobile was manufactured.
    (e) The date it was shipped to a retail distributor.
    (f) The name and address of the retail distributor to whom it was shipped.
    (g) The name and address of the purchaser of said automobile from the retailer.
    (h) The names and addresses of those persons who have the care, custody and control of production records of this automobile.
    (i) The records and how they are described which the defendant has as to this particular automobile.

Interrogatory No. 2.

Did the 1961 Chevrolet Station Wagon Model No. 1836 bearing Identification Number 11835F138206 include in its assembly what is commonly known as an "X frame"? If not, state the kind and type of frame this vehicle contained. (If the answer to this interrogatory is in the negative, all interrogatories subsequent hereto are amended to change said interrogatories from "X frame" to the kind of frame given in defendant's answer thereto).

Interrogatory No. 3.

How many models of this type of automobile did the defendant manufacture?

Interrogatory No. 4.

Did all of the defendant's 1961 Chevrolet Station Wagons have an "X frame"? If not, state:
    (a) The kind of frame used.
    (b) The number which did not use the "X frame."
    (c) The reason for using a different type of frame.
    (d) The kind of frame used in place of the "X frame."
    (e) The reason for using a different type of frame.

Interrogatory No. 5.

What are the names and addresses of each person who participated in the original design of the "X frame" used in the 1961 Chevrolet Station Wagon?

Signed_____
        Attorney for Plaintiff
        [Address]
        [Telephone Number]

LAW OFFICES OF
SMART & WHITE
One Schoolhouse Square
Suite 23
P.O. Box 1119
Evansville, IN 47708-1234

January 8, 1991

Grant and Pawlyk
Post Office Box 502
Evansville, IN 47708-1234

RE: Our Client: Alex Martin
     Insured: Juanita White
     D/Incident: 4/1/90

Gentlemen

Mr. Smart and I are interested in pursuing settlement discussions concerning the claim of our client, Alex Martin. I have taken the liberty of supplying you with medical information, medical bills, and photographic information concerning Mr. Martin's injuries. We would like to give you and XYZ Insurance Company an opportunity to compromise and settle this claim prior to the incurrence of defense costs, and settle this claim for the policy limits.

Facts of the Collision: On April 1, 1990, Alex Martin was the owner and operator of a 1985 Buick Regal sedan. He was traveling in a southerly direction on Pennsylvania Avenue. As he approached the parking lot of Bailey's Tavern in Evansville, Indiana, Juanita White, pulled directly into the path of his vehicle, intending to execute a left turn. She completely blocked Mr. Martin's lane of travel, and he had nowhere to go to avoid the collision.

Immediately after the collision, your insured stated that she looked both ways but did not see Mr. Martin. She acknowledged that she pulled directly into his path and that the accident was her fault. Sometime later someone told her that Mr. Martin may have been drinking, and this was the first time she attributed any fault to Alex Martin.

As your client's vehicle exited into his lane of travel, Mr. Martin instinctively veered to the left. There was not sufficient time to do anything else. The right front of your client's vehicle struck the right passenger side of the Martin vehicle, causing it to go out of control. I have enclosed two of the official police photographs depicting this damage.

I have also spoken with Justin Williams, the passenger who was riding with

Mr. Martin. He verified that your client pulled directly into the path of the Martin vehicle. He stated that Mr. Martin's only options were to strike the truck in the driver's side in a "T-bone" configuration, or to try to avoid the collision by trying to steer to the left of the truck. He informed me that no matter what course of action Mr. Martin took, the collision was inevitable because of the actions of Ms. White.

Injuries Sustained by Alex Martin: I have enclosed copies of the medical records that detail Mr. Martin's very severe injuries. As you can see from the enclosed records, he had a gaping laceration on his forehead and a fractured jaw. His most severe injury was a "burst fracture" of one of the vertebrae in his lower back, L1. The fracture of the vertebra caused portions of the bone fragments to be driven in to the spinal canal and damage the area of the spinal cord known as the cauda equina.

Mr. Martin was taken by ambulance to the Ames Community Hospital. He was seen and treated by Dr. Banpote Saw. Records show that he had a deep laceration on his forehead and a fracture of his left mandible as well as the fracture of the L1 vertebral body. Dr. Saw repaired the severe laceration over the forehead. Fixation devices were placed on his teeth and his jaw was wired shut. He continued to have difficulty with his lower extremities, i.e., weakness of both legs and numbness of his legs below the knee area. He was also complaining of severe pain.

Dr. Saw contacted Dr. Watson Lane, who maintains offices in Evansville, Indiana. Dr. Lane's consultation notes are enclosed. The consultation notes show that Mr. Martin had numbness below the knees and he was unable to urinate. The doctor felt that a CT Scan should be performed. Sensory tests showed numbness over the foot areas and very poor ability to distinguish sensations in the legs. The x-rays showed a fracture of L1 with a large bone protrusion into the spinal canal. The doctor felt it was quite probable that Mr. Martin would require surgery on his back.

Dr. Lane had Mr. Martin transferred to Black Hospital for surgery. Copies of those records are also enclosed. Suffice it to say the automobile collision crushed his vertebra and caused damage to his spinal cord, Dr. Mary Lamb, an orthopedic surgeon, was also contacted, and she and Dr. Lane performed surgery on Mr. Martin. Those operative notes are enclosed. As you can see from the records, a very lengthy surgery, over five hours, was performed. The fracture was so severe that metal bars known as Harrington Rods were placed in his spine. I have enclosed a page from a medical encyclopedia that describes and depicts Harrington Rods.

The bone spurs and chips caused a compression at the bottom of the spinal cord. This is the area known as the cauda equina. I have also enclosed a diagram depicting the location of the cauda equina. As you can see, the cauda equina divides into many nerves that extend into the pelvis and the lower extremities.

After the surgery, Mr. Martin was a paraplegic. He was unable to walk and had numbness throughout his entire body below the level of the fracture. He was unable to urinate. The surgery was quite lengthy and complicated, causing him much pain during his rehabilitation process.

As with all spinal cord injuries, the physicians did not know the extent of Mr. Martin's paralysis nor the extent of his recovery. After surgery, he was referred to physical therapy. When he was released from the hospital, he was unable to walk without using a back brace (depicted in two photographs) and a walker.

After he healed from his surgery, Mr. Martin continued follow-up treatment with Dr. Lane. Dr. Lane referred him to Community Hospital for in-depth physical therapy. I invite you to review the physical therapy notes. They show that he began his therapy in July of 1990 and continued until the end of November 1990. The physical therapist noted some improvement in certain muscle groups.

I know that it is quite difficult to review medical records and obtain an accurate description of the injuries suffered by a person. Because of that difficulty, I have taken the liberty of enclosing with this letter approximately five minutes of videotape that depicts Alex Martin as he is today. When Mr. Martin was released from physical therapy, he was instructed to perform exercises a minimum of three times per day in order to strengthen his legs and to learn how to walk. He does perform those exercises, sometimes five to six times per day. Mr. Martin has noticed absolutely no improvement in his walking, his standing, or his leg strength in the past two months. He has continued to visit with Dr. Lane on a regular basis. Dr. Lane, as of Mr. Martin's last visit in September 1990, feels that there has been little or no improvement.

You will note from the videotape that Mr. Martin is unable to walk on his toes. The doctor has felt that the weakness in his feet has remained unchanged for the past several months. He has difficulty standing still. He has a tendency to lose his balance and needs external support. You will note from the tape that he stands in a very rigid manner. This is because of the Harrington Rods. I have also enclosed several still photographs that depict the surgical sites, and you can see that the scars are quite extensive.

Mr. Martin is unable to run. I have asked him to do so and invite you to review the tape. It is a very sad sight to see. Mr. Martin is thankful that he is able to walk, but from a review of the tape, it is obvious that he is basically unemployable in many types of jobs, is unable to run, is unable to walk fast, and has much difficulty.

The tape does not show his additional difficulties. He still has severe pain in his back. He becomes physically exhausted after twenty minutes of exercises. After he does his physical therapy for approximately twenty minutes, he must lie down for forty to sixty minutes. Once he regains his strength, he is able to continue his physical therapy exercises for another twenty minutes. It totally and completely exhausts him to do his exercises three to five times per day.

Mr. Martin is unable to urinate. He has to utilize a catheter, which as you know is a long plastic tube. It is boiled in order to sterilize it, coated with medicated oil, inserted in his penis through his ureters and into his bladder. He must then tap himself in the side until the urine flow starts. After his bladder is empty, he must take the catheter out, boil it in water to kill all of the germs, and wait until he needs to urinate again. This is quite a degrading experience for this young man. Mr. Martin also has problems with his bowels. If he is unable to reach a bathroom immediately upon feeling his bowels move, he soils himself. This has happened to him on several occasions while riding in automobiles with friends, while sleeping, and while walking near his home for exercise.

Another unfortunate incident of his injuries is the fact that he is now having sexual problems. He is able to attain an erection, but since the injuries he has been unable to have an orgasm. I have enclosed information from a medical encyclopedia that discusses this unfortunate but common occurrence in people with spinal cord injuries.

Medical Specials of Alex Martin: I have enclosed the medical bills of Alex Martin. They are as follows:

Dr. Banpote Saw	4/1/90 - 5/1/90	$ 665.00
Evansville EAS	4/1/90	1,902.30
Ames Community Hosp.	4/1/90 - 4/3/90	3,681.54
Dr. Watson Lane	4/2/90 - 9/15/90	3,163.00
Ames Ambulance	4/3/90	175.00
Black Hospital	4/3/90 - 4/20/90	16,869.85
Dr. Mary Lamb	4/4/90 - 4/6/90	5,056.00
Ames Med. Radio	4/4/90 - 4/6/90	336.00
Ames Physical Therapy	7/15/90 - 11/8/90	700.85
Ames Physical Therapy	11/23/90	36.00

TOTAL MEDICAL SPECIALS....................................$ 30,785.54

You will note from the office notes of Dr. Watson Lane that he has recommended foot orthotics with a platarflexion spring. These are basically braces that fit onto specially made shoes. The specially made shoes will then bend forward because of springs. Mr. Martin has lost all use of the muscles that allow the foot to go up and down. Consequently, Dr. Lane feels these shoes are needed. Mr. Martin has been informed that the shoes cost approximately $4,000.

From a review of the medical bills, medical records, photographs and videotape, it is quite obvious that this gentleman has sustained severe, excruciating, and permanent injuries. He is left with multiple scarring on his face, his back, and his hip area. He has constant pain in his back and has little or no use of his legs. He cannot function sexually and cannot urinate. He has noticed no change in his walking ability for at least two months. It physically exhausts him to do his exercises.

<u>Settlement Demand</u>: We have been authorized by Mr. Martin to compromise and settle his claim for bodily injuries for the sum of $500,000 or the single limits of the policies of insurance that were in full force and effect covering Juanita White and the vehicle she was operating. It is my understanding that you have informed Mr. Smart that the applicable coverage in this case is $25,000 on Ms. White and $25,000 on the vehicle she was driving for total insurance benefits of $50,000.

Mr. Martin has sustained devastating injuries. There is insufficient insurance to compensate him for his injuries in this case. Please be advised that the offer to compromise and settle the claim for the applicable policy limits will remain open for a period of thirty (30) days from the date of this letter. In order to compromise and settle the claim on those terms, we will need not only your drafts but also certified copies of the policies of insurance including the declaration sheets. We will also need affidavits executed by your insured stating that there are not additional insurance policies that cover this accident, the vehicle involved, or Ms. White.

Please be advised that the videotape and the photographs enclosed are being lent to you with the understanding that they remain my property and will be surrendered to me upon my request.

If there are any items that I have in my file that may aid you in the evaluation of this claim, do not hesitate to call and I will see that they are provided. Thank you for your consideration in this matter. I will look forward to hearing from you.

Very truly yours

Sam White
Attorney At Law

SW/jw

Enclosures

LAW OFFICES OF
SMITH, TOLENTINO & SHORT
402 Williamson Blvd.
Evansville, IN 47708-1234

November 7, 1990

UNIVERSAL INSURANCE SOCIETY
One Bank Plaza
Suite 1187
P.O. Box 7007
Hartford, Connecticut 46240-7007

Attn: Mr. James South

Re: Claim Number: 33456
      Insured: Noland Sandefur
      Claimants: Jessica and Donald Morely
      Date of Loss: January 3, 1990

Dear James

On Thursday, November 6, 1990, I met with the insured, Noland Sandefur.
Based on my meeting with the insured, and a review of the investigation
file, I submit the following preliminary report concerning this case.
Please note the comments and suggestions contained at the end of the report
for your consideration.

FACTS

On January 3, 1990 at 2:55 p.m. Noland Sandefur completed his school day at
Harrison High School on the east side of Newburgh, Indiana. Noland went to
his 1980 Olds Cutlass and left school to go home. In the car with him was
Sean Clark, son of Frederick Clark, who resides at 203 South Garfield
Avenue, telephone 555-1678. Noland took some of the back roads to the west
of the high school to arrive at the intersection of Tyler and South Lake
Road. Tyler is a two (2) way, two (2) lane residential street that runs
east-west and dead ends to the east into another north-south road of homes
and to the west into South Lake Road. South Lake Road is the main north-
south artery on the east side of Newburgh, which provides access to several
fast food restaurants and shopping malls/stores. South Lake is actually
five (5) lanes, two (2) north, two (2) south, and one (1) center turn lane
for traffic going both north and south. Traffic is light on Tyler, but is
almost always heavy on South Lake Road; and, if the traffic is not heavy on
South Lake Road, there are always several cars and trucks turning off and
onto this Road.

As Noland arrived at the intersection of Tyler and South Lake Road he
stopped at the stop sign that controls the traffic coming onto South Lake.
He had the front of his car partially sticking into the east lane of the

UNIVERSAL INSURANCE SOCIETY
Mr. James South
November 7, 1990
Page 2

north lanes of South Lake, as his view to the north was blocked by cars
parked on a car lot on the northeast corner of Tyler and South Lake. Also,
his view to the south was partially blocked by a ceiling fan and lighting
retailer located on the southeast corner of Tyler and South Lake. Noland
watched for oncoming traffic from the south, while his passenger, Sean
Clark, was watching the traffic coming from the north. As Noland and Sean
waited for the traffic to clear, a white delivery van or truck in the east
lane of the north bound lane of South Lake, approached the intersection
with its turn signal on indicating its intention to turn right or east onto
Tyler. Sean then informed Noland that there was no traffic coming from the
north, and Noland saw no traffic coming from the south other than the slow-
ing truck with its turn signal on, so he glanced north and then proceeded to
pull across the north bound lanes of South Lake and into the center turn
lane to go south. As his vehicle was almost all the way into the center lane
going south, the driver's side rear of his car was struck behind the wheel
well opening by the driver's side front of a car driven by Louise Johnson
and occupied by her mother-in-law, Jessica Morely.

It seems that the 1972 Olds Cutlass driven by Mrs. Johnson was directly
behind the delivery truck and was not visible to Noland as he pulled from
the intersection. Further, Noland describes the impact as being rather
mild and not doing much damage to either car (i.e., each car was able to be
driven from the accident scene; the impact did not really move Noland's
car). As soon as Noland's car came to a rest, he got out of his car and went
to the Johnson car a few feet away. Louise Johnson was having difficulty
opening her driver's side door, and it was at this time Noland noticed Ms.
Johnson had a passenger in the front seat (Jessica Morely). Also present in
the car were an infant in a car seat in the rear seat of the car and a child
seated on Ms. Morely's lap in the front seat. The child seated on Ms.
Morely's lap was crying, and it was apparent to Noland that Ms. Morely was
trying to comfort the child. Noland did notice that Ms. Morely was not wearing a shoulder harness while seated in the car, but that she could have had
a lap belt on as he could not see her lap since the child was sitting on it.

When Louise Johnson got out of her car, Noland told her that he ''couldn't
see her'' when he pulled out. The only comment Noland recalls Ms. Johnson
made was ''thanks a lot.'' They then went to call the Newburgh Police
Department. About twenty (20) minutes later, the police arrived, had them
move their cars, and then talked to Louise Johnson and Noland in the police
cruiser. Responding to the officer's question, Louise stated that everyone
in her car was okay. The officer then filled out a short form police report.
He told Noland the accident was Noland's fault, but he did not issue a
ticket to Noland, and he let the parties go. During the entire time, Ms.
Morely stayed in the vehicle of Louise Johnson.

UNIVERSAL INSURANCE SOCIETY
Mr. James South
November 7, 1990
Page 3

After the accident, Noland and Sean Clark were contacted by an investigator
employed by plaintiff's counsel and each of them did give a recorded statement to the investigator. Neither Noland nor Sean has a copy of his
statement.

MEDICAL EXPENSES AND INJURIES

The medical expenses incurred by Ms. Morely relating to the accident are
primarily for diagnostic purposes and noninvasive treatment. Ms. Morely
has not been admitted to the hospital and has not had any surgery as a
result of the accident.

A. Protestant Hospital Emergency Room:

Ms. Morely first sought medical care on the same day as the accident
(January 3, 1990) at the Protestant Hospital Emergency Room. She was at the
Emergency Room from 10:24 p.m. to 11:27 p.m. Her chief complaints were of
neck pain, right knee pain, and headache. X-rays of the right knee and cervical spine were taken. She was also noted to have multiple contusions. The
history she gave as contained in the nurses' notes was of being in a motor
vehicle accident at 2:30 p.m. where she was a "restrained" passenger in a
vehicle that was hit by another car in the side. She said she had been
"thrown around in" the car but did not lose consciousness, and also gave a
"Hst cervical spine surg" or history of cervical spine surgery. Her
neurological examination was normal and she had "no obvious --------" (I am
assuming this means no obvious injury). The x-ray findings were normal except for some "reversal of the usual cervical lordotic curve" the
significance of which was listed as "uncertain." The doctor discharged her
with prescriptions for Flexeril and Naprosyn (muscle relaxant and an-
tiinflammatory), and told her to apply heat to her neck, rest the weekend,
and be rechecked at Protestant or with her family doctor, Ronald Hawk, if
needed after three (3) days.

Her primary care has been provided by Family Practitioner Ronald Hawk, M.D.
However, she has also been seen since the accident by Anthony Jacoby, M.D.,
an internist who holds himself out to be a pain specialist, and a
neurologist, Steven Saint, M.D.

B. Ronald Hawk, M.D.:

1. Treatment before the accident:

Ms. Morely has apparently been a patient of Doctor Hawk's for some time. The
most complete copy of Hawk's office notes that we have show he has seen her
at least since November 23, 1988. Before this accident, on January 23, 1989
she complained of "constant frontal HA (headache) under stress -- husband

UNIVERSAL INSURANCE SOCIETY
Mr. James South
November 7, 1990
Page 4

in hospital, doesn't sleep well. Plan -- Elavil 25 mg - 50 - (?)." On January 19, 1989, she was also prescribed the painkiller Darvocet; and on February 3, 1989 she reported that her "HA's (headaches) not as bad no (?)," but she was still taking the antidepressant Elavil at this time.

2. Treatment since the accident:

Hawk's office notes establish he treated Ms. Morely with ultrasound, heat, injections and medication following the accident from January 24, 1990, at least until June 27, 1990. During this time, the patient was seen by Dr. Jacoby on February 9, 1990 (it is unclear whether this was of her own doing or a referral by Dr. Hawk), was scheduled to see Dr. Jacoby again on April 11 to have a thermogram performed on April 27, 1990, and to be seen by Dr. Saint on April 18, 1990. Two (2) MRIs have been performed at Protestant Hospital, one on May 19, 1990, at 2:30 p.m. for her lower back (i.e., L4-5, L5-S1 vertebrae) and one on May 20, 1990 at 1:00 p.m. for her neck (i.e., C4-C7 vertebrae). The office notes of Hawk for May 14, 1990 say that Dr. Jacoby concluded the thermogram was "abnormal" and an MMPI was "abnormal" showing "depression" and "somatic form pain disorder." The MRI results were both negative for ruptured discs according to a May 23, 1990, office note. Her symptoms during the time Hawk has treated her ranged from acute pain to being pain free. She experienced tremendous relief from pain after obtaining and using her TENS unit in May of this year.

A letter from Hawk dated July 20, 1990, says that he started treating Ms. Morely on January 16, 1990. However, the earliest office note we have is January 24, 1990. This letter chronicles the changing nature of the patient's symptoms during the time he has seen her (headache and neck pain; sacroiliac back pain; back pain and headaches; dysesthesia of the right thumb).

C. Anthony Jacoby, M.D.:

Doctor Jacoby's February 9, 1990, letter says there was no sign of injury according to the lumbosacral spine and left hip x-rays; but that he believed as a result of the accident she was having back, neck, hip and headache pain that could be treated with medicine, injections, exercise, education, and "psychophysiologic reactivation." A later letter, dated May 2, 1990, refers to thermography having been performed on Ms. Morely which "objectify the patient's subjective complaints." An MRI, EMG and nerve conduction study of the right and possibly left arm were then recommended by Jacoby. Jacoby's last letter was dated August 29, 1990, and based on her history and "psychological testing" he gives her a nineteen percent (19%) whole body partial permanent impairment based on problems "involving neck myofascial pain, headaches associated with trauma, occipital and/or radicular neuralgia as well as significant psychological factors affecting her physical condition."

UNIVERSAL INSURANCE SOCIETY
Mr. James South
November 7, 1990
Page 5

D. Steven Saint, M.D.:

Steven Saint's consultation letter reviews the objective testing done on Ms. Morely, which was found to be normal, and then concludes:

> She does have tenderness of the occipital nerve on the right side, causing severe pain over the suboccipital and occipital area on the right side.

> Impression: This patient does have an occipital neuralgia as manifested by the tender right occipital nerve. Secondly, she has a sensory loss which does not conform to any dermatome pattern; but it is more in keeping with a psychophysiologic reaction or conversion reaction, which could also account for the heavy feeling in the right arm and difficulty using it also.

> My recommendation at this time is strictly conservative treatment. I have no objections to heat or some ultrasound; as far as subjective treatment, I do not feel that she is a candidate for multiple injections at trigger points. She also just picked up a TENS unit and I have no objection if this gives her some relief. I think more important, however, that she remain on some type of a muscle relaxer, perhaps an antidepressant or nerve type pill; and I think that as soon as she gets back to her normal activities the better off she will be. I think this is more of an emotional type problem rather than a true physical injury.

E. Medical Expenses:

The documented out-of-pocket medical expenses appear to be, according to plaintiffs' counsel's most recent calculation, $9,245.70, itemized as follows: Anthony Jacoby, M.D. $565.00; Ronald Hawk, M.D. $5,465.00; Ambulance (City of Newburgh) $161.75; Meny's Pharmacy $155.90; Paul's Pharmacy $111.83; Tri-State Radiology $40.00; Newburgh Medical Radiological Services $375.00; Protestant Hospital, Inc. $2,285.07 [$1,826.00 of which was for the two (2) MRIs]; Neurological Consultants (Steven Saint, M.D.) $86.00.

PROPERTY DAMAGE AND SUBROGATION INTERESTS

Plaintiffs' insurer, Farm Bureau Insurance, has paid its medical limits of $1,000. The file reflects that a draft in the amount of $1,719.88 was sent

UNIVERSAL INSURANCE SOCIETY
Mr. James South
November 7, 1990
Page 6

to the plaintiffs' attorney on or about November 6, 1990. According to the file, this settlement amount attributed to $1,000 for personal injury and $719.88 for property damage. There also was a letter that accompanied this draft explaining it was for settlement of ''your Property Damage & Bodily Injury claims.'' Please confirm whether this draft was sent and cashed. If it was, then we may be able to argue plaintiffs have released the insured from any further liability.

SETTLEMENT NEGOTIATIONS

Plaintiffs' attorney offered to settle their claims for $75,000 by letter dated September 20, 1990. A counteroffer was made by UNIVERSAL Insurance on October 31, 1990 of $11,750. This offer was rejected by letter dated November 9, 1990.

PLEADINGS

A two (2) Count Complaint was filed in the Vanderburgh Circuit Court in Newburgh on October 9, 1990. Count I of the Complaint seeks damages for Jessica Morely for the negligence of Noland Sandefur; while Count II is a claim for loss of services and consortium for the spouse of Jessica Morely, Donald Morely. Plaintiffs requested trial by jury. Served with the Complaint were Interrogatories and a Request for Production of Documents which I have discussed in previous correspondence to you. Our Answer to the Complaint is presently due December 7, 1990.

LAW OF THE CASE

A. Liability:

As you know, this case will be decided under Indiana's statutory form of modified comparative fault. Under this system, a plaintiff can be prevented from recovering if her fault for the accident was more than 50%. If plaintiff's fault is less than 50%, she may still recover, but her recovery will be reduced by an amount equal to her fault for the accident.

The liability issues in this case are: whether Mr. Sandefur acted as a reasonable man under all the circumstances; whether Jessica Morely was negligent; and whether Louise Johnson was negligent, and if so, may this negligence be imputed to Jessica Morely? There are sufficient facts for the plaintiffs to argue Mr. Sandefur was negligent even though we have an argument that he acted reasonably.

1. Negligence of Jessica Morely:

It will be very difficult to prove that Jessica Morely was negligent:

> . . . a passenger is required to exercise reasonable care for his own safety and will be barred from recovery if he voluntarily rides with

a driver he knows to be intoxicated, reckless, or incompetent, or unreasonably fails to warn the driver of danger which he discovers, or, in the exercise of reasonable care, should discover. A passenger is required to use that degree of care for his own safety that an ordinary prudent person in like circumstances would use. An occupant may have a duty to warn the driver of a danger of which the occupant is aware. However, an occupant may ordinarily rely on the assumption that the driver will exercise ordinary care and caution and need not generally keep a lookout for approaching danger.

Goodhart v. Board of Commissioners of County of Parke, Ind. App., 533 N.E.2d 605, 610, (1989), transfer denied.

2. Ability to impute any negligence of Louise Johnson to Jessica Morely:

It will likewise be difficult to argue that any negligence of Louise Johnson should be imputed to Jessica Morely under Indiana law. As the **Goodhart** case cited above explains,

It was settled law in Indiana at the time of this accident (i.e., 1989) that the negligence of a driver will not be imputed to the passenger absent facts which would make the passenger vicariously liable as a defendant, such as ability to control or joint enterprise.

Id. In other words, for us to impute the fault of the driver to the passenger, we will have to discover some facts to establish they were on a trip where they each had an equal opportunity to decide or control where they were going, when they would leave, what route they would take, etc.

B. Damages:

1. Lost wages:

Our best arguments will be with respect to the issue of damages. From the Complaint it appears Ms. Morely was not employed at the time of the accident. Therefore she should have no lost wage claim.

2. Impairment of earning capacity:

She will still have, however, a claim for impairment of earning capacity. Impairment of earning capacity is distinguished from the concept of lost earnings, since the term ''impairment of earning capacity'' means the impairment of the ability to engage in a vocation rather than past and future earnings lost as a result of the injury. **Dunn v. Cadiente**, Ind. App., 503 N.E. 2d 915, 918-919 (1987). The measure of damages for the impairment of

UNIVERSAL INSURANCE SOCIETY
Mr. James South
November 7, 1990
Page 8

earning capacity is the difference between the amount which the injured person is capable of earning before the injury, and the amount which he is capable of earning thereafter. **Id**. In short, the Indiana substantive law recognizes that an injured claimant may not only have been deprived of lost past and future earnings, but of the ''enjoyment of employment and earning capacity he once held.'' **Id**.

However, this does not mean that a jury may consider the injury's effect upon loss of enjoyment of life as an independent basis of recovery. **Id**. In fact, it is error to include in a jury instruction that the jury may consider the effect of the plaintiff's injuries upon the quality and enjoyment of plaintiff's life as a separate element of damages when the jury is also instructed they may award damages for pain and suffering or for permanent injury as this constitutes an ''impermissible duplication of damages'' and therefore makes for an erroneous instruction. **Canfield v. Sandock**, Ind. App., 546 N.E.2d 337, 338-340 (1989), **Seifert v. Bland**, Ind. App., 546 N.E.2d 342 (1989), **Marks v. Gaskill**, Ind. App., 546 N.E.2d 1245 (1989).

I am hopeful, given Ms. Morely's age of 64, that we will be able to argue that these damages are *de minimis*.

3. Pre-existing injury:

From what little records we have, it also appears that we may be able to argue that we only aggravated a pre-existing injury. The office notes of Hawk show she had problem headaches before the accident, and the nurse's notes from Protestant also say she had had previous neck surgery. The law in Indiana concerning liability for pre-existing injuries or conditions is as stated in **Skaggs v. Davis**, Ind. App., 424 N.E.2d 137, 140-141 (1981), and **Louisville, N.A.&C. Ry. v. Jones**, 108 Ind. 551, 9 N.E. 476 (1886) (cited in **Skaggs** at 424 N.E.2d 140-141). This law is as follows:

> If you find that Plaintiff had a pre-existing condition or disease . . . and that the accident in question did in fact aggravate such pre-existing condition, you should assess only those damages directly and proximately resulting from such aggravation and not from the disease or pre-existing condition itself.

> If, however, you find that the Plaintiff had a pre-existing condition or disease . . . and that the accident in question did not aggravate such pre-existing condition, then you should find for the Defendant and against the Plaintiff on that issue. **Id**.

4. Continuing damages, pain and suffering:

However, our best argument for limited damages has been supplied by Steven Saint's report letter wherein he states,

UNIVERSAL INSURANCE SOCIETY
Mr. James South
November 7. 1990
Page 9

Impression: . . . Secondly, she has a sensory loss which does
not conform to any dermatome pattern; but it is
more in keeping with a psychophysiologic reaction or conversion reaction, which could also
account for the heavy feeling in the right arm
and difficulty using it also.

. . ., I think more importantly, however, that she remain on some
type of a muscle relaxers, perhaps an antidepressant or nerve
type pill; and I think that as soon as she gets back to her normal
activities the better off she will be. <u>I think this is more of an
emotional type problem than a true physical injury.</u> (emphasis
added)

This information gives us the opportunity to argue that the principal cause
for her continuing complaints is her over-reaction to the limited physical
injuries she suffered in the accident.

Finally, she has not undergone any surgery, has not been told she needs
future surgery, and has not been admitted to the hospital.

5. Right to Request a Change of Judge or Venue:

Under Indiana law we have the right to take an automatic change of venue of
the case or a change of judge. My experience with the judge handling the
case is limited as he has been on the bench a little over a year. However, as
this matter will be tried to a jury, my experience with Vanderburgh County
juries is that they are conservative. Given these reasons, I do not recom-
mend taking either a change of judge or venue and will assume this recommen-
dation meets with your approval unless instructed otherwise.

SETTLEMENT EVALUATION

Given the information currently in our possession, and based upon the
relatively conservative jurors in Vanderburgh county, the settlement value
on this case would be between $15,350 and $19,500; while the possible jury
verdict ranges would be $23,250 to $32,500. These opinions may vary as the
case progresses.

COMMENTS AND SUGGESTIONS

A Request for Production of Documents needs to be served upon the plaintiffs' attorney so we can obtain a copy of our client's transcribed statement. We also need to contact Mr. Sean Clark to see if he will agree to obtain a copy of his statement as well and then furnish us with a copy.

Interrogatories need to be served upon plaintiff, Jessica Morely, in an effort to find out the names of her health care providers for the last several

UNIVERSAL INSURANCE SOCIETY
Mr. James South
November 7, 1990
Page 10

years. Given what we have already discovered, I am hopeful we will discover additional beneficial information.

We need to seek to obtain a medical authorization from the plaintiff, Jessica Morely, so we can obtain a complete copy of her medical records from Doctor Hawk (i.e., missing office notes for January 16 to January 24, 1990, and office notes previous to 1988, if any); and from Doctor Jacoby (i.e., all his office records, and especially the test results from the MMPI).

A deposition of Jessica Morely should also be scheduled to determine if she did have a child on her lap when the accident occurred and if the child was injured. If the child was not injured, this would imply that Ms. Morely was not injured; or if Ms. Morely says she was injured because she was trying to hold onto the child, then we would have an argument that Ms. Morely did engage in contributory fault; or if the child was injured, then we may have an argument that the child suffered most of the impact and injuries.

Also, as noted above, we need to confirm whether the settlement draft sent for payment of all claims of bodily injury and property damage was cashed.

I will assume the above recommendations meet with your approval and will proceed accordingly. I would also appreciate the benefit of your thoughts as to my analysis of this case and as to its further handling.

Very truly yours

SMITH, TOLENTINO & SHORT

By: Marcia E. Short

MES/rer

GARP LAW OFFICES
STEVEN P. GARP — DRUCILLA W. GARP
16 Lakeside Park
Piedmont, IN 47709-1234

February 21, 1991

Mr. John Doe
17 XYZ Street
Evansville, IN 47708-1234

Re: Tomorrow Corporation, Account No. 62-156-7, $376.25

Dear Mr. Doe

This office has been retained to liquidate the above claim. Your creditor requests that you direct full payment to this office without delay.

You must make payment or contact us either by telephone or by mail within seven days. This will avoid increasing your indebtedness by the addition of the costs involved in litigation.

If we do not hear from you within seven days, we will assume that you do not wish to resolve this matter amicably and will proceed accordingly.

Very truly yours

GARP LAW OFFICES

Steven P. Garp

SG/jw

LAW OFFICE OF RALPH L. DOWNER
111 N.W. Hudson Street
Evansville, Indiana 47708-1234
Telephone 812/422-0000

January 4, 1991

Mr. and Mrs. John C. Chang
123 4th Street
Evansville, IN 47708-2345

Description: The following described real estate located in Vanderburgh
County, Indiana:

Lot One (1) in Block Two (2) in Walkway Subdivision, an Addition to the City
of Evansville, as per plat thereof, recorded in Plat Book D, page 111, in
the office of the Recorder of Vanderburgh County, Indiana.

Tax Code: 11-111-11-111   City Center Township

Fee Title: Joseph P. Quarrels andd Ida Quarrels, husband and wife, as
tenants by the entirety

Abstract: No. 91,111 under cover of Indiana Abstract and Title Company Inc.
finally dated and certifying to December 31, 1990 at 8:00 A.M.

Dear Mr. and Mrs. Chang

I have examined the abstract of title to the above described real estate and
based on the abstract, I find that title is as above stated, subject to the
attached Schedules I and II and Exhibit A.

This opinion is for your use and benefit exclusively.

Yours very truly

Ralph L. Downer

Abstract No. 91,111
Page 2

SCHEDULE I

LIENS, ENCUMBRANCES AND CERTAIN OTHER MATTERS AFFECTING TITLE

1. Entry 20, page 40, shows that the real estate taxes for the year 1989, payable in 1990, are unpaid, as follows:

May Installment	$278.50
Delinquent, Subject to Penalty	
November Installment	$278.50
Delinquent, Subject to Penalty	

Real estate taxes for the year 1990, payable in 1991, are now a lien. Real estate taxes for the year 1991, payable in 1992, will become a lien on March 1, 1991.

2. Entry 5, page 25, shows a mortgage executed to Indiana State Bank dated March 15, 1980 and recorded in Mortgage Drawer 2, card 55555, securing an original indebtedness of $45,000.00 You must have this mortgage released of record.

3. Entry 2, page 3, shows the plat of Walkway Subdivision with building and use restrictions. In addition, the plat shows a building setback line along Main Street.

4. There are easements affecting the captioned lot as follows:

    a. The plat shows an easement for public utilities along the rear of the captioned lot.

    b. Entry 10, page 30, shows an easement in favor of Southern Indiana Gas and Electric Company recorded in Deed Drawer 1, card 11111, to construct, inspect, maintain, operate, enlarge, rebuild, and repair a pole and wire line. It is impossible to determine from the language of this easement whether this easement actually affects the captioned lot. Southern Indiana Gas and Electric Company has complete maps showing the location of all their easements. By contacting Southern Indiana Gas and Electric Company, you will be able to determine whether this easement directly affects the captioned lot.

5. Entry 15, page 35, shows a coal lease titled "underground coal lease" recorded in Lease Drawer 1, card 321. Although it is titled as an underground coal lease, a review of the lease discloses that in certain circumstances the lessee has the right to use the surface of the captioned lot, including to discharge water and to core drill. You may wish to consider requesting that the lessee release the lessee's surface rights under this lease. Otherwise, you must recognize that these are continuing rights that may affect your use and enjoyment of the surface.

Abstract No. 91,111
Page 3

6. Entry 18, page 44, shows an oil and gas lease dated October 15, 1961 and
recorded in Lease Drawer 1, card 543. In the event there is still production
under this lease, title to the captioned lot is made subject to the rights
under this lease. You should reach an understanding with the present owners
as to whether they intend to sell to you any of the current royalty interests they may be receiving under this lease. However, in the event this
lease is no longer in effect, under the current status of law, you should
either obtain a release of this lease or an affidavit confirming that this
lease has expired by its terms. Pursuant to such an affidavit, a request to
the Recorder of Vanderburgh County, Indiana, to release this lease should
be made.

Abstract No. 91,111
Page 4

SCHEDULE II

OBJECTIONS AND OTHER QUESTIONS CONCERNING TITLE

1. There are various defects in the early chain of title to the captioned lot, all of which because of passage of time can be safely waived.

Requirement: None.

2. The captioned lot was formerly owned by Sam L. Jones. The abstracter discloses a judgment against a Sam Jones, which is unreleased of record. There is nothing to confirm whether the former owner, Sam L. Jones, is the same person as the judgment defendant, Sam Jones.

Requirement: Either information must be placed of record to establish that the former owner of the captioned lot, Sam L. Jones, is not the same person as Sam Jones against whom there is an unreleased judgment or said judgment must be released of record.

3. One of the present owners, Ida Quarrels, has filed an action against Joseph P. Quarrels to dissolve their marriage as Cause No. 82D04-9009-DR-1234 of the Vanderburgh Superior Court. As of the final continuation date of the abstract, no court order prohibiting the sale of the captioned lot has been entered nor has a decree relative to said action been entered.

Requirement: Before completing the purchase of the captioned lot, you must again review the current proceedings in this dissolution of marriage action to determine that no orders of any kind have been entered that would in any way limit or prohibit the sale of the captioned lot by the present owners.

EXHIBIT A

GENERAL EXCEPTIONS AND COMMENTS

This title opinion is based on the examination of an abstract. As a consequence, the information and conclusions set forth herein are based solely on the matters certified to by the abstracter, which matters primarily include records in the offices of the County Recorder, Auditor, Assessor, Treasurer and Clerk. Some abstracters also certify bankruptcy court records. There are other matters that may affect, either directly or indirectly, the captioned real estate, but no coverage or protection is furnished for such either by this title opinion or said abstract. As a consequence, you may wish to obtain additional information, instruments, or other protection. These matters include, but are not limited to, the following:

1. Survey: This title opinion is subject to such information that would be disclosed by a current and complete survey. Although the information included in a survey varies, information that should be set forth in such a survey includes, but is not limited to: (a) the existence and location of improvements, visible easements, rights-of-way, drains, and ditches; (b) evidence of encroachments, overlaps, and shortages in area; and (c) whether the captioned real estate abuts and lies adjacent to a street, roadway, or other easement providing access.

2. Parties in Possession. In the event there are occupants or users of the captioned real estate other than the record owners, then you must determine to what extent they may have any interest in and to the captioned real estate.

3. Mechanic's Lien. In the event any material, machinery, work, or labor has been furnished within the last 60 days for the captioned real estate, then the title is subject to the possibility of a mechanic's lien being filed and becoming a lien on the captioned real estate. This lien must be filed within 60 days from the time the material, machinery, work, or labor was last furnished. No lien for such material, machinery, work, or labor shall attach to real estate purchased by an innocent purchaser for value without notice, provided said purchase is of a single or double family dwelling for occupancy by the purchaser, unless notice of intention to hold such lien shall be recorded as provided under the Indiana Mechanic's Lien Law prior to the recording of the deed by which such purchaser takes title. However, this applies only to new construction.

4. Real Estate Taxes. The current status of real estate taxes for the captioned real estate is set forth under Schedule I. However, pursuant to I.C. 6-1.1-9, if the captioned real estate has been undervalued in the assessment or omitted from an assessment, there is the possibility of an increase in assessed value or an assessment of the captioned real estate.

5. Restrictions and Covenants. Recorded restrictions or covenants affecting the captioned real estate that have been included in the abstract

Exhibit A (cont'd)

are referred to under Schedule I. However, I do not certify whether the captioned real estate and the use thereof are in conformity with any such restrictions and covenants.

6. Zoning and Thoroughfare Ordinances. The abstract does not certify as to the present zoning of the captioned real estate nor to what extent any thoroughfare ordinances may affect the captioned real estate. You should determine through the Area Plan Commission whether the intended use of the captioned real estate is in compliance with said zoning and thoroughfare ordinances.

7. Availability of Utilities. An independent investigation is necessary to determine the availability of water, electricity, gas, sewer, and other utility services to the captioned real estate.

8. Sewer. The abstract may disclose that there are agreements for the construction of sanitary sewers that directly or indirectly affect the captioned real estate and a general reference to such agreements may be included under Schedule I. However, the abstract does not certify as to: (a) the availability of a sewer line to the captioned real estate; (b) if any tap-in and connection charge for the use of any sanitary sewer line has been paid; or (c) if such sanitary sewer line has been accepted for maintenance by appropriate governmental authorities. This information may be obtained from appropriate governmental authorities unless the sewer line is a part of a private sewer system, in which event the owner of the captioned real estate must be contacted. The abstract does not certify as to whether any improvements located on the captioned real estate are actually connected to and using any such sanitary sewer line. A plumber would be able to advise you of this. If a sanitary sewer line is available to the captioned real estate and a tap-in and connection charge has not been paid or if said charge has been paid and the line is not being used by the improvements upon the captioned real estate, there is a possibility that appropriate governmental authorities in enforcing applicable laws and regulations may eventually force the use of said sewer facilities and require the payment of any unpaid tap-in and connection charges.

9. Streets. The abstract does not disclose whether or not any streets adjacent to or which serve the captioned real estate have been accepted for maintenance by appropriate governmental authorities. Until the owners of the real estate adjacent to any such streets improve such to minimum standards, then the applicable governmental authorities will not accept such streets for maintenance. If access is from private streets that have not been dedicated to the public, then appropriate governmental authorities will not assume the maintenance of such streets.

10. Minerals. Irrespective of any information that may be referred to under Schedule I concerning minerals, this title opinion does not certify and assumes no responsibility whatsoever as to the ownership and title to minerals, including but not being limited to coal, oil, gas, and all other

Exhibit A (cont'd)

minerals of every kind and nature. Without limiting the generality of the foregoing, this title opinion does not cover and assumes no responsibility for: (a) the validity or existence of any oil or gas leases; (b) the validity or existence of any coal or mining leases; (c) any rights that may exist under any instruments affecting mineral rights, including for the development of the captioned real estate and the use of the surface in such development.

11. Uniform Commercial Code. Except to the extent pointed out under Schedule I, according to the abstracter, there are no financing statements filed in the Fixture Index covering any fixtures on the captioned real estate. However, the abstracter's certificate is limited by the possibility that there may not have been an adequate legal description filed in the Fixture Index and as a consequence, the abstracter may not have been able to determine the existence of a fixture filing for the captioned real estate. In addition, the search of the abstracter does not cover or include crops or other farm products.

12. Laws, Ordinances and Governmental Regulations. This title opinion affords no protection for whatever effect laws, ordinances, and governmental regulations may have upon the captioned real estate, including but not being limited to the following:

   a. City or County: Building codes, subdivision control, flood and surface water drainage, health, sanitation, land planning, and development.

   b. State: Usury, building codes, subdivision requirements, consumer protection, land planning, and development.

   c. Federal: RESPA, truth-in-lending, consumer protection, interstate land sales, environmental protection, land planning, and development.

13. Period of Coverage. The coverage of the abstracter extends to a specific date. There will be elapsed time between the date of the abstract and the completion of your intended transaction. Title is obviously subject to such matters that occur subsequent to the date of the abstract and the completion of your intended transaction. Title is obviously subject to such matters that occur subsequent to the date of the abstract and prior to the proper recording of instruments relative to your transaction.

14. Title Insurance. This title opinion is merely an opinion and in no way represents a guarantee of title. It is not comparable to a title insurance policy and does not give the protection afforded by such a policy. For example, this title opinion affords no protection against any defects that may exist but that cannot be ascertained by the examination of an abstract, including such things as forgeries, alterations of instruments, incompetency of parties, improper execution of instruments, the failure to deliver

Exhibit A (cont'd)

instruments, fraud, duress, coercion, errors in public records in governmental offices, or inaccurate or misleading information from affidavits,
deeds, and other instruments of record. A title insurance policy, however,
would give protection against loss or damage by reason of such in addition
to certain other protections and coverage.

The foregoing General Exceptions and Comments are not all-inclusive and
other matters may also affect, either directly or indirectly, the
captioned real estate.

MINUTES OF THE FIRST ANNUAL
MEETING OF THE SHAREHOLDERS OF
XYZ CORPORATION

The first annual meeting of the Shareholders of _____ was held at _____ Evansville, Indiana, on _____ 199_ , at _____ P.M.

The meeting was called to order by _____ President of the Corporation, who presided and who also acted as Secretary of the meeting and recording the minutes thereof.

The Secretary submitted to the meeting the following:

a) A Waiver of Notice of this meeting, waiving the time, place, and purpose thereof signed by _____

b) A complete list of the holders of the common shares of the Corporation as of the close of business _____ 199_ , the record date fixed by the Board of Directors for the Shareholders entitled to notice of and to vote at this meeting.

The Chairman directed that a copy of the waiver be annexed to the minutes of the meeting. Inasmuch as the list of holders of the common shares of the Corporation contains only the name of _____ it is not appended to these minutes.

The inspector of elections examined the list of shareholders and made a poll of the shares represented at the meeting in person or by proxy. It was reported that 1,000 shares were entitled to vote at the meeting and that all shares were present in person. The Chairman announced that a quorum was present for all purposes, and that the meeting was lawfully and properly convened and competent to proceed to the transaction of the business for which it had been called.

A motion was duly made, seconded and carried waiving the reading of the annual report.

The Chairman called for nominations for directors to serve for one (1) year or until his successor or successors are elected and qualified. On behalf of management, _____ was nominated to serve as the sole director of the Corporation.

The Chairman called for further nominations, but none were made. The inspector of elections was instructed to take a ballot and acted as teller.

After all ballots had an opportunity to vote, the Chairman declared the polls closed. Upon inspecting the report of the inspector of elections, the Chairman reported that the holder of 1,000 shares of the Corporation have voted in favor of _____ as the sole director of the Corporation, inasmuch as no other votes were cast in opposition. The Chairman declared that _____ _____ had been elected to serve as the sole Director of the Corporation for one (1) year and until his successor was elected and qualified.

The Secretary then made the following motion:

> ''RESOLVED that the firm of _____
> continue to serve as auditors of the Corporation in 1983.''

On motion duly made and seconded, and since there was no objection, a voice vote was taken and the Chairman declared the motion was unanimously accepted.

The Secretary and Treasurer then presented for review the Interim Financial Report as well as the Minute Book of the Corporation. On motion duly made and seconded, a voice vote was taken and it was unanimously:

RESOLVED that all proceedings of the Board of Directors as set forth in the Minute Book of the Corporation and all actions pursuant thereto taken by the members of the Corporation or by officers of the Corporation are hereby ratified and approved in all respects.

Upon motions duly made and seconded and upon vote duly taken, the following resolutions were passed:

RESOLVED that the Resolution of the Board of Directors assuming the duties and responsibilities of the Employment Agreements with _____ and _____ are hereby ratified and approved.

RESOLVED that the Resolution of the Board of Directors regarding the salary of _____ adopted at the meeting of _____, 199_, be ratified and approved.

RESOLVED that the offices of this Corporation be changed from _____ , Suite _____, Evansville, Indiana, to _____, Evansville, Indiana.

RESOLVED that the Corporation be authorized to designate the initial 1,000 shares of the Corporation issued by the Corporation as 1244 stock.

There being no further business before the meeting, the meeting was adjourned.

_____, 199_____
Dated

APPROVED:

_____
Secretary

GLOSSARY

achieving document† Document that records a transaction and provides a framework for a future relationship; *e.g.*, a lease, option, or contract.

***ad hominem* attack†** Personal attack in which a writer denigrates the opposing party without focusing on real issues.

affiant A person who makes a sworn written statement or affidavit.

affidavits Voluntary statements reduced to writing and sworn to or affirmed before a person legally authorized to administer an oath or affirmation.

answer A pleading in response to a complaint. An answer may deny the allegations of the complaint, demur to them, agree with them, or introduce affirmative defenses intended to defeat the plaintiff's lawsuit or delay it.

appellant A party who appeals from a lower court to a higher court.

appellee A party against whom a case is appealed from a lower court to a higher court.

articles of incorporation The charter or basic rules that create a corporation and by which it functions.

averment The act of alleging, pleading, asserting, or stating.

barristers In England, lawyers who are permitted to try cases in court; an informal term for lawyers in the United States.

bilateral agreements Agreements in which each party promises performance to the other, the promise by the one furnishing the consideration for the promise from the other.

brief A written statement submitted to a court for the purpose of persuading it of the correctness of one's position. A brief argues the facts of the case and the applicable law, supported by citations of authority.

certificate of service† A signed statement at the end of a pleading indicating that the certificate and the pleading have been mailed to or otherwise served on all other parties at the time it is filed.

classification† In a document, the arrangement of information under the appropriate grouping or subgrouping.

complaint The initial pleading in a civil action, in which the plaintiff alleges a cause of action and asks that the wrong done him or her be remedied by the court; a formal charge of a crime.

consideration The reason a person enters into a contract; that which is given in exchange for performance or the promise to perform; the price bargained and paid; the inducement. Consideration is an essential element of a valid and enforceable contract. A promise to *refrain* from doing something one is entitled to do also constitutes consideration.

***contra proferentem* rule†** A court rule providing that ambiguity in a document be construed against the document's author.

contract of adhesion A contract prepared by the dominant party (usually a form contract) and presented on a take-it-or-leave-it basis to the

389

weaker party, who has no real opportunity to bargain about its terms.

corporate bylaws† Rules that establish a corporate board of directors, identify officers and their duties, and set forth requirements regarding voting or shareholder issues.

counterclaim A cause of action on which a defendant in a lawsuit might have sued the plaintiff in a separate action.

court order A determination made by a court.

cross-claim A counterclaim against a coplaintiff or a codefendant.

decree The final order of a court of equity, as opposed to a judgment, which is the final order of a court of law.

deductive logic† A form of reasoning wherein specific conclusions are inferred from accepted general principles.

defendant The person against whom an action is brought.

demand A claim of legal entitlement or a request to perform an obligation; the assertion of a right to recover a sum of money.

design† The format according to which ideas are organized within a document.

discovery process A means for providing a party, in advance of trial, with access to facts that are within the knowledge of the other side, to enable the party to better try his or her case.

division† The main headings of an outline for a document.

doctrine of unconscionability Doctrine prohibiting contracts in which a dominant party has taken unfair advantage of a weaker party, who has little or no bargaining power, and has imposed terms and conditions that are unreasonable and one-sided.

ejusdem generis† Of the same kind or class; specific words limit the meaning of more general words.

elegant variation† The use of more than one word (synonyms) to indicate a single meaning within a document; courts assume different words intend different meanings.

emotive language† Language meant to provide an emotional response; *e.g.,* a sales pitch or an attorney's summation to a jury.

encircling the concept† Using a string of words to capture the concept of a provision.

expressio unius est exclusio alterius† A rule providing that if a writing specifies an exception or condition, then other exceptions or conditions not mentioned were intentionally excluded.

form book† Book that provides forms for court-related documents (*e.g.,* complaints, answers, motions) or transaction-related documents (*e.g.,* wills, trusts, leases).

freedom of contract A phrase relating to the contract clause of the Constitution, which provides that "no state shall . . . pass any . . . law impairing the obligation of contracts." This provision is a constitutional guaranty of the right to acquire and possess property and to dispose of it as one wishes.

fulfilling document† Document that records an event; *e.g.,* a deed.

guest acts State statutes that govern the liability of the owner or operator of a motor vehicle for injury to an automobile guest. Under such statutes, the owner or driver is liable to a guest only for injury resulting from gross negligence.

inductive logic† A form of reasoning wherein general conclusions are drawn from particular situations.

interrogatories Written questions put by one party to another, or, in limited situations, to a witness in advance of trial.

lease A contract for the possession of real estate in consideration of payment of rent, ordinarily for a term of years or months, but sometimes at will.

legal drafting† The preparation of transaction documents.

local rules Rules of court that are applicable in a single judicial district.

loose sentence† Sentence that contains its main idea at the beginning.

macro editing† Checking the broad content of a drafted document for order, sense, and coherence; *e.g.*, examining the flow of an argument or considering whether a transaction will work.

memorandum A writing made for the purpose of preserving events or ideas in one's memory or communicating them to someone else; a writing made for the purpose of recording and evidencing the terms of an agreement prior to drafting it.

micro editing† Checking the details of a drafted document: spelling, grammar, punctuation, consistency, citations, word usage, capitalization, and tabulation.

motion An application made to a court for the purpose of obtaining an order or rule directing something to be done in favor of the applicant.

motion in limine A motion made before the commencement of a trial that requests the court to prohibit the adverse party from introducing prejudicial evidence at trial.

nominalization† A verb or an adjective changed into a noun.

nonemotive language† Language that lacks emotional content.

noscitur a sociis† A rule suggesting that the meaning of a word or phrase be interpreted by surrounding words.

notice pleading† Pleading under the modern rules, which provide that the primary purpose of a pleading is not to frame issues but to notify another party of a claim.

obiter dicta Means "comments in passing."

on point Refers to a judicial opinion that, with respect to the facts involved and the applicable law, is similar to another case.

overreaching conduct Taking unfair advantage in bargaining. Overreaching by one party might cause a contract to be voided.

parol evidence rules Rules stating that evidence of prior or contemporaneous oral agreements that would change the terms of a written contract are inadmissible.

periodic sentence† Sentence that contains its main idea at the end.

plain-English movement† A movement away from so-called legalese; *e.g.*, plain English activists promoted the passage of laws calling for consumer documents to be written in understandable language.

plaintiff A person who brings a lawsuit.

pragmatics† The effect of words on those who hear or see them.

prayer Portion of a bill in equity or a petition that asks for equitable relief and specifies the relief sought.

preamble† Introductory part of a legal document, which identifies the parties and the type of document.

primary authority† Rules of law contained in constitutions, cases, statutes, court rules, regulations, and ordinances.

procedural form book† Book that provides forms for court-related documents such as complaints, answers, motions, interrogatories, and jury instructions.

procedural posture† The section of a case brief that tells at what stage of a case the dispute was decided.

prolixity† The state of being unnecessarily wordy, often the result of strung out prepositional phrases.

ratio decidendi† A holding or principle of law decided by a court.

recitals† Statements that follow the preamble in a transaction document, outlining the purpose of the agreement and providing a brief background for the reader.

regulating document† Document that provides for a means to resolve future problems; *e.g.*, a collective bargaining agreement or corporate bylaws.

remand The return of a case by an appellate court to the trial court for further proceedings, for a new trial, or for entry of judgment in accordance with an order of the appellate court.

request for admissions† A method of discovery in which one party submits a written request that another party admit to the truth of facts, the genuineness of documents, or the application of law to fact.

request for examination† A written request that the opposing party in a legal action be examined by an impartial physician; part of the discovery process.

request for production of documents† A written request to examine documents held by the opposing party in a legal action; part of the discovery process.

rhetorical paragraphs† Within a pleading, numbered paragraphs reciting the supporting facts and the basis for the pleading.

second authority† Something written about the law (*e.g.*, encyclopedia, article, or book).

semantics† The meaning of words.

semiotics† The study of the rules of our speech community.

signals† Abbreviated notations that tell the reader how legal authority supports an argument.

solicitors In England, persons trained in the law who prepare briefs, draft pleadings and legal instruments, and advise clients, but who are limited with respect to the courts in which they may appear.

squinting modifier† A modifier placed ambiguously between two possible referents.

statutes of frauds Statutes, existing in one or another form in every state, that require certain classes of contracts to be in writing and signed by the parties.

style† The individualized way someone writes.

subpoena A command in the form of written process requiring a witness to come to court to testify.

subpoena *duces tecum* The *Latin* term *duces tecum* means "bring with you under penalty." A subpoena duces tecum is a written command requiring a witness to come to court to testify and at that time to produce for use as evidence the papers, documents, books, or records listed in the subpoena.

substantive form book† Book that provides forms for transaction-related documents such as wills, trusts, leases, and contracts.

summary judgment A method of disposing of an action without further proceedings.

summons In a civil case, the process by which an action is commenced and the defendant is brought within the jurisdiction of the court.

syntactics† The relationship of words to one another.

table of authority† An alphabetical list of every case cited in a brief.

transaction documents† Documents that memorialize events: *e.g.*, deeds, wills, trusts, contracts, bills of sale, and corporate minutes.

ultraquistic subterfuge† The use of a word with multiple meanings to express different ideas within a single document.

INDEX